KENDAL: A HISTORY

PLAN
OF
KENDAL
MADE BY JOHN WOOD
1833.
Tenter Fell
Green Bank
Mr. B. Atkinson
Dockray Hall Mills
Chapel Row
Union Tavern
Busher
Ro. Benson Esq.
John Wilson Esq.
Beezon Field
Union Row
Castle Street
Stramongate Bridge
Stramon Gate
Market Place
Finkle Street
New Road
Old Shambles
Sepulchre
Allhallows Lane
Nethergraveship
National Schools
Sandes Hospital
Mount Pleasant
Bowling Green
Highgate
Stricklandgate
Canal Warehouses
Castle Mills
Allan Simpson Esq.
Castle in Ruins
Cricket Ground
Gilling Grove
Blind Beck
Abbot Hall
Church
Vicarage
Kirkbarrow
Nether Bridge
Gas Works
Jacob Wakefield Esq.
From Ulverstone
To Penrith 26 miles
To Orton
Stock Beck
River Kent
Skewbarrow
REFER
No. 1 Messrs. Wakefields
2 United Secession
3 St. Georges Chap
4 Town Hall
5 Unitarian Chape
6 Friends Meeting
7 Roman Catholic
8 Whitehall
9 Independent Cha
10 Dispensary
11 Post Office
12 Theatre
13 Bank of Westm
14 Glassite Chapel
15 Messrs. Crewdso
16 Primitive Metho
17 Duke of Cumber

KENDAL

a history by
Andrew White

CARNEGIE

Kendal: a history

First edition

First published in 2013 by
Carnegie Publishing Ltd
Chatsworth Road,
Lancaster LA1 4SL
www.carnegiepublishing.com

British Library Cataloguing-in-Publication data
A catalogue record for this book is available from the British Library

ISBN 978-1-85936-150-4 *softback*

Designed, typeset and originated by Carnegie Publishing
Printed and bound in Malta by Gutenberg Press

Contents

Acknowledgements

A NUMBER OF PEOPLE have helped me in the research and writing of this book. Among them are the staff of the Cumbria Record Offices at Kendal and at Barrow-in-Furness, and of the Carnegie Library at Kendal.

I am most grateful to Rachel Newman, Director of Oxford Archaeology North, for useful discussions on recent archaeological excavations at Kendal Castle and in the town, and to Jonathan Ratter for his comments on the built environment. Mrs Pat Hovey and members of Kendal Civic Society, especially Trevor Hughes, have kindly helped me in specific enquiries. Dick White has researched Kendal and Sizergh marbles and the connections with Sizergh Castle.

My wife, Janette, has been most forbearing over my mid-evening absences for more than two years while I was writing.

Introduction

KENDAL'S GREAT FAME is disproportionate to its modest size. Ask anyone about Kendal and they might well mention Kendal Mint Cake, Kendal Green cloth or Kendal and the Lake District. As for the latter, 'Kendal, Gateway to the Lakes', a concept beloved by tourism promoters, the idea of a gateway as something that limits rather than aids access is always at the back of one's mind. The tourism connection has now been around for well over two hundred years, since the Lake District came into public consciousness and its previously forbidding aspect, its beetling crags and mighty mountains became a positive selling point. Indeed, Kendal gained one of the first museums in the country soon after Keswick gained its own pair. Each was entirely dependent upon tourists for its survival.

But there has always been another side to Kendal; a workaday community which got on with its business regardless of Lake poets and visitors. The town's motto says it all: *Pannus mihi panis* or 'cloth is bread to me' was a close approximation to the truth. We must think of this in its widest sense, for there were many trades which supported the cloth industry, such as the fullers, tenters, dyers, shearmen and drysalters, as well as the packhorsemen who carried it away. It has long been said that Kendal's main trade was woollen cloth of a coarse type, right at the bottom of the market (which economists tell us is not a bad place to be), and known confusingly as 'Kendal Cottons'. However, historical analysis now suggests that Kendal may also have had a hand in the production of better-quality cloth. Even history does not stand still.

Other trades associated with Kendal included horn-working, brush-making, tobacco-processing (particularly for snuff), and limestone-working. The latter became a very significant trade when the art of cutting and polishing the local limestones into marble and ashlar for building was perfected at the end of the eighteenth century. Hosiery and bootmaking also became important in the eighteenth and nineteenth centuries, the former the domain of hand-knitters in the town and surrounding villages, the latter perhaps an offshoot of the significant tanning industry which developed along the riverside. By the later nineteenth century shoe-making had become one of the principal trades and it remained so until the 1980s.

The town has a number of myths, handed down with unwarranted veneration by successive historians. Every town has such a parallel history, which modern historians carefully challenge but which show few signs of dwindling away in popular belief. In Kendal's case four myths seem especially resilient. These are, in no particular order, that the Kendal yards were built as a defence against the Scots; that Queen Katherine Parr was born at Kendal Castle and spent her youth there; that the Kendal woollen industry was established by a Flemish émigré in 1331; and that there was a notorious character called Dicky Doodle who carried the town's first charter, given by King Richard I. As a thoroughly modern historian, I shall endeavour to dispose of each of these myths in appropriate place.

Kendal, though the largest place in Westmorland for eight centuries, was *not* the county town. That honour went, for reasons of post-Conquest politics, to Appleby, but that small town was remote from most of its county and for practical purposes, and in particular because of its greater ease of access, Kendal served as a surrogate in many ways. It had a very large rural hinterland, for which it was a service centre, and it accumulated a good range of doctors, lawyers and banks in the process, as such places do. We know a good deal about the inhabitants of Kendal over the centuries, partly because there are a number of excellent lists of names from 1577 onwards, including a detailed 'census' of 1695 and a partial one of 1787. These help us to identify the names and trades of a part of the population who rarely appear, in any detail, in other records.

The origins of Kendal are still obscure—though of course the same is true of most towns. There was a Roman fort and civilian settlement at nearby Watercrook, and these

The earliest prospect of Kendal, drawn by Gregory King in 1665. The view claims to be taken from the Ambleside road, but seems to be from Beast Banks. All the main features of the town are shown, including Stramongate Bridge, the parish church, and the earlier Abbot Hall.

BY COURTESY OF THE COLLEGE OF ARMS

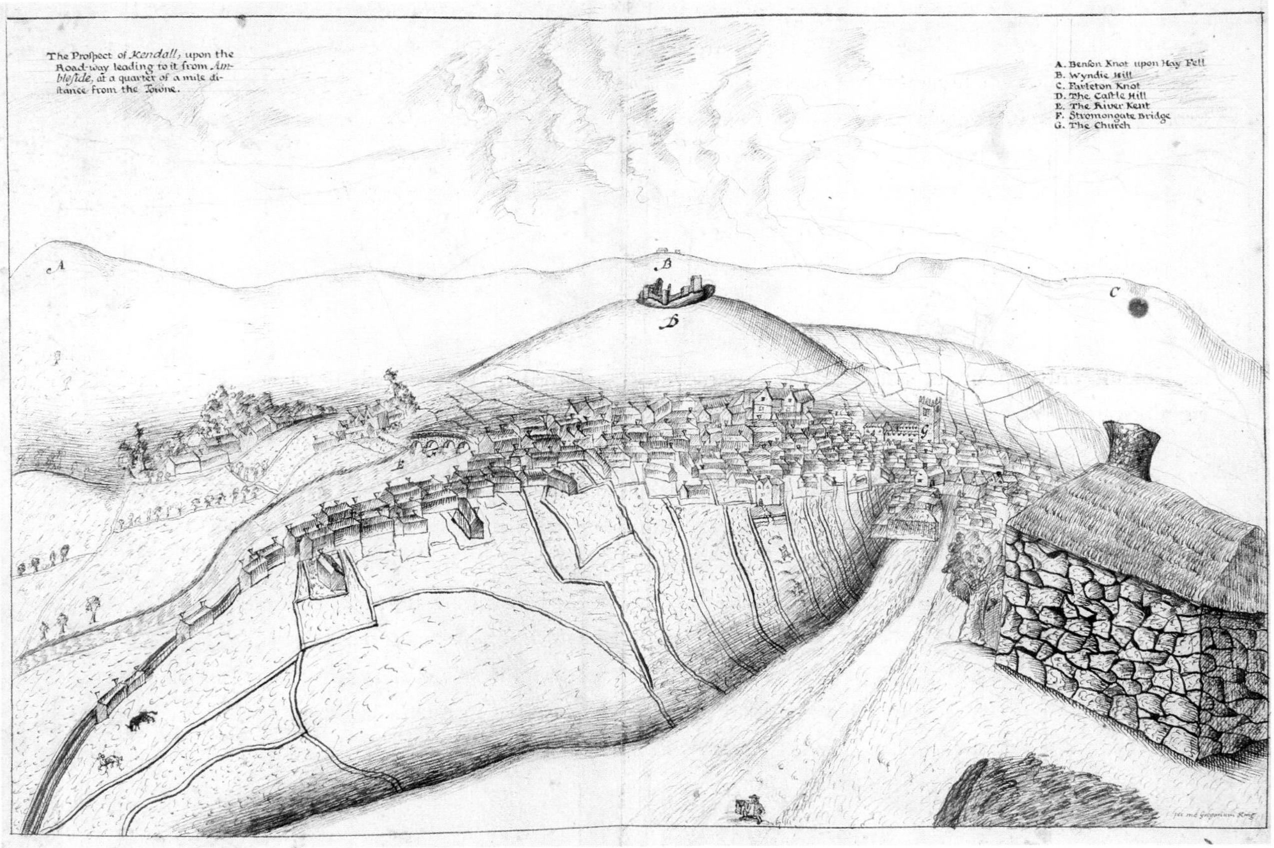

are sometimes seen as the town's predecessor, but whether there was any connection between this and the origin of the borough is quite unclear. In any case, there is no doubt that urban life in the civilian settlement, such as it was, died out in the third century. There are two possible explanations of the origins of the medieval town. One is that there was a significant settlement, dating from perhaps the seventh or eighth centuries, in the area of Kirkland, which emerged as a proto-town in the eleventh century and from which a borough was formally created just to the north in the years around 1200. The other is that the town, borough and all, was wholly a creation of the new charter at the end of the twelfth century, and developed on an essentially non-urban base though incorporating an earlier church, village and earthwork castle.

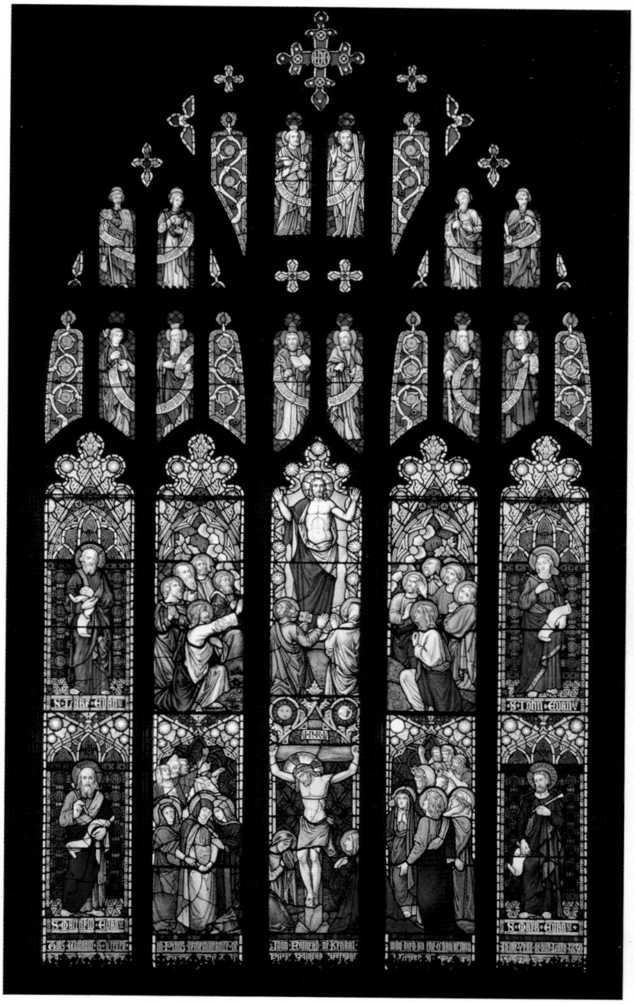

East window, Kendal parish church.

PHOTOGRAPH CARNEGIE, 2012

Archaeological excavation in the area of the parish church might resolve this issue once and for all. What is not in doubt is that the church and its environs, whatever its status (incipiently urban or not) represents a church-settlement of the type which was typical in the Norse period. It was called Kirkby Kendal (the church-town of Kentdale), a type of name found widely in the north-west (other local examples are Kirkby Stephen and Kirkby Lonsdale). The 'Kirkby' element says little or nothing about the size of settlement, only about its status as the possessor of a church in an area where places of worship were few and far between, and were necessarily supported by large parishes because of their poverty and low density of population.

In the following chapters we will look at Kendal's origins; its two castles; the river Kent and its bridges, which were the lifeblood of the town; and how the borough was created and the way in which it functioned. We will also see something of its religious life, which had such an impact on trade and social history. The history of the built environment is covered in chapters on shops and businesses and on houses, while the range of industries, one of Kendal's great surprises to outsiders, and the transport network which grew up to serve it, form the background to further studies. The evidence of maps occupies a chapter on its own, as it is such a fruitful source. We also consider health and education, food and entertainment, and the cultural and artistic life of the town. Life was often harsh—so we investigate the ups and downs of fortune as the town experienced fire, flood and the actions of hostile armies.

Kendal belongs to that class of towns which are small enough to be manageable, friendly and accessible, but large enough to have a good range of amenities and facilities—the best of both worlds. In such towns the quality of life is generally held to be highest, and on several occasions Kendal has been voted the place in England with the best quality of life. Of course this is very subjective, and not everyone living here at the time would share that opinion. Indeed, as everywhere, most people are quite scathing about their own town, even if they would not choose to live anywhere else, and even those who are most content often feel that essential qualities are being lost day by day. It must be said that the weather also plays a part for, though Kendal on a fine day presents a splendid aspect, when the weather is wet—which is not infrequently—the very stone of which it is built seems to suffer from depression.

From the point of view of historians and archaeologists Kendal has benefited very greatly from several institutions. One is the Cumberland and Westmorland Antiquarian and Archaeological Society, generally known as 'the C & W', one of those great English institutions and now well into its second century. It was founded in 1866 and has published a wealth of articles in its annual journal, together with a long series of supplementary volumes on a wide range of historical subjects. A much more recent body devoted to local history is the Curwen Archives Trust, which has produced a range of important texts on the town and its neighbourhood. There are also two institutions of immense value to anybody interested in Kendal and its people in the past and the present. One is the splendid Local Studies Library and the other is the Kendal branch of the Cumbria Record Office, both of them deserving the fullest praise for their friendly, helpful and extremely knowledgeable staff. Any student of Kendal must be glad that in 1974 the new county of Cumbria took the brave decision to maintain a series of local branch record offices, rather than centralise its archives in Carlisle. Then there is the Museum and the Abbot Hall Art Gallery complex, which contain much vital local material.

The story of Kendal is a narrative of hard work and comparative peace. There have been exceptions to both, of course, and its position on one of the main roads to Scotland means that the town has had a few shocks in its time. The phrase, 'a hive of industry' is often misused, but in Kendal's case the tradition of getting on with things in your own way seems to have a long history. This is that history.

Origins | 1

KENDAL lies in the valley of the fast-flowing river Kent, between two areas of higher ground. To the west is the limestone Kendal Fell and to the east an isolated hill that is now crowned by Kendal Castle. The medieval town was quite constricted by its position, standing on a shelf of ground gently inclining from west to east between Kendal Fell and the river. The main streets—Kirkland, Highgate and Stricklandgate—run roughly north–south and cross several streams, tributaries of the Kent, which rise from springs that break out on the slope to the west. Most of these streams are now culverted, although a short but vigorous beck runs from the Anchorite Well and into the river Kent just to the south of the parish church. A little to the north is Blindbeck, an important boundary that divided Kirkland from the borough (of which more later). Most of the time it is dry or almost so, hence its name, but for a few days in the year it is a raging torrent. On old maps it can be seen rising in Gilling Grove, and it was reinforced about halfway to the river by Buttery Well.

The river Kent has played a large role in Kendal's history and indirectly gives the town its name. The name of the river probably dates back to before the time of the Romans, and is thus from Celtic roots. Ekwall, the place-name expert who did much work on north-west England in the 1920s, considered it to have the same origin as the river Kennet in Berkshire and the place-names East and West Kennett in Wiltshire.[1] The former also seemed to be the origin of the Roman place-name *Cunetio*, now Mildenhall in Wiltshire. But opinion is divided as to the meaning of the name. Celtic river names rarely seem to have deep meanings and usually have an obvious descriptive purpose, such as 'swift' or 'dark', so perhaps we should look for some simple interpretation. More recently, however, it has been suggested that the derivation of the Westmorland river-name Kent is not the same as that of the central-southern Kennet.[2] The lack of early forms, as is so often the case in the North West, hampers our search.

The river has a short course of only some 20 miles (32 km) from its source in the Kentmere Fells to its last windings among the sands of Morecambe Bay. For the final few miles, from around Heversham, it joins with the waters of the Gilpin (which rises behind Crosthwaite and Crook) and together they form a wide estuary with a recognisable channel, albeit one which constantly shifts, through the low-tide sandbanks. It flows alongside the promenade at Arnside and then crosses over to Kents Bank before turning south and crossing the bay almost to Morecambe. In its short course to the sea the Kent descends some 2,000 feet (610

The Blind Beck, which forms the boundary between the borough of Kendal and Kirkland. Often dry, this beck rises very rapidly in wet weather.
PHOTOGRAPH: AUTHOR

metres), which means that it flows very fast and also rises quickly if there is heavy rain in the hills. In the past this has led to serious flooding. Where it reaches the lower ground just north of Kendal the Kent is joined, at Burneside, by the river Sprint (which rises on Harter Fell and Gatescarth Pass and flows down Long Sleddale). Its name is from an Old Norse word that means 'to jump' or 'to spurt', appropriate for its mountainous course. After another mile the Kent is joined by the Mint, a name of which the oldest recorded form is *Mimet* and which seems to be from a Celtic root meaning 'making a sound'. It is possible that the modern form of the name Sprint was formed in order to imitate the older name Mint—such pairings are not uncommon.[3] The Mint flows down from lonely Bannisdale, west of the A6 as it climbs from Watchgate towards Shap.

From ancient times the dwellers on the banks of the Kent have used the river as a means of defence, as a source of power for machinery, to supply tanpits, and for washing wool and cloth. No fewer than fourteen mills in the vicinity of Kendal have used the river as a source of power at some time during the past 400 years, and some of these sites date back to the early medieval period. Most of them have used some indirect method of taking water for power, because the river is too variable in its flow and often far too powerful and dangerous for direct use. The medieval Castle Mill in Kendal itself, for instance, used a leat that drew water from the river upstream and returned it to the main channel downstream from the mill site. Several sets of washing steps remain on Waterside, a few of the many that once existed in Kendal when wool was its daily bread. On these steps the wool would be washed, allowing the oils and impurities to be removed by very clean and fresh moving water, rather than by steeping it in vats. But of course wool was not the only thing washed in the Kent—the river served any and every purpose for which the townsfolk needed it, and often their different needs and requirements were in conflict. For example, the river was an important source of fish, but the outfall of noxious effluent from tanneries might kill the fish. Conflict was often inherent.

Above and below the main streets stretched the burgage plots, the very long and narrow plots which were typical of a medieval planned borough. They had a narrow street frontage and an elongated rear yard. Originally they were developed only along the street end, and thus had a relatively low population density, but by the eighteenth century they were becoming more intensively built-up, forming the well-known Kendal yards. Heading northwards, Highgate rises steadily to its summit at the junction with Stricklandgate, and then falls away again to the north. Near the highest point lies the Market Place, now much reduced in size compared with its original extent. Finkle Street (the name means 'winding street') leads to Stramongate and the river crossing, and there was a small suburb on the east bank in Longpool and Far Cross Bank, with a road—which very much later became the A6—leading out to the north-east. Around this central core various other streets have developed, leading up to the Fell and the irregular suburb of Fellside, or down to and then across the river.

The Stock Beck rises on the eastern side of the Kent and runs under Castle Street, entering the Kent near Goose Holme.

PHOTOGRAPH, AUTHOR

On the other side of the Kent, which runs in a series of looping meanders through the town, is the Stock Beck, flowing in from the north just above Goose Holme, a former island in the river. To the south of this is a wide area of low-lying ground known as The Aynam, whose name comes from a Scandinavian word meaning 'land separated from a main estate'—in this instance, cut off by river channels and streams. It was later to become an industrial suburb based upon the Canal Head, divided by the ancient mill-leat feeding the Castle Mill, which comes out of and returns to the river, to the north and south respectively. More recent development has led to huge extensions of the built-up area towards Oxenholme, down the Milnthorpe Road, behind the Castle Hill, and particularly to the north and north-east in suburban growth along the Windermere Road and in industrial estates linking with Burneside. Despite this radical change in the overall size of Kendal, the shape of the medieval town is still very evident. It looks as if it has always been there, but in fact it was brought into being by a series of deliberate acts, and to understand the chronology and motivation, we have to look closely at how and when this happened. The following chapters trace the evolution of the town over the centuries, charting the reasons why it grew and developed.

The Roman period in the Kendal area

At first glance Kendal, like many other towns, appears to have a Roman predecessor, insofar as the well-known fort at Watercrook lies just to the south of the medieval borough, and on the southern edge of the modern town. However, it is doubtful if there was any direct connection between the Roman settlement and the later town. There is a long and understandable gap in the records, both documentary and archaeological, between the early fourth century and the foundation of the present parish church of Kendal, no earlier than the eighth century and possibly somewhat later. It could well be that the close positioning of the two sites—Roman Watercrook and later Kendal—is largely fortuitous, resulting only from a common dependence upon the river Kent and the obvious natural advantages of the general location. Therefore the existence of a Roman predecessor is likely to have had little or no influence upon the location of the town. Some evidence might one day be found to demonstrate a physical migration from one site to the other, but if so it will only be found by archaeological excavation and research.

The Roman fort at Watercrook has been known to antiquarians since the seventeenth century and it was described in 1692 by the Reverend Thomas Machell:

> There are foundations of a great Roman fort as may be discovered by a great bulwark (where the marks of the trenches do yet appear) of seven score yards square, within which the foundations of houses are found in great abundance. ... And hereabouts, to wit at Watercrook, many Roman coins have been dug [up] and some presented [to] me by Mr Harry Guy of Watercrook formerly of Queen's College.[4]

Bishop Richard Pococke came here in 1750 and reported that:

> A small mile below Kendal is a farm-house called Watercrook, the river washes three sides of the ground about it, and it must have been some ancient Roman place, for many foundations of buildings, coins, and other antiquities have been found there, and I saw in the yard an altar with a festoon on two sides of it, the other being cover'd by the walls, so as that I could see no sign of an inscription; but I copyed a very imperfect one in the garden.[5]

Plan of Watercrook Roman fort showing areas so far excavated and features revealed by aerial photography. The excavations diagonally across the north-east corner took place in 1974–75.

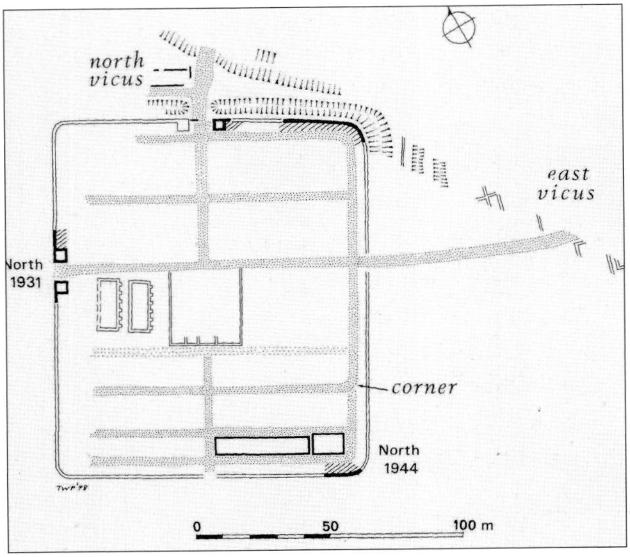

The fort lies in a loop of the river Kent, which surrounds it on three sides. As is usual with Roman military sites, it is almost square in shape, and it occupies some 3.87 acres (1.5 ha). This is quite small in comparison with other forts occupied by the *auxilia* (the non-legionary forces derived from provinces elsewhere in the Roman Empire), and this indicates that its garrison must have been correspondingly small. Today the fort platform lies some 3–5 feet above the level of the surrounding field.

The Roman name of the fort is not known for certain, but David Shotter, in his detailed work

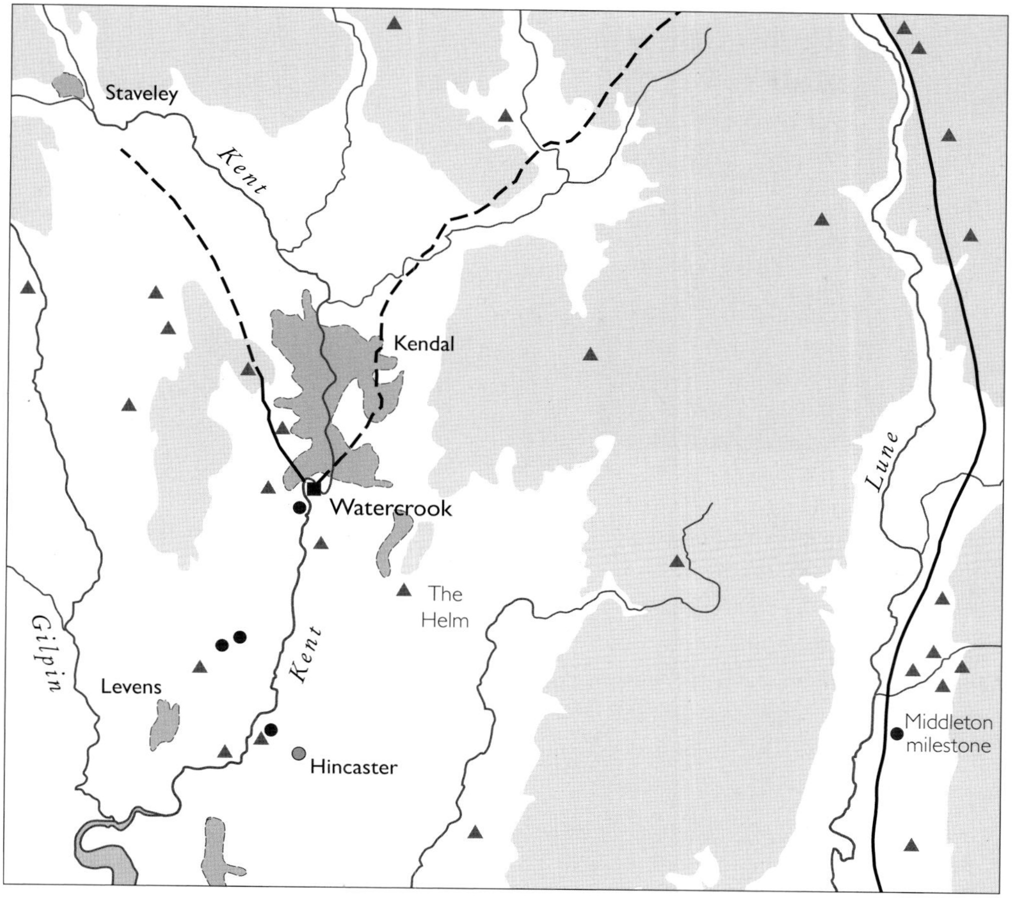

Watercrook Roman fort in relation to Roman roads and other Roman features.

on the Romans in north-west England, suggests that it might well have been *Mediobogdo*, a name which appears on the seventh-century Ravenna Cosmography, a listing of roads and places which was in turn probably derived from a late Roman road map. The name *Mediobogdo* means 'fort in the middle of a bow [in a river]', which is an exact description of the site and, perhaps very significantly, is exactly the same as the present name Watercrook, 'the place in the crook or bend of the water'.[6] It was once thought to have been called *Alauna*, a place-name that occurs in the Antonine Itinerary, a compilation of routes thought to date from between AD 100 and 300, but this might have been the name of the fort at Burrow-in-Lonsdale. The evidence is limited, and any attempt to tie down the name of one site seems to lead to a mismatch somewhere else in the region. This evidence is reviewed in Rivet and Smith.[7] The only certainty for place-names in the Roman period is when an inscription gives an explicit reference. These are very rare finds indeed, and not to be expected in the present case.

Trial excavations by Colonel O.H. North took place on the site of the west gate of the fort in 1931, and he and E.J.W. Hildyard excavated the south-east corner in 1944. Further major

Excavations under way on the north-east corner of the fort at Watercrook in 1974–75 under the direction of Dr Timothy Potter.

AUTHOR COLLECTION

excavations were carried out in 1974–75 under Dr T.W. Potter, focusing on the peripheral areas of the fort along the riverbank to the east, north and west where erosion had taken place. Further research excavations were intended to follow in subsequent years, investigating the interior of the fort, but these never took place due to a change in excavation policy. However, in the two exceptionally dry summers of 1887 and 1975 the parch marks allowed the layout and arrangement of internal buildings to be plotted, so the plan of the fort is known with reasonable confidence.[8] The fort is aligned north-east/south-west, presumably to allow its north and west gates to open on to roads leading to fords or bridges across the river. In the north-west and north-east angles, between the fort and the river, lay the main area of the *vicus*, or civilian settlement, although there was another to the south-east which was partly excavated in 1974. According to the antiquarian literature, the military bath-house stood south of the fort. This would have been an important building, capable of serving all the soldiers of the garrison on some sort of rota system, but it probably underlies the present farm buildings and has never been excavated.

We do not know who comprised the garrison of the fort—where the troops came from and how long they were there. The size of the fort suggests a quingenary cohort—that is, a unit of infantry nominally 500-strong—but it is becoming clear that the garrisons of Roman forts were often under-strength, with some of the men serving on detached duty, and they may also have been garrisoned by more than one unit at a time. The discovery of six arrowheads within the fort area perhaps signifies that its garrison at some stage comprised archers from the eastern Mediterranean, but this is unproven. The use of bows may have been more common than we think, but there were some specialised units within the Roman army, which fought with their customary weapons, such as the slingers of the Balearics or the Hamian archers.[9]

In contrast to some of the other forts in north-west England, the site at Watercrook was not chosen by the first wave of invading Romans under the governors Cerialis and Agricola in AD 69–75. Instead, it seems to have been part of a later strategy to fill other key points in order to guard the Lake District, which had been bypassed by the earlier invasion but was being subdued in the late 80s and early 90s.[10] In its initial phase it was a simple turf and timber construction, a turf rampart being topped by vertical tree-trunks, but this was replaced in stone in the middle of Hadrian's reign (*c.*AD 130). As well as being a late addition to the sequence of forts, it also had a relatively short life, perhaps being demilitarised as early as AD 320.

It is axiomatic that Roman roads will have linked this fort with other forts in the area, but almost nothing is known about these roads and their routes. Partly because Watercrook lies in good agricultural land, the road system in general is less well understood than that of many forts in more rugged country. Indeed, in several published maps of the Roman road network the fort appears to be unconnected with its neighbours, but it is quite clear that this was not the case. A confirmed road runs north-west from the fort of Burrow-in-Lonsdale in the general direction of Watercrook, and although it is not known in detail beyond Lupton there can be no doubt that it is heading for the Kendal area, broadly along the line of the present A65. Another road is known to have extended south-west from the fort of Low Borrow Bridge, near Tebay, and again Watercrook is the only plausible destination.[11] A road clearly led north from the major Roman fort and settlement at Lancaster, one branch leading down to the shore at Hest Bank but another pointing towards Kendal. Lancaster stood on a key strategic route from Cheshire, via the Mersey and Ribble crossings at Wilderspool near Warrington and Walton-le-Dale, and today more or less matched by the A49 and A6. It is thought that this road and another high-level one which runs parallel to it through the Bowland Fells from Manchester to Carlisle both date from the period of initial conquest in the years around AD 69. Logically, the fort at Watercrook must also have been linked with the important site on the head of Windermere at Ambleside, the key to the southern Lake District, but here, too, no definite trace of the road has yet been found.

Only a handful of Roman inscriptions have been found from Watercrook, but nonetheless these have considerable interest.

An altar found in 1687, and now lost, read:

... DEAB ... ... SACRV ... ... VALENS ... AVG V S L M
'Sacred to the goddesses...Valens [ ] of the emperor ... freely fulfils his vow'

left Roman sculpture from Watercrook, probably representing Bacchus, god of wine.
PHOTOGRAPH CARNEGIE, BY COURTESY OF KENDAL MUSEUM

below Roman tombstone of Publius Aelius Bassus, former centurion in the Sixth Legion, from Watercrook, RIB 754.

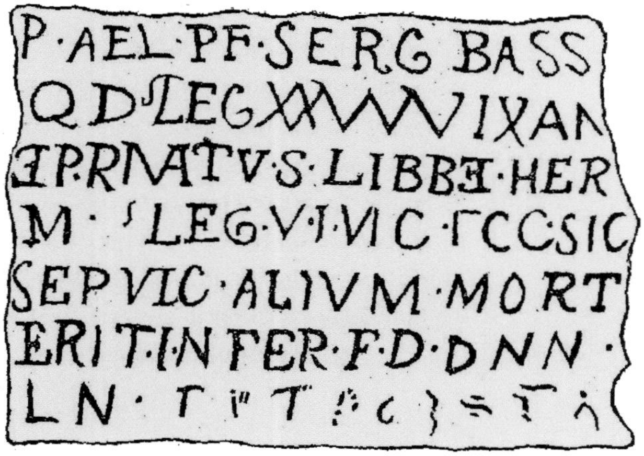

A small altar seen 1732 in Watercrook House, now lost, read:

> DEE N AELIT V V
> 'To the goddess … … [someone's name] …'

A funerary slab seen at Watercrook in 1688, later built into a barn there, and now in Kendal Museum, reads:

> [D M S] P AEL P F SERG BASS[VS MVRSA] QD > LEG XX V V VIX AN …
> … S ET PRIVATVS LIB ET HER [PER AEL SVRIN]VM > LEG VI VIC F C SI
> Q[VIS IN HOC] SEPVLC ALIVM MORT[VVM INTVL]ERIT INFER F D N HS
> … INS AEL SVRINO …
> 'Sacred to the spirits of the departed. Publius Aelius Bassus, son of Publius, of the Sergian voting-tribe, from Mursa, once centurion of the Sixth Legion Valeria Victrix, lived … years … [ ] … and Privatus, his freedmen and heirs, through Aelius Surinus, centurion of the Sixth Legion Victrix, had this erected. If anyone brings another corpse into this tomb, let him pay to the treasury of our Lords [ ] Set up under the direction of Aelius Surinus'

This tombstone, part of a larger monument to Publius Aelius Bassus, a centurion of the Sixth Legion which was based in York, was set up by another centurion of that legion, Aelius Surinus, perhaps at the expense of his two freed slaves and heirs, one of whom, Privatus, is named. Surinus might have been commandant of the fort, but why Bassus was buried here is not clear. Legionary centurions were highly regarded and well paid. 'Our Lords', if that is the correct reading, must refer to joint emperors, sometime in the third century AD.[12]

There is also a very weathered sculpture from the site, now in Kendal Museum, which depicts a figure—perhaps Bacchus—in high relief, together with a fine and very unweathered altar without inscription.

Like the majority of Roman forts, Watercrook was built with its strategic position very much in mind, and was initially purely for military purposes, but it soon acquired a civilian settlement at its gates. The residents included the common-law wives and children of serving soldiers (soldiers could not officially marry while in service, but unofficial relationships were numerous), merchants, shopkeepers, officials, retired soldiers and others who were attracted to the relative prosperity and security of the fort. These helped to romanise the area, being the acceptable face of the Roman occupation. Many of them, including the soldiers' wives, would have been native Britons, whose families had long lived in the area. Conversation in the civilian settlement would be conducted in Celtic as well as in Latin, while Greek and other Mediterranean languages would not be unknown.

Roman forts did not exist in isolation. They could only survive in the long term because they were supported, willingly or unwillingly, by the output of many small farms producing food and drink, animals and leather, as well as industries which supplied metals and other raw materials. Relatively few such farms are known around Kendal, although some must almost certainly be marked by modern farm sites for the same reasons of position and water supply. Forts in wilder locations, such as that at Low Borrow Bridge in the upper Lune Valley, can be seen much more clearly in their context of native farmsteads, of which the deserted earthworks often survive.

The Watercrook fort was abandoned by its garrison in the early fourth century, but life may have continued for civilians, given the tenacity of settlements once they are established. It is conceivable that the site was occupied into the sub-Roman period, but there is no specific evidence for that. Indeed, it has been suggested that a worsening climate in the late Roman period might have led to the abandonment of the low-lying site at Watercrook in favour of a drier position further north. That might, ultimately, give us evidence for the origin of the site now known as Kendal, but at present we simply do not know.[13]

The early Anglo-Saxons

In north-west England there was a long interval between the collapse of Roman rule in the later fourth century AD and the arrival of the Anglo-Saxons. In some places during the fifth and sixth centuries Romanised ways might have taken a long time to fade, with old Roman forts forming centres of power amid an increasingly lawless area, but on the other hand a strong native culture, often called Romano-British, had survived throughout the four centuries of Roman rule, and elsewhere this must rapidly have reasserted itself. The archaeological record is as yet almost silent, and there is no written record. The Germanic settlers did not reach north-west England until the beginning of the seventh century, and even then they spread only slowly. Numerically they were few, and place-name evidence suggests that a substantial British population remained in areas such as Cartmel and Dent for generations.

The British kingdom of Rheged included Kendal and surrounding areas. At its largest extent Rheged stretched from central Scotland to the Manchester area, and was centred on Carlisle; it remained independent until the early seventh century, when it was conquered by Northumbria. Another British kingdom, the territory of the people whom the Saxons called the *Dunutingas*, was centred on Dent and the great hillfort of Ingleborough, and its territory extended to the edges of the Kendal area. It, too, lost its separate identity in the seventh century. It is very likely that the Cartmel peninsula was also a separate mini-kingdom in the seventh and eighth centuries, and there is a possibility that the territory of Kentdale, stretching from the heart of the Lake District to the sea, was another such small political unit for a relatively brief period.[14]

The first substantial historical evidence which we have in Kendal comes from the parish church, where there is a small fragment of an Anglo-Saxon cross-shaft with a pattern of vine-scroll carved upon it in high relief. It dates from the late eighth or early ninth century. The problem with this small piece is that it has no archaeological context and in principle could have been carried here from elsewhere. Collingwood was confident that it was found during the restoration work on the church in 1850, and then spent some years in the rockery at the Unitarian Chapel in the Market Place before being brought back to the church in 1901.[15] There is no direct proof of this, and it could easily have come from another site such as Lancaster, where fragments of Anglo-Saxon crosses are plentiful and there is other archaeological material such as coins to provide a context. This piece must await corroboration before we can assign it full weight as evidence for that very evidence-free period of Kendal's history, what used to be called 'the Dark Ages'.[16] Assuming, however, that it does come from the site of the church, or from Kendal town, it will have considerable significance as a lone representative of a period otherwise largely unknown here.

right Anglian cross of late eighth- or ninth-century date, decorated with a vine-scroll pattern. This is now in the parish church and may be the earliest Christian relic from the Kendal area, but the circumstances of its discovery are far from clear.

PHOTOGRAPH CARNEGIE, 2012

The origins of Kendal

It is certain that there was no significant Roman site in the area of the modern town for, as we have seen, the Roman fort of Watercrook lies outside the present built-up area, and in the Middle Ages that separation was even more marked. That site clearly had little significance in the context of the medieval town, the development of which belongs to the centuries before and after the Norman Conquest. However, it is perhaps relevant that the earliest focus for the growth of Kendal was at Kirkland, closer to the site at Watercrook, for there is considerable evidence elsewhere for connections between the ruins of Roman military installations and the establishment of the early church.

We must look first at place-names. 'Kendal' is a modern shortening of the older formal title of the town, which was 'Kirkby Kendale [or Kentdale]'. It means 'the settlement with the church in the valley of the Kent'. The name Kirkby incorporates the Scandinavian word 'kjirk', rather than the Anglo-Saxon 'church' and indicates that the church goes back in origin at least to the period of Norse influence. The earliest significant Scandinavian presence in the area was at the beginning of the tenth century, when Norse Vikings from Dublin settled along the Irish Sea coast from Wirral to Morecambe Bay. However, it is very likely that the newcomers simply renamed, in their own language, an existing place—so the probability is that the foundation of the church predates the tenth century, which would accord with the ambiguous presence of the carved cross-shaft mentioned above. The church at Kendal became the focus of a huge parish, covering the whole of southern Westmorland. Even today the parish is large, but in the Middle Ages it included places as far away as Windermere and Grasmere, which eventually were detached and became separate parishes in their own right.

Places named Kirkby, or with the word 'Kirk' in their name, at the head of very large parishes, are often found in north-west England—examples include Kirkby Lonsdale ('the church town in Lonsdale—the valley of the Lune'), Kirkby Stephen, and Kirkby Ireleth in Furness, as well as Kirkham and Ormskirk in Lancashire. The present town of Cartmel was once called Kirkby Cartmel for similar reasons, as Cartmel was the name of a substantial area. Kirkby Kendal, then, was a settlement containing the mother-church of Kentdale, to which several daughter churches and chapels were subordinate. The parish church is in the area known as Kirkland—'the church land'—which is now no longer distinguished from the rest of the town, but which once had its own jurisdiction, beyond that of the borough. Indeed, it was already in existence when the borough was created in the thirteenth century. One consequence was that small tradesmen who did not wish to pay the large fine [fee] to be allowed to trade in the borough could freely trade in Kirkland, in competition to the traders of the town proper. A similar arrangement existed with Kendal's southern neighbour, Lancaster, which maintained an uneasy relationship with the village of Skerton immediately to the north, outside the borough but near enough to enjoy some of its benefits.

Kirkland therefore not only included the parish church of a very large parochial area, but it pre-existed the medieval borough, and its origins are therefore to be sought in the pre-Conquest period. Also at Kirkland is another important and misunderstood feature, the Anchorite Well, which has produced a substantial literature of its own, and much speculation. Machell repeats an old tradition that here there was a chapel even older than the parish church:

> By whom the church was founded I have not yet learned, but they say there was a chapel before the church was built, which stood North West of the church near the head of Well Sike in Kirkland, from which place there is a lane, called Cappelane, which leads down to the great street.[17]

The name *Cappelane* seems to be a red herring, for it really means 'Capper Lane' and has nothing to do with a chapel. An anchorite was a medieval hermit, often walled up in a church or occupying some place close to it, and supported by food and drink given by well-wishers. It is perhaps more likely that the first anchorite, whoever he or she was, came to this site because of its existing holy associations. The Anchorite Well and house formed a sacred site from early times, but it was not the site of a church, although it has been suggested that a chapel of St Mary stood here.[18] The Anchorite Well still survives, in the rather incongruous surroundings of the Kirkbarrow Estate. There was a wellhouse and a deep wide basin (until the late 1940s, some 2 metres deep) receiving the waters of a constant spring. In Wales there would be no difficulty in classifying this as a holy well with lodging house.[19] Such a site, where sick people bathed in and drank the waters, lodging in a nearby house with a priest or warden, can be seen at St

The Anchorite Well now lies in the middle of a housing estate and was once much deeper. It seems to bear comparison with the holy wells of Celtic Christianity to be found in Wales and the South-West and was always associated with an Anchorite House.
PHOTOGRAPH: AUTHOR

Cybi's Well near Criccieth or St Winefride's Well at Holywell in Flintshire. Many such wells had very early pagan origins as healing places, and were later taken over by the Christian church. In the case of the Anchorite Well, though, we have little historical evidence. It is first mentioned in 1430, when a commission was issued to the Prior of Cartmel 'to confine Alice Skawseby in a certain house built for anchorites near the church' of Kendal.[20] This reference is somewhat ambiguous, and archaeological excavations in 1992 were inconclusive as they did not reach below modern deposits.[21]

Another source of confusion lies in something called 'Tholde Warke', which is sometimes adduced as evidence for the remains of an older church at the Anchorite's Well. 'Tholde warke' is mentioned in a survey of the chantries in the parish church in 1546 and is there clearly identified as the chantry of St Mary in the church.[22] It is possible that some further reference is missing, but there is really nothing there to suggest a site outside the present building. The meaning of 'Tholde Warke' is uncertain, for such a phrase usually describes the ruins of former buildings, so it probably means that there was a fragment of a structure which looked notably old.

Kirkland contains not only the church but also an ancient manorial site, known as Abbot Hall from the long period when it was in monastic hands and held by St Mary's Abbey, York. Abbot Hall was later rebuilt by Colonel George Wilson as a Georgian villa, and it is this building, converted as an art gallery, that survives today. As noted earlier, the boundary between Kirkland and Kendal proper lay along the Blind Beck, which now flows through a culvert under the road and for most of the year is dry. Kirkland is probably the original focus of settlement in the pre-Conquest period, and the kernel to which the new borough of Kendal was attached.

The earliest written record: Domesday

In some parts of the country substantial quantities of written records survive from before the Norman Conquest, but in the North West these are very rare. Few places in Cumbria or Lancashire have any detailed record—or even a passing reference in a document—before the Domesday Book of 1086. Even this record, so detailed for most parts of England, is only in outline form for the area north of the Ribble, and is extremely sketchy for the area which is now southern Cumbria. Northern Cumbria is not covered at all, since in the 1080s it was still part of the kingdom of Scotland. The counties of Lancashire, Cumberland and Westmorland did not yet exist, so the lands north of the Ribble and into the southern Lake District are listed following the detailed coverage for Yorkshire, to which they were administratively attached. This is how Kendal enters written history. The original Domesday entry reads:

TERRA REGIS IN EVRVICSCYRE
In Stercaland. Mimet. Cherchebi. Helsingetune. Steintun. Bodelforde. Hotun. Bortun. Daltun. Patun. Haec habuit Gilemichel. In his sunt xx car[ucatae] t[er]rae ad g[e]ld[um]. In Cherchebi Duuan vi car[ucata] ad g[e]ld[um]. In Aldingha[m] Ernulf vi car[ucata] ad g[e]ld[um]. In Ulurestun Turulf vi car[ucata] ad g[e]ld[um]. In Bodeltun vi car[ucata]. In Dene i car[ucatam]

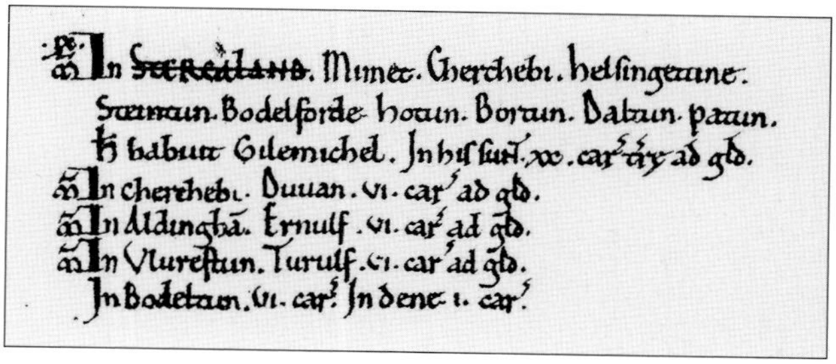

The entry from Domesday Book showing the Kendal area in 1086, our earliest record by a considerable margin.

This, with its formulaic and heavily abbreviated Latin, can be translated as follows:

Land of the King in Yorkshire
In Strickland, Mimet [Mint], Cherchebi [Kirkby Kendal], Helsington, Stainton, Bodelforde [now lost], [Old] Hutton, Burton-in-Kendal, Dalton [now part of Burton], Patton. Gilemichel had all these. In these there are twenty ploughlands to be taxed. In Cherchebi [Kirkby Cartmel] Duuan had six ploughlands to be taxed. In Aldingham Ernulf had six ploughlands to be taxed. In Ulverston Turulf had six ploughlands to be taxed. In Bolton [Urswick] are six ploughlands. In Dendron there is one ploughland.[23]

The interpretation of this is fraught with difficulties, in part because there is nothing with which to make contemporary comparisons, and in part because the information is so terse. The first section deals with the great manor of Strickland, under which are listed nine other settlements including *Cherchebi*. Each is measured in *carucates* (or ploughlands), a unit that varied according to the character of the land, but roughly equalled 100–120 acres. The total of twenty ploughlands is suspiciously round, and suggests that figures should not be taken too literally. The names of the pre-Conquest holders of the land are given, as it was customary to indicate the values when King Edward the Confessor was alive and dead (AD 1065). The significant name here is *Cherchebi*, the alternative Anglo-Saxon name for Kirkby Kendal, and almost certainly signifying Kirkland. *Strickland* clearly declined in importance in subsequent centuries, but at this date was the head of an extensive landholding. The medieval townships of Strickland Roger and Strickland Ketel recall this pre-Conquest holding, as does the name Stricklandgate, 'the road that leads to Strickland'. *Mint* must be the area to the north of Kendal, around the river of the same name. *Helsington* is still with us as a township to the south. The place called *Bodelforde* ('the ford by the bothy or cottages') is now unidentifiable, but almost certainly lay at the southern end of Kendal or further south in Natland. The other names in the first listing are those of villages or townships more distant from Kendal and Strickland, but still in the lordship of Strickland. The other listings cover Cartmel and Furness, the second *Cherchebi* being Kirkby Cartmel, or Cartmel town.

The information given in the entries is frustratingly limited. Its name indicates that Kendal had a pre-Conquest church, although it is not specifically mentioned, and the same applies to Cartmel. However, throughout the country, Domesday does not systematically record churches, so the absence of references in the other places listed does not mean that they had no church. We do not know how large, or relatively important, the places in the first list were, because they are all grouped together in the 'twenty ploughlands' total, and no indication at all is given of the number of inhabitants or their other economic assets. It is now recognised that the listings for north Lancashire and south Cumbria were not the result of a personal survey of the area by the king's commissioners—rather, they made use of some earlier Anglo-Saxon tax listing, which is now lost, and simply copied the outline details.[24] Thus, we have the merest glimpse of a familiar landscape more than nine hundred years ago, before the Kendal we know took shape. If only the commissioners had come and looked more closely!

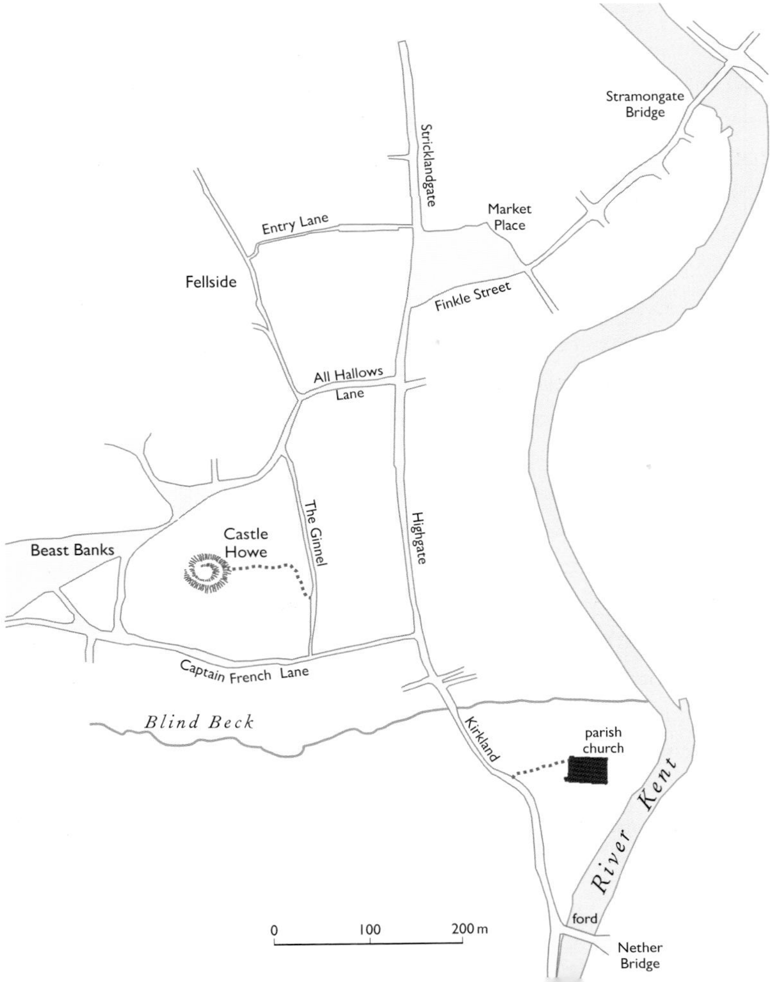

Early features of the Kendal townscape.

The borough and town government | 2

ONE OF THE most important events in the history of medieval Kendal was the granting of the borough charter in the early thirteenth century by William of Lancaster, its principal landowner. This had a major effect on the growth and development of the town, as well as on its governance and its influence in the wider world. To understand these processes we have to look at the circumstances and pattern of borough-creation in medieval England.

In the early Middle Ages landowners often sought to establish a borough on their lands in order to increase the income which they could draw from their estates. Boroughs were places with special rights and privileges (often called 'liberties') which were granted by charter. Many existing settlements were entirely within the jurisdiction of a single lord, who thereby held considerable power over the inhabitants—essentially, the feudal controls that were typical of the early medieval period. This power was usually in the context of rural communities and, for example, obliged tenants to use the landlord's mill, to owe him exclusive loyalty, to pay him individual rent, and to do boon services (that is, to work for certain days upon his land without payment). Furthermore, the feudal system of landholding, or tenure, meant that all land was ultimately owned by the lord, and tenants could not freely buy or sell, bequeath and inherit, without the consent of the lord. This represented an exasperating limitation upon the more ambitious and entrepreneurial tenants, and a constraint upon the growth of an incipient urban community. In a place with potential, which happened to lie upon an important road or commanded important resources, feudal limitations could hold back development and self-government.

Many landlords realised that it was to their advantage to free their tenants from rural or feudal services by granting them a borough charter in return for a fixed communal payment. If the place already had urban characteristics the townsfolk could then diversify their interests, engage in more extensive mercantile activities, govern themselves and, if all went according to plan, prosper. In other cases there was no pre-existing settlement, but the landlord saw the possibility of creating one, especially in the years of expansion before 1300. He would therefore offer potential settlers the benefit and security of a charter, along with freedom from the nuisance of arbitrary or interventionist control. In such cases the granting of borough status was in the nature of a speculation, based on the hope that these advantages would attract settlers and encourage the growth of a town. Many medieval boroughs, therefore, were recognisably towns, even if in terms of size many of them would by our standards have been mere villages. As with any speculative activity, not all boroughs succeeded. Some were in the wrong place, or were chartered at the wrong time, or were too close to existing centres, to make a long-term success.

Studies of medieval boroughs in north-west England reveal the regional pattern of which Kendal was part.[1] In some of the newly created boroughs, such as Carlisle, Preston and Lancaster, the lord was the king, and these were therefore granted royal charters. In others, such as Appleby, Kendal or Ulverston, the charter was granted by a noble landowner, and these are known as 'seigniorial' boroughs. Others, such as Kirkham and Ormskirk, were chartered by monasteries. There was a considerable difference in status between them, and royal charters tended to give away much more in the form of benefits and to retain less in terms of services. It was in any case necessary to obtain a royal sanction for the granting of a charter, and the records of such grants were written up in the 'charter rolls', central government records that are a key source for the history of the period. At law, the king was landlord of all landlords, and it was a common, somewhat cunning, device of the medieval Treasury, guided by perennially hard-up monarchs, to query the rights of towns in court and then to make them pay for an expensive charter of confirmation. Consequently the piece of parchment on which the text of the charter was inscribed became one of the community's most valuable and important possessions and, with later charters, the basis of its legal existence, to be guarded fiercely.

Kendal's borough charter was given by William of Lancaster III, holder of the barony of Kendal. The barony was much more extensive than the town, covering large tracts of Westmorland east of Windermere and up into the heart of the Lake District, though in the early Middle Ages most of that huge area was part of the great parish of Kendal. The exact date of the charter is not known, but it must have been granted between 1222, when William succeeded to the barony, and 1246, when he died.[2] Nationally, this period—the second quarter of the thirteenth century—was the peak time for the issuing of charters and the creation of new boroughs.

When William died in 1246 he left no male heirs, and the lands of the barony were therefore divided between his three sisters, one of whom herself died without children. Ultimately, therefore, the two surviving sisters each inherited one half of the barony. In 1274 one of the sisters, Helwise, died and left only two daughters, each of whom acquired one-half of her mother's share, or one-quarter of the original barony. At a much later date the two half-portions became known, through marriage descent, as the 'Marquis fee' and the 'Richmond fee', and the post-1274 quarter-share as the 'Lumley fee'. All these names derive from later holders of the land, and it is anachronistic to name them thus in a thirteenth-century context, but so custom dictates.

In this way the main landholdings of the Kendal area became confusingly complex, and the rights of landowners within the borough even more so. In practice, the castle and its environs lay wholly in the Marquis fee, while the Lumley fee was acquired by the owners of Levens Hall. The Richmond fee and, for a time, the Marquis fee fell into Crown hands, the former in the fourteenth century, the latter in the sixteenth. This meant that three-quarters of the Barony lands, including most of Kendal town, became royal property. Although from time to time the Richmond fee was granted by the Crown to others, it reverted to royal ownership no fewer than eight times because of the death of grantees without heirs.

The original borough charter for Kendal does not survive, but its text has been reconstructed from a copy that is held at Levens Hall.[3] Its provisions are very similar to those of two other boroughs in the neighbourhood, Ulverston and Warton near Carnforth. The latter, now a village and bearing little evidence of its ancient status, can be seen as an example of a failed borough. These grants were also made by barons of Kendal, so it is not surprising that they have features in common. Royal and seigniorial charters often refer to each other, since having obtained a good model it was cheaper and easier simply to copy its provisions and apply it to other places rather than to draft each time from scratch. The charter for Kendal has a number of clauses, which cover burgage tenure; rights of timber, of woodland and of pasture; limitations of forfeits; the price of ale; use of the lord's oven and the lord's mill; contributions to aids, taxation and feudal levies; the lord's justice and the limitation of his credit; agreements with fullers and dyers; and forced service as officials. The mixture perhaps seems a little odd to us today, including matters we find unfamiliar and trivial, and excluding some significant ones that we might expect to see.

The central aim of the charter was to regulate the relationship between lord and tenant, which in a rural manor might be arbitrary and vexatious (at least to the tenant), but in a borough was designed to retain the lord's most valuable rights without frightening off potential tenants. A town built largely of timber, and with only wood to burn, clearly had a great interest in

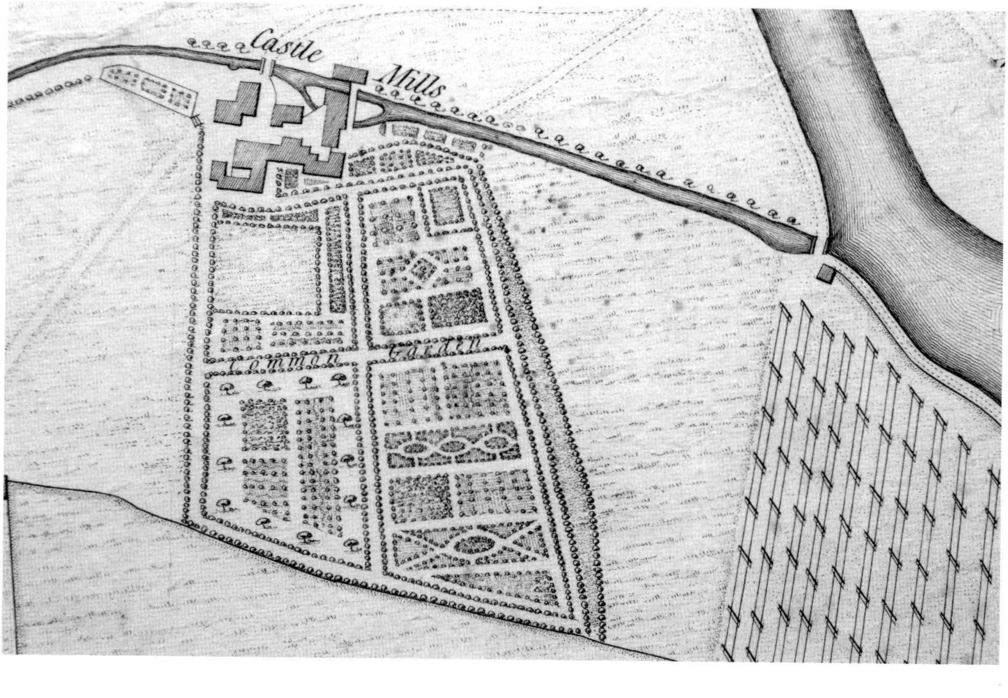

Castle Mills and common garden, as depicted on Todd's map of Kendal, 1787. The site of Castle Mills went back to a corn mill belonging to the medieval lords of Kendal.

PHOTOGRAPH CARNEGIE, FROM AN ORIGINAL HELD AT WESTMORLAND RECORD OFFICE, KENDAL

access to legitimate supplies of wood, which, in the Middle Ages, were a closely guarded right. Likewise, in a rural manor the enforced use of the lord's mill and of the common oven was an expensive monopoly and a burden to the population, and the freedom which the charter gave *not* to use them emerged as a valuable concession. The most important element in some ways was the freedom to take ownership of as many burgage plots (known as tofts) as an individual wanted (or could afford) and to sell them to whoever one would, reserving only a rent of sixpence per year per toft to the lord. This freedom to buy and sell property, if not ownership of the freehold, was normally a rare feature in the Middle Ages, and its granting by charter was one of the factors that made for a prosperous urban environment. It also led to the creation of a distinctive unit of urban property, which can still be seen in many medieval boroughs. This was the burgage plot, a long narrow strip of land running back from the main street and containing a house, workshop, warehouse or garden, with other unseen adjuncts in the form of rights in the common fields and woods. The first few elements of this will be immediately familiar to many Kendalians as the basis of their townscape—the Kendal yards—but changes over the centuries have stripped out some of the other valuable rights, such as in the fields.

One question about medieval Kendal concerns the extent to which there was already an existing settlement when it became a borough, and to what extent it was an artificial creation. Arguments can be assembled to support both viewpoints. Medieval new towns, laid out on virgin sites and with a substantial degree of careful design and planning, are numerous, with examples known from all over the country (ones not too far from Kendal include Appleby,

Beast Banks and locality, from Wood's map of Kendal, 1833.

PHOTOGRAPH CARNEGIE, FROM AN ORIGINAL HELD AT WESTMORLAND RECORD OFFICE, KENDAL

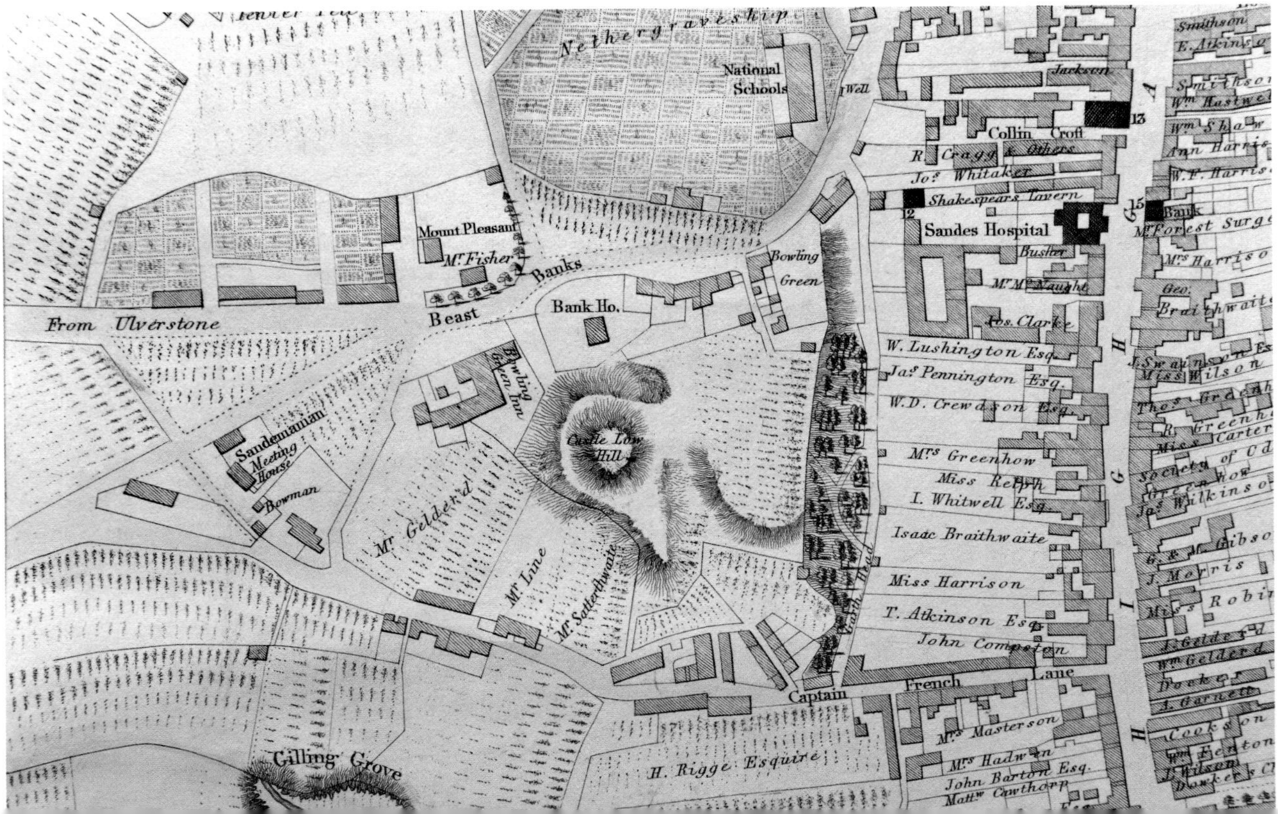

Barnard Castle and Liverpool). So a medieval landowner might indeed lay out and create a borough where there had been none before. But many other boroughs developed around a pre-existing nucleus, an older organic development where the landowner saw the advantages of granting rights to a town already emerging on his doorstep. Preston and Hexham are examples. Still others were places with no real evidence of coherent planning, where a substantial existing community was simply upgraded in status—Ulverston is a good instance.

At Kendal there are persuasive indicators of an earlier, and important, pre-burghal settlement: the early existence of the market, the position of the first earthwork castle, the nature of Kirkland, and possibly even the topography of the Beast Banks area. These and other clues suggest the earlier emergence of an urban environment, but the wording of the charter itself does not give us any help. Perhaps sustained archaeological investigation will eventually provide more information, both by demonstrating a strong physical element of planning after the creation of the borough, and the presence of earlier buildings and property boundaries beneath the main streets.

The borough

So much for the legal aspects of borough status. What about the physical appearance of the town in the early medieval period? The town lies principally upon a sloping platform of land above the west bank of the river Kent and below Kendal Fell. The single very long main street formed by Kirkland, Highgate and Stricklandgate rises northwards as far as Finkle Street and the Market Place and then falls again to its northern extremity. Finkle Street itself drops sharply north-east towards the river and becomes Stramongate, then turns into Wildman Street on the further bank. This characteristic 'Y' pattern is clearly very ancient and persistent, probably going back to the borough's origin or even earlier. On the western side of the main spinal route there have long been lanes leading up towards Kendal Fell, in particular to the irregular settlement of Fellside, the layout of which contrasts sharply with the tidy pattern of the borough. A little further to the south of Fellside is the curious feature known as 'Beast Banks', which some have interpreted as an early village green that became fossilised in the later townscape. It seems more likely that this was an area where cattle could be grazed and penned at the end of a long drove-road over Kendal Fell, before being brought down the hill into the market. That would accord with the unusual name.

To see a ghost of the medieval layout of Kendal it is only necessary to look at Todd's map of 1787 or Wood's map of 1833. Here we can see, relatively uncluttered by the later development, a town based on a pattern of long narrow burgage plots running up to the Fell or down to the river. Burgage plots varied considerably in size but averaged about ten to twenty metres along the street frontage and about four or five times as great in length. Originally these were the units of a burgess's land-holding, the very stuff of a chartered borough, providing a house or shop on the frontage and space for a narrow passage beside it leading through to the land at the back which might form a garden, a yard, or space for stables or for a trade to be carried out.

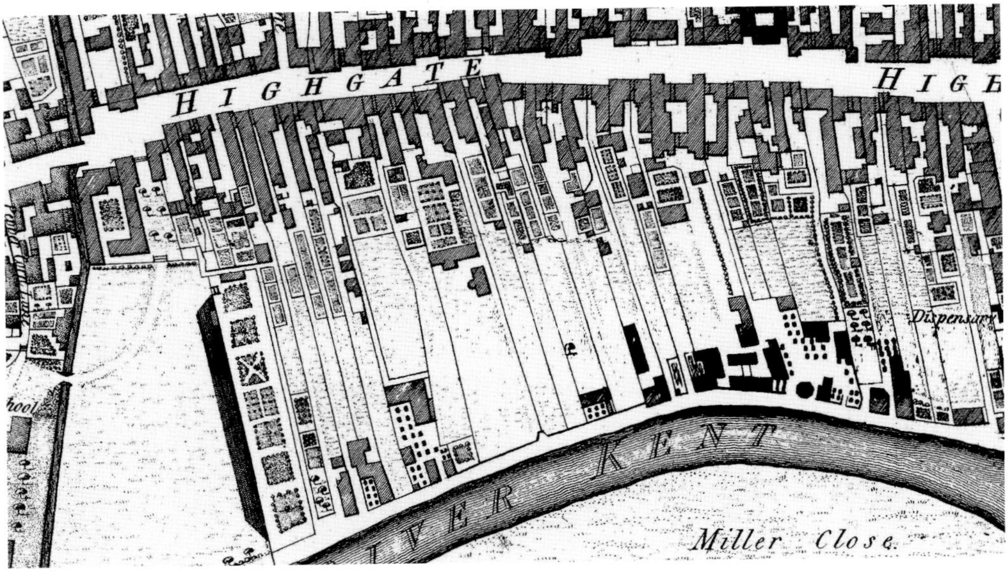

Burgage plots on the east side of Highgate, from Todd's map of Kendal, 1787.
AUTHOR COLLECTION

Associated with such a plot would be rights to pasture cattle, sheep or pigs on the common, a share in arable land surrounding the town, access to timber for building or for firewood, and (very importantly) a role in the government of the borough.

In the early Middle Ages the town, though extensive, was very thinly occupied by modern standards, with a discontinuous building line to the street and much open space. The characteristic burgage plots were later to become built up and, as the population increased, they became the equally characteristic Kendal yards. In these the frontage owners often capitalised on their increasingly valuable backland by building industrial premises or cottages for rent. The infill started quite late, probably no earlier than the last quarter of the seventeenth century. The yards were thus the result of urban infill and, despite often-repeated popular belief, were absolutely *not* a medieval creation to protect the townsfolk from raiding Scots.

Perhaps inevitably, the situation on the ground is never as clear-cut as the text-books imply. In principle a burgage was a plot of land within a borough boundary, but in practice the term began to have a wider usage at an early date. Thus, there are several references to 'burgages' in Kirkland, which technically could not have had any because it was outside the borough boundary. For example, Thomas Chaumer was enfeoffed in 1487 of 'one burgage and a garden adjacent upon le Kyrkland for 79 years'.[4] In 1700 Thomas Preston, joiner of Kirkland, left 'two burgage houses situated on Kirkland', while in 1719 Edmund Gibson, grocer, left a 'burgage house' in Kirkland.[5] The use of the term in Kirkland probably reflects its role as an increasingly important suburb of the growing town.

Another area that lay outside the borough, although closely related to it, was the Nether Graveship. The origins of this are quite uncertain, but in general terms it lay south of Kirkland and extended east of the river. There were also detached portions at the head of Allhallows

Lane, containing the chapel of Holy Cross and All Hallows,[6] and two sections south-east of the Appleby road. It appears to have been specifically defined by *not* being within the borough, and might therefore have represented some ancient separate jurisdiction, such as the demesne lands (directly held and managed estates) of the castle. The office of 'grave' existed in various places, as a minor parish officer, and 'graveship' was not uncommon as a term for an administrative district in medieval Cumbria. Other examples were found in Kinniside, Netherwasdale and Setmurthy, for example.[7] The term 'Nether', meaning 'lower', was presumably used in relation to either Kirkland or the borough itself. One might expect that it was complemented by an 'Upper' or 'Over' Graveship, but no such entity seems to be recorded. Could it be that such a name was used before the borough existed, for the area to the north of Kirkland? In 1880 the Nether Graveship was reduced in size and in 1908 it and Kirkland ceased to have a separate existence, being joined with Kendal proper as a single civil parish.

Garth Heads, a lane which runs along the backs of burgage plots on the western side of Highgate, originally providing rear access to them.

PHOTOGRAPH: ELLIE GODDARD

Another area closely related to the borough but outside its boundaries was 'the Hay', including the townships of Scalthwaiterigg to the north-east, and Hay and Hutton-in-the-Hay to the east,[8] a very considerable extent of 'forest' (in 1272) which was partially enclosed in 1812–15 and at that time amounted to 900 acres. Some of these terms need explaining. A 'hay' was a private enclosure, the word being related to hedge. Such a usage occurs at Hay-on-Wye on the Welsh Border. The Hay may have been a hunting park in origin, but it also provided wood supplies for Kendal tenants and pannage (or grazing) for pigs owned by the Hutton and Scalthwaiterigg tenants. 'Forest' does not necessarily imply trees, although there clearly were trees here—a forest in medieval England was an area with special laws which protected it as a hunting chase, and placed tight and legally enforceable restrictions on other uses, such as agriculture and the taking of wood or game.

Nearer to Kendal was an area known as Castle Lands, lying east of the castle. The 1834 Corn Rent map shows that this comprised a number of farms and their fields, including Kendal Park, High Park, Murley Moss, Birds Park and Singleton Park, representing a discrete block of land outside the common-field system, all of which originally belonged to the castle. The farm-names suggest that some of this area may also have been given over to deer-parks as well. In the late twentieth century, though, much of this land provided space for the south-easterly expansion of the town, and it is now largely built over.[9]

Closely associated with borough charters were those for markets and fairs. Fairs rarely had a permanent location, or only acquired a 'fair ground' at a later date, but markets required a

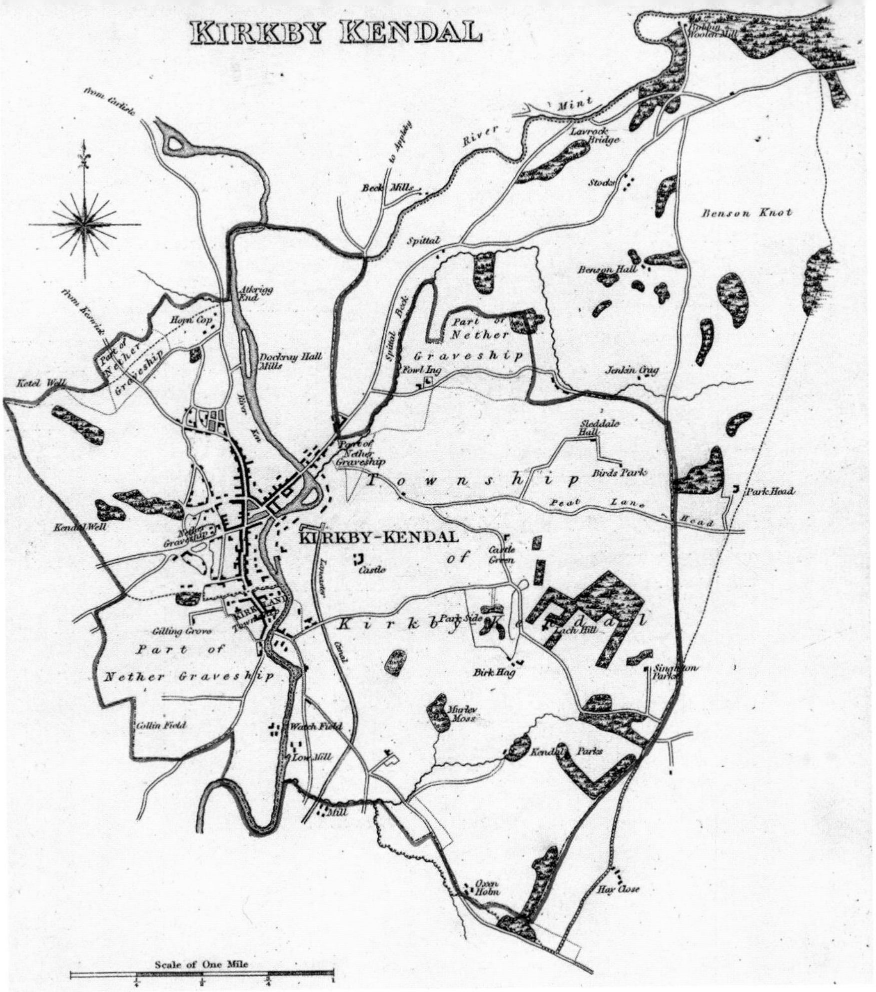

The Nether Graveship, from Lewis' map of 1835, showing the bounds of the borough. The Nether Graveship shows up as a series of rather odd scattered areas at the fringes of the borough, and so looks as if it represents something much older, carved up in the thirteenth century when the borough was created.

AUTHOR COLLECTION

market place and a tollbooth or market house where market tolls were taken. It was usually centrally placed within the settlement. Kendal had a market charter as early as 1189, and two charters for fairs were granted in 1268 and 1333. The market charter therefore predates the creation of the borough, and the first market place cannot have been where the present market place stands, as that was laid out after the borough was established. It was therefore elsewhere, possibly adjacent to or even within the churchyard at Kirkland, before being moved to its current location in the thirteenth century.

It is probable that the new market place, laid out at that date, originally occupied all the space between the present Market Place and Finkle Street. It was very common for the large open spaces of successful medieval market places to be encroached upon by temporary stalls, which gradually became permanent and were eventually refigured as shops. Even so, the market stalls were not confined to the Market Place proper, and they spread out along nearby streets. Different commodities were sold in different places, there being designated areas for certain types of trade such as fish-selling, butchering and hay and straw. It is noticeable that the main streets adjacent to the market place are unusually wide, and they were probably laid out seven centuries ago with trading in mind. In the twentieth century they became clogged with traffic, but partial pedestrianisation has now allowed us to appreciate their full width once more. Inns were also required to accommodate the merchants and farmers who came to town and to feed them and their horses. The pattern of burgage plots included many inns with long yards behind: Kendal's pre-eminence in Westmorland in accommodation for travellers, which we shall consider further in chapter 6, dates from as far back as the Middle Ages.

To the east of the main spinal route was the river. Stramongate bridge led to a small transpontine suburb on the road to the north but apart from this, and the castle, there was no medieval building beyond the river. The western (town side) bank was used for tenter frames for cloth, while access to the river from the backs of the burgage plots in Highgate was important for all sorts of industrial processes including tanning. The river made two large bends through Kendal. On one of these, below the castle, a leat was cut across the low ground to provide a controllable supply of water to the corn mill that stood there. The existence of this mill is implied in the foundation charter of the borough and it may well be older. The lord's mill was a valuable source of revenue in most manors, since all his tenants were obliged to

Elizabeth I's Charter of 1575. This charter of incorporation gave Kendal its right to self-government and established its corporate status.

PHOTOGRAPH TREVOR HUGHES; REPRODUCED BY COURTESY OF KENDAL TOWN COUNCIL

have their corn ground there at a charge set by the manorial steward. In Kendal's case there is no mention in the charter of any such obligation, but purchased corn was to be ground there at a charge of one-sixteenth part (that is, that portion went to the lord). From this mill and its water supply on the Aynam has grown up the industrial suburb that stands there today.

The charter of 1575

Although Kendal was chartered from the early thirteenth century, as a seigniorial borough it had fewer privileges than those enjoyed by royal boroughs such as Preston and Lancaster. These had a greater measure of self-government, and also had the privilege of parliamentary representation. The next step was incorporation, whereby the borough council became a legal entity in its own right, with a formal constitution, a borough seal, and a higher degree of civic dignity. Kendal was granted its charter of incorporation by Queen Elizabeth in 1575. Preston and Carlisle had gained theirs a few years earlier, in 1566, but Lancaster not until 1604. Under the 1575 charter the government of the borough was to be headed by twelve burgesses, one of whom was chosen as alderman or chief magistrate, but it did not include the office of mayor. There was also to be a recorder, or chief legal officer, and twenty-four 'assistants' or ordinary councillors. This sort of arrangement was not uncommon in town government, providing in effect two groups, one senior and one junior. In 1636 a further charter, granted by Charles I, created the office of mayor, and at this time too the twelve burgesses became 'aldermen', while a junior set of twenty became 'chief' or 'capital burgesses'.

Earlier documents are largely absent, but upon incorporation in 1575 the new borough council began the so-called 'Boke off Recorde', the minutes of its proceedings and decision-making.[10] With the beginning of corporate status came a centralisation of records and powers, which, as we have seen, had been tremendously fragmented by the medieval division into 'fees'. For the first time Kendal could see itself as a unit, with common interests. It also first recorded the powerful trade guilds, designed to control quality and access to individual trades, which probably existed before 1575 but were now formally part of the governance of the town. In the course of time they became a dead hand upon innovation.

There was nothing democratic about the new corporation. From 1636 new aldermen, to fill vacancies, were to be chosen by the mayor and the other aldermen; the mayor was to be chosen from among the aldermen; and the capital burgesses appointed by the mayor and aldermen. In other words it was an entirely closed, self-electing and self-perpetuating body. Nor was it particularly required or intended to have the general good of the town at heart. It served the interests of its ruling elite, and nobody else had any formal voice. This elite was made up mainly of those who had served an apprenticeship and been made freemen of the borough, together with a much smaller group of those who bought their freedom or who had been given it as a mark of respect. This again was standard practice for corporations throughout the kingdom until the Municipal Corporations Act of 1835, which drastically restructured the whole system of urban government in England and Wales.

Some corporations were more effective than others, and some were notoriously corrupt, but we should not look at them in modern terms. Their nature meant that they were not inclined to change with changing economic or political forces, and there was no requirement for them to do so. In particular, they were generally unwilling to take on new responsibilities involving heavy costs, especially those relating to the infrastructure of urban living and the maintenance or support of the poor. Although the titles and offices may apparently have remained unchanged over the centuries, modern forms of local government are in reality very recent creations. Historically, corporations were there to serve the needs of a small group of free tradesmen, often organised into self-governing trade guilds. There was no obligation to act for the greater good of the wider body of inhabitants, who had no say at all.

Other official bodies

This helps to explain the creation of the Kendal Fell Trustees in 1767, established to undertake the new tasks essential to civilised urban life. In 1767 a local Act of Parliament was secured, to enable the town to manage its own poor relief and other local affairs through a body called the Kendal Fell Trust. It provided for 'enclosing a piece of waste ground in the Borough and township of Kirkby in Kendal for the benefit of the poor, and cleansing the streets of the town, and for confirming a rule or order of assize and order of the high court of Chancery, relative to the rates and assessments to be raised for the relief of the poor, by the inhabitants of the said township, and the owners of lands, called Park and Castle Lands'. Under this Act, the mayor of Kendal and twelve other inhabitants were empowered to make orders for maintaining and employing the poor, along with a range of other matters such as setting out roads, cleansing and lighting the streets, levying fines for nuisances and so on, a combination of Poor Law activities and others of the sort carried out in other towns by Police Commissioners or Improvement Commissioners. This is dealt with further in chapter 9. By 1848 the town council and Fell Trust were amalgamated into a Sanitary Commission, while a second Act (The Kendal Fell Act, 1861) allowed the town to extend beyond its earlier boundaries to accommodate new inhabitants.[11]

The mock corporation

At some time in the late eighteenth century a 'mock corporation' was founded, its aim being to lampoon the real corporation and to poke fun and its pompous ways and self-important personalities. In the words of Charles Kightly, 'the custom of electing "mock mayors" [was] particularly popular in communities which had a large proportion of poor, underprivileged and "rough" inhabitants'.[12] The area east of the river, in Longpool and beyond (for which this description is very apt) became known as 'Doodleshire', and a central and completely unhistoric figure called 'Dickie Doodle' was alleged to have secured the town's market charter from Richard I. Each year a mock mayor and recorder were elected, and horse-races were held here into the early nineteenth century.[13] The whole entertainment was intended as a satire on the borough folk west of the river, and their fancy mayor-making ceremonials. It was perhaps helped along by disaffected members of the local establishment, as the proceedings do have a slightly intellectual cast. Mock corporations were surprisingly widespread: north-western examples include Sefton, Clitheroe, Worston, Walton-le-Dale and Chester, all either chartered towns or villages just outside them. In many there was an additional, more shadowy, dimension—they served as amusing fronts to clandestine Jacobite meetings and were occasions for the gathering of Stuart supporters.

The 1835 Municipal Corporations Act

The old corporations, with their focus on the narrow interests of a single powerful group, were abolished in 1835 as a result of the Municipal Corporations Act. This imposed uniform standards and procedures on 178 corporations up and down the country, including Kendal. It required a democratic process for the election of councillors, regulation and scrutiny of financial matters, and a coherent structure of administration. From that point on the government of the municipal borough of Kendal was not only reformed, but also became more modern and more effective. There was an emphasis on the provision of services, even though the franchise was still very restricted by our standards—not until the twentieth century was one citizen, one vote the rule. Measures were introduced centrally to promote better health and to police the town, following the government's adoption of national patterns and national standards and their imposition on local authorities. The 1848 Public Health Act, for example, had far-reaching consequences, as it was devised centrally, and the municipal boroughs found that they were required to enact its provisions. The hold of central government over local government had begun, and it has tightened its coils ever since. Until 1894 the borough was also an urban sanitary authority under the Public Health Act of 1872. This gave it further responsibilities for services such as the provision of water and sewerage. The civil parishes of Kirkland and Nether Graveship were abolished in 1908 and absorbed with Kendal civil parish (and the Kendal Fell Trust transferred its powers to the Mayor and corporation at the same time).[14] The boundaries of the borough itself were extended slightly in 1935.

The 1972 Local Government Act

The 1835 Municipal Corporations Act changed the nature of local administration, but it retained and reinforced the concept of separate urban-based borough authorities. But the reforms that came into effect on 1 April 1974, under the terms of the 1972 Local Government Act, were far more radical in terms of local identity. In the search for larger units of local government, which were thought to be more efficient and economical, the identities and existence of many ancient boroughs were lost. The municipal borough of Kendal, like the urban districts of Windermere, Lakes, Grange and Ulverston, was dissolved, and all were merged, with the surrounding rural districts, into a new South Lakeland District. The town, losing its separate administrative identity after more than seven centuries, was now joined with other towns and large swathes of rural territory which had previously included parts of three counties—Westmorland, Lancashire and the West Riding of Yorkshire. At the same time, the new county of Cumbria was created, so Westmorland itself disappeared.

Although Kendal retains a 'town mayor' with apartments in the town hall, this office is largely ceremonial. Kendal as a proper administrative unit officially ceased to exist almost forty years ago—though loyalty to the town's identity remains firm and strong. The story does not end here, for over the years there have been more opportunities for change, including the proposals for a Morecambe Bay unitary authority which would also embrace Lancaster and Barrow. Something on those lines already happens in the field of healthcare, but the county boundary still remains significant in determining the shape of local government. Another important trend over the years has been the bleeding-off of many of the old functions of a local authority; police and fire, water, electricity and gas, housing and transport, either to new public bodies or to the private sector. In this way the character of the modern South Lakeland district council would be almost unrecognisable to the local politicians of a hundred years ago, and the pace of change grows rather than slackens.

Trade companies

Kendal's trade companies or guilds appear at first glance to be a product of the 1575 charter: the numbers given in various sources suggest that there were at least seven of them, and a list of 1578 includes twelve companies.[15] These are:

1 Chapmen Marchannts and Salters
2 Marcers and Drapers Lynnen and Woollen
3 Shearmen Ffullers Dyers Websters
4 Taylers Imbrodyrers and Whilters [quilters?]
4 Cordyners Coblers and Curryers
6 Tanners Sadlers and Girdlers
7 Inholders and Alehowsekepers and Typlers
8 Butchers and Ffishers
9 Cardmakers and Wyerdrawers
10 Surgons Scryveners Barbors Glovers Skynners Parchemt and Poyntemakers
11 Smythes Iron and Hardwaremen Armerers Cutlers Bowyers Ffletchers Spuryers Potters Pannrs Plumbrs Tynkers Pewterers and Metallers
12 Carpenters Joyners Masons Wallers Sclaters Thatchers Glasiers Paynters Pleysterers Dawbers Pavers Myllers and Cowpers

The structure of these companies seems rather confused, and there are some rag-tag groupings especially as we get to the end of the list, which suggests that there may have been attempts to tidy up an unsatisfactory range of small companies, as well as to include the more important trades such as drysalters and shearmen. In fact, this confusion very probably reflects much older origins, and it is likely that there was merely a documentary 'new beginning' in the 1570s, rather than a real innovation.

The various companies regulated trade and training within their own fields, including the taking of apprentices and the recognition of 'masters', those who had served an apprenticeship to an accredited master in the town. They also had a social function, offering charitable support to old, widowed or sick members and families, parades and the performance, until the seventeenth century, of the Corpus Christi plays.[16] As in other towns the guild events were the occasion for extravagant processions, junketings and public festivities. Here, as at some other places, the sheer cost of this probably led to the pattern of holding full-scale celebrations at infrequent intervals. The most famous instance is the Preston Guild, which still survives and has been held every twenty years since 1542 (1942 excepted). At Kendal the Guild Merchant celebrations took place every twenty-one years,[17] the last being held on 4–6 June 1759 'with extraordinary and ruinous magnificence'.[18]

Apprentices were usually taken at the age of thirteen: their father or another relative would hand them over, accompanied by a written agreement, to a master of a particular trade. The terms varied, but usually an apprentice or his family paid a fee to learn the trade, but was given his keep for the seven years of apprenticeship. There were some female apprentices, but by and large it was a male preserve. The quality and nature of the training varied. Some masters were slovenly and regarded their apprentices as skivvies or mere servants, while others employed the older apprentices to train the younger ones (thus abdicating their own responsibilities). The apprentices formed a large and sometimes unruly group within the youth of the town, as we shall see. However, at the end of seven years the apprentice was entitled to claim the freedom of the borough, which brought with it the right to trade there and other valuable assets such as the vote and freedom from tolls in certain other boroughs (a useful advantage for merchants and traders). Most then went on to become journeymen for a few years, working as paid employees for others, until they could set up in trade on their own account. During this period they would be considered sufficiently stable financially to marry, if they chose. Enrolments of apprenticeships within the borough became significant, because in order to enjoy the privileges of a freeman the former apprentice had to be able to prove that he had served his time with a Kendal master. A list of apprentices enrolled in Kendal between 1571 and 1645 appears in the 'Boke off Recorde'.[19] These contain some 600 names and include 140 shearmen, 66 cordwainers and 45 mercers, the rest being smaller numbers in other trades. Later apprenticeship enrolments remain unpublished but are to be found in Kendal Archives Office.[20] One example is that of Isaac Wilson of Hawkshead whose apprenticeship to Roger Wakefield, shearman-dyer, was enrolled in 1729. Typically the apprentice was moving in from a smaller place with fewer opportunities to a known centre of trade, where chances might be better.[21]

In many towns the system of apprenticeship went on into the nineteenth century, although it was beginning to break down by the middle of the eighteenth. There were many reasons, but the decline had much to do with the greater mobility of labour, the widening of horizons, and the gradual decay of the old rigid divisions between trades as new ones came in. In much the same way modern governments have found it increasingly difficult to control working conditions when there is global competition. The boundaries have continued to move outwards.

Elections

During the latter part of the eighteenth century and into the early nineteenth the political situation in Kendal became highly polarised. More anger and venom were injected into the contested election of 1818 than at any time before or since. The underlying factor was that for over 150 years from the early eighteenth century the Lowther family, earls of Lonsdale, who owned a huge estate in Cumberland and Westmorland (by 1873, nearly 40,000 acres in Westmorland alone) controlled a collection of nine parliamentary boroughs, some 34 seats in the House of Commons.[22] The Lowthers were dedicated to the Tory cause, as were (in the main) the lesser landowners of the county, but the townspeople, and especially those of Kendal, tended to support the Whigs. In the case of Kendal many people were relatively radical in their politics, which created growing tension. Unlike the tiny 'pocket borough' of Appleby, Kendal was not represented separately in parliament—its voters were included among the county electorate for the two Westmorland seats—and it formed an island of urban Whiggish opinion in a rural Tory sea. Because of the property qualifications, which greatly restricted even the county franchise, the Whigs were normally unable to field enough votes to counter the Tory dominance, but in 1768 Kendal, the most outspokenly Whig area in Westmorland, was able against the odds to have its Recorder, Thomas Fenwick, returned as one of the MPs for the county.

The two main political factions in the town each erected an obelisk to mark their feelings. The earlier of the two, put up by the Whigs in 1788, is on the site of Castle Howe, the Norman motte just west of the town. It was erected to mark the centenary of the Glorious Revolution of 1688, which drove out King James II and the Stuarts, and brought to the throne William III of Orange and Mary his wife. The obelisk itself was known at one time as 'Bill Holme's Bodkin' after its builder, William Holme, partner of Francis Webster (the Websters and their circle are more fully described in chapter 5) and because of its rather diminutive size, resulting from a shortage of donations.[23] The Tory obelisk was put up by James Bateman of Tolson Hall, and can be seen from the A591 Windermere road just outside the town. It ostensibly commemorates the defeat of Napoleon and his exile to Elba in 1814—in that it was somewhat premature, as Napoleon escaped soon after and returned to France, only to be defeated at Waterloo. However, the real purpose of the monument was to commemorate the Tory hero William Pitt the younger, who had died a few years earlier, and had been the main prosecutor of the war against Napoleon.[24]

In 1818 the town was almost comically divided between the two factions. Many of the local gentry supported the Lowther nominees, while the Whig candidate was Henry Brougham, a

left
Inscription on the monument on Castle Howe, set up in 1788 to commemorate the 'Glorious Revolution' of a century earlier. It was Francis Webster's earliest known work.

right
Monument at Tolson Hall, just to the north of Kendal. This was in part a Tory riposte to the monument on Castle Howe, and was to commemorate the capture of Napoleon and his imprisonment on the island of Elba in 1814.

charismatic though erratic character. The battleground was over reform, the great battle-cry of what was to become the Liberal Party. The two politically opposed local newspapers, the *Kendal Chronicle* and the *Westmorland Gazette*, fought a very dirty battle. The reputations of each other's contributors and editors were muck-raked, and all Tory triumphs were ignored by the *Chronicle*, those of Whigs disregarded by the *Gazette*. In the election time the road at Nether Bridge was barricaded by the Whig mob to keep out the Lowther party, based locally at Dallam Tower in Milnthorpe, and a riot took place when the Lowther horsemen and carriages arrived.[25] Dorothy Wordsworth, herself a Tory and daughter of a Lowther employee, wrote about the coarseness of the Kendal women who supporting the 'Blues' (at that time the colour of the Whigs):

> [Independence] Oh! that is a mischievous word. It is the motto of servants, of the Girls working at trades, comb-makers, straw-hatmakers, etc, and really walking Kendal streets in the evening of one of these bustling days of Easter week … I could not have believed it possible that so many impudent women and girls were to be found in Kendal.[26]

One of the oddest figures to be thrown up by these times was Jimmy Wiggins, the radical rhymer. A weaver by trade, this little crooked man shaped, as he himself said, like a question mark, produced much political doggerel during the feverish elections of the early nineteenth century. A mere threat to put his enemies in verse was enough to keep them quiet. He was also involved in the Doodleshire elections and sports, a haven for slapstick humour, being elected 'recorder' in 1829 and 'mayor' in 1830. He died in poverty in the workhouse in 1838, saying, 'Had I but served my God as I served Harry Brougham, the workhouse never would have been my doom'. Even his dying words were in rhyming couplets.[27]

The pressure for parliamentary reform culminated in the great Reform Act of 1832, which

Lowther's Entry into Kendal, painted by Richard Stirzaker in 1820. It shows an incident in the fiercely contested election of 1818, when Lord Lowther fought the Kendal seat for the Tories and Henry Brougham for the Whigs. Lowther's coach is outside the Commercial Inn, after a battle to get past Nether Bridge where the opposition and canal navvies had built a barricade. The navvies got into the Commercial Inn and started eating the Lowther voters' dinner, then moved to the White Hart where they did considerable damage.

PHOTOGRAPH TREVOR HUGHES: REPRODUCED BY COURTESY OF KENDAL TOWN COUNCIL

gave Kendal its own borough seat. Although this pleased radical Kendal in principle, the Act in fact did little to extend the franchise beyond the more prosperous middle classes. Kendal might now have its own MP, but even in 1861 the electorate numbered a mere 432 voters.[28] The existence of a strict property qualification led to the implementation of plans for the building of houses, whose new owners would swell the Liberal vote.[29] These houses, at the north end of the town in streets near the workhouse and the house of correction, were known originally as the 'Blue Buildings', after the then Whig colours. They are dealt with more fully in chapters 4 and 5.

After it gained its own parliamentary seat in 1832 Kendal elected a series of carpet-bagging Whig MPs, and then finally one of its own industrialists, the Liberal John Whitwell, who represented the borough from 1868 to 1880. But in the later nineteenth century Parliament began the move towards equal representation based on constituency population, the first step in this being the abolition of smaller borough seats. Under the Redistribution of Seats Act 1885, Kendal's parliamentary independence was removed, and the borough was absorbed into the new Southern Division of Westmorland—once again, submerged in a rural Tory sea.[30]

In most subsequent years Tory MPs were elected for the constituency, with only occasional exceptions. As the Liberals declined in the town, in the early decades of the twentieth century, they were not replaced by Labour to any great extent. In 65 years from 1922 South Westmorland (from 1983, Westmorland and Lonsdale) had just three MPs, all Conservative: Oliver Stanley (1922–45), W. Fletcher-Vane (1945–59), and Michael Jopling (1959–97), an extraordinary indication of political stability.[31] From 1997 to 2005 the MP was the Conservative Tim Collins, but in the latter year it was narrowly won by Tim Farron, for the Liberal Democrats, a victory he repeated in a much more convincing manner in 2010 with a huge majority. Whether this foreshadows a return to Kendal's old Liberal tradition, or whether this represents a personal following, only time will tell.

3 Kendal's castles

KENDAL is among the relatively few towns in England which had two medieval castles. Here, an early earthwork castle was replaced by a later structure on a different site. Another example is Middleham in Yorkshire, and probably the best known is York with its Baile Hill and Clifford's Tower. At Kendal there was a castle on either side of the river Kent, and in the past this has led to some confusion among antiquarians and historians. The stone ruins on the eastern hill are the more familiar, especially through the spurious antiquarian tradition of a connection with Queen Katherine Parr, but the other earthwork on the western side in fact raises more intriguing questions than its better-known neighbour.

The concept of castle-building was introduced into England and Wales from the Continent in the mid-eleventh century, shortly before the Norman Conquest, under the influence of a few powerful Norman favourites of King Edward the Confessor. After the Conquest, however, the building of castles went through a boom period, as the new lords sought to impose their control over newly acquired territories. Seventy years later, during the troubled period known as The Anarchy ('when God and all his angels slept'), there was incessant civil war between adherents of Stephen de Blois and the Empress Matilda, and many more castles were constructed, mostly without any record at all.

Map showing castle mottes in Cumbria and north Lancashire.

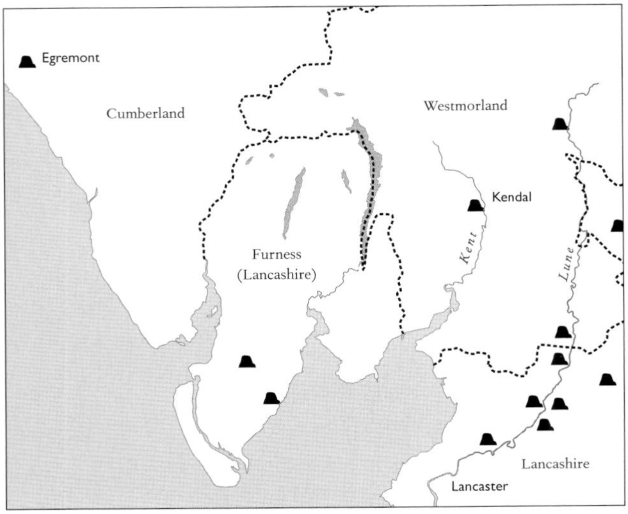

With relatively few exceptions (mainly the principal royal strongholds) these early castles were earthworks, with timber stockades, towers and gates. They fall into two main categories—motte-and-bailey castles and ringworks—with some combining the two features, or utilising natural or earlier defences, such as the banks and ditches of Roman forts. Motte-and-bailey castles consist of a high mound (the 'motte') and a larger enclosure (the 'bailey'). The motte provided both the defence of last resort and the location for private chambers, while the bailey offered the space for a hall, kitchens, stables, barns and workshops, thus becoming the focus of everyday life in the castle community. Ringworks were simpler, with a bailey, usually circular or almost so, and a strong gatehouse as the focus of the defences, perhaps providing some accommodation. The two Kendal castles represent successive sites, rather than being in use at the same time, although their chronology must as yet be based on what can be gleaned from experience elsewhere, as the motte unfortunately remains unexcavated.

Castle Howe

The older of the two castles is the site known as Castle Howe, which dates from after 1066 and probably as late as the 1090s. It is of the motte-and-bailey type and lies on the edge of the high ground west of the present town—though the town itself, as we have already seen, is largely a later creation. Judging by its date the castle would therefore relate to the Kirkland settlement rather than to the later borough. Indeed, by the time the borough received its charter, sometime between 1222 and 1246, Castle Howe was probably already deserted. However, its position raises the question of whether there was a settlement, perhaps an incipient urban community, immediately below it in the area of modern Highgate, or around Beast Banks. If so, it was perhaps this that gave rise to the borough.

Castle Howe is a motte-and-bailey of traditional type, constructed on a natural ridge and situated between Low Beast Bank and Captain French Lane. Access can be gained from Garth Heads, a narrow track running north to south below the eastern edge of the earthwork. The name 'Garth Heads' suggests that this formed the back lane servicing the burgage plots of Highgate. The motte is some 46 metres in diameter at its base and 18 metres at its summit, and it rises about 15 metres above the bailey, from which it is separated by a ditch. It has been created by developing the existing ridge by adding material to heighten the mound, but also by lowering the level of the surrounding ground surface. Traces of the natural ridge survive on either side of the motte. The whole site covers roughly 1.5 hectares.

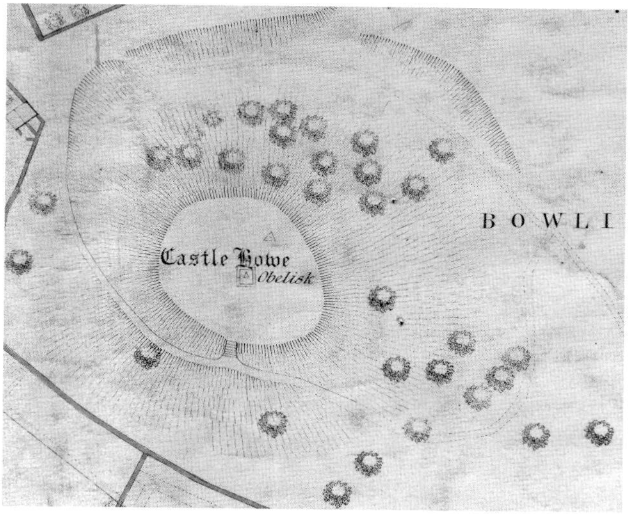

Plan of Castle Howe, from the Ordnance Survey map of 1861.

PHOTOGRAPH CARNEGIE, FROM AN ORIGINAL HELD AT WESTMORLAND RECORD OFFICE, KENDAL

There is virtually no recorded historical evidence for this site, but it closely resembles several other earthwork castles on either side of the county boundary in the nearby Lune valley, such as Castle Stede at Hornby (overlooking the river at Loyne Bridge) and Castle Hill in Halton, where the bailey still survives, and those where the bailey is now lost, as at Arkholme, Melling, Whittington, Kirkby Lonsdale and Sedbergh. All of these seem to date from the period between the Norman Conquest and the end of the Anarchy in the mid-twelfth century. Such castles had the merit of being swiftly constructed in a hostile

Castle Howe and the monument from the west.

environment, as the newly conquered lands clearly were, using an unskilled forced labour under skilled supervision and with readily available materials. Few documentary records survive from this period, and in the civil wars of 1135–50 there was no coherent central authority that could authorise castle-building, so many unofficial castles were constructed by local lords.

Tradition assigns the Castle Howe motte-and-bailey castle to Ivo de Taillebois, who died in 1094, or to his successors, but in reality we are quite in the dark about this—certainly, no written evidence of this survives. However, Castle Howe may have been the first *caput*, or 'head-place', of the Barony of Kendal. On Speed's map of Kendal of 1610 the motte is marked as 'The Mount', while a deed of 1767 refers to the site as 'Catcastle'. The earthworks were much altered in 1788 when the obelisk was built on top of the motte to mark the centenary of the Glorious Revolution, while the subsequent use of the bailey as a bowling green and a public park caused further changes.[1]

Kendal Castle

Kendal's other castle, on the east side of the town, probably replaced Castle Howe in the later twelfth century. The surviving fabric suggests that it more closely resembled a fortified manor house than a true castle. It stands on the dominant hill but is rather divorced from the town which it overlooks, and indeed there was little or no other settlement on this side of the river during the Middle Ages. Kendal Castle consists of an approximately circular earthwork, which has a wide dry moat or ditch and is surmounted by a stone curtain wall with stone interval towers. The shape seems to be determined by the existence of an earlier ringwork, to which the stone was added later. The ringwork also has traces of a small annexe to the north, perhaps protecting the main gate.

Kendal Castle seen from Castle Howe.

There is no keep as such and, except for its prominent position, the castle is remarkably weak in all defensive and military aspects. The towers are insufficient in number, and do not project far enough, to *enfilade* the outer walls (that is, to allow archers and other defenders to intercept attackers before they reached the foot of the curtain wall). This is an inherent weakness in all circular castles, but is particularly obvious at Kendal. While the earthen bank and the lower courses of the curtain walls are original, much of what we see today is in fact a rather poor early nineteenth-century restoration, perhaps dating from 1813, which in places does not even quite follow the original lines.

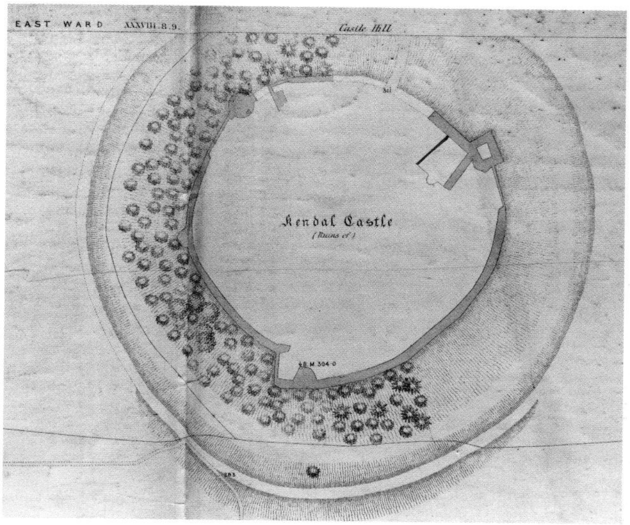

Plan of Kendal Castle, from the Ordnance Survey map of 1861. It is very lacking in detail, perhaps because of the overgrowth and fallen masonry at the time.

PHOTOGRAPH CARNEGIE, FROM AN ORIGINAL HELD AT WESTMORLAND RECORD OFFICE, KENDAL

Familiarity with the site should not stop us recognising that this is actually a strange and unusual castle. Recent interpretation has helped to make the site more accessible, but it is quite difficult to gain a sense of what it originally looked like, partly because of its very ruined state. One of the best potential sources is a bird's eye view by Thomas Machell of the castle in 1692, which shows the twin-towered gatehouse, now wholly gone—but this is only a potential source because in reality it is unlikely that the buildings stood so complete in his day. One would like to know how much he saw and how much was conjecture, for in all probability Machell used the ruins themselves and a liberal measure of imagination to recreate the appearance. On his drawing are two pencil comments: 'Kendal Castle gathered from the Ruines for deli[very?]' and, referring to the south tower,

South-west view of Kendal Castle from Todd's map of 1787.

PHOTOGRAPH CARNEGIE, FROM AN ORIGINAL HELD AT WESTMORLAND RECORD OFFICE, KENDAL

'This is too Big a Tower'. Nevertheless, subsequent reconstructions seem to have taken his drawing at face value.[2] In his picture, almost all the defences seem directed towards the ridge north of the castle (the most likely line of approach) with very little to east and west and a just single lodging tower to the south, which contains a postern gate.

Today the castle is surrounded by the broken line of the curtain wall—there is a large gap in the northern defences left by the collapse of the twin-towered gatehouse. To the east is the most impressive surviving element, the hall block, with two parallel vaulted cellars, the remains of four which originally existed. Immediately south-east of this is a small rectangular tower projecting outside the curtain, with garderobe shutes (toilet outfalls) leading into the outer ditch. A long stretch of featureless curtain wall follows until, on the southern side, we reach the fragmentary remains of a tower, shown by Machell as rectangular in plan, with an offset in the curtain providing a postern gate, accessed by a vaulted passage which survives in part. It appears that this tower predates the curtain wall, so there may have been a phase when the enclosure was protected by stone towers linked by a timber stockade on an earthen base.

A further stretch of curtain wall runs round towards the west, where a half-round outward-facing projection might be a fragment of another tower, or an artillery platform. The degree of rebuilding makes it difficult to interpret, while Machell's drawing is equivocal. A little further on there is a projecting circular tower, still retaining stumps of the original thick curtain wall on either side. Excavation has shown that on both sides of this tower the curtain had been robbed down to foundation level by the nineteenth century. The tower has a spiral staircase in its south wall and a fireplace and garderobe at first-floor level. Known in 1409 as the Troutbeck

The romantic castle ruins, which command a panoramic view over Kendal and a large swathe of countryside.

Kendal Castle in about 1900, showing the Hall complex and its vaults.

GLASS SLIDE, BY COURTESY OF KENDAL TOWN COUNCIL

Tower, it seems too small to have provided lodgings, so may have simply been quarters for the garrison.[3] On the other hand, the quality of its accommodation could mean that it was an office for the receiver of the rents for the estate. As the most senior and regular occupant of the castle, he would clearly occupy the best rooms. A William Troutebek, esquire, is listed in 1431 as one of the co-tenants of land on the Parr property, which perhaps included the castle, and the tower was perhaps named after him or one of his ancestors.[4]

Excavations by boys from Heversham Grammar School, under the direction of J. E. Spence took place in 1951,[5] and further excavations under Barbara Harbottle in 1967–71.[6] Finally, there was limited excavation, survey and interpretation in 1995–96 under the auspices of the Lancaster University Archaeological Unit.[7] The results of these three investigations have helped to fill out the picture. There was probably a rectangular structure, matching the great hall, on the other side of the gatehouse, although not on the same scale. The great hall itself seems to have gone through two phases. In the first it was probably a ground-floor room, with no vaults. Subsequently, it was raised to first-floor level, over vaulted cellars. In front of the hall, at its south-western corner, a passage was constructed, probably linking it with the gatehouse. A massive stone platform in front of the hall block formed the base of an external staircase leading into the modified hall at first-floor level. The chamber block, providing private accommodation for the lord's family, has not been located, but was probably close to the great hall, at the upper end nearest the dais. Even allowing for the fact that many of the castle's internal buildings are likely to have been of timber, there seems remarkably little living accommodation. One wonders whether the castle can ever have been the main residence for the various owners.

Other features are identifiable from documentary evidence, such as the existence of a chapel, a well, a dovecote, stable, and granary, the last three all listed in a document of 1409.[8]

Undoubtedly there were many other features within the courtyard, either robbed out to below ground level for their stone, or built of timber. Quite substantial timber structures could have leaned against the inside of the curtain wall without leaving any trace, especially since much of what we see of the curtain is itself a nineteenth-century restoration. The chapel, a substantial building according to Machell, stood close in front of the great hall. A circular mark near the centre of the castle, shown on an aerial photograph, could be the site of the dovecote, while the same picture shows the earthwork of a large rectangular building inside, and to the west of, the main gate.

Some of the more interesting finds discovered during the three periods of excavations since the 1950s are now in Kendal Museum. They include a sixteenth-century majolica altar vase, made on the Continent and clearly associated with the chapel; German stoneware drinking vessels, of a type popular in the sixteenth and seventeenth centuries; a packhorse bell, perhaps a relic of Kendal's extensive use of packhorse transport; and a 'wrestler' slate from the ridge of one of the internal buildings.

The owners of the castle

It has to be said at the outset that we do not know who built the castle. There are no documents, and archaeology has not yet given us the answer. Perhaps it was Gilbert, son of Roger Fitz Reinfrid, who seems to have been a 'coming man' in the late twelfth century, but there is evidence to suggest that the major development of the relatively new 'second castle' was associated with the foundation of the borough. One possibility is that the seat of local power quite soon shifted from its original site at Castle Howe, the 'first castle', because the creation of the new borough, and a general lack of space, meant that the older complex became too cramped. It is possible that it was this eastern castle which in 1216 Gilbert, son of Roger, had to render up to King John, together with that of *Morhull* (Mourholme, in Warton near Carnforth) and the payment of a huge fine of 12,000 marks, having backed the wrong side in the civil warfare of that troubled reign.

left The south tower and postern gateway of Kendal Castle.

right The Troutbecke Tower, a circular tower on the western wall of the Castle, perhaps used latterly as the receiver's office for rents.

PHOTOGRAPHS: AUTHOR

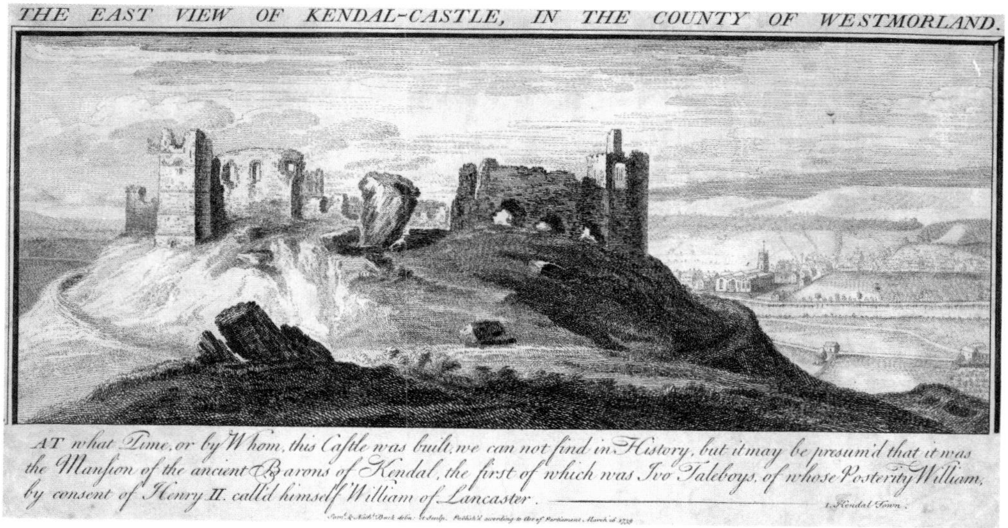
THE EAST VIEW OF KENDAL-CASTLE, IN THE COUNTY OF WESTMORLAND.
AT what Time, or by Whom, this Castle was built, we can not find in History, but it may be presum'd that it was the Mansion of the ancient Barons of Kendal, the first of which was Ivo Taleboys, of whose Posterity William, by consent of Henry II. call'd himself William of Lancaster.
1. Kendal Town.

Samuel and Nathaniel Buck's engraving of the Castle, 1739. The view is from the east, ie towards the town, and shows a somewhat exaggerated mound, especially at the north end.

KENDAL LIBRARY, CUMBRIA COUNTY COUNCIL

Notwithstanding this little difficulty, in due course William de Lancaster, son of Gilbert, inherited the castle and estates, and it was he who established the borough between 1222 and his death in 1246. In the latter year the Kendal portion passed into the hands of Peter de Brus, and on his death in 1272 it went to his sister and brother-in-law Margaret and Robert de Ros.[9] Robert died just two years later, and in 1297 Margaret then conveyed the castle to her son William de Ros. He inherited it outright on her death in 1307. When he

William Stukeley's prospect of Kendal showing Parish Church and Castle, 1725.

THE BODLEIAN LIBRARY, UNIVERSITY OF OXFORD, MS TOP GEN D.14, FOL. 20R

Prospect of Kendale Church & Castle from Kirkbarrow hill Aug. 14. 1725.

in turn died in 1310 the castle was said to be 'in bad repair'. The new owner was William's son Thomas, only 3½ years old on his father's death. He was taken into wardship, in 1325 (when he came of age) petitioning to take possession of his property. He had to wait another three years to get it, but having done so he enjoyed the benefits for many years, not dying until the age of 84 in 1390.[10]

His granddaughter Elizabeth, wife of William de Parr, succeeded him as owner of the castle and its estate. This is the first occurrence of the Parrs, famous as the ancestors of Queen Katherine Parr and inextricably associated in popular legend and belief with the history of the castle. Elizabeth predeceased her husband William, who himself died in 1404. Their son John succeeded to the property, but he was dead in 1409, leaving a young son, Thomas. Having come of age, Thomas negotiated a deal over his mother's dower in 1431. He was succeeded by his son William (who inherited in 1461 and died in 1484) and grandson Thomas.[11] It was this Thomas who was the father of Queen Katherine Parr. He was made steward of the king's lands in Kendal in 1509 and was granted free warren in his manor of Kendal in 1511. In 1513 he obtained a forty-year grant from the king for many of the economic assets of Kendal which for centuries had been separated by divided inheritance, including tolls, fairs and markets, and the profits of the borough itself.[12]

When Thomas Parr died in 1518 his son, William, was five years old (and his daughter, Katherine, just six). William became Marquis of Northampton and died in 1572, but by then the castle had already been abandoned a few years earlier and its grounds disparked. In popular stories and legends over the past three centuries, Katherine Parr has become inextricably associated with Kendal. Although she was of course a member of the family that had owned the castle and estate since the end of the fourteenth century, her own influence and presence in the town has been much exaggerated.

The legend of her close connections with Kendal, including her being born there, started with Sir Daniel Fleming in the seventeenth century,[13] and has been enthusiastically maintained ever since. Machell states that Kendal Castle 'has been the seat of some notable families and here the famous Queen Katherine was born, the sixth and last wife of Henry VIII whom he married at Windsor Castle in 1543'.[14] In Kendal Museum we are shown a German stoneware drinking mug, alleged to have been used by Katherine at Kendal. In fact, she was born elsewhere and probably never even visited Kendal, a remote and not especially convenient family estate where the castle was already well on the way to ruin. However, antiquarians liked to create such connections, and just as John of Gaunt will forever be associated, in a spurious relationship, with nearby Lancaster, so Katherine and Kendal will always go together.[15]

In 1572 a survey was commissioned by William Parr's widow, the dowager marchioness of Northampton. It states that

> The Castle of Kendal is situate on the knowl of a hill, within the park there, and on the east side of the town, with a fair and beautiful prospect. The out walls embattled 40 ft square ... within the same no building left, saving only, on the north side is situate the

> front of the gatehouse, the hall with an ascent of the stairs to the same, with a buttery and pantry at the end thereof; one great chamber and 2 or 3 lesser chambers, and rooms of ease, adjoining the same, all being in decay both in glass and slates and in all other reparations needful. Under the hall are two or three small rooms of cellars ... The walls are circular, guarded by three towers and a keep, with a large square area in the centre, being all in a state of dilapidation ... There is a dove cot in the south side thereof in good repair.[16]

Another description of 1588, in a letter from Edward Bradyll to Lord Burghley, adds to the picture of decay:

> The moste parte of the rouffs of the said Castell are falne downe, the tymber and sclayte pitifully broken, the gutters of lead, iron in windowes and doors pilfered and stoln away.[17]

Evidence of this pillaging came in graphic form with the archaeological discovery in 1996 of a small lead-melting hearth set on top of the vaulting under the great hall. At some stage in its decay the castle might have provided accommodation for a tenant farmer, since parts of the hall complex would still have been habitable—a midden, perhaps of the sixteenth century, was located in excavations outside the hall.[18] Further ruination followed, including the partial destruction or collapse of the gatehouse, apparently after Machell's 1692 drawing. A huge fragment survived until a great wind in 1824 blew it down and shattered it. Since the gatehouse was probably the most massive part of the castle, it is hard to imagine that it originally fell of its own accord. One wonders whether it was slighted during or after the Civil War to make it indefensible, although the rest of the castle would not have offered much resistance. Perhaps it was merely the victim of stone-robbing, or even destroyed to allow carts access into the interior for that purpose?

In 1692 Machell described how

> The Castle stands on a round hill on the East side of the river Kent having a pleasant and delightful prospect of the town of Kendal ... and was heretofore so surrounded with trees, standing in the midst of the park, that no part of the house but a single turret could be seen afar off. But now there is neither wood nor deer and the very castle is become a ruin.[19]

This is the only description of the emparked area around. The wood made its reappearance in 1813 when the curtain wall was rebuilt and trees were planted around the castle in a clump, at the behest of the owner Mrs Thomasin Richardson. In 1830 the young John Ruskin made a visit here: 'we shortly arrived in Kendal, where we stayed till the next morning; in the afternoon, we took a walk to the Castle which looks very well from the town, but is a disagreeable nettly place, when you are at it.'[20]

In the nineteenth century the Corporation acquired the site and in 1897, to mark Queen Victoria's Diamond Jubilee, it was opened to the public. It had been used by the people of Kendal much earlier, as can be seen from the long series of photographs in Kendal Library showing leisure activities there, and it was also in demand as a space for the Volunteers to camp or to parade and drill. Nothing much was done with the ruins until a century later, when interpretation and some visitor information were provided. Recent work has made the castle more accessible and comprehensible, and it is, as it has been for two centuries, a popular attraction to locals and visitors alike.

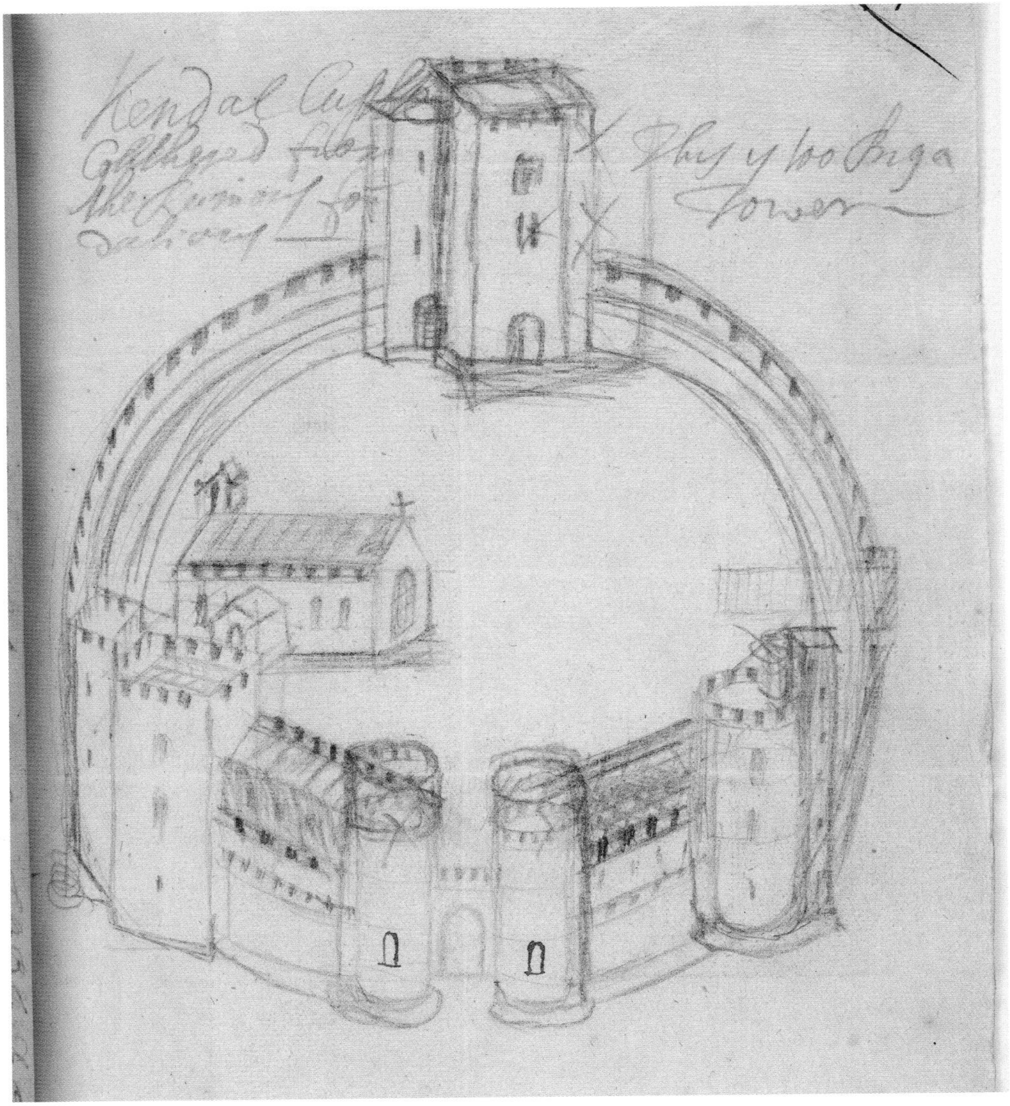

Thomas Machell's drawing of Kendal Castle in 1698. The tower at the top of the picture (south) is annotated in pencil 'This is too Big a Tower', and there are a number of features which seem incorrect, but it has the merit of being the earliest detailed image of the Castle.

REPRODUCED BY KIND PERMISSION OF CUMBRIA ARCHIVE SERVICE

Kendal on the map | 4

KENDAL IS FORTUNATE in having a succession of detailed town plans from which we can deduce much about its settlement history. Unlike many other towns it retains to a high degree the layout that was established in the late medieval period, and which in turn goes back to roots in the early thirteenth century, when it received its borough charter. Many roads have been added, and the town has expanded greatly from its original core, but the simple pattern of central streets, which gives the town its essential character, remains instantly recognisable from early maps.

No medieval maps of Kendal exist—the Gough Map of about 1360, which is preserved in the Bodleian Library, shows only a conventionalised picture-image for 'Kirkebie Kendale'—but it is possible to use some of the later maps to project backwards in time. The earliest surviving plan is Speed's little map of the town in 1611–12. Although it is not itself medieval in date, it belongs to a time before the great growth of Kendal in the eighteenth and nineteenth centuries. It therefore records a situation not far removed from that of the fourteenth or fifteenth centuries, although it must of course be used with care. Among other features it shows a very simple street pattern with conventionalised houses occupying the street-frontages. A key beside the map lists thirty-two names, of streets, fields and individual buildings. In this way it helps us to 'fix' the names then current, indicating for instance that even in 1611 the main street north from Kirkland was known as Highgate and not Soutergate, although this name was so beloved of antiquaries such as Curwen that even in 1900 he used it in preference.

It is not only through the maps themselves that we learn things. By comparing them we can offer dates for significant growth or change, at least within limits. Each new map reveals new

John Speed's map of 1611-12. Speed is now known to have surveyed the town himself in 1607 and his original manuscript plan is in Merton College, Oxford.

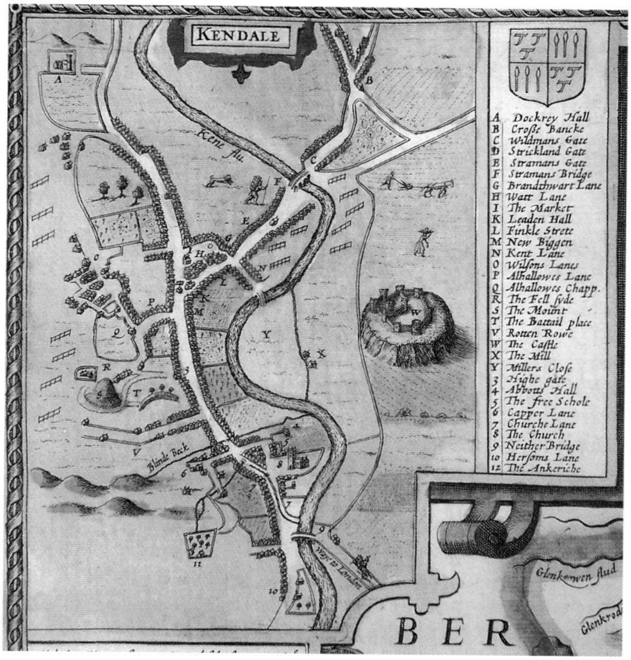

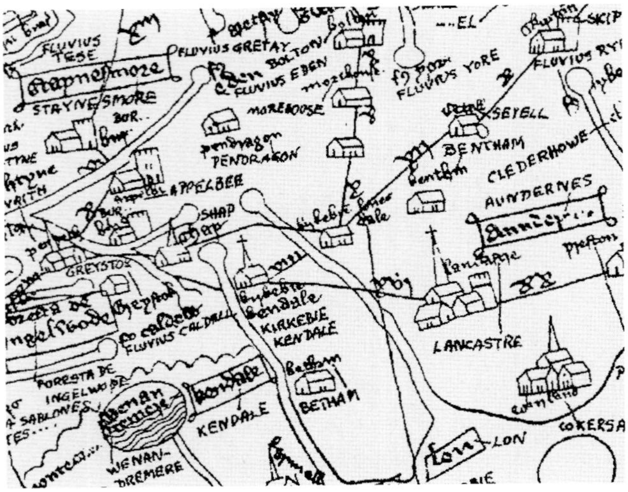

Detail from the Gough map of c.1360. North is to the left. Kendal is shown as 'Kirkebie Kendale' with a conventionalised church.

SKETCHED FROM THE ORIGINAL IN THE BODLEIAN LIBRARY, OXFORD

features. Of course, maps are always out of date. From surveying to publication is usually a matter of years, so that by their date of publication things will have changed, often radically. However, they are often the best available source for the appearance and disappearance of elements of the townscape and landscape.

John Speed, 1611–12

This, the earliest plan of Kendal by a considerable margin, appears in the corner of John Speed's Westmorland map in his *Theatre of the Empire of Great Britaine*, which was published in 1611–12. The Kendal plan is often given the date of 1614, but this seems to be wrong. The maps were completed by 1610, and the atlas itself published the next year. Speed's county maps were largely derived from the surveys of others, but in producing the town plans which are fitted into blank corners of these sheets he was often a pioneer. Usually these plans were of the county towns, but Westmorland was provided with a plan of Kendal rather than of Appleby, the county town, presumably because Kendal was much the larger and more prosperous of the two. The number of such town plans depended upon the shape of the county, and thus how much space was left in the corners or margins. Of seventy such town plans some 44 were surveyed by Speed himself. The remainder are derived from other sources, some of which are known, others not. Kendal is now thought to be among the former, surveyed by Speed on his way south from Carlisle on 15 August 1607. The original manuscript survey is in Merton College Library, Oxford, along with others from this series.[1] The scale is not shown on the printed map, but must be about 5 inches to the mile. The Merton College draft is surveyed at a scale of 50 paces to the inch, or 1:3,000.

Speed's plan shows an entirely recognisable Kendal, with the constituent parts we still see. To the south there is Kirkland, south of Blind Beck, with the parish church. Further north is the main street of Highgate and Stricklandgate, with the market place to the east, and east of this Stramongate leads in a north-easterly direction out across the Kent. To the west is the straggle of houses that makes up Fellside. On all sides, in the meanders of the river and on Kendal Fell, stand the tenters for cloth, which was by then the mainstay of the town's economy. The houses all hug the street frontage, except in Fellside, where

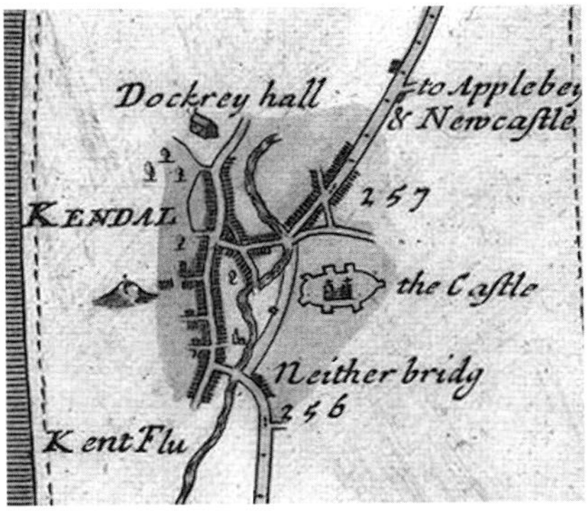

Miniature plan of Kendal from Ogilby's strip map of the road from London to Carlisle, 1675.

there is no perceptible pattern. The yards had yet to develop behind the frontage houses, and to this extent the map shows a town that would also have been recognisable to its medieval inhabitants.

The key to the map uses all the letters of the alphabet except J, U and Z, and the numbers 3–11, so a total of 32 features are identified. These letters and numbers are deployed roughly from north to south, although somewhat unsystematically. Why 1 and 2 were omitted is unclear—perhaps 1 could have been confused with 'I', but the same cannot be argued for 2. The principal streets are all named: Stricklandgate to the north, Highgate to the south, and Stramongate with its extension, Wildman's Gate (Wildman Street) to the east, leading to '(Far) Cross Bancke'. The main road to the south divides at Nether Bridge and is shown as 'Waye to London' (the modern A65) and 'Hersoms Lane', presumably for the road to Heversham (the modern A6). To the east is the castle, its perspective somewhat difficult to disentangle, with Dockray Hall to the north, Fellside to the west and 'The Ankeriche' to the south, all at least in name features of modern Kendal.

Jefferys, 1770

Apart from the very basic plans used by Ogilby (1675) and Bowen (1720) in their road-books, both of which are almost certainly derivative, the next map after Speed does not appear for over a century and a half. It is the small plan that occurs in the corner of Thomas Jefferys' map of Westmorland, dated 1770. Since it serves the same purpose as Speed's plan—something to occupy an empty corner of a larger map—it is awkwardly shaped and rather tightly confined within its borders. Nevertheless, it shows some interesting detail, particularly individual buildings that seem to be realistically proportioned rather than simply conventionalised. Among these are outbuildings, and presumably industrial premises, set at the further ends of the burgage plots, especially between Highgate or Stramongate and the river. Interestingly no tenter-frames relating to the woollen industry are marked, although they certainly existed here. In fact the plan betrays little of Kendal's industrial base, and we have to obtain information on this from other sources.

Jefferys' plan occupies the left-hand half of sheet 3 of his map. The survey took place in 1768, and it was the first of his three county maps (the

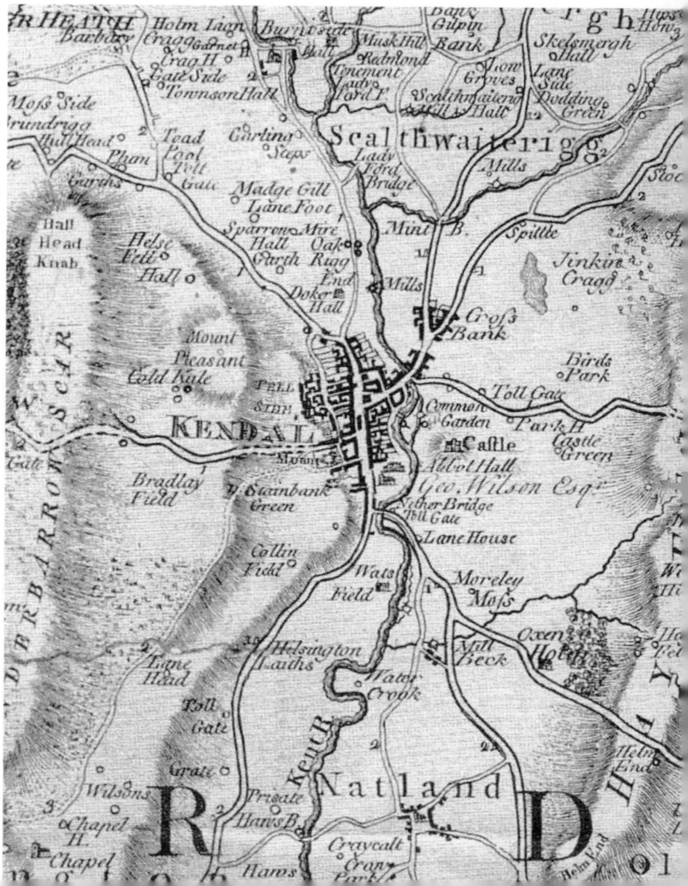

Detail of the area around Kendal from Jefferys' one-inch map of Westmorland, 1770.

others being of Yorkshire and Cumberland) at the new scale of one inch to the mile, encouraged by prizes offered by the Society of Arts. The effort bankrupted Jefferys, the London publisher, who died in 1771. The actual surveyor was John Ainslie, perhaps assisted by Thomas Donald, who was responsible for the adjacent parts of Yorkshire. A facsimile has recently been published by the Cumberland & Westmorland Antiquarian & Archaeological Society.[2]

The plan shows the traditional area of the town, from Kirkland in the south to Dockray Hall in the north, and so closely copies the Speed outline. It is partly in the style of a block plan, showing an undivided frontage to the main streets, and partly showing as individual buildings, where they are on back land. Its scale is just over 135 yards to the inch, or about 13 inches to the mile. There is no key, all the names being on the plan itself. Individual buildings identified include Abbot Hall, the church, the vicarage, the free school and the meeting houses and chapels (these being the chapel in the Market Place (St George's), the Dissenting Meeting House off Branthwaite Brow, and the Presbeterian (*sic*) Meeting House at The Banks. The Friends' Meeting House is not shown.

Outlying features include the Poors House at the very top of the plan, near a common garden. Another Common Garden is shown in the bend of the river below the castle. The castle itself is marked purely conventionally, as a regular hexagon. Below it is the mill leat leading off the river, and also the mills it served. A brewery stands in Wildman Street, and a tollgate is marked on the far side of Nether Bridge, on what is now the A65. Two bowling greens lie on the west side of the town, one off Low Fell Side, the other occupying what was once the bailey of the Mount or Castle Howe, the old Norman castle-mound. For the first time there is an attempt to delineate the fields surrounding the town, which is useful when we come to interpret later developments, since these are often determined by pre-existing boundaries.[3]

John Todd, 1787

John Todd's map of 1787 is on a much larger scale—slightly less than 70 yards to the inch, or roughly 25 inches to the mile. It can thus be readily compared with the maps of Wood (1833), Hoggarth (1853) and the Ordnance Survey (1914). A facsimile of this map has been produced by the Curwen Archives Trust. Todd's plan, unlike any of the others, is orientated with north to the right and west to the top, creating a landscape format. It is headed 'A Plan of Kendal in the County of Westmorland, from an Actual Survey Anno 1787 By John Todd' in a cartouche in the top left corner, which also shows the corporation seal. At three blank points in the lower part (the fields east of the town) are placed vignettes of the church, the castle and Abbot Hall. The source from which these vignettes were derived is unclear, since the view of the castle by Samuel and Nathaniel Buck, dating from 1739, was drawn from the opposite side. Despite its relatively late date no map illustrates better the pattern of medieval burgage plots making up the town.

This very detailed and attractive plan contains a great deal of useful information. Its focus is upon the usual area, lying roughly between Nether Bridge (to the left) and the workhouse

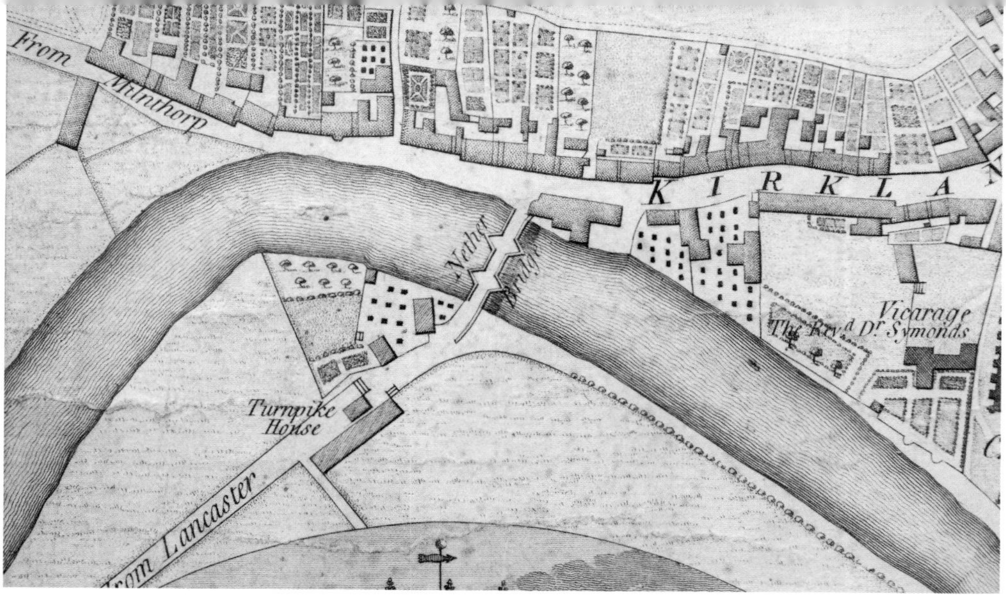

Detail from John Todd's map, 1787.

PHOTOGRAPH CARNEGIE, FROM AN ORIGINAL HELD AT WESTMORLAND RECORD OFFICE, KENDAL

(to the right), now joined by Dockray Hall Barn and the House of Correction. There is much more interesting information, including names of roads, chapels, bowling greens and common gardens, of which there are several. A workhouse, a house of correction and a dispensary have also appeared, heralding the growth of provision for the poor, the criminal and the sick. The boundaries between individual burgage plots are shown, as are the shape of buildings, and many industrial features. The fields are shown in some detail, and the tenter-frames are marked beyond the workhouse to the north, by the river at the northern end of Stricklandgate, on Kendal Fell to the west, and in two places to the east of the town near Castle Mills and on an island in the river (Goose Holme) opposite Thorney Hills. The map even includes such minor but intriguing features as 'Willow Wand Tarn', just below the castle, presumably important for the local basket-making trade.

Because of the large scale of the map there is some attempt to show garden layouts, though these are unlikely to be accurate and are possibly invented by the engraver to fill in otherwise blank spaces. 'Common Garden' is shown just to the east of Castle Mill and 'New Common Garden' immediately to the south of the bend in the Sedbergh Road. Another set of symbols, this time consisting of small black rectangles, is more likely to be significant. These are only found by the riverside fronting Waterside or New Road; near the vicarage in Kirkland; and across the river where Beezon Road now stands. There are some fifteen such groups, and from contemporary evidence and later maps we can identify these as tanyards with their tanning pits, which were undoubtedly filled from the river and their noisome contents returned there after use.

J. Lowes, 1798

This little map was engraved by J. Lowes, but the surveyor is unknown. It fills a gap between the plans by Todd (1787) and Wood (1833). It is probably derivative and was used to illustrate a book. At the two lower corners of the map are a very crude image of Abbot Hall and an

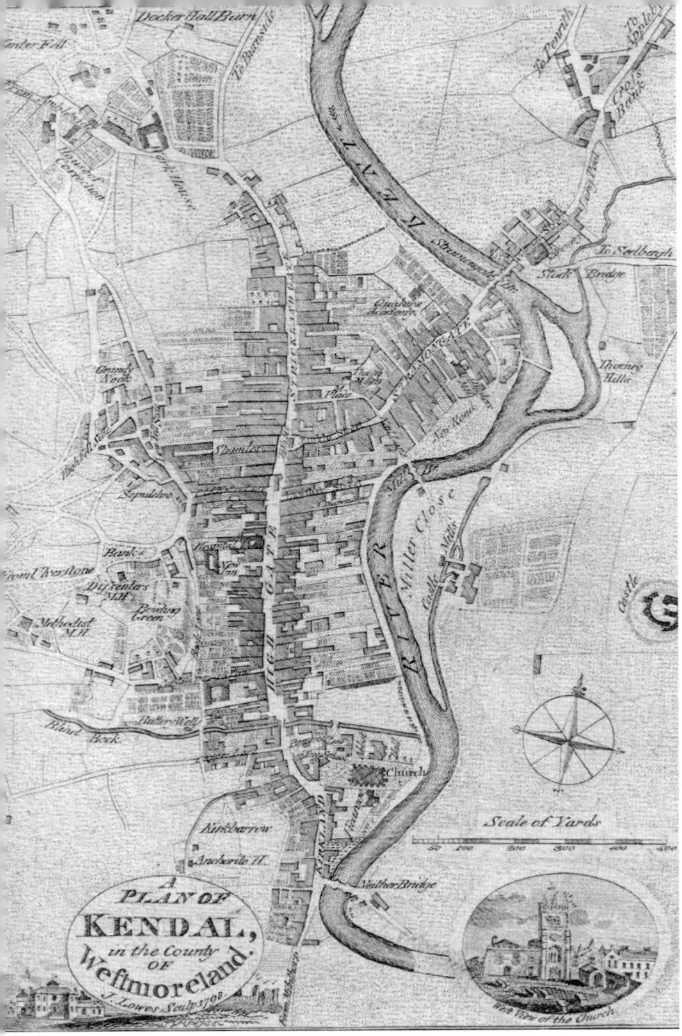

Lowes' map, 1798.

even cruder vignette of the parish church. The scale is 300 yards to the inch, or just less than 6 inches to the mile, and although it usefully fits between the other two maps its small scale and the basic cartography means that it adds little to our detailed knowledge of Kendal.

John Wood, 1833

In 1833 another map appeared, surveyed by John Wood, an interesting character whose life is somewhat shadowy. His maps are always rare, many apparently existing only in a single copy, and it is not easy to understand how he managed to make a living, since it was usual to have a sufficient number of subscribers before embarking upon a project of this sort. Wood was a Yorkshire surveyor, born in the early 1780s, who was later based in Edinburgh. He surveyed some 52 towns in Scotland, 48 of which appeared in his Town Atlas of 1828, and another 59 in England and Wales, mostly in the north and west. Surveying was done in the field, and the engraving was carried out by a number of firms in Edinburgh, a centre of the map and printing trade.[4] A facsimile of this map has been produced by the Curwen Archives Trust.

The map is headed 'Plan of Kendal made by John Wood 1833', while at the bottom is 'John Wood, Surveyor, Northallerton, Yorkshire'. It is at a scale of about 75 yards to the inch or slightly less than 25 inches to the mile, comparable to those of Todd (1787), Hoggarth (1853) and the Ordnance Survey. As well as the very detailed captioning, which includes most of the yard and inn names on the main streets, and the owners of the surrounding fields, there is a set of seventeen numbers in the right margin listing key buildings (such as chapels and banks) which would otherwise have been difficult to label individually.

By 1833 Kendal had begun to break out of its ancient bounds, with the extension of building onto the eastern bank of the river. This process started in a tentative way with Castle Buildings and Kent Terrace, two rows of genteel houses east of Goose Holme, and with the beginnings of a small agglomeration of industry around the Canal Head, from 1819 the northern terminus of the Lancaster Canal. The canal itself is one of the more significant additions to the map. Further industry had appeared south-east of Nether Bridge—a tannery; the Netherfield works, which was later to become very important; and the gasworks, reliant on canal-borne coal.

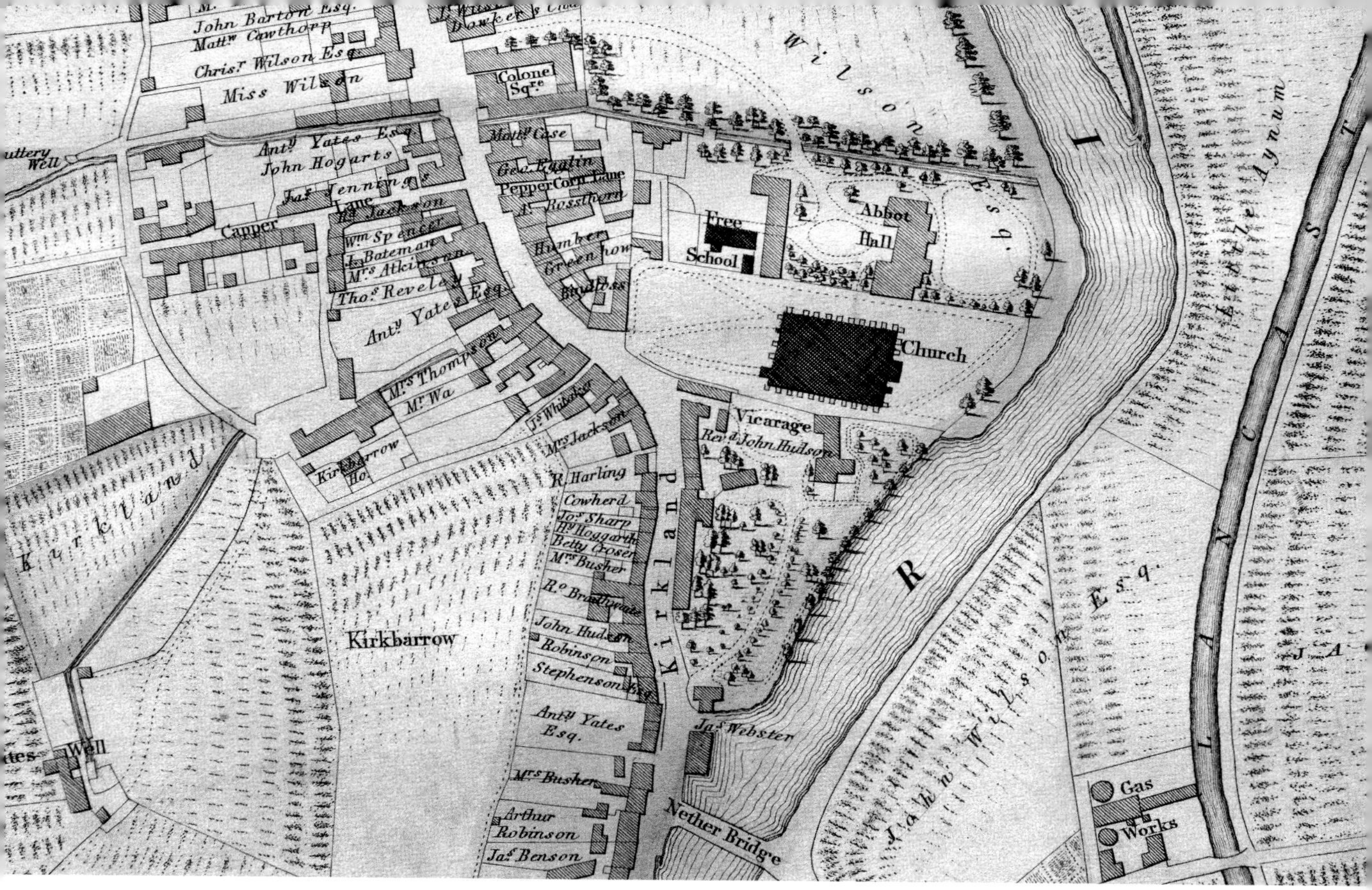

A detail of Wood's map of 1833, showing the parish church and Kirkland.

PHOTOGRAPH CARNEGIE, FROM AN ORIGINAL HELD AT WESTMORLAND RECORD OFFICE, KENDAL

To the north, beside the road to Windermere, were now the series of terraces (Union Street, Caroline Street, Strickland Street and Cross Street) resulting from the activities of the Union Building Societies in the 1820s, which had sought to increase the number of freeholders in the town and thereby add to the Liberal vote.

Corn Rent map, c.1834

The production of this map was necessitated by a large and expensive legal dispute.[5] It is one of the forerunners of the great series of tithe apportionment maps which historians use so extensively as evidence for field-names, property ownership, and farming practices in the early Victorian countryside.[6] As with the post-1836 tithe apportionments and maps, it was associated with a scheme to establish monetary payments based on land values in lieu of paying tithes in kind to the incumbent of the Established Church, which had become complex, tiresome, and unwieldy. The map is to be dated to about 1834 and its scale is less than half that of Hoggarth's map of 1853 (see below), at about 12 inches to the mile. It is also less than half the scale commonly used for the major tithe surveying of the 1840s (26.7 inches to the mile). As it is concerned with agricultural produce it shows the fields surrounding the town, 730 of them in all, but omits large parts of the built-up area, such as most of Kirkland and all of Highgate. Of those parts that are shown, the principal ones are the northern end of Stricklandgate, the

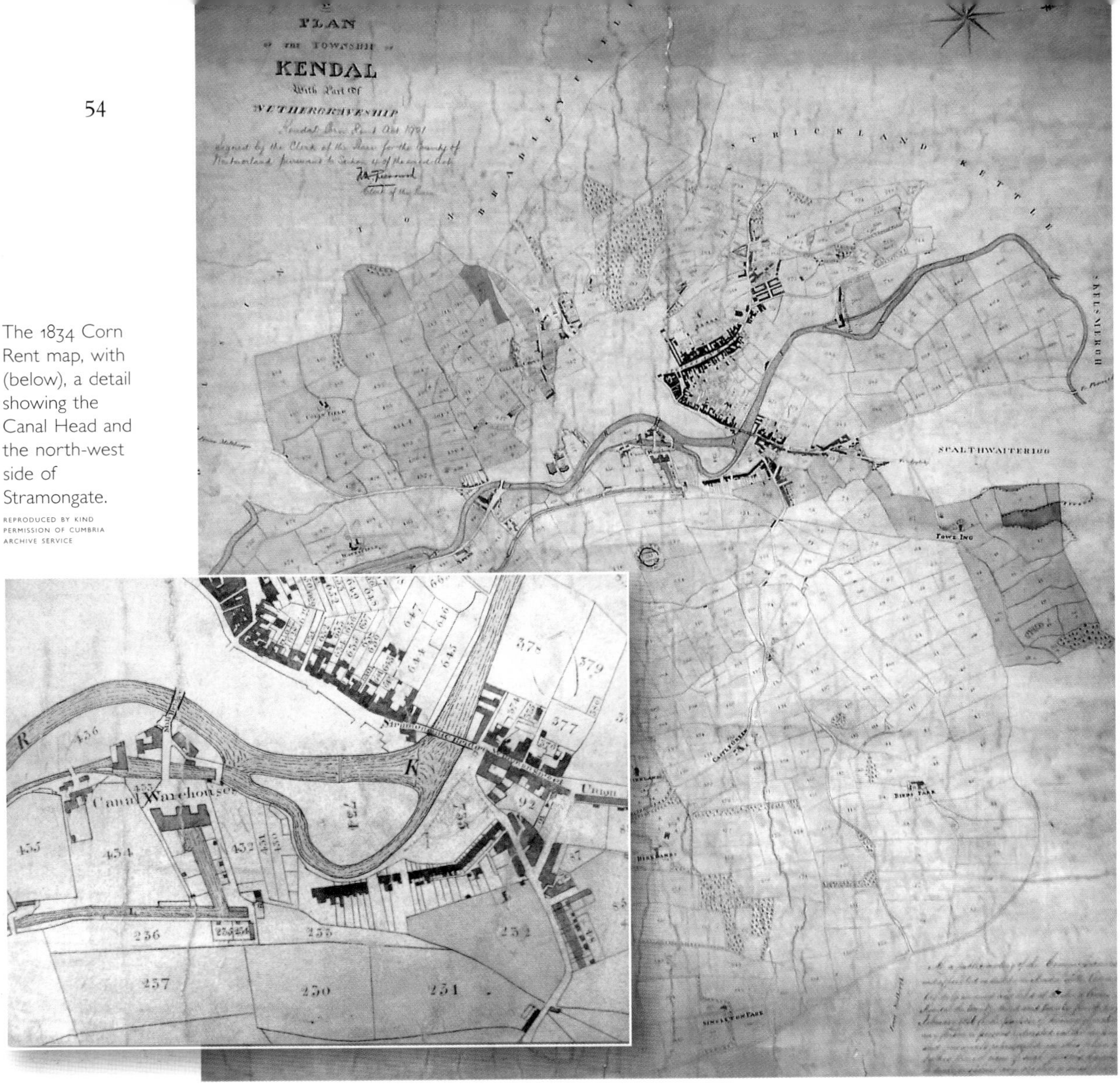

The 1834 Corn Rent map, with (below), a detail showing the Canal Head and the north-west side of Stramongate.

north side of Stramongate, Beast Banks, and the whole of the built-up area east of the Kent including Thorny Hills and Far Cross Bank.

The fields include many east of the town which had 'Park' names—for example, Kendal Parks, Singleton Park and Birds Park—and these reveal the location of the deer parks that were associated with the medieval castle estate. Interestingly this area can be compared with a plan of about 1700 which shows the 'Castle & Park Lands' to the east of the Kent and has differently sized and shaped fields.[7] There are other oddities in the 1834 plan, such as fields 79 and 80 which are named Organ Close, presumably because the rent from them paid some or all of the salary of the organist at the parish church. The accompanying schedule lists owners, tenants, field and building names, and the actual area measurement, to contemporaries the most important part of the survey.

Henry Hoggarth, 1853

By the mid-nineteenth century private mapmakers had to compete with the Ordnance Survey, which produced maps of Kendal on a range of scales: six inches to one mile (1863), 25 inches to one mile (1860 and 1914) and the exceptionally large scale of 1:500 (roughly ten feet to one mile) in 1861. Nonetheless, in 1853 the surveyor Henry Hoggarth published his 'Plan of the Town of Kendal in the County of Westmorland from an actual survey', lithographed by Waterlow & Sons of London. The scale is about 75 yards to the inch or just under 25 inches to the mile, comparable to Todd's and Wood's earlier maps and that of the Ordnance Survey seven years later. The original map was coloured to show the ward divisions: Kendal, Park and Castle Lands, Nether-Graveship, Scalthwaiterigg, Strickland Ketel and Kirkland. Again, a facsimile has been produced by the Curwen Archives Trust.

The map extends further to the north and east than that produced by Wood. There may have been changes in the intervening two decades, but there is a surprising lack of new building outside the town area. For the first time the woodland above High Fellside is marked as Serpentine Walks. These woods, and particularly the little summerhouse built in about 1833, were very popular for picnics and represent part of the growing social amenities of Kendal. Two new terraces have appeared—Castle Park Terrace to the east and Cliff Side Terrace to the west, above Low Beast Banks—and other new features were the two churches, St Thomas in Stricklandgate (1836–37) and St George on the east bank of the river, on the former Tenter Holme (1839–41). The Roman Catholic presence was also more visible, with their new church of Holy Trinity and St George on New Road (1835–37).

However, the biggest change was undoubtedly the arrival of the Kendal & Windermere Railway, connecting Windermere with the main line at Oxenholme and opened in 1846. It cut diagonally across the eastern part of the town, with a station at Longpool serving Kendal town. Like the earlier canal, the railway soon attracted industrial concerns. Fields containing tenter-frames for cloth are still to be seen at Green Bank, Low Tenterfell, High Tenterfell, Martin Croft, and Goose Holme. At the very bottom of the map is the Lound Foundry, set between the canal and the river. Two more iron foundries lie to the west of Kirkland.

Titus Wilson, 1861

The surveyor of this map is unknown, but it was produced to illustrate the second edition of Nicholson's *Annals of Kendal*, which was published in 1861.[8] The scale is about 280 yards to the inch or about 6¼ inches to the mile. Due to its small scale, and because it was published only eight years after Hoggarth's plan, this map adds little to our knowledge, although it is certainly a more convenient size.

Ordnance Survey, 1861

Kendal is indeed fortunate to have been among the places included in the project for the largest-scale town mapping ever systematically undertaken in this country. A start had been made in the late 1840s with surveying large-scale maps for all towns with a population over 4,000 (that threshold being determined by the need for sufficient detail to plan sanitary improvements). Kendal, like Appleby, was surveyed in 1861 and Carlisle in 1866 at a slightly smaller scale, but Lancaster and Preston, for example, had to wait until 1892, when the maps appeared almost simultaneously with the 25-inch series.[9] The scale of this mapping, 1:500 or just over ten feet to the mile, means that individual buildings, including the details of back yards and gardens, street furniture and even the interior plans of some public buildings, are shown in enormous and impressive detail. The disadvantage is that even for a modestly sized town such as Kendal the map occupies many sheets, so it is difficult to gain an overview because each covers such a limited area. However, the benefits of such a source far outweigh any practical problems, and apart from its inherent interest the map is a key primary source for all sorts of themes. There are two sets locally, both incomplete: one at the Cumbria Record Office and another (more complete) set of photocopies at Kendal Reference Library.[10] The latter set consists of twenty-eight half sheets, the numbering of which is related to the 25 inch mapping.

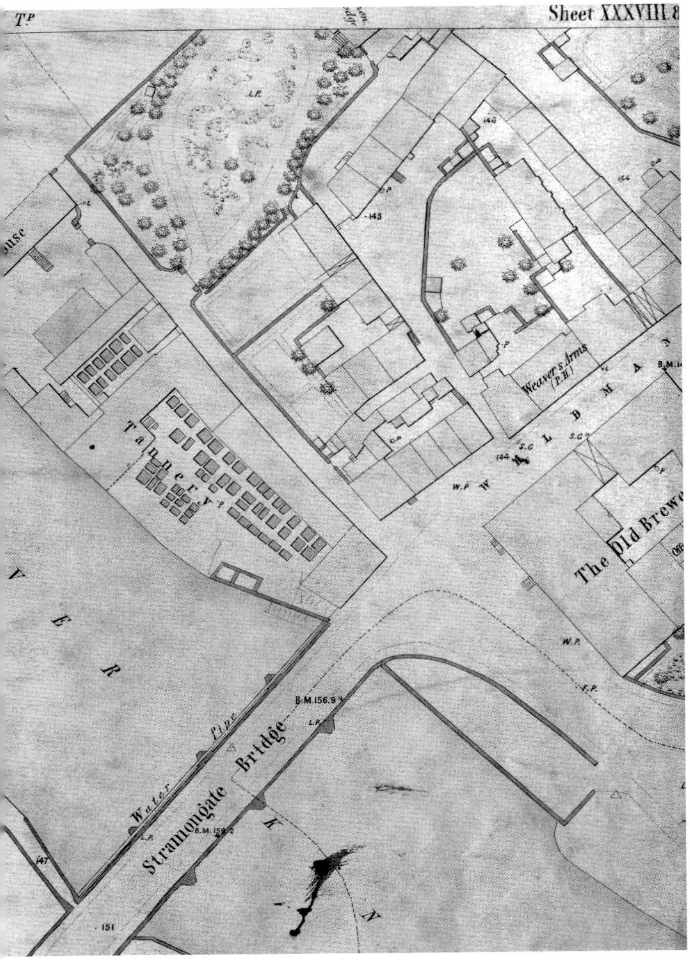

A detail of the Ordnance Survey 500" map of Kendal, 1861, showing Stramongate Bridge and tannery.

PHOTOGRAPH CARNEGIE, FROM AN ORIGINAL HELD AT WESTMORLAND RECORD OFFICE, KENDAL

Because of the huge cost of surveying less of the urban fringe is mapped than on those at a smaller scale, but this series is remarkably useful for its depiction of the yards and the many inns in the town centre, and also for its detailed depiction of industrial premises. The cluster of works around Canal Head and the various tanneries along the riverside are particularly well shown, the latter having every tanpit delineated. As noted above, public buildings, including the main churches, chapels and schools, the house of correction, the workhouse, the market house and town hall, the almshouses, and even the New Shambles, are all shown in ground-floor plan, with the interior layouts. Thus we can see exactly how much space each individual was allowed in Sandes Hospital, and the various wards of the workhouse.

Mapping on this scale was ruinously expensive, but what a joy it is for the local historian! After

1894 it was decided that all towns as yet unmapped would be surveyed at only 1:2,500 or smaller—in other words at a fifth of this scale—unless the local authority paid for a larger scale. Few did![11]

Ordnance Survey, 1914

In 1914 the Ordnance Survey published a map at the scale of 25 inches to one mile, revised in 1911 from an earlier survey. Although this is of course a much smaller scale than the magnificent 1861 sheets, it is still respectably detailed and is comparable in scale with the earlier maps by Todd, Wood and Hoggarth. Two sheets were required to show the built-up area of Kendal, since growth had been considerable between 1861 and 1914. Facsimiles of both have been conveniently published by Alan Godfrey Maps as 'Kendal North' and 'Kendal South', at a reduced scale.

The changes between 1861 and 1914 had been profound. There was very extensive recent

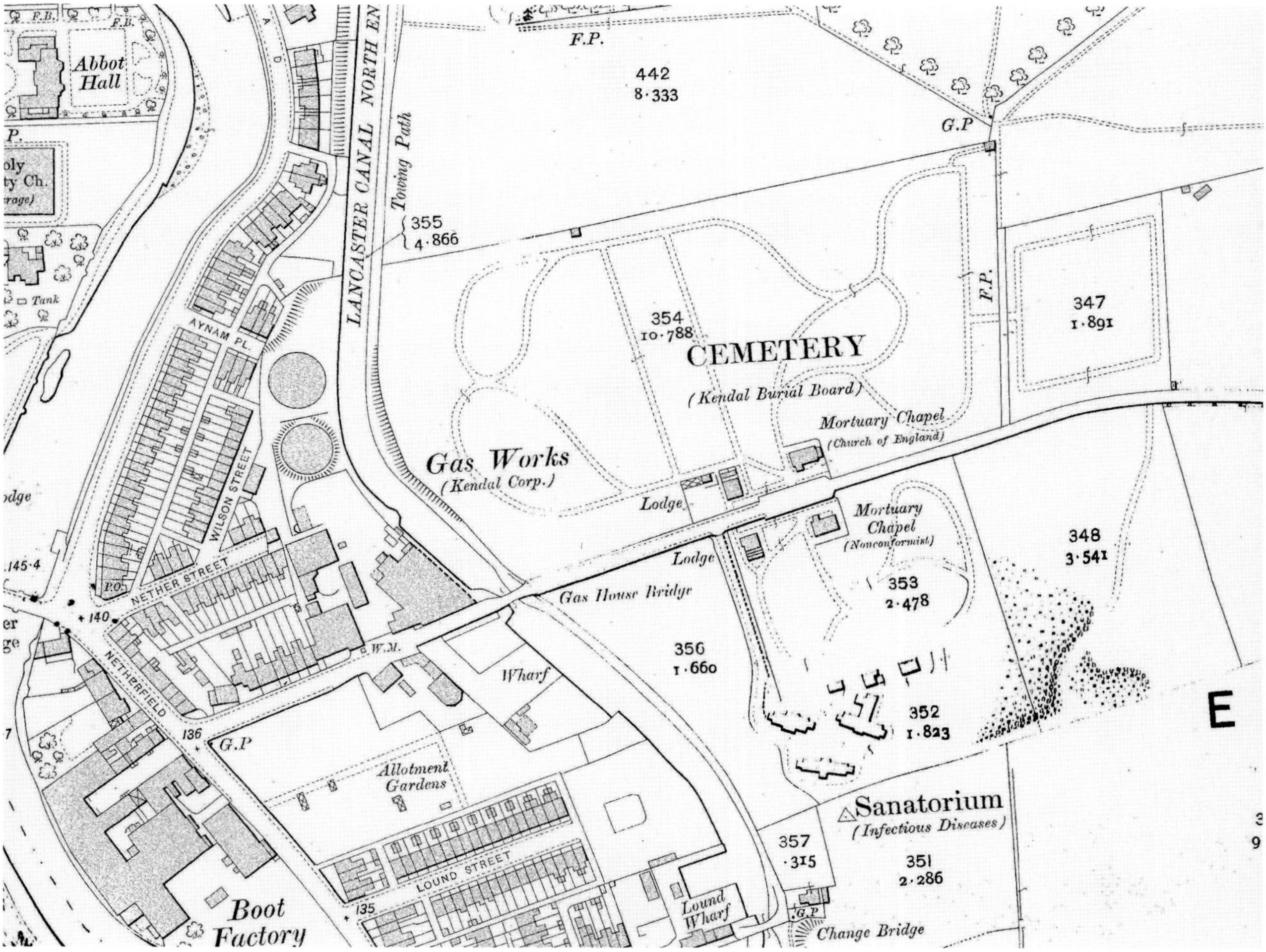

Ordnance Survey 25" map of Kendal 1914 showing gasworks, cemetery and Netherfield Boot Works.

housing around the fringes of the older built-up area. A block of new streets had appeared between Milnthorpe Road and the river, including Romney Road, Park Street, Park Avenue and West Street. On the opposite bank there was by 1914 a more or less continuous frontage of houses, with other streets at right angles such as Garden Street, Lound Street, Nether Street, Aynam Place, Parr Street, Sunnyside and Queen Catherine Street. Ribbon development of larger houses now lined the road to Sedbergh, beyond the railway line. On the western side of the town the boundary at the upper ends of the old burgage plots, long established except for the ragged sprawl of Fellside, was now broken. Gilling Gate, a new creation of 1861, and Captain French Lane were lined with houses running up the hillside. Green Side, Summer Hill, Victoria Terrace, Serpentine Road, Queen's Road and Grandy Nook all represented favoured positions overlooking the town. To the north semi-detached houses fronted the road to Windermere at Highfield Villas, while on the other side of the road several new terraces had appeared at Shaw's Brow. To the east, beyond Far Cross Bank, new terraces appeared at Mint Street, Crescent Green, Westfield, East Bank and Ash Meadows.

A considerable number of small commercial and industrial businesses had been established around the railway station and goods station, and at Canal Head. Aynam Mills, and Bridge Mills and Lees Croft Mills at Stramongate Bridge, had all appeared in the half-century before 1914. Also new were the grammar school at The Lound, the cemetery just east of the canal, and the county hospital south-west of the Norman earthworks of Castle Howe. Apart from the new residential roads to the west of Fellside, the most important additions to the road network were Gilling Gate and Sandes Avenue, the latter replacing the older Sands Close Lane. With the growth of the town new bridges had been built over the river, although this was still a significant traffic barrier. Among them were the footbridges at Romney Bridge and at Abbot Hall recreation ground, and Victoria Bridge, linking Sandes Avenue with Beezon Avenue and the railway station.

Since then, of course, the expansion of the town has been even more marked, especially with the major spread of housing eastwards and of industrial estates to the north-east. These expansions can be tracked on various later versions of the 25-inch and 6-inch Ordnance Survey maps, allowing direct comparison at the same scale.

House and home | 5

KENDAL today can show examples of many different styles and periods of domestic buildings, from the late Middle Ages up to the present, in a great variety of building materials. Some periods are obviously better represented than others, while the gradual rebuilding of many houses and shops has hidden but retained traces of earlier phases. The town has an unusual wealth of domestic and vernacular architecture, which contributes greatly to its attractive appearance and historic interest.

An aspect of the town which is not unique, but which gives a very strong visual character, is the great series of long yards running back from the street frontages of the central area. These 'Kendal yards' have their origin in the long burgage plots, the urban landholdings which the burgesses owned in the Middle Ages and later, and on which they could build, carry out their daily trade or craft, keep animals, or stable horses. There is a widespread, but totally erroneous, belief that the yards were intended as a form of defence against Scottish invasion in the Middle Ages. At that stage, in the mid-fourteenth century, they had in fact hardly begun to take shape: they had been laid out, but were mostly undeveloped. Furthermore, comparable layouts were to be found in hundreds of other towns throughout England, and the notion that this was a defensive arrangement in completely untenable. Their infilling, and the resultant density of building, was in reality a feature of the major growth of the town in the eighteenth and nineteenth centuries. In the twentieth century there was extensive clearance of what had often become sub-standard accommodation, and several of the more central yards were converted into retail developments, as in the Westmorland Centre, Woolpack Yard and Elephant Yard, a process that removed further evidence of their complex and fascinating evolution.

The Middle Ages

A number of small archaeological excavations have now taken place in the yards of Kendal, so it is now possible to see a clearer picture of how the simple burgage plots of the Middle Ages, with their garden plots to the rear, became the location of industrial or craft processes, and were later developed for housing—although at what date each of these changes took place is often a matter of dispute or continuing uncertainty. This picture is by no means unique, and in many towns we can, using title deeds, trace the gradual change from open spaces including gardens and orchards, to a densely built area of housing and workshops.

Although excavations have usually been small, and have been in places affected by disturbance for new building rather than necessarily in the most archaeologically promising locations, several in Kendal have told us a great deal about the earlier state of sites where no documentary evidence survives. The most fruitful in that respect were in Stricklandgate, such as the investigations on the site of the Westmorland Centre in 1987–88. There the early boundaries of burgage plots were found, in the form of a series of stone walls, built one on top of another. These suggest strongly that when the borough was created the burgage plots were marked out in a clear and unequivocal manner, then perhaps occupied piecemeal and over quite a long period. No very early pottery has been found, but it is surprising, and significant, to realise that burgage plots were occupied in the fourteenth century so far north within the town, beyond the Market Place.[1]

The earliest buildings on that site were constructed on sill beams, large horizontal timbers which were laid in shallow trenches and which carried all the main structural uprights. Internal partitions were marked by earthfast posts of small scantling. No stone was used until the post-medieval period, showing that the houses and shops must have been entirely of timber-framed construction. However, their appearance is unknown—not all the timbers may have been left visible, and the walls were perhaps rendered or harled all over with a lime-based wash. It is difficult now for us to appreciate that four hundred years ago Kendal, which might seem the archetypal stone-built town, was in fact a place of timber-framing. Indeed, the same was true of most Cumbrian towns. At some later stage, perhaps in the sixteenth century, the early timber buildings in Kendal were replaced by structures with walls of a clay or cob construction mixed with small stones. Such clay construction is well known in the Solway area, where the buildings are known as 'clay dabbins', but clearly this technique might also have been used in more southerly areas of Cumbria.[2] Whether it simply formed a dry base for a timber construction, or made up entire walls, is unknown.

The yard surfaces were already metalled in the medieval period. At Elephant Yard, the excavations in 1998 revealed a small circular kiln of medieval date with a long flue set in banking at the back of the plot. Its purpose is unclear, as no residues from a manufacturing or production process were identified, but presumably it marks some early industrial activity.[3]

In recent years many small excavations have been carried out in the central area of Kendal and are now usefully reported in the Cumberland & Westmorland Society Transactions, published on an annual basis. In 2004 work went on at 147 Highgate, 119 Stricklandgate, Yard 2 Stricklandgate, Yard 52 Stramongate and Yards 110 and 112 Stricklandgate, in 2006 at 98 Highgate, in 2007 at Collin Croft, and in 2008 at 130–36 Stricklandgate.[4] Many of these were carried out in tandem with 'desk-based' surveys and had a limited purpose connected with planning and redevelopment.

None of these excavations has yet been fully published, so we must await a fuller analysis of the findings. However, with a couple of exceptions where larger sites could be examined, most of the excavations have been upon backland and not upon the street frontages, where the earliest and most significant evidence is likely to be found, if it survives. Where later buildings on the site had deeply excavated cellars, their construction is likely to have destroyed most or all of the evidence for underlying medieval structures. Furthermore, the survival of earlier fabric in the buildings on street frontages is often a matter of chance, while the evidence is often slight and all too easily destroyed. Archaeology has, however, revealed some specific examples of when yards were built up. It appears that infilling of the backlands by cottages was not significant before the late eighteenth century, as confirmed by the findings from the site of the Westmorland Gazette offices.

Individual larger houses

There were, and to some extent still are, a number of larger, higher-status houses of medieval and Tudor date, which were once on the fringes of the town but are now surrounded by the later expansion of the built-up area. In addition, a few at a greater distance from the town centre had a close relationship with the life and business of Kendal. The use of stone immediately distinguishes most of these houses from the majority of burgage houses.

One of the strangest houses in Kendal is the so-called 'Castle Dairy', which stands on the north-western side of Wildman Street. It is clearly in part a medieval house of some pretensions, but its history and purpose have been greatly confused by later legend and half-truth. It merits a closer look. The house, built of stone rubble, consists of a central hall of one storey flanked by two-storey wings projecting forwards. Originally built in the fourteenth century, it was extensively altered in the sixteenth and seventeenth centuries when a rearward extension was added behind the south-west wing and to the north-east. The fireplaces are of sixteenth-century date, with massive cylindrical 'Lake District-type' chimneys above them. The name 'Dairy' name has caused much confusion, and there does not seem a simple explanation, although a possible derivation from 'Dowry' has been suggested. It is, however, certain that the building was never so humble as to be used for a dairy. A fine view of the house, drawn by Edward Blore in 1847, is now in the British Library.[5]

Cunswick Hall, lying far from modern roads

Two images of Castle Dairy: above, from a drawing by Edward Blore; lower, as the building is today.
AUTHOR COLLECTION

north-west of the town, is an example of an ancient gentry house which has now come down in the world. The plain exterior belies its long history. It belonged to the Leyburne family, who were very influential in Kendal affairs, and it may have had a medieval defensive tower. The surviving house is much reduced, appearing now to be principally of nineteenth-century date with a few surviving older fragments and a gatehouse, which in itself signifies the gentry character of the house.[6]

Sadly, Dockray Hall is now just a name. Parts of it survived in the seventeenth century, and were mentioned by Machell,[7] and it is marked on Speed's map of 1611, but it was already falling into disuse, and by the time Todd's map was surveyed in 1787 only a barn remained on the site. Dockray Hall Mills, some distance away the north-east, are named after it.

Burneside Hall, which lies a little to the north of the town, is one of the handful of medieval houses around Kendal with the chamber block in the form of a tower for defensive purposes. Such towers were common features after the troubles with Scotland in Edward II's reign, and represented the response to danger by those among the gentry who did not own proper castles. They are at the lowest level of defensive capability, but their high walls and fire-resistant structure could buy valuable time and perhaps put off all but the most determined attacker. It is likely that the many such houses in Westmorland were never tested in earnest, but nearer the Scottish border the risks were and remained higher. Burneside was built, perhaps in the fourteenth century, by the Bellingham family. The north end of the present house is a ruined tower, containing two parallel vaults, with a hall to the south, originally at first-floor level and approached by outside steps, and with a southern cross-wing which, according to the drawing by Thomas Machell in the 1690s, also once took the form of a tower.[8] In front of the hall, enclosing a triangular area, are walls and a medieval gatehouse.[9]

Helsington Laithes, just beyond the southern end of the town, is a late medieval house which was extended for Colonel Grahme of Levens in about 1690. The west end is the oldest, with very thick walls. Could this also have originally formed part of a tower? It contains a plaster wall panel with initials and date I & A B 1538 (for 1583), matched by identical plasterwork at Levens carried out for the Bellinghams.[10] Levens Hall and Sizergh Castle, both major houses and the centres of large estates held by higher-ranking gentry, are some distance from the town, but still had a significant influence upon its affairs. Both originated in the Middle Ages with defensive towers or, more precisely, chamber blocks constructed as towers, within a more complex range of buildings. They were extensively altered in the sixteenth and seventeenth centuries, and it was that period which created the principal 'flavour' which they have today. Colonel Grahme of Levens had the famous topiary gardens laid out in the years around 1700 and, bypassed by the

Sizergh Castle, from a glass slide.

GLASS SLIDE, BY COURTESY OF KENDAL TOWN COUNCIL

Wattsfield House (*left*) from a glass slide and (*right*) as it is today.

GLASS SLIDE, BY COURTESY OF KENDAL TOWN COUNCIL

many intervening changes of fashion and taste when the house became a secondary residence, these still survive today, to delight visitors and garden historians.[11] At both houses the original defensive towers remain, now attached to and embedded within ranges of undefended residential and ancillary buildings.

Collinfield, south-west of the town, was probably built in the late sixteenth century, but was considerably remodelled by George Sedgwick, secretary to Lady Anne Clifford, Countess of Pembroke, after he acquired it in 1668. It has typical 'Lake District' cylindrical chimneys. An inscription on the porch reads, very appropriately, 'NVNC MEA MOX HVIVS SED POSTEA NESCIO CVIVS I & M/G 1663' (*Now mine, soon his, but afterwards whose I don't know*). Unfortunately, the ambience of the house has been totally destroyed by the over-dense modern building close beside.[12] The same fate has befallen Wattsfield (formerly Watchfield), a seventeenth-century stone house with a central full-height porch, which now lies in the southern suburbs of the town, surrounded by modern houses.[13] Bleaze Hall at Old Hutton, four miles south of Kendal, is a late sixteenth-century winged stone house with a fine plaster ceiling. For many years it was the home of the Bateman family, who maintained one of the packhorse trains to London, and was thus vital to the cloth trade of Kendal.[14]

Building materials

Until the seventeenth century Kendal was a town of timber-framed buildings, with only a few exceptions such as the parish church, Castle Dairy, and some substantial yeoman or minor gentry houses on the outskirts, such as those we have just noted. The timber would not have been very apparent to the observer, as it was usually coated, as were the plaster infills, with a uniform limewash. The image of a dramatic 'black and white appearance', as in places such as Chester and Shrewsbury, is largely a creation of the Victorian imagination.

The timber for building Kendal's timber-framed houses came from relatively near at hand. While there can have been few really large oak timbers in the vicinity, most of the demand was supplied by the extensive woodlands of the southern Lake District and Furness. Not until the late eighteenth century were large supplies of Baltic fir imported for ship-building and house-building, and even then places such as Kendal, somewhat further from the ports where the timber was landed, were at a relative disadvantage.

There were few sources of building stone in the vicinity except for Carboniferous Limestone, the material which, with rendering and limewash, came eventually to dominate the appearance of the town. Kendal's distinctive greyness owes much to this stone, which has no natural 'grain' and is consequently difficult to split in predictable directions. For this reason it was nearly always used in the form of rubble, with occasional dressed blocks as lintels or quoins at corners. Only when the Websters, the town's major late eighteenth- and early nineteenth-century dynasty of craftsmen and architects, began to adopt methods of sawing the stone was dressed ashlar available. This happened at the end of the eighteenth century, and is very obvious. Much of the rubble masonry was probably rendered or limewashed originally, as for instance were both the interior and exterior of the parish church. The standard material was Kendal Fell limestone, a fairly intractable medium. Several beds seem to have been used, ranging from a featureless grey to the very shelly bedded limestone that can be seen in Lowther House at the bottom of Lowther Street and several houses in Highgate. By the end of the eighteenth century local limestone could also be cut and 'polished' (that is, smoothed) for decorative work such as fireplaces, and several local sources produced limestone that could take a high polish and be labelled as 'marble'.

Other sources of stone in Westmorland were inaccessible because of transport difficulties—thus Shap granite was not worked until after 1868, and even the ubiquitous slate of the Lake District was fragile and difficult to carry. Indeed one of the first loads of Burlington slate (from Kirkby Ireleth) came to Kendal via the Lancaster Canal in 1826, having been brought across Morecambe Bay to Glasson Dock by ship and thence along the canal. Other building stones had to wait for the development of the railway system which, for example, allowed the importation of inexpensive Welsh slate, or the Eden Valley sandstone that was used in the building of the Carnegie Library. Kendal 'proper' never adopted the use of brick, at least as an external material. Although the railway terraces at Oxenholme are of red brick and, as so often, the railway company introduced building styles more common elsewhere, most brick in Kendal is rendered or roughcast over.[15]

There was a long tradition of limewash, harling or rendering, one which suited the rather unattractive limestone rubble or composite timber, plaster and stone of which much of the town was built before the late eighteenth century. Its use today, however, is questionable, since what has often been used in new developments or urban replacements such as Waterside or Fellside is in fact wet-dash, which turns a particularly depression-inducing damp-stained grey in the wet weather from which the town all too often suffers. Few places can present such different aspects in sun and rain as does Kendal!

Tudor and Stuart Kendal

Unlike its southerly neighbour Lancaster, Kendal has retained a considerable number of timber-framed buildings of the sixteenth and seventeenth centuries. Among these are 7 Stramongate, now Henry Roberts booksellers, a sixteenth-century town house that was owned by the Bellingham family of Burneside. It retains much of its original timber roof and was restored in 1985. Pembroke House, Kirkland, is a timber-framed and jettied house with three gabled dormers, the upper part based upon reused cruck blades. It too was restored in the mid-1980s, by the Kendal Civic Society Building Preservation Trust.

No. 7 Stramongate, a sixteenth-century house once belonging to the Bellingham family, now a shop.

It seems that Kendal did not experience any disastrous fires in the post-medieval period of the seriousness that prompted other towns to rebuild in stone, while it may have been the intractable nature of the local limestone that discouraged rebuilding for its own sake until the end of the eighteenth century, when the new technologies of cutting and polishing made it useful and desirable to build in this tough stone. The consequence is that the main streets of the town exhibit a number of notably 'old' features, banished from many towns in the Georgian period: irregular frontages, gable ends to the street, dormer windows, and steeply pitched roofs. Most of the original framing is no longer apparent from the outside, and such as is, paradoxically, is probably the product of nineteenth-century romanticism. However, behind the façades, roof structures and interiors retain quite a lot of ancient fabric. Clearly there was a lengthy transitional period between timber-framing and stone construction, and many of the timber-framed houses belong to the seventeenth and eighteenth centuries when building techniques had changed quite radically from their medieval origins. Composites of jointed and nailed timbers, stone, lath and plaster and rough-cast may not be so much battered relics of older styles as newer features.

Detail of roof gable, showing the Bellingham family crest.

PHOTOGRAPHS: ELLIE GODDARD

A survey of Kendal carried out in 1695 gives us a good deal of evidence about the structure and functioning of contemporary households, where in prosperous mercantile or trading families the man worked at his craft or business on the premises, often helped by servants and apprentices who, like the wife, children, and domestic servants, all lived in. At the lower end of the spectrum, members of the family may have worked for someone else, and there were no servants.[16] The following examples of Kendal households of the end of the seventeenth century come from Highgate:

Christopher Wallace, a weaver, lived with Isabell his wife, their three children, and three servants (Thomas Jackson, Edward Bell and Agnes Wiggin)

John Gaitskell, a poor glover, lived with his wife Agnes and their two children

William Wilson, a wealthy man with a personal estate of £600, lived with Jane his wife, George his son, and three servants (Obediah Thornbecke, Michael Barrow and Isabell Holme)

Probate inventories, which listed the personal and household effects of an individual immediately after his or her death, give us valuable insights into life within Kendal houses of the seventeenth and eighteenth centuries. They do not tell us about the plan or layout, but they list rooms and so give us a good impression of the size of the house and way it functioned. For example, the inventory of Allan Wilson, gentleman, of Highgate (1675) lists a hall, little kitchen, buttery and passage, milkhouse and drinkhouse, new loft, hall-loft, floor-loft, high loft, study and old kitchen. The study contained books and other specialised items, giving a sense of a house with considerable comfort and some luxury.[17] By contrast, in 1688 William Gruby or Grewbye, a weaver of Fellside, Highgate, had only a house loft, back chamber and parlour, suggesting that he perhaps occupied just part of a shared house.[18] John Gilpin, a waller (the Kendal term for a stonemason), who died in 1700, rented two houses in Stricklandgate and Highgate. In one of them (it is not clear which) he had a kitchen (with fire irons, a table, a chest and two buffet forms), a 'bodystead' (the main hall chamber of the house), a buttery containing pewter,

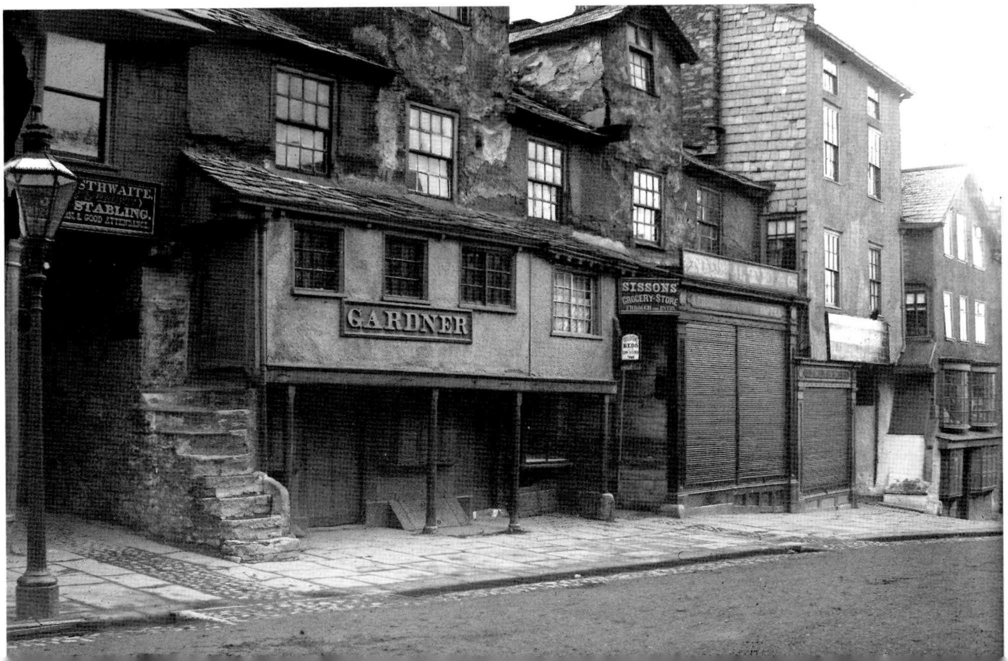

The White Lion, one of a small group of buildings claimed to be 'galleried' on the Chester model. This is probably an oversimplification, and never gave rise to Rows as in Chester.

GLASS PLATE NEGATIVE, BY COURTESY OF KENDAL TOWN COUNCIL

parlour, house loft, buttery loft, kitchen loft, roof loft, and cowhouse.[19] In 1769 Robert Green, silk man, had a hall, front parlour, parlour loft, hall loft, servants' room, kitchen loft, cellar, buttery, kitchen and back kitchen.[20] All these houses, or part-houses, seem essentially to have had a series of main ground-floor rooms with storage in the roof space above, the various lofts being named after the rooms above which they lay. The disposition of furniture between rooms is, by our standards, unpredictable and confused, beds in particular appearing in what we would consider unlikely places. This in turn bears witness to the lack of privacy and personal space which most accepted as normal at this time.

One feature of seventeenth-century Kendal, which survived into the nineteenth, was its so-called galleried houses, which made some visitors equate it with Chester. William Stukeley came here in 1725, though his words were not published until over fifty years later: 'This town has been built mostly with pent-houses and galleries over them all along the streets, somewhat like Chester.'[21] Gray, somewhat later, drew a different parallel: 'My inn promised sadly, having two wooden galleries, like Scotland, in front of it; it was indeed an old ill-contrived house.'[22] This was probably the White Lion, described later by Cornelius Nicholson thus: 'There is no doubt that the first floor of the front of this house was one of the open galleries ... and the tinman's shop ... which is now beneath a penthouse, was under the gallery.'[23] Galleries are mentioned in deeds of the seventeenth and eighteenth centuries. One such was in the north-east corner of the Market Place, and appears in a deed of 1636 where James Warde of Kendal, tailor, sold four shops and a gallery to Thomas Sleddall, Mayor and aldermen, but was to have 'free power and liberty for a way through the said gallery to his house or chamber'. This group of buildings was to house the first theatre, the *Football Inn* and later the Working-Men's Institute.[24]

No. 54 Stricklandgate, from a glass slide of the 1870s. This shop appears to be a survivor of the Kendal 'galleried' type, with a shop on the ground floor and an upper level lit by bow windows and reached by steps at the side.

PHOTOGRAPH BY PERCY DUFF, BY COURTESY OF KENDAL TOWN COUNCIL

Two of these galleried houses survived on the east side of Stricklandgate until demolition in 1818 and 1822.[25] It is not clear how they functioned, but it seems that both lower and upper floors projected into the street with open frontages, and with stone steps up to the first floor. They do not seem to have been part of any form of continuous walkway, as in Chester, and in any case all trace has long since vanished, so it is not possible to assess their design or purpose.[26] The resemblance between Kendal and Chester seems to have been merely superficial, Chester being a city very familiar to contemporary travellers. Closer parallels should instead be drawn with nearby towns such as Kirkby Lonsdale and Sedbergh, which at one time apparently had similar features,[27] or Dent, where they are well-attested.[28] It might therefore be more worthwhile to pursue parallels with other types of external timber galleries (so-called 'spinning galleries') on Lakeland farms, and those commonly indicating division of a building into separate tenements, as in Whitby, Yorkshire.[29] The evidence for surviving galleries in the area as a whole is well summarised in Allen's *Old Galleries of Cumbria*.[30]

By the early eighteenth century demand for housing was rising. The town's industries needed labour, and the population was growing appreciably. There was nowhere to build outside the existing 'footprint' of the medieval town except on the common fields, and these were still too useful for tentering cloth and grazing to allow them to disappear under houses. Therefore many of those who owned properties on street frontages responded to the demand by building cottages for rent behind their main house, typically accessed through an arch from the street. Industrial premises, too, began to develop on these plots. The result was that, westwards to Fellside, and eastwards all the way to the riverbank, the hitherto open backlands of the burgage plots began to fill up. The effect of all this building is unmistakable even today, despite major programmes for the clearance of the insanitary slums that had been the common result of the infilling. The impact of the eighteenth- and early nineteenth-century backland development still gives Kendal a major element of its character. Few yards are now left in their fully built-up state, Dr Manning's Yard to the east of Highgate being the best surviving example.

One feature which seems to be unique to Kendal was the system, established in 1861, of numbering the yards consecutively, street by street (although in a number of larger towns and cities, such as Liverpool, the tiny courts were numbered in this way). Elsewhere, as at Carlisle

left
The former *Football Inn* in the corner of the Market Place, for which seventeenth-century documentary evidence exists for a first-floor gallery.

right
Dr Mannings Yard, an attractive and not necessarily typical example of a Kendal yard. Those on the downhill side of the main streets received all the rubbish and cess from those further up the hillslope.

left Yard 153, with a typical arched entrance to allow waggons through. Many yards have setts and two lines of smooth slabs to guide the wheels. There are also many devices for stopping waggons from crashing against arches or walls.

right Yard 24, Highgate, from a glass slide. Unlike most towns with burgage plots, Kendal has mostly numbers rather than names for its yards, the number being derived from that of the house or shop on the frontage. Kendal Town Council.

GLASS SLIDE, BY COURTESY OF KENDAL TOWN COUNCIL

or Preston, people relied on names for the yards, often those of the inn or the business owner on the frontage. These tended to change with a change of owner, and must have presented an intractable problem for the authorities in maintaining addresses. Some Kendal yards also have names of that type, but the numbering system persisted and has even survived the demolition of much of the yard property. Later in this chapter we will look at Woolpack Yard in detail as an exemplar of the yards in general.

The Georgian period

As we have seen, Kendal saw no concerted 'great rebuilding' in stone, and all sorts of materials continued to be used, while many older houses survived along the street frontages. The limited move towards the use of stone in the years around 1800 was prompted, as noted

earlier, when the problems inherent in cutting the local limestone had been solved in the late eighteenth century, and the more ambitious work of several families of architects and craftsmen began to appear in the town (most notably, the celebrated Webster family, who are discussed in the next section).

By far the grandest house is that known as Abbot Hall, occupying an ancient site in Kirkland outside the borough itself, and rebuilt—a short distance from the site of its predecessor—in 1759 by Lieutenant Colonel George Wilson at a cost of £8,000. Wilson was a member of the gentry family that owned Dallam Tower near Milnthorpe, and had married a Lancaster heiress, Anne Harrison, whose money undoubtedly helped him pay for the house. They did not enjoy it for long. Their only daughter died aged six (her memorial can be seen in Lancaster priory church) and they then moved to York, letting the house to tenants. There are portraits of all three, by Romney. The design of Abbot Hall is often attributed to John Carr of York, and this is reasonably plausible, although it cannot be proved. Indeed, many absolutely deny this attribution. A contemporary description, published in the *Lonsdale Magazine* of 1821, certainly describes it as 'rebuilt in 1759, under the superintendence of Mr. Carr of York ... In 1801, it came into the possession of the present inhabitant, Christopher Wilson, Esq. who, at a considerable expense, has made it a very comfortable residence ...'[31] Does this mean that it was not comfortable in its original form? It is now an art gallery and has recently been beautifully restored to its original condition.

Numbers 134–136 Highgate, a pair of three-storey houses of six bays, were built in 1798 by Francis Webster for John Davidson, using beautifully cut limestone ashlar that had been polished at the Websters' Helsington works. These houses demonstrate how this previously intractable material, thanks to new technologies, had now become manageable. Blindbeck House, which stands at the junction between Kirkland and Kendal proper, is a large vernacular house of the sort commonly seen in Cockermouth or Whitehaven, with a coat of painted render and painted stone sills and surrounds. It was built for Christopher Wilson in 1785, (the initials C M/W for 'Christopher and Margaret Wilson' can be seen on the rainwater heads) but subsequently

Nos 134–6 Highgate, a pair of houses by Francis Webster, of about 1797. They exhibit the finely cut limestone blocks in which the Websters specialised.

left Blindbeck House, built for Christopher Wilson and his wife Margaret in 1785. The rendered and painted stonework belongs to a period when the local limestone could only be used as coursed rubble, and so was covered up.

right Stricklandgate House, a dignified seven-bay town house, built for the banker Joseph Maude in 1776 and one of the best houses in Kendal.

GLASS SLIDE, BY COURTESY OF KENDAL TOWN COUNCIL

it served for many years as the *Queen's Hotel*. The *Highgate Hotel* (128 Highgate) is dated 1769 and bears the inscription TO THE DWELLERS IN THIS PLACE GOD GRANTE PEACE. A house near the Brewery has an unexpected pair of massive Doric columns framing the door up the yard.

Near the top of Highgate is Farrar's Teashop, an outstanding and very rare survival of a shop of about 1820, with two shallow bow windows. It was built by Francis Webster, as was also the frontage of the Highgate Pharmacy, no. 41 Highgate, with another 1820s shopfront added to a much older building. A number of very long stair windows, typical of northern vernacular architecture, can be seen at the rear of buildings in Lowther Street. They are best viewed from Tanners' Yard, which runs parallel. Lowther Street was new in 1782, so these features can be dated exactly. Another very long stair window is visible on the side of the house standing next to the Friends' Meeting House in Stramongate. Stricklandgate House, substantial and dignified, of seven bays with a rusticated lower storey, was the home of the banker Joseph Maude in 1776. Later, in 1854, it became the home of the Literary & Scientific Society's Museum and Library. The early eighteenth-century Brewery House was originally a town house belonging to the Wilsons of Dallam Tower, with a long garden behind. In 1758 this land was converted to brewery uses, and the premises were operated by Whitwell Mark & Company for many years until the firm was taken over by Vaux. The complex is now a thriving theatre and arts centre.

Other important houses can be seen on the north side of Stramongate. One is the so-called 'Ladies' College', in which the architectural composition extends across two adjacent buildings, with rather fine detailing and attractive doorcases set in the sides of the carriage entries, each one different. Aynam Lodge of 1824, also by Francis Webster, is placed in an eye-catching position at the end of Miller Bridge and shows very well the use by the Websters of beautifully cut limestone ashlar blocks. No doubt this also served as a splendid advertisement for what the firm could do.

During the 1820s there was major population growth in Kendal, and the built-up area at

left Aynam Lodge, a Francis Webster building of 1824.

right Aynam Lodge, detail of the limestone ashlar blocks cut by the Websters.

last began to expand onto adjacent open land. The new locations included the smart houses on the east bank of the river in Thorny Hills, where plots were being sold by Mr Cookson in 1823 at two shillings per square yard;[32] the less ambitious Castle Crescent; Union Row in Longpool of 1820;[33] and, to the north near the union workhouse, the group of streets built by the Union Building Society to increase the Liberal vote.[34] These include Union Street, Caroline Street, Cross Street and Strickland Place, all dated 1820 or 1821. They bear the street-names and dates in Roman numerals cut elegantly into the limestone, rather than on attached plates.

In 1787 the county magistrates ordered a household census of Westmorland, one of the earliest for any English shire. This gives valuable evidence for the household structures of the period, highlighting the great diversity that existed. Take these three examples from Stricklandgate:[35]

left Thorny Hills, a row of elegant houses of the 1820s, all different but in limestone ashlar.

right Street name for Cross Street, part of the Union Building Society development at the north end of the town, with the date 1820 in Roman numerals.

A shopkeeper's household:
Mr Batty Hodgon, grocer; Ann Hodgon, his daughter; William Adlington, an apprentice; Henry Middleton, a servant; Margaret Rodick, a servant.

An inn:
Edward Willan, innkeeper; Thomas Bellos; Edward Hurd; John Storey; Robert Willan, a servant; Margaret Willan; Mary Willan, daughter; Mary Parker, servant.

An odd shared household of unrelated bachelors:
Mr John Todd, gentleman; Mr William Gothrop, ironmonger; John Plumber, shearman; Thomas Robinson, weaver.

The Websters and their circle

The Websters have already been mentioned, and their importance now merits a lengthier discussion. Beginning as artisan craftsmen and graduating to ambitious architecture, the family always retained a close interest in stone-working and was responsible for polishing marble and cutting the difficult local limestone to make it a building material of some distinction.

There were three generations. Francis Webster (1767–1827) had two sons, George (1797–1864) and Francis II (1805–80), the last-named managing the family marble works. George had several children including Francis III (1829–72), who took over the marble works from his uncle and namesake. Francis the elder had come to Kendal from Furness. He was a stone-mason rather than an architect, and made his family's fortune by skill and good workmanship. With the family were associated William Holme, Francis Webster's partner, and Miles Thompson, whom George promoted from draughtsman to a partnership in 1845.[36]

There was also a group of skilled craftsmen and draughtsmen who backed up these principals. William Coulthart, who later practised in Lancaster, was probably one of their protégés, and it is known that Richard Stirzaker, described in the section on local artists in chapter 11, was employed by the Websters to produce images of how their proposed buildings would look.[37]

The Websters had a huge influence on the building of Kendal and were responsible for many buildings in the surrounding area and in parts of Lancashire and the West Riding of Yorkshire. They seem to have had little competition except from those architects associated with wider interests, brought in by their patrons. One exception was John Richardson (1774–1864/65),

The somewhat battered gravestone of Francis Webster, architect, in the parish church graveyard.

Kendal from Thorny Hills, painting by William Brown, 1819. The new development of Thorny Hills lay across the river from the town. Tenters for cloth can be seen on Goose Holme in the foreground, while to the left of Miller Bridge is the windmill tower at the foot of Yard 65.

a contemporary of Francis I, who designed at least four competent buildings, including the new theatre in Woolpack Yard (see below).[38] A remarkable photograph of him and his wife in old age survives. He died in his nineties, and his epitaph is notable.

My earthly house has fallen to decay,
The base was shaken, and the walls gave way;
The pillars that had borne its weight for more
Than fourscore years, were mouldered at the core;
The rafters crumbled, and the light was faint
That crept in at the windows old and quaint;
While seam and crevice in the tottering shell
For years let in the wind, when down it fell;
The roof-tree, strong and sound, being last
To topple beneath the resistless blast.
Then, past repairs, I looked for no new plan
Whereby to have rebuilt the outward man;
But calmly waited, with the world at peace,
Nor would, when death approached, renew the lease;

But humbly sought for my departing soul,
Beyond the grave, eternally a place,
Where it might still the grand creations trace
Of God, the first great *Architect* of all.[39]

Otherwise there was only Thomas Harrison from Richmond, more famous for work in Lancaster and Chester, who designed Stramongate Bridge in 1793–94, and Richard Pedder, who was paid for plans and a model for the new workhouse in 1767 with additions in 1776.[40] It is possible that more Kendal buildings should be attributed to Richardson and Pedder, who have been entirely overshadowed by the remarkable Websters.

Victorian developments

As we have seen, the town grew rapidly outwards during the nineteenth century, while the yards and any corners of undeveloped land in the central area were soon filled. Those who could afford to do so fled the increasingly insanitary yards of the town centre, stimulating growing demand for new housing on the higher ground to the west, and on the town fringes elsewhere. Gillingate, Summer Hill, Greenside and Beast Banks are full of large houses, mostly in short terraces or groups. Cliff Terrace is a typical irregular development of plain stone houses of three storeys, some with projecting bays, its date of 1851 testified by a plaque on the corner of the southernmost house, although the terrace was not all built at once. The deeds of no. 16 suggest that the first two houses were completed in 1856.[41] In Gillingate, built from 1861 onwards, there are several highly imaginative houses with spiky towers and wilful rooflines, making the most of the fine views and elevated position. Plots of land for building were being sold in the early 1860s on House of Correction Hill under the terms of the Kendal Fell Act of 1861.[42] Serpentine Terrace also belongs to this decade. Plans were approved for no. 1 for Mr James Leighton by the Kendal Board of Health (an embryonic planning authority) in 1867.[43]

Houses were constructed along the eastern bank of the river as well, with long terraces lining the riverside road. An excellent example is Church View, dated 1879. Other streets extended to the east, such as Queen Katherine Street and Parr Street, the former with three-storey houses with dormers flat to the street, the latter also three-storeyed and dormered, but with lower bay

Cliff Terrace, a development of 1851 off Beast Banks with a view over the town.

windows and continuous outshuts forming roofs to bay and porch. This more spacious design can also be seen in Sunnyside, the continuation of Parr Street east of the canal. Similar designs, though smaller, can be seen in Park Avenue, Ford Terrace and Howard Street, all near Romney Bridge.

There are terraces of small houses at the other end of the town, in Windermere Road, in the vicinity of Shaw's Brow. Highfield Villas, a little further north, show the late nineteenth-century trend towards large semi-detached houses with long gardens front and behind. A larger development was Kendal Green, opening out east of Windermere Road and occupying the land acquired by Kendal Fell Trustees which had formerly been Low Tenterfell and even before that waste ground called in 1683 'Dob Freer'. The large irregular green forms the focus of a mixed development that includes a terrace of large three-storey houses on the west side, looking for all the world like a seaside promenade. There are further terraces on the east side, while more modern groups fill in those sites originally left vacant.[44]

A few individual houses are worth highlighting. Bridge House, no. 65 Castle Street, is the last house before the railway embankment heading east, and was built for the first Kendal stationmaster. Despite its date of 1846–47 it is entirely Georgian in style, of two storeys and three bays, with a hipped roof. In the old Sedbergh Road no. 103, Little Holme, was built by the famous Arts and Crafts architect C. F. A. Voysey in 1909 for Arthur Simpson, the distinguished Kendal furniture maker. Although small by Voysey's usual standards, it shows all his care for Arts and Crafts detailing and has a splendid porch. Voysey knew the area, having built several distinctive houses in the Lake District.[45]

More large villas are further north in Sedbergh Road, including Brantholme, Heathfield and Eller Lea, or on Queen's Road, below Serpentine Walks, including Brantfield, Hollin Garth and Underwood. Others face the terrace in Green Side, above Beast Banks, among them Underfell, Ghyll Close and Larch Howe. All are distinguished by an elevated position on the town's edge, and they have large gardens with shrubberies. These were the homes of successful town businessmen and shopkeepers, who could now afford to live well away from

left
Summerhouse at Bowling Fell.

right
Summerhouse at Monument House.

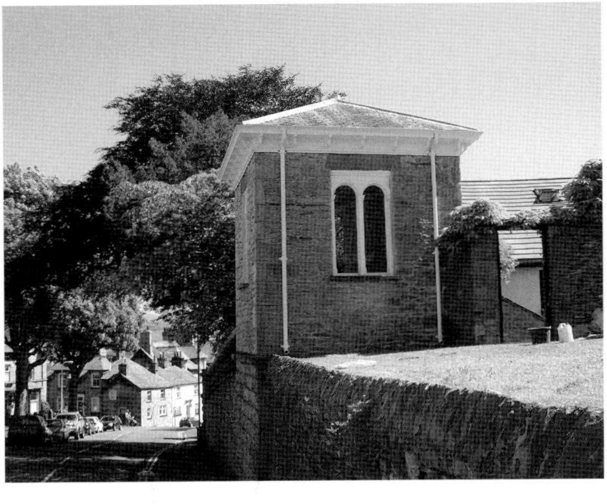

their work, an sign of the increasing trend in the later Victorian period whereby those who could chose to make a break from living over the workplace and escaped the increasingly noisy, insanitary and downright unhealthy town centre.

One remarkable feature of Kendal is the wealth of summerhouses built in the eighteenth and nineteenth centuries, of which many examples survive. The fashion may have its origins in the long sloping gardens created by the medieval burgage plots—with the land rising steeply to the west of the town, these gave delightful prospects. There is a splendid survey of these delightful features of the townscape, carried out by David Butler at the end of the 1970s.[46] Gardens themselves were of course a luxury. The tightly packed high-density nature of the town centre meant that most folk saw little or no greenery, but the larger houses often had long gardens which, because of the sloping sites, allowed terracing, steps and other landscaping features, with summerhouses playing their part. In a few gardens there are still traces of what might once have been commonplace—stone stances for sheltering straw bee-skeps, also known as 'bee-boles'. Examples can be seen at the rear of 45 Highgate and at Prospect Terrace, Rosemary Lane.[47]

A Kendal yard in the 1860s

Of all the Kendal yards Woolpack Yard is one of the best examples for studying. Not only is there unusually good documentary evidence for it, but also this yard, with its neighbours, was largely gutted and replanned a few years ago to create a shopping centre named after the neighbouring Elephant Yard. This gave the opportunity to investigate aspects of its history and development both architecturally and archaeologically. Taking the 1860s as a period of study allows us to compare and contrast evidence from two excellent contemporary sources. It also coincides with the period when Kendal was at its densest in terms of population. The yard is probably quite typical of living conditions for the majority of Kendalians at the time, and offered neither the best nor the worst of environments in the town. Indeed, even within the yard there is evidence for sharp social gradation.

Woolpack Yard, from the 500" 1861 Ordnance Survey map.

PHOTOGRAPH AUTHOR, FROM AN ORIGINAL HELD AT WESTMORLAND RECORD OFFICE, KENDAL

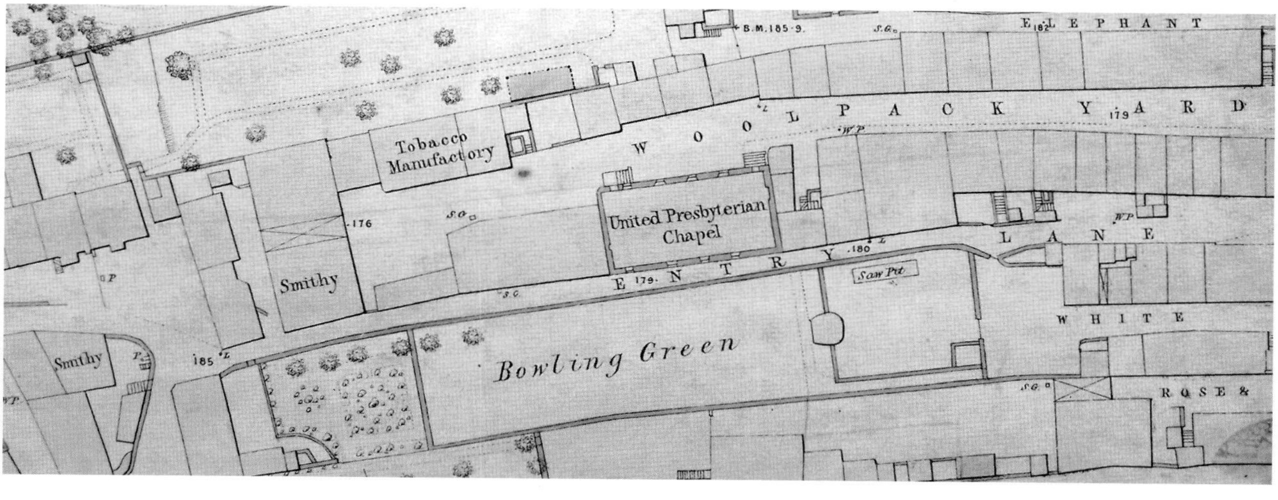

The former Woolpack Inn with a projecting window and a large arch giving access to the yard behind.

The first of these sources is the 1:500 Ordnance Survey map of 1861, which was discussed in chapter 4. This shows that on the street front stood the *Woolpack Inn*, its name commemorating the town's most important industry. The inn itself was known as the *Shipp Inn* in 1716, but by 1737 had become the *Crown and Woolpack*.[48] An arch under the building gave access to the long yard behind, running westwards towards Fellside and accommodating a very characteristic diversity of uses. Behind the inn itself was a range of buildings that probably included kitchens and stables, and then there were some thirty cottages, ranged on either side of the yard and thus leaving only a narrow central passageway. At the rear was a smithy, extending at right angles across the yard and blocking any further access, while on the north side was a tobacco manufactory. Facing this on the south side, a little nearer the front, was a building marked on the map as 'United Presbyterian Chapel'. This is thought to have been built about 1778 as a theatre, and probably reconstructed some ten years later. In 1823 it ceased to function as a theatre, having been closed down under pressure from the religious interests in the town, and ironically became the chapel of the Scotch Presbyterians. Most of the buildings on the south side of the yard have survived in some form, including the former theatre, while the former tobacco manufactory, now part of Martindale's the builders' premises, appears to be a pair or triplet of Georgian houses once of higher status, with long stair windows at the rear. While the majority of the cottages have gone, enough survive to show that the standard was a tall narrow three-storeyed house, indicating that the very real degree of overcrowding was still not as severe as in towns where two storeys were the norm.

The information from this map can be correlated with that in the exactly contemporaneous census, the returns for which give the raw data collected on the doorstep from the residents.[49] Of course, the census was concerned with household details, and therefore does not record businesses except where they coincided with the home, so neither the smithy nor the tobacco manufactory are listed in the census. However, it does give us a fascinating picture of the very varied population both of the yard and of the *Woolpack Inn*, 166 people in total. The occupants ranged from the very poor, with large families and often a number

Georgian houses in Woolpack Yard, now part of a workshop. They have characteristic long stair windows on their rear elevations.

left Houses in Woolpack Yard, providing when new cheap accommodation within the old inn yard.

right Entry Lane is not a conventional yard, being a throroughfare. It backs on to Woolpack Yard and provided access to Fellside.

of lodgers to help them pay their way, to owners of small businesses, seven of whom appear in the 1858 *Post Office Directory* and are indicated by asterisks in the following table.[50] The density of people per house varied from one to twelve, two houses having eleven occupants and two nine. The densest occupation was by families with children, but in a couple of cases—the houses of Thomas Mackinch and Michael Dougherty—the overcrowding was exacerbated by the presence of five boarders in each case. Ironically, the poorest and largest families with least space had often to take in boarders to make ends meet.

There were a few servants, most of whom were apparently working in domestic or commercial service elsewhere but living at home here with their families (in other words, they were 'living out' servants who went to work on a daily basis). Five of them, however, including two at the *Woolpack Inn*, do seem to have been servants employed on the premises. It is not at all clear how the privies were allocated, but there seems to have been a small group of them, perhaps five or six, between the back of the *Woolpack Inn* and the cottages, and perhaps three or four further ones projecting out into Entry Lane to the south. All this points to them being shared. Nor are there any signs of drying facilities for washing, although there may have been access to the lower slopes of the fell for this purpose. Only twelve years earlier George Clark had reported, 'The Woolpack Yard, visited by cholera in 1832, has a large open cesspool of about 100 feet area filled with mixed nightsoil and stable manure, and above, on the upper floor, is a privy and a pigsty'.[51]

Woolpack Inn and Woolpack Yard, Kendal (1861 census)

Name	*Age*	*Occupation*	*Place of birth*
John Jackson	56	Publican*	Silverdale
Mary	50	Wife	New Hutton
1 child			
Jane Atkinson	18	House servant	Crooklands
Sarah Hunter	19	House servant	Kendal
Joseph Atkinson	20	Ostler	Kendal
Michael Castelo	40	Shoemaker	Ireland
Jane	37	Wife	Ireland
John	16	Factory hand	Ireland
William	14	Factory hand	Ireland
4 other children			
George Wilson	45	Agricultural labourer	Whinfell
Jane	41	Wife	Strickland Ketel
4 children			
Joseph Holden	72	Tailor*	Northumberland
Sarah	70	Wife	Maulds Meaburn
Mark	42	Agricultural labourer	Kings Meaburn
John Ramsden (grandson)	13	Woollen factory operative	Kendal
William Braithwaite	39	Agricultural labourer	Patton
Margaret	38	Wife	Patton
3 children			
Ann Thwaite	12	House servant	Hutton
Ann Nicholson	61	Charwoman	Lupton
William	18	Currier's assistant	Lupton
John	14	Currier's assistant	Lupton
Robert Sill	40	Marine store dealer	Wigan
Margaret	29	Wife	Lancaster
3 children			
Thomas Cragg	49	Worsted spinner	Whinfell
Isabella	48	Wife	Kendal
Ann	23	Warehouse girl	Crook
John	19	Painter's assistant	Kendal
Robert	14	Girth weaver's assistant	Hutton
6 children			
William Casson	48	Woollen weaver	Cumberland
Mary	48	Wife	Cumberland

Name	*Age*	*Occupation*	*Place of birth*
Mary	21	Daughter	Kendal
Elizabeth	19	Woollen weaver	Kendal
William	16	Woollen finisher	Kendal
James	14	Errand boy	Kendal
6 other children			
Jane Hunter	63	House keeper	Yorkshire
Henry Airey (s in law)	25	Schoolmaster	Kendal
Eliza Airey	26	House servant	Kendal
1 child			
Mary Lancaster	67	Muffin baker	Barton
Thomas	31	Groom	Kendal
Jeffery	26	Coachman	Kendal
Seamus Mallon	36	Shoe maker	Ireland
Robert Wilson	42	Whitesmith	Kendal
Mary	35	Wife	Kendal
William	15	Pupil teacher	Kendal
4 other children			
John Addison	75	Blacksmith	Levens
Frances	66	Wife	Cumberland
1 grandson			
John Yearis	37	Chimney sweep	Lancaster
Jane	25	Wife	Milnthorpe
5 children			
William Jackson (boarder)	23	Hawker	Lancaster
James Prickett	54	Wood cutter	Preston Patrick
Elizabeth	54	Charwoman	Kendal
Francis Jackson	43	Ostler	Silverdale
Sarah	41	Charwoman	Warton
3 children			
Mary Cullen (boarder)	50	Household nurse	Scotland
Joseph Young	28	Hawker	Great Asby
Mary	28	Wife	Scotland
Thomas Tomlinson	42	Joiner	Kendal
Elizabeth	40	Wife	Beathwaite Green
George	14	Errand boy	Kendal
Mary A.	11	Seamstress	Kendal
4 other children			

Name	*Age*	*Occupation*	*Place of birth*
Thomas T. senior	64	Blind	Kendal
Edward Nelson	47	Carpenter employing 2 men 1 boy*	Hutton
Ann	37	Wife	Kendal
Edward	13	Ironmonger's assistant	Natland
John W	12	Carpenter's boy	Natland
4 other children			
Thomas Kendall	50	Soda water manufacturer*	Middleton
Anne	41	Wife	Kirkby Lonsdale
John	17	—	Kirkby Lonsdale
Thomas Mackinch	60	Porter	Grasmere
Elizabeth	54	Wife	Yorkshire
Thomas	22	Accountant	Sedbergh
Catherine	17	House servant	Sedbergh
Robert Murgatroyd (boarder)	52	Linsey weaver	Kendal
William Davison (boarder)	30	Chaise driver	Beetham
John Winder (boarder)	20	Nail maker	Ireland
Joseph Hawkings (boarder)	58	Farm servant	Shap
John Lynch (boarder)	60	Blacking maker	Ireland
Michael Dougherty	40	Shoe maker	Ireland
Hannah	45	Wife	Kendal
Richard	25	Rag gatherer	Kendal
Thomas	23	Groom	Kendal
3 other children			
Henry Wallace (boarder)	35	Hawker	Ireland
Mary (boarder)	23	Hawker	Whitehaven
Mary (boarder)	50	—	Scotland
Mary Killan (boarder)	68	Hawker	Ireland
Agnes Troughton (boarder)	22	House servant	Sedbergh
George Hully	32	Corn dealer*	Kendal
Eleanor	29	Wife	Hutton
3 children			
Elizabeth Parker	19	General servant	Kendal
John Marsden	32	Inland Revenue officer	Manchester
Lydia	32	Wife	Derbyshire
2 children			
James Bindloss	55	Grocer etc.*	Helsington
Elizabeth	64	Wife	Bentham
James	22	Wine merchant's clerk	Kendal

Name	*Age*	*Occupation*	*Place of birth*
George Dinsdale	62	Boot maker employing 4 men 1 boy*	Kendal
Margaret	62	Wife	Heversham
Isabella	39	Sewing machine hand	Kendal
George	26	Shoe maker	Kendal
William	23	Shoe maker	Kendal
Thomas	24	Draper's assistant	Heversham
Margaret	20	Boot binder	Heversham
Robert Dent	67	Stone mason	Hutton Roof
Margaret	58	Coffee house keeper	Crosby Ravensworth
1 child			
John Botham (boarder)	37	Printer	Lancashire
John Wilson	31	Cabinet maker	Kendal
Mary A	35	Milliner	Lindale
3 children			
George Huller (boarder)	30	—	Braithwaite

* listed in 1858 Post Office Trade Directory

The past hundred years

The twentieth and twenty-first centuries have seen an inexorable expansion of the built-up area of Kendal, as new housing, including the 1970s Heron Hill, has lapped up to and around Castle Hill, stretching all the way to Oxenholme and covering most of the erstwhile Kendal Parks. Council housing, built for rent in the period between 1920 and 1970, has left its highly visible mark in large estates. Sandylands, north of the town, was developed from the late 1930s, and building carried on in the 1950s once wartime restrictions had been lifted. Three other large council estates were developed between the wars, at Underley to the north-west, Castle Park to the east, and Kirkbarrow to the south-west.[52] The Hallgarth estate was entirely post-war. These are all marked by features that are familiar from many other towns but are distinctively different from the Kendal tradition. They are relatively spacious, with large areas of green, and houses mainly in pairs and short rows, built of brick with rendered exteriors, contrasting vividly with the tightly packed yards of small stone cottages, which they largely replaced. Jenkin Rise, on Sandylands, is very spacious, and before widespread ownership of cars, must have seemed even more so. Kirkbarrow and Anchorite Fields now occupy a large part of south-west Kendal, with housing rising up the steep slopes to the west of the parish church.

Private housing has followed a similar pattern in the town, with more spacious developments leading to a huge increase in the area of the town without a matching rise in the population. Standardised designs, beginning in the later nineteenth century, turned away from the local vernacular. Semi-detached houses and bungalows in standard materials, varying only in scale and size of garden, mean that there is little to tell you that you are in Kendal rather than some other town.

However, some of the more recent developments do incorporate a few vernacular elements, as at least a nod to the traditions of the area. Houses in Wasdale Close are tall and have rendered exteriors, but also have semicircular stair turrets in stone at one side, in some vague copy of Lake District vernacular. Perhaps surprisingly, there has been a recent move to refurbish and modernise, or rebuild, houses in some of the yards, in order to bring people back into the town centre. This is in addition to those yards that have been developed for shopping, such as Elephant Yard and Wainwright Yard. Kendal Civic Society's Building Preservation Trust led the way in 1977 with the purchase and refurbishment of houses in Collin Croft, on the west side of Highgate, and there have been a number of recent commercial developments in other yards, such as Webster's Yard, also in Highgate, marked by its very ornate iron gates. The aim of clearing the old yards was originally to remove some of the greatest risks to public health. Conversely, the move to repopulate at least some of them comes from a desire to minimise the endless extension of the town into green fields, and to reduce town-centre crime by smartening up what had become lurky back-alleys.

The high-tide mark of Kendal's council housing was reached in the mid-1970s, when some 2,800 houses were in council ownership (almost as many as the total number of houses in the borough in 1901). However, the 'right to buy' legislation of the 1980s rapidly eroded this figure, and this decline in outright public ownership was matched by the growth of tenanted property owned by housing associations.[53] After a long period when governments single-mindedly espoused the idea of universal home ownership, the rented sector has more recently been revived—in part because of the exceptionally high price of property in desirable towns such as Kendal, with its highly favoured geographical position. Kendal is not within the Lake District National Park, with all its planning constraints, and so it feels the pressure of demand for building houses within easy reach of the park. Locally, many houses have been bought to rent in recent years, but what the long term holds is quite unclear, with the post-2008 turmoil in the housing market and the wider financial world. It is clear, though, that Kendal will never be a cheap place to live.

Shops and businesses | 6

The Market Place

THE MARKET PLACE was at the heart of medieval Kendal, both physically and economically. Today it is hard to envisage how it might have looked six hundred years ago, because of the way in which buildings have encroached upon its original extent. There is also some uncertainty about its exact origins. Farrer, writing in 1923, stated that Richard I granted Roger Fitz Reinfrid a charter for a weekly Saturday market in return for 20 marks as early as 1189 (at a time when the king was anxious to raise money for his Crusading adventures).[1] The documentary evidence appears to be lost, but the date is plausible—other places in the region which were definitely granted market charters at this period include Preston (1179), Lancaster (1193), Brough (1201) and Cockermouth (1221). A date of 1189 was before the creation of the borough and hence the market at that date was probably held somewhere other than its present location, perhaps in Kirkland, in or immediately outside the churchyard—such places were commonly used for early markets, as at, for example, Preston and Burnley. At all events, there was a further grant in 1309 by Edward II of a Saturday market to Marmaduke de Thweng and William de Ros, heirs of Peter de Brus, to be held in the manor.[2] All we can say is that from fairly early in its medieval history Kendal had a Saturday market, and a market place in which to hold it.

Markets were of fundamental importance to medieval towns. This was especially so before the fifteenth century, since in many places fixed and permanent shops only began to develop at that time. Even after the emergence of shops, markets remained vital to economic well-being. Among the main things sold, in Kendal as anywhere else, were dairy products such as butter, milk and cheese, produced in the surrounding countryside, together with basic staples such as bread, beer, vegetables, beans and corn. Cattle and sheep were also sold, both on the hoof and as meat, as were fish from the rivers, lakes and shores, and poultry of all sorts. Markets also dealt in goods other than foodstuffs, such as shoes, wooden goods, baskets and cloth. Some of those who held stalls on the market were not freemen of the borough, and they paid a small fee for the privilege, known as the 'stallenge'. Goods passing into or through the town on market days had also to pay a toll, unless the traders were exempted for one reason or another, and both of these were a useful source of income to the town or to its lord.

The requirements of a medieval market place included, of course, a large open space in which stalls could be erected; a market cross, on the steps of which the egg and cheese sellers might sit and countrymen and women might offer small quantities of goods for sale, spread on a cloth. The market cross was also the place from which friars and other passing preachers might address the crowds, and for centuries the cross was also used for public proclamations of laws, byelaws, and official news such as the deaths of kings and the denouncing of traitors. Markets needed space not only for people and goods but also for the wagons, horses and mules that carried them. A tollbooth, the ancestor of many town halls, was also close at hand for taking tolls and fees, and for regular checks on goods sold in the market—the assizes of bread and beer, when both weight and quality might be examined by the mayor and officers of the borough, suddenly and without warning. Goods that were defective or underweight would be confiscated and destroyed, and their sellers punished. It was important for the good name of the town and the continued prosperity of its market that this should be so.

On the whole people seem to have welcomed the chance to buy 'in open market' where others could witness their bargain, in case things should go wrong later. The borough or manorial authorities had a vested interest in overseeing the process. Otherwise 'forestallers', those who bought up goods before they came into market and avoided the tolls; or 'higglers' who bought up goods such as dairy products and then acted as wholesalers; or 'regraters', who bought from one stall and then resold in small portions at a hefty profit, could seriously damage their income. A necessary concomitant to petty crimes was the means of summary justice, such as stocks, pillory or whipping-post. These might be the punishment for short weight or

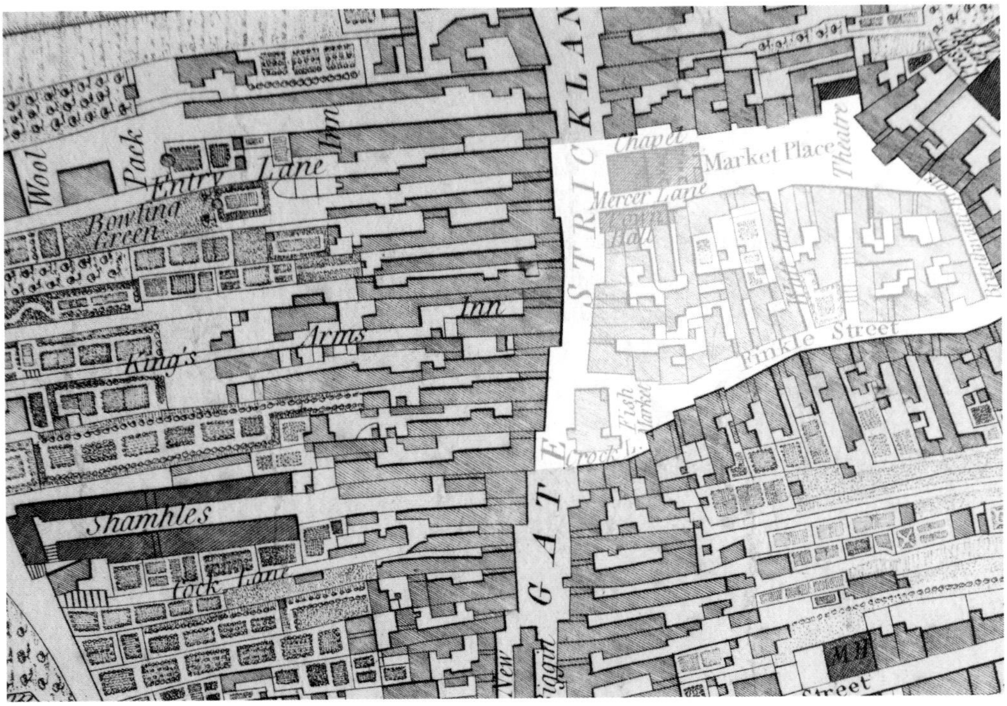

Schematic plan of the Market Place, based on Todd's map of 1787, and showing the area which had probably been encroached upon in the middle.

PHOTOGRAPH CARNEGIE, FROM AN ORIGINAL HELD AT WESTMORLAND RECORD OFFICE, KENDAL

The Moot Hall, by Robert Abbot, 1821. The Moot Hall was the earliest town hall, built in 1591, remodelled in 1729 and used until 1859 when the former White Hall was adapted. The remaining portion was destroyed by arson in 1969, but partly rebuilt.

PHOTOGRAPH CARNEGIE, 2012, BY COURTESY OF THE MUSEUM OF LAKELAND LIFE

poor quality of goods, or for drunkenness or affray. Some of these punishments outlived the Middle Ages and were still in use in the early nineteenth century.

Speed's 1611 plan of Kendal does not give much detail about the buildings and other features of the market place, but later maps show how its original area was steadily reduced in size. The basic shape of the original market place was a large irregular opening eastwards from the junction of Stricklandgate and Highgate at the summit of the hill, its north side defined by the present Market Place, its south side by Finkle Street (which becomes Stramongate further east) and by Branthwaite Brow to the east. On its south-west corner was the Tolbooth or Town Hall, which was burned down and replaced by a look-alike shop in 1969. It now lies at the edge of the Market Place but, since the extent of the open space was once so much greater, it originally stood in the centre, as the only intrusion into the trading space.

A considerable depth of shops and buildings has therefore taken over the southern half of the medieval market place, an area that is now threaded by two lanes, New Shambles and Police Yard. By the eighteenth century the various entrances to the Market Place from the west were also constricted by buildings, that to the south by the *Pump Inn* and the Fish Market in Finkle Street and that to the north by St George's Chapel. Another encroachment in Highgate was an extraordinary structure known as the New Biggin, which may also have arisen from permanent building on what had once been space for stalls. It occupied the centre of the roadway of Highgate, just opposite the site of the present Town Hall, and is said to have dated from about 1500. There is little reliable evidence apart from a picture drawn from

Detail of the entrance to the Finkle Street, with the Pump Inn and the Fish Market, from the 500" Ordnance Survey map of 1861.

PHOTOGRAPH CARNEGIE, FROM AN ORIGINAL HELD AT WESTMORLAND RECORD OFFICE, KENDAL

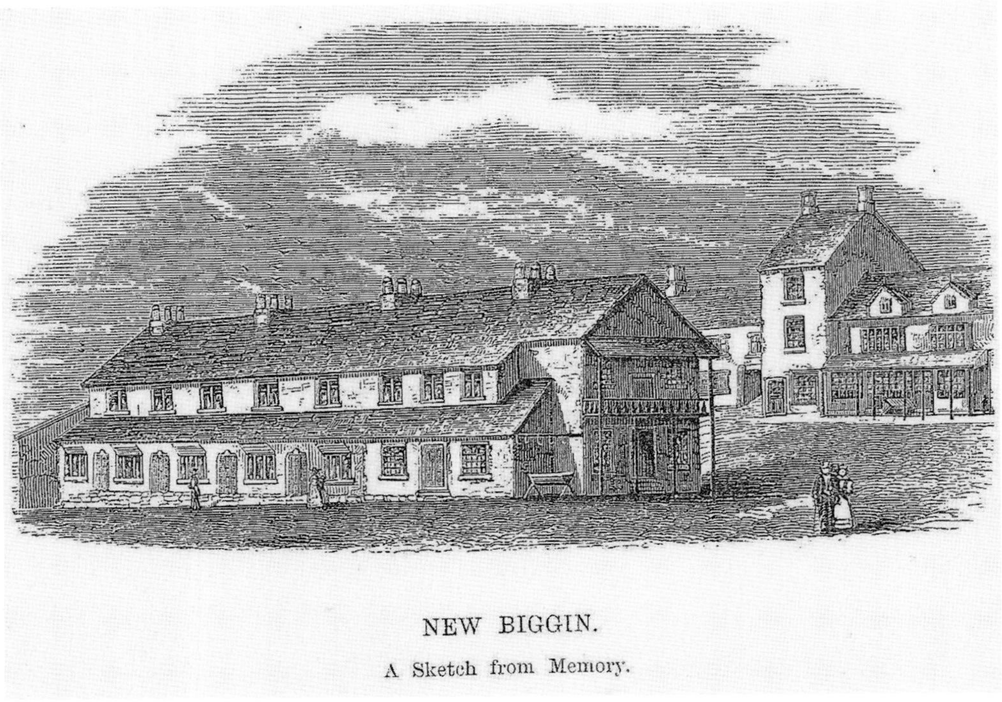

Drawing of the New Biggin from Nicholson's 'Annals', the only surviving image of this remarkable building.

memory in 1845 by John Richardson, and showing mainly seventeenth- or eighteenth-century features. It was some 30 yards (27.5 m) in length by 9½ yards (8.7 m) in breadth, of two storeys with shops beneath and a hall above for the Cordwainers' (shoemakers') Company. The road divided around it, leaving a very narrow passage to the west and a wider one to the east. The eastern elevation included a pentice roof on columns, providing shelter for customers of the shops on that side, while the northern end also had a gallery on the upper floor carried out on columns. On the death in 1803 of its owner, Lord Lonsdale, the New Biggin was given to the Corporation and immediately demolished. Its footprint can be seen on Todd's map of 1787, and the widening of the roadway in this area still shows where it stood.[3]

Encroachment on market places in this way is normally regarded as a sign that the commercial life of a town was vigorous and buoyant. The demand for permanent shops, or for stalls which were fixtures rather than being erected and dismantled weekly, inevitably tended to reduce the area of open space at the heart of a thriving community. To what extent this was the case in Kendal we cannot say, but it seems to be a strong likelihood. The same process has been recognised in many other towns and can be seen in Preston and Skipton, for instance. That this was seen as a problem at the time is made clear from a borough ordinance of 1577 which complained about 'the great streitninge [restricting] off the Markett places within [Kendal] by ... Dyvers howses shoppes Taverns grecis stayres and buyldinge heartoafore beinge sufferide to bee sett upp made and fframyd by sundrye personns'.[4]

As the Market Place shrank in size, it also became divided into specialised areas, and trading spilled out along the adjacent streets. In 1829 it was stated that the Market Place proper

Fish market in Finkle Street, from a glass slide.

GLASS SLIDE, BY COURTESY OF KENDAL TOWN COUNCIL

Potato market in Stramongate, from a glass slide.

PHOTOGRAPH BY PERCY DUFF, BY COURTESY OF KENDAL TOWN COUNCIL

was now used almost exclusively as a corn market, while sheep and cattle were sold in New Road, meat in the Old and New Shambles, fish at the head of Finkle Street, and potatoes and vegetables in Stramongate.[5]

St George's Chapel stood at the western entrance to the market place from 1754, and when it was removed in 1855 a covered market was built in its place, in part replacing the space under the rear porch of the chapel that had been used previously as the corn exchange. The new covered market also provided space for the market women with their butter and eggs, who had previously been exposed to the elements.[6] This building has had a curious afterlife, being first used as a library until the new Carnegie Library was built in 1909, then rebuilt in Sandes Avenue with the original front and side elevations opened out to produce one long façade. It still serves as a shop. A new market building was provided on the north side of the Market Place to mark Queen Victoria's Golden Jubilee in 1887. The open market in the Market Place still survives, with stalls set up here on Wednesdays and Saturdays, and an occasional 'farmers' market'.

For many years the town stocks stood behind St George's Chapel, while the pillory and market cross stood in the middle of Stricklandgate, outside the formal area of the Market Place.[7] The last relic of the base of the market cross is said to be the 'Call Stone' (or 'Cold Stone' in some older documents), now standing outside the present Town Hall at the junction of Highgate and Lowther Street. It is completely shapeless and highly polished, and does not look much like any part of a former cross base. From this stone important announcements are still made from time to time. Until 1859 the Town Hall building was known as the White Hall, an 1825 rebuilding by Francis Webster of a structure which may once have been a cloth

left Former Market and later Library building, rebuilt and 'opened out' in Sandes Avenue.

right The 'Call Stone' outside the Town Hall, and moved from the corner of the old Market House near the Moot Hall. Possibly from the base of a former cross, it was used as a platform from which to make official proclamations.

below Kendal Hiring Fair, Whitsuntide 1891, by Cuthbert Rigby. The fair was on New Road, with the Catholic church in the background.
PHOTOGRAPH BY PERCY DUFF, BY COURTESY OF KENDAL TOWN COUNCIL

hall, where small masters sold cloth to wholesalers. In 1859 it was converted and enlarged to become the town hall, and was further extended in 1893.[8]

As was the case in almost all medieval towns, Kendal had fairs as well as its weekly markets. In 1268 Peter de Brus, the lord of the barony, was granted the right to hold an annual fair by Henry III. It was to be at Holy Trinity in Eastertide, and in 1309 the grant was confirmed by Edward II when he also reconfirmed the town's market charter. In 1333 Edward III granted Cristiana, widow of Ingelram de Gynes (one of the heiresses of the divided barony) the right to a second fair, to be held on the Feast of St Luke the Evangelist (18 October). Fairs such as these were an occasion for socialising and entertainment, as well as the serious business of selling livestock and fixing major deals on the sale of produce. They also dealt in people, for these fairs were the ancestors of the great hiring fairs which, by the middle of the eighteenth century, had become a key event in the farming year throughout northern England.

As a centre of employment, both domestic and industrial, Kendal had hiring fairs twice each year. Many of those hired were employed in agriculture in the countryside around, but others worked in the town itself. The hirings took place in an area between the Market Place and the top of Finkle Street, where farmworkers would congregate, each wearing some distinctive item, such as, for example, a piece of whipcord to show that he was a horseman. All enjoyed a brief holiday between being signed off from one term and hired again for the next. Kendal therefore saw some lively social activity at these times. A pleasure-fair with rides was held on

Highgate with White Hall, later to become the Town Hall, engraved by William Westall in 1829.
AUTHOR COLLECTION

The Hiring Fair, with booths for the sideshows on New Road.

REPRODUCED BY COURTESY OF KENDAL TOWN COUNCIL

the riverbank in New Road, and indeed this has outlived the hirings. During the Victorian period there are accounts of the fairs: in November 1870, for example, the hiring sessions were part of a series of fairs held over two days, the 8th and 9th of the month. There were fairs for cattle, then the sale of onions, then horses, and finally the hiring. On that occasion it was noted that there were plenty of men servants but fewer women. High wages were asked and obtained.[9] By that time, too, there was also a Kendal Fortnight Fair, somewhat overshadowed when it coincided with one of the hirings. The two hiring fairs were held at strategic times in the farming year, on Whit Saturday in May, and around 11 November, or Martinmas. These are two of the quarter-days recognised in Scotland and adjacent areas of northern England. Northern farmers preferred a six-month hire to a year, as it deprived the servant of any claim on local poor relief.[10] Eventually, though, hiring fairs died out, with the reduction in the number of farm workers, longer term employment, and the use of agencies to mediate between employer and employed. Between the wars this time-honoured element in the town's life came to an end.

The inns of Kendal

At first sight Kendal seems to be crammed with inns and public houses, although this is perhaps because there are few main streets. Many inns are placed prominently on the street frontages, so it is difficult to avoid seeing them. But if there seems to be a large number now, in the past the impression must have been even more marked. In parts of upper Highgate and lower Stricklandgate, for example, the inns stood contiguously. The large-scale Ordnance Survey map of 1861, for example, shows the *Fleece*, *Exchange*, *White Hart*, *Crown*, *King's Arms*, *Rose & Crown*, *White Lion*, *Woolpack* and *Elephant* more or less side by side on a short stretch of the western side of the street.

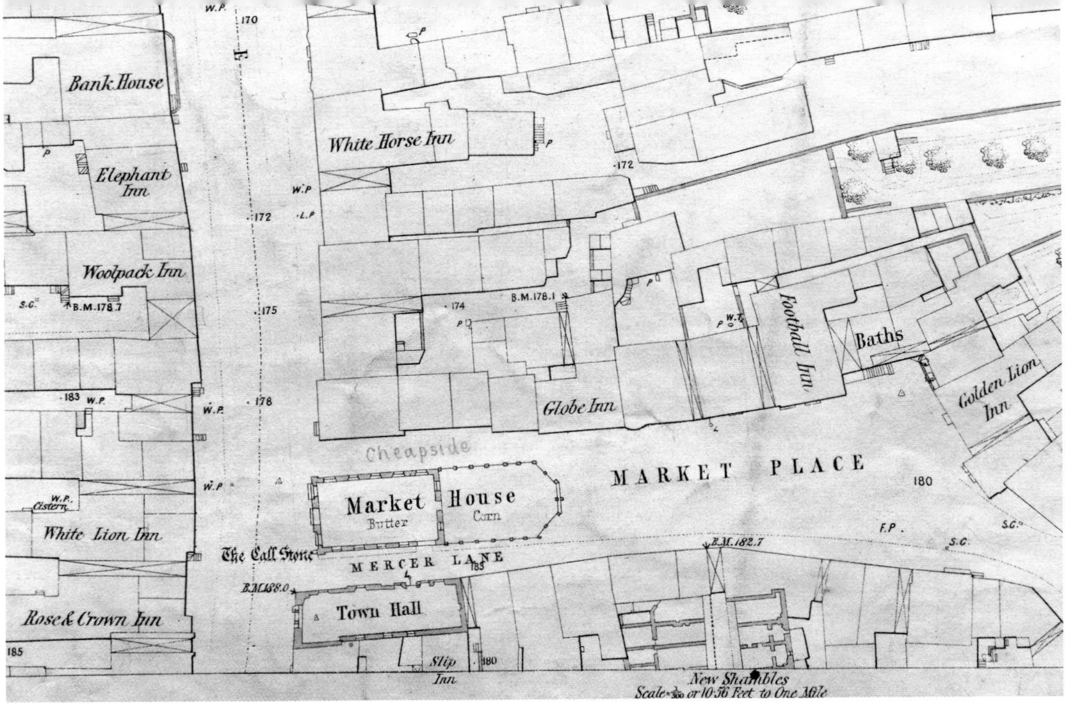

Detail from the 500" Ordnance Survey map of 1861, showing the density of inns in Highgate and Stricklandgate.

PHOTOGRAPH CARNEGIE, FROM AN ORIGINAL HELD AT WESTMORLAND RECORD OFFICE, KENDAL

left The Ring of Bells Inn is set on the edge of the churchyard in Kirkland and may represent an ancient inn site.

right The Shakespeare Inn was built in 1829 and very appropriately has a theatre at the end of the yard behind it.

Many of these inns were very old-established, and they all contributed to Kendal's position as the town with greatest quantity of accommodation for travellers in all Westmorland, although it was not the county town.[11] The importance of the inns is not surprising, given the location of the town on the main western road to Scotland. The detailed and specific origin of many of the inns is quite unclear, but innkeepers are mentioned in many documents from the sixteenth century onwards, and at least some of the inns go back to the Middle Ages. But which? The evidence is equivocal, and early records are lost. Few sites can be proved to be ancient, but one candidate for longevity is the *Ring of Bells* (known as the *Eight Bells* in 1790) next to the parish church in Kirkland. This has every indication of being on an ancient site, perhaps even as a place where church-ales were held in the medieval period. Nevertheless,

there are conflicting traditions which claim that it was established as late as the eighteenth century. Another long-established inn is the *Duke of Cumberland* at Far Cross Bank, the name at least of which goes back to 1745 when the duke and his army followed the retreating Jacobites through Kendal. However, there is evidence for an earlier *Duke of Cumberland* on the south side of the Market Place in 1757, perhaps a renaming of the *Wheat Sheaf*.[12] So perhaps the present inn of that name is not so old. Only rarely was the opening of a new inn announced in the press, though one such was the *Shakespeare Inn*, appropriately fronting the new theatre in Highgate and opened in August 1829.[13]

In the late sixteenth century the supremacy of the traditional English ale was challenged by new types of beer, which soon became popular. Paul Clark, the leading historian of alehouses, has noted that, 'In the early part of Elizabeth's reign (or before) beer was a popular tipple in [the Midlands] and the following decades saw beer advancing to ... Kendal'.[14] Some travellers rated Kendal ales very highly. In 1705 Joseph Taylor, passing through the town, reported that 'We staid only to dine and refresh ourselves, and found there the best Malt liquor we had drunk in all our Travells'.[15]

The Pump Inn occupied most of the junction of Finkle Street and Highgate and the Fish Market was just behind it. This sixteenth- or seventeenth-century building became the Pump Inn in about 1740 and was demolished in 1877.

GLASS SLIDE, BY COURTESY OF KENDAL TOWN COUNCIL

In 1578 it was agreed that one of the 'Twelve Severall Companyes', the trade guilds of the town, was to be for 'Inholders and Alehowsekepers and Typlers', suggesting that there were already a substantial number of people employed in this trade.[16] In 1686 a survey of guest-bed and stabling space, undertaken for military purposes, shows Kendal with 279 of the former and 439 of the latter, all in inns and ale-houses. This is by far the greatest number in Westmorland, and in the modern area of Cumbria only Carlisle had more.[17] A survey of 1695 lists eleven innkeepers, but does not identify their premises. However, four were in Highgate, six in Stricklandgate and only one in Stramongate. The 'census' of 1787, which only covers Stricklandgate, lists ten innkeepers. These lists are very unlikely to be complete. Occasionally innkeepers and their ilk appear in other records: for instance, in 1696 the refusal of the excisemen at Kendal to take the old coins in payment of beer duty precipitated a riot led by the alehouse keepers.[18]

The probate inventories of innkeepers give us useful information about their premises and their social status. Two examples are instructive. That of Robert Wilkinson of Highgate (died 1678) records a house (that is, a main living room), parlour (wherein were a 'rapier and swordbelt' and a 'chaff bed'), tavern (containing wooden and earthenware vessels and a lantern), a kitchen, a loft over the house, another loft, and a loft over the parlour. This was a modest establishment, and even the drinking vessels seem old-fashioned for the period.[19] By contrast, when he died in 1742 Henry Fletcher, innkeeper of the *Royal Oak* in Highgate had a kitchen, hall, far parlour, middle parlour, first parlour, a parlour over the cellar, a 'Coffyhouse' (containing 'Eleven Chaires one table Long settle and picters'), garrets, a buttery, a best room, a 'green room', a billiard room, a 'red room' and a long loft, with wine, ale, casks and brewing vessels. The coffeehouse and billiard room are examples of how relatively new fashions had reached Kendal by the reign of George II, and had been adopted by town inns as an additional source of income.[20]

As well as catering for travellers, the inns of the town also served the farmers who came to market, while the carriers who distributed goods to and from the villages and, before the advent of the railways, over longer distances as well, mostly started from the main innyards. Inns were the natural venues for meetings, auctions and other public business. Many of their names reflect the trades of the town, and were calculated to appeal to men working in particular trades. For example, the *Woolpack* and the *Bishop Blaise* (later the *Kendal Bowman*, but now defunct) reflected the dominant wool trade (Bishop Blaise was the patron saint of woolcombers, as he was martyred by having his flesh torn with woolcombs), and other trades are reflected in the *Sawyers' Arms* in Stricklandgate, the *Masons' Arms* in Stramongate and the *Weavers' Arms* in Wildman Street.

Another view of Kendal's inns comes from the diary of George Hilton of Beetham, by his own admission a rake, gambler and drunkard. This is one of the few diaries to need its own index of inns, such was his usage of them. He mentions four Kendal inns in the period 1699–1704—the *King's Arms*, *New Tavern*, *Queen's Arms* and *White Lion*—although relatively little of his hard drinking was done in the town, perhaps because his mother lived here![21] In 1795, when Sir Frederick Eden was gathering data for his book on the poor, Kendal and Kirkland between them had 48 alehouses in which 6,620 barrels of ale (totalling some 225,080 gallons) were drunk annually.[22]

The *Dog & Buck* inn in Finkle Street is described thus in 1834;

> ... all that newly built and well accustomed inn or public house and coaching house called the Dog and Buck Inn with the coach office, adjoining yard, three stalled stable, brewhouse three stories high, and out offices behind the same, situate on north side of Finkle Street, Kendal late in occupation of Elizabeth Dixon, deceased; also all that newly erected and commodious stable on south side of Finkle Street, containing accommodation for 6 horses with the hayloft above and a privy and dunghillstead adjoining—all subject to payment of 10s. yearly burgage rent.[23]

From 1794 trade directories give us useful comparative information, although even with these there are likely to have been omissions. In that year 39 innkeepers or victuallers are listed, not all with the name of their inn, and by 1829 there were 44 inns. In 1834 these had been supplemented by 25 beerhouses, established under recent legislation. Beerhouses in this period did not usually have names, and later on, when they did acquire them, the distinction between inns and beerhouses was disappearing. By 1849 there were 47 inns and 15 beerhouses;

in 1873, 41 inns and various beerhouses; and in 1914, 32 inns and 3 beerhouses. Although there were inconsistencies in directory coverage, it is clear that there was a steady reduction over the course of the century. Today that trend continues, and several old-established inns are either standing vacant or have changed tenants very frequently. Hybrids and variations, such as eating establishments with alcohol licences, nightclubs, or pubs showing sport on large-screen televisions, have largely taken over the role of the traditional inn.

Until the mid-nineteenth century many inns brewed their own beer. Kendal also had its own specialist brewery from the mid-eighteenth century, where the Brewery Arts Centre now stands, and in 1805 the town had two: the New Brewery, run by Hoggarth, Barns, Long & Co., and the Old Brewery, run by Whitwell, Pennington & Co., who later became Whitwell Mark & Co.[24] In the 1873 directory, however, the Old Brewery, of J. J. Banks, is listed in Wildman Street. After this time local brewing declined rapidly in the face of competition from the big national brewers in London and Burton-on-Trent.

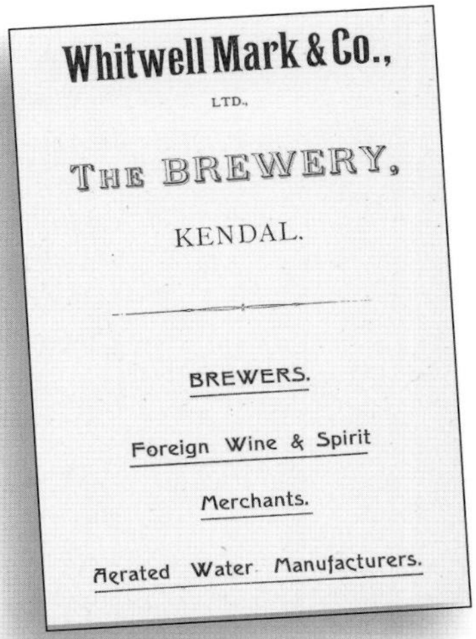

Advert for Whitwell Mark Brewery in 1906. This became the site of the Brewery Arts Centre.

Businesses

A very useful list of trades and businesses in the town was produced in 1695,[25] following Acts of Parliament of 1694 and 1695 which authorised a tax on marriages, baptisms and burials, as well as on bachelors over the age of 25 and widowers with one child. The lists which were drawn up are arranged by district (Highgate, Stricklandgate, Stramongate and Kirkland) and seem to be complete as far as the first three are concerned. This survey is unusual, in that most lists of the period cover only heads of households, but for the first three areas at least the lists name individual adults and their occupations, and also servants, but give only the number of children. The list for Kirkland, however, seems only to list the actual money received. Women are also listed, both wives and single women (the latter designated as spinsters, which in the case of Kendal might actually mean their occupation, not their status). Some of the 'servants' at least would have been engaged in their master's trade, rather than being domestic servants. The tables below show the trades and occupations of the Highgate, Stricklandgate and Stramongate areas, as identified in the 1695 survey. Variations in the use of terms and the crudeness of the three-part division of the borough probably conceal the true geographical distribution of trades, however.

Highgate

Apothecary	1	Butcher	1	Currier	2
Apothecary	1	Chandler	1	Doctor	1
Attorney	2	Chapman	3	Dyer	1
Bailiff	1	(Wool) Comber	2	Farrier	1
Barber	2	Cordwainer	25	Glazier	2
Brazier	4	Curate	1	Glover	11

Harper	1	Personal estate	1	Surveyor	1
Husbandman	2	Schoolmaster	1	Swordbearer	1
Innkeeper	4	Shearman	3	Tailor	2
Labourer	3	Shoemaker	1	Tanner	6
Lime burner	2	Slater	2	Waller	9
Maltster	2	Smith	2	Weaver	24
Mercer	5	(Wool) Stapler	2	Whitesmith	3
Musician	1	Stockiner	1	Yeoman	5

Stricklandgate

Apothecary	2	Innkeeper	6	Tailor	9
Baker	1	Labourer	4	Tin man	1
Barber	1	Mercer	14	Waller	1
Butcher	1	Minister?	1	Wigmaker	1
Cardmaker	3	Personal estate	1	Wire drawer	1
Commissioner	2	Pewterer	1	Woolstapler	1
Currier	1	Saddler	1	Yeoman	2
Gent	2	Shearman	29	Younger son of a knight	1
Glover	2	Shoemaker	10		
Haberdasher of hats	2	Stockiner	1		
Hookmaker	1	Stuffweaver	12		

Stramongate

Barber	6	Glazier	1	Saddler	2
Blacksmith	1	Glover	1	Shearman	13
Butcher	2	Hatter	2	Shoemaker	1
Carpenter	2	Innholder	1	Smith	5
Cobbler	2	Ironmonger	1	Tailor	2
Comber	1	Joiner	3	Tanner	3
Cooper	2	Knight & baronet	1	Weaver	25
Cordwainer	1	Labourer	27	Yeoman	9
Dyer	4	Mercer	3	Younger son of a knight	1
Fletcher	1	Pewterer	3		

We have another snapshot of trades, this time those practised by Roman Catholics, in 1767,[26] in the 'Return of Papists' for that year. The list of 'reputed Papists' for Kendal covers the four main divisions of the town and lists names, trades and ages. The numbers are small (about 150 in total), and many of those listed were wives or children, with no stated or actual trade. However, the concentration of weavers in Highgate and Stramongate, evident in 1695, seems to be replicated here also. It is interesting to see the number of women apparently running businesses, marked below with (f).

Highgate

Apprentice, trade unknown	1	Butcher	1	Dry salter (f)	1
Blacksmith	1	Cordwainer	1	Female servant	2
		Corn factor	1	Hosier	1

Inn keeper	1	Weaver	1	Woolcomber	3
Midwife (f)	2	Weaver, journeyman	1	Worsted spinner	1
Tanner, journeyman	1	Whalebone cutter	1		

Stricklandgate

Brasier	1	Paviour	3	Yeoman	2
Card maker (f)	1	Shoemaker	2		
Miller	1	Weaver	2		

Stramongate

Baker (f)	1	Labourer	1	Woolcomber	1
Carpenter	2	Waller	1		
Gent	1	Weaver (1 f)	8		

Kirkland

Barber	1	Female servant	1	Whipmaker	1
Bread baker (1 f)	2	Glove cutter	1	Works at silk engine	1
Datalman	1	Weaver	1		

For Kendal the so-called 'Westmorland census', commissioned for unknown purposes by the Westmorland Court of Quarter Sessions in 1787 only covers Stricklandgate, but it too lists occupations:[27]

Stricklandgate

Attorney	2	Dealer in grain	1	Millwright	4
Banker	1	Doctor	1	Nailer	2
Barber	4	Draper	6	Officer of Excise	3
Blacksmith	3	Dry salter	1	Ostler	6
Book keeper	1	Dyer	4	Plumber	1
Brandy merchant	1	Earthenware dealer	1	Reed maker	1
Brazier	3	Fiddler	1	Rope maker	4
Breadbaker	5	Gardener	2	Saddler	5
Butcher	4	Gent	6	Schoolmaster	1
Captain	1	Grocer	5	Shay driver	1
Card maker	2	Hatter	1	Shearman	27
Carpenter	4	Hook maker	2	Shoe maker	8
Carter	1	Horn comb maker	1	Shopkeeper	3
Chair maker	2	Hosier	6	Smith	1
Clerk	3	Huckster	1	Stationer	1
Clockmaker	3	Innkeeper	10	Staymaker	2
Clogger	2	Ironmonger	4	Tailor	17
Clothier	1	Joiner	4	Tanner	1
Cobbler	1	Labourer	62	Thrower	1
Cooper	4	Lime burner	1	Tobacconist	1
Currier	1	Maltster	1	Twine spinner	1
Dealer in blue	1	Mercer	1	Waller	18

Watchmaker	1	Wine merchant	1	Woolcomber	19
Weaver	90	Wire drawer	3	Wright	2
Wheelwright	2	Wood monger	1		

In the main streets the various shops and businesses lay in an apparently haphazard manner. The unusual plan of the town, with only three main streets but an exceptionally linear form, did not lend itself to the patterns of subdivision by trade that were to be found in many other towns. However, the lists of inhabitants in 1695 and 1787 do show a degree of concentration, with, for example, most of the shearmen in 1695 being resident in Stricklandgate (29), fewer in Stramongate (13) and least in Highgate (3). In contrast, among the shoe-making trades (shoemaker, cobbler or cordwainer) Highgate had the greatest number. Surprisingly few butchers are recorded, but it is likely that many butchers in earlier periods had no fixed premises, simply operating from open stalls in the market area, on either side of Highgate from the *Pump Inn* down to the New Biggin.[28]

The butchers increased in significance with the building of the (Old) Shambles on the west side of Highgate in 1779–82, two rows of shops totalling forty units, with a grander building at the top forming the *Butchers' Arms* public house. Later came the New Shambles, just to the south of the Market Place, built in 1803. This consisted of twelve small single-storey shops in two rows running between the Market Place and Finkle Street. They are still there, but some are now combined and none is now a butcher's shop. The new facilities might have been better than the open stalls which they replaced, but in hygienic terms there was little improvement. Slaughtering was still carried out on the premises, and the blood, guts and offal had no natural escape except by running down the steep roadways towards the river, or by being carried away periodically. Such a gory mess in the very centre of the town was not only aesthetically unpleasing but a real health hazard. However, it was no different from the situation in most towns … and a wet and rainy climate must have been a real help in this case, helping to flush away the debris.

Several of the seventeenth-century tradesmen of Kendal left brass tokens, issued at a time

left The Old Shambles, off Highgate.

right Finkle Street and the New Shambles, from the 500" Ordnance Survey map of 1861.

PHOTOGRAPH CARNEGIE, FROM AN ORIGINAL HELD AT WESTMORLAND RECORD OFFICE, KENDAL

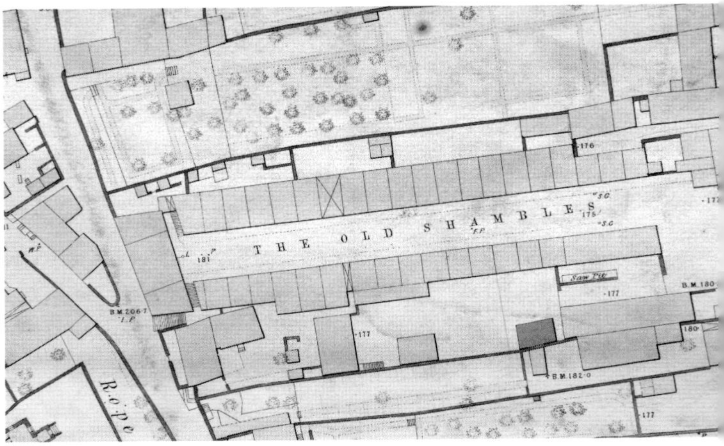

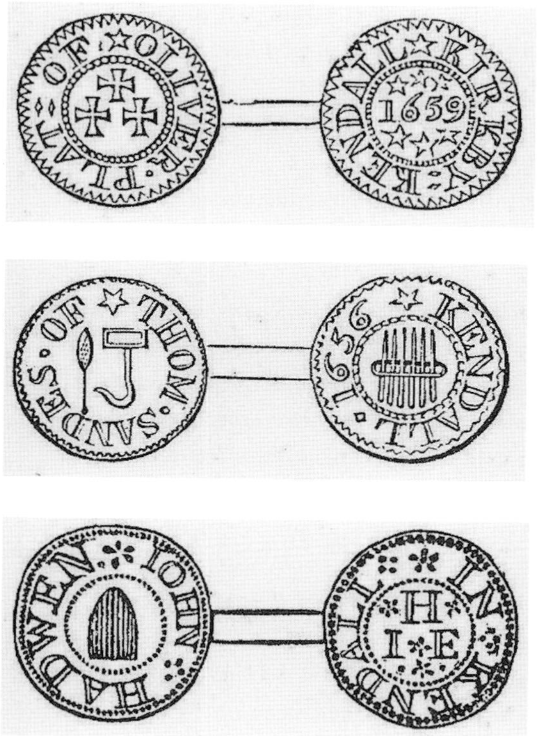

left
Seventeenth-century trade tokens of Kendal issuers John Hadwen, Thomas Sandes and Oliver Platt.

right
One-handed lantern clock which was given to the town by James Cock, Mayor, in 1654.

GLASS SLIDE, BY COURTESY OF KENDAL TOWN COUNCIL

when there was a shortage of official small coinage. The tokens were usually for a farthing or a halfpenny and would be accumulated by other traders and shoppers, to be exchanged periodically for silver. Those issuers for whom examples are known include Thomas Sandes, the founder of Sandes Hospital (token of 1669), Edmond Adlington, dyer (1659), Oliver Plat (1659), John Hadwen, grocer? (undated), Thomas Wilson & Thomas Warde of Kirkland (1666) and James Cocke junior, mercer (1667). In addition both the Mercers' Company and the Shearmen's Company struck tokens, in 1657 and 1667 respectively.[29]

From the mid-seventeenth century new trades began to appear, particularly those connected with the growing demand for consumer goods and luxury items. For example, clock-making became a significant craft trade in the late seventeenth century, Kendal having many more clockmakers than any other place in Westmorland. This trade itself created new opportunities, and some local cabinetmakers branched out in case-making. In the early days the local clockmakers produced everything themselves, but by the late eighteenth century specialised parts, such as brass gears and

Handbill of James Newby, clockmaker, c.1800, from the Soulby Collection.

SOULBY ZS, 22, BY COURTESY OF BARROW ARCHIVES

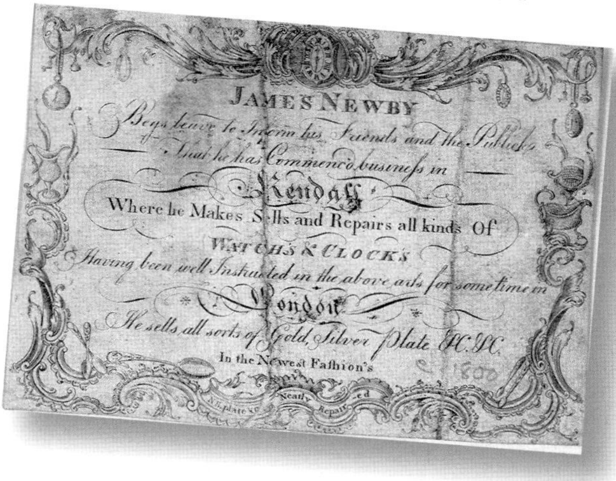

enamelled dials, could be bought ready-made from Clerkenwell, Coventry or Birmingham, while springs and other mechanical elements came from Prescot in south Lancashire.[30]

Shops

Until the nineteenth century most of the shops were associated with production, in workshops set behind in the long yards, or above the main building. Relatively few dealt with the sale of items made elsewhere and imported to Kendal. Indeed, there was a healthy distrust of middlemen, who took a profit without adding anything to the goods. Nonetheless, luxury items and exotic goods could not be produced locally, and from quite an early date a few Kendal shops did specialise in the imported goods. By the early seventeenth century, too, Kendal had become a major regional shopping centre, a role testified by entries in the diaries and account books of county families. For example, in 1612 Lord William Howard of Naworth near Carlisle sent to Kendal for 'one pound's worth of wax candles for My Lady's devotions',[31] while in the 1670s Sarah Fell at Swarthmoor Hall near Ulverston bought a variety of goods from the town, including bellows, pans, soap and shoes. Her account books record money paid to Daniel Cooper 'for carrying 2 petticoats to Kendal and bringing them again, and that he payd for dieing them ash colour, of sisters Susannah and Rachael, 1s. 6d'.[32]

We know a good deal about some businesses, because they have left detailed records. One such was Joseph Symson, mercer, who flourished in the early eighteenth century.[33] Symson was typical of traders of his time in that, although described as a mercer, he sold a great variety of goods, ranging from buttons, silk and shoelaces, to tea, coffee, snuff and books, all of which he obtained from London by packhorse carrier during the period 1711–20, for which time his business records survive. The probate inventories of such tradesmen often leave us puzzled as to what exactly was their principal business. In truth they were probably general entrepreneurs, and any formal description (such as 'mercer') can be misleading.

An old rhyme, preserved by Whitwell, gives us a list of businesses in Highgate, probably in the late eighteenth century (the name 'Barrow & Milton, linen-drapers', appears in the 1784 trade directory).[34] Fitzgibbon tells us that Betty Wilson was a maker of 'Kendal wigs', a local delicacy which was in the form of a yeasted bun, enlivened with caraway seeds or currants.[35]

Cuddy Coupland, smith and farrier;
Benjamin Newton, Kirkby carrier;
Barrow and Milton, linen drapers;
Jossey Lockey, periwig maker;
Betty Wilson, bread baker.[36]

Until at least the end of the seventeenth century the shops that were in the town were usually of the open-fronted type, with a large shutter that could be dropped to form a counter. They were staffed very largely by apprentices, who were a central element in the guild system. In

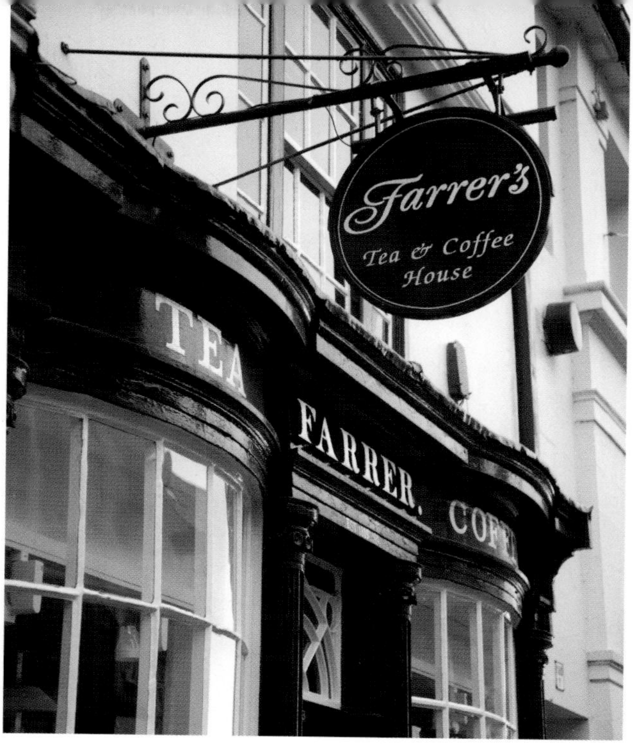

left
Shops in Branthwaite Brow with cast-iron front panels, cast at the Lound Foundry.
PHOTOGRAPH: ELLIE GODDARD

Farrer's Tea and Coffee shop, something of an institution in Kendal.
PHOTOGRAPH: ELLIE GODDARD

order to trade it was necessary to have served an apprenticeship with a recognised master, usually for seven years. Towards the end of their time apprentices might teach and control younger ones, freeing the master to do other tasks. Shop hours were long, and apprentices lived and slept in the shop, on call to serve early or late customers. Not surprisingly, there are no survivors of this type of shop in Kendal. Most went in the 1820s, the victims of renewal and improvement, but a few, with windows inserted at first-floor level, survived into the age of photography. These probably had lock-up shops in the medieval tradition on the ground floor, and the upper floors in separate ownership.

Improvements in glass-making, and the breakdown of the guild system, brought changes to shops in the later eighteenth century. Larger windows for display required new façades: in 1822, for example, the Websters refronted a group of shops on the east side of Stricklandgate (nos 13–17), of which Farrers' tea and coffee shop is an exceptional survival, in terms of its two bow display windows and its fine interior fittings. Another notable shop front is that of the Highgate Pharmacy, no. 41 Highgate, a building also refronted in 1826 and with a contemporary or slightly later shop window, complete with its trade sign of a pestle and mortar over the door. In the early nineteenth century plate glass display windows, better lighting, and larger staffs of paid employees, rather than apprentices, continued the process of change. However, this was not a uniform progression, and older types of shops survived alongside the new. In part it depended upon what they sold, as some goods were still hand-made, while others, such as metal goods and china, were now being produced by developing industrialised methods.

Some Kendal shops defy categorisation, as there seems to have been an early taste for the 'quaint' or 'antique', giving us, for instance, 26–28 Highgate, a sixteenth-century building with a shop front in three windows, possibly built by the Websters in 1828. In Branthwaite Brow nos 39–45a form an exceptional group of shops dating from 1853. Their timber framing carries a frontage made up of cast-iron plates, said to have been designed to reduce their projection into the street. Is it not more likely that their builder, the iron-founder Joseph Winder of the Lound Foundry, was giving a very visible showcase to his wares? By the late nineteenth century there was a host of small trades, some highly specialised.

Several 'fried fish' proprietors appear in the 1894 directory, including William Lever and John Williams in Allhallows Lane, heralding the arrival of fish and chips as a popular dish, the saviour of the poor. Photographers also became commonplace during the later nineteenth century, and bicycle manufacturers and dealers start to appear.

Recent years have seen many changes in the nature and type of shops in Kendal. As in most towns the twentieth century saw the arrival of national chain stores, replacing many local shops. However, Kendal was too small to attract all the main high street businesses, and also suffered (or perhaps benefited) from the narrowness of the sites available, mostly still determined by medieval burgage plots. Ancient property boundaries can be extremely resilient, so that a prospective developer, without the support of a local authority's compulsory purchase powers, can find it very expensive to assemble enough contiguous properties to make a sufficiently extensive site upon which to build a large store.

Inevitably, the other main driving force behind change has been the motor car, and the desire of shoppers to park in the town centre, or to use shops which have their own car park. This has led to out-of-town shopping, which is inimical to a healthy town centre. Although local authorities might try to resist this, using their planning controls, they are facing rich and powerful companies and fluctuating government policy. Even in a place such as Kendal, in many ways the classic country market town set in lovely scenery, the cheaply built large sheds out of town, set in a sea of parking, are a highly visible demonstration of late twentieth-century trends. This is especially true in the trading estates, such as those on Burton Road near the hospital, or at Mints Feet and Fell View off the Shap road, for which the use of a car is unavoidable.

In more recent times, partly in an effort to counter these trends, larger-scale central developments have taken place, first at the Westmorland Centre in 1989 and then at Elephant Yard, where the whole fabric of the townscape has been changed by the combining of plots and the reorientation of the building lines. Such developments are superficially attractive and seem popular with shoppers, especially when shopping and car parks are closely linked, but there may be serious side-effects, such as blight in other areas of the town. In recent years the main victim in this respect has been Kirkland and the southern part of Highgate. The rebuilding of the so-called 'K Village' on the site of the K Shoes factory in 2009–10 might, when opened, have a similar effect upon the town centre. Perhaps there is simply not enough trade in the town to support all these new developments simultaneously; nor do shoppers these days choose to walk far. Notwithstanding this, though, some of the new developments are a credit to the town centre and make a genuine effort to enhance its appearance and its commercial viability—the new Booths store and Wainwright's Yard are especially noteworthy.

But nothing is for ever. In recent years many buildings in the town centre, including a number that were built for industrial purposes, have been converted and adapted for residential use, increasing the population of the central area after years of steady decline, and revitalising parts of Kendal that were experiencing decay. Who knows whether, in the fullness of time, changing circumstances may mean that shopping will return from the fringes?

Banks

In the late eighteenth and early nineteenth centuries several banking businesses were established in Kendal.[37] They were privately owned, founded by merchants of the town, and issued their own banknotes, examples of which survive. Banks such as these, to be found in every town in the country, facilitated the major expansion of trade and commerce. The banknotes, which were essentially promissory notes, could be sent where gold could not, and all local banks also drew on London bankers, creating an embryonic national network. It was very difficult for traders and merchants to carry out long-distance buying and selling when gold was almost the only means of exchange. The arrival of systems of credit and the use of notes was therefore of crucial importance. Without banking and the associated financial arrangements it would never have been possible to build the terraces of houses, the canals or the railways, which so symbolise the Industrial Revolution and the economic vigour of the nineteenth century.

Kendal one pound banknote bearing engravings of Kendal Castle and a beehive, a symbol of industry.

In Kendal two main banks were established in the same year, 1788. Wakefield's Bank and Maude, Wilson and Crewdson's Bank were resilient: both survived the disastrous economic crisis of 1825–26, which was caused by a wave of bank failures across the country (both of Lancaster's banks crashed, in 1822 and 1826). George Smith of Hornby recorded in his diary for 1826 'a severe run upon Kirkby and Kendal banks'.[38] In 1840 the two undertakings amalgamated to form the Kendal Bank, with its main premises in Highgate (now Barclay's). This bank also issued its own notes. In 1833 the Bank of Westmorland had been founded, as a joint stock bank with 144 proprietors, in Lowther Street. The principle of a joint stock company, which was far more secure and legally defined, became popular after the failure of so many private banks in the previous decade. In 1835 it moved to the new building in Highgate, designed by George Webster, which its successor the HSBC still occupies. In the course of time the smaller local banks were swallowed up by a handful of nationwide banks. Now we have much the same limited choice as anywhere in the country.

7 ‘Pannus mihi Panis’: Cloth is bread to me

The people of Kendal are generally industrious, so that it is a very rare thing to see any person standing idle, as is too usual in other thorough-fare towns, or other places of public resort.[1]

Any study of Kendal and its industries will confirm that it was indeed a town of many trades and crafts, pursued with a single-minded intensity that puts many larger places to shame. The woollen industry was Kendal’s principal business from the Middle Ages right through until the later nineteenth century,[2] but one of the great strengths of the town was that it never depended entirely upon one trade. The range of goods produced here, in addition to woollen cloth, is impressive, helping to tide it over the hard times in the staple trade. When woollens were eventually toppled from prime position, their place was taken by shoe-making but, for example, tanning and leather had long been an important industry.

The Flemings

One of the great myths about the town’s history, first propagated in Nicholson’s *Annals of Kendal* in the mid-nineteenth century and extraordinarily resilient since then, is the story that a Fleming, John Kemp, who had been licensed by Edward III in 1331 to establish his weaving business, introduced the weaving of woollen cloth to Kendal.[3] There is absolutely no basis for this claim. Kemp was a real person, and he did indeed establish himself—in Norwich, then a great centre of the cloth trade—but had nothing at all to do with Kendal. Neither are there any surnames of recognisably Flemish origin in the area.[4] Whatever the beginnings of the English cloth trade it certainly did not originate from this, because there is a wealth of archaeological and historical evidence to show that cloth production was well established long before the Norman Conquest. The legend, for such it is, typifies the simplistic Victorian approach to history, which sought to assign single causes or specific origins to complex or undocumented matters. Even so, the Kemp story still regularly surfaces and seems to have life left in it.

The emergence of Kendal's woollen industry was an entirely local, or home-grown, process. The industry itself has been extensively described and analysed in several excellent books, and there can be no doubting its central place in the town's economic and commercial development during the medieval period.[5] Kendal's motto, 'Pannus mihi panis', says it all. It means 'cloth is bread to me', the Latin offering a small pun on the similarity of the two words. This has been variously mistranslated as 'wool is my bread' or 'cloth is my bread', but without labouring the point, if the coiner of the phrase had wanted to say the latter he would have said 'pannus meus panis'.

The locally produced woollen textiles are sometimes confusingly referred to as 'Kendal Cottons'. However, they did not include any cotton—rather, the cloths were made from a coarse wool with the nap raised in a process known as 'cottoning'. They were at the very bottom of the market in terms of quality, but there is always good business to be done in cheap and affordable goods, and Kendal's products were sent far and wide, finding a ready market among sailors and the poor of cities such as London. Initially they were distributed by packhorse, but later by carriers' carts and also by ship—for example, a new market in the West Indies opened up, producing coarse woollen caps for slaves. It was reckoned that in 1770 in excess of 3,500 pieces of Kendal cottons were exported to America and the West Indies each year. Davies-Shiel suggested, however, that the woollen cloth produced in Kendal was much more varied than hitherto believed, and that it included some of much higher quality.[6]

Until the eighteenth century the production of cloth was a cottage industry, the textiles being woven in small workshops and homes. As in Yorkshire, 'little masters' put out the raw materials to be processed into yarn and cloth by individual weavers, then collected in the finished cloth. This was also true of the countryside around the town—at this stage there were no particular benefits to being in the town as the process was unmechanised. Many traces of small-scale manufactories survive in Kendal's yards, in the remains of rather anonymous workshops. In Kendal the yarn was turned into cloth by the many weavers who worked as family units within their own homes, no fewer than 61 of these being listed in the 1695 survey of inhabitants.[7] Wholesalers bought up the finished cloth, and chapmen distributed it.

Reconstructed handloom in the Museum of Lakeland Life. Much of the early cloth production of Kendal was on such handlooms by self-employed weavers.

PHOTOGRAPH CARNEGIE, 2012, BY COURTESY OF THE MUSEUM OF LAKELAND LIFE

Several examples of probate inventories for Kendal weavers give a flavour of the industry in the later seventeenth century. In 1688 William Gruby or Grewbye, weaver, of Fellside, Highgate, left property including two pair of looms with 'furniture' (shuttles and other equipment) valued at £1 5*s.*, bobbins and yarn, and 'Linnen and woollen yarne and one peice of Stuffe'.[8] Richard

Collinson of Kirkland (who died in 1700) left 'Loomes and other goodes in the workhouse', but he was also a small farmer, to judge from the 'swine, sheepe, bigg, oates, hay and a dunghill' that all feature in his inventory. Such dual occupations must have been quite common, particularly on the fringes of the town.[9] An impressive early eighteenth-century inventory is that of John Crewdson of Stramongate, stuffweaver (1718), with woollen yarn valued at £37 and linen yarn at £15 16*s.*, stored in his garret, and in the 'Waying roome' another £40 worth of woollen yarn and £23 of linen yarn. He was a wealthy man, with personal possessions which were valued in total at £895 3*s.* 6*d.*[10]

Sometimes inventories give more detail about the cloth itself. For example, that of Edward Curwen, weaver, in 1724, lists '18 Hanks blew yarn, a Frame and Bobbins, 60 Hanks of blew Linn yarn 14 white, 18 yards of tow cloth a peece more, 1 peece Check 26 Check napkins, a webb & loomes, Raddles & reeds 24 pair of Geare wheel & spels, 16 yards fine Cloth Stall, and 75 Hanks of Scotch yarn'.[11]

The table below shows the cloth, and weaving equipment, owned by two Kendal weavers of the 1730s:

Henry Gibson of Stramongate, 1730[12]		*George Knipe of Wildman Street, 1738*[13]	
Lin yarne	£30 14*s.* 9*d.*	2 Leads 4 pair of Looms 2 Wheels Gangs Bobin Frame Chub & Spells	£3 2*s.* 6*d.*
Woollen yarne	£10 11*s.*	16 score and half of Linnen yarn at 1*s.* 6*d.* per score	£13 4*s.*
29 white linseys at 18*s.* per peice one Broad at 28*s.*	£36 10*s.*	a parcel of Wool and Woolen yarn	£13 9*s.*
16 Broad skipper at 24*s.* 3 ditto narrow at 20*s.*	£22 4*s.*	2 Chests healboards Yarn Cords Bobins & yarn bruches & locks & Reeds	£2 12*s.* 6*d.*
a Warping Mill	£0 12*s.*	7 Grogehams 3 white 2 blew 5 strips 3 warps	£17 6*s.* 6*d.*
A beam and scales and Weights	£0 6*s.* 6*d.*	10 Brods at 27*s.*	£13 10*s.*
13 Grograms	£18 4*s.*	Credits by Simple Contract	£282 6*s.* 1*d.*
5 pair of Loomes att 6*s.* per pair	£1 10*s.* 0*d.*	[overall] Total	£404 7*s.* 5*d.*

The high value of stock held by these men, and the scale of their operations (with up to five pairs of looms) emphasises the significance of the Kendal woollen industry by the 1730s. The references to debts and credits reveals an increasingly sophisticated system of finance, long before there were any local banks. We can also see a gradual spread of new technologies, devices for speeding the process—from the woollen wheels and looms of the early inventories to the 'warping mill' and 'bobin Frame' of the later ones.

Yarn was supplied to Dent and other villages such as Orton and Ravenstonedale by mills to the north of Kendal, and these villages long kept up the tradition of hand-knitting. This

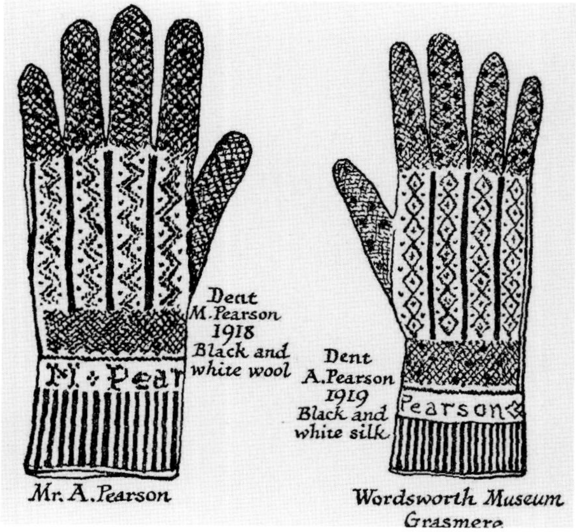

left
Wensleydale hand-knitters, from the *Costume of Yorkshire*, 1814. All around Kendal, in Dent and in Wensleydale, men, women and children knitted as they worked or walked, using a wooden knitting-pin holder tucked in the belt.

right
Two pairs of knitted gloves from Dent, a place closely associated with hand-knitting, but only one among many.

was an exceptionally fast method using metal needles and a wooden knitting sheath, practised by young and old alike, and led to an outstanding production of items such as gloves, hats and stockings, for which machinery did not yet exist.[14] It became a speciality of the area, and although it is most closely associated with 'the terrible knitters of Dent', Kendal also had many knitters: 'There is a meritorious spirit of industry amongst them, and the country people, both men and women, were knitting stockings as they drove their peat carts into town.'[15]

None of this activity, whether in weaving or in knitting, was possible without the 'little masters'. One such was John Crewdson of Stramongate, stuffweaver, whose will and inventory of 1718 we have encountered above. His son Richard was said to employ 700 people in woollen manufacture.[16] Another fanciful local tale says that the great Stourbridge Fair near Cambridge originated in the seventeenth century with a group of Kendal clothiers whose stock was spoiled with damp on the way to London. They allegedly sold the stock *al fresco* at Stourbridge, were amazed at the amount of money they took, and subsequently made the fair a regular port of call. It is also said that the Cambridge area shows a number of surnames more usually associated with Kendal, implying that Westmorland traders settled there. In reality, Stourbridge Fair was a major international trading location since the early Middle Ages, while the second proposition has been demonstrated to be without foundation. The name Docwra, associated in Kendal with Docwra Hall, does indeed appear in Cambridgeshire and Hertfordshire, but only because a branch of the family (associated with the Order of St John) moved there for entirely different reasons.[17]

We also learn something of the industry from the observations of travellers. When Bishop Pococke came to Kendal in 1751 he noted that, 'They have a Manufactory of a sort of frieze call'd Cotton, at eight pence a yard sold mostly for the West Indies, for the use of their slaves, and Linsey Woolseys, made of thread and yarn, mostly strip'd, and much used for

Metal tenter frame in the Museum of Lakeland Life.

PHOTOGRAPH CARNEGIE, 2012, BY COURTESY OF THE MUSEUM OF LAKELAND LIFE

waistcoats; they have also a manufacture of knit stockings from 2*s*. 6*d*. to half a guinea a pair, and lately they weave coarse white silk stockings at 7*s*. 6*d*. a pair.'[18]

Arthur Young described the industry in 1771:[19]

> They reckon one hundred and twenty wool-combers, each employing five spinners, and each spinner four or five knitters ... They make two hundred and fifty dozen [stockings] a week the year round, or twenty eight thousand six hundred dozen annually. The price *per* pair is from 22d. to 6s., but in general from 22d. to 4s. ... They send all the manufacture to London by land carriage, which is said to be the longest, for broad wheel wagons, of any stage in *England*. The earnings of the manufacturers in this branch are as follows:

	s	*d*
The combers, per week	10	6
The spinners, women	3	0
Ditto, children of ten or twelve years	2	0
The knitters	2	6
Ditto, children of ten or twelve years	2	0

During the eighteenth century the Kendal woollen trade grew steadily, and new mills and commercial dyehouses appeared. Most were small, and all were operated by water power. Steam-powered looms were not introduced into Kendal until 1860, when they were installed at Dockray Hall and Highgate Mills. Many smaller businesses continued, tucked away in yards.

Tenters on Tenter Fell, from Todd's map of 1787.

PHOTOGRAPH CARNEGIE, FROM AN ORIGINAL HELD AT WESTMORLAND RECORD OFFICE, KENDAL

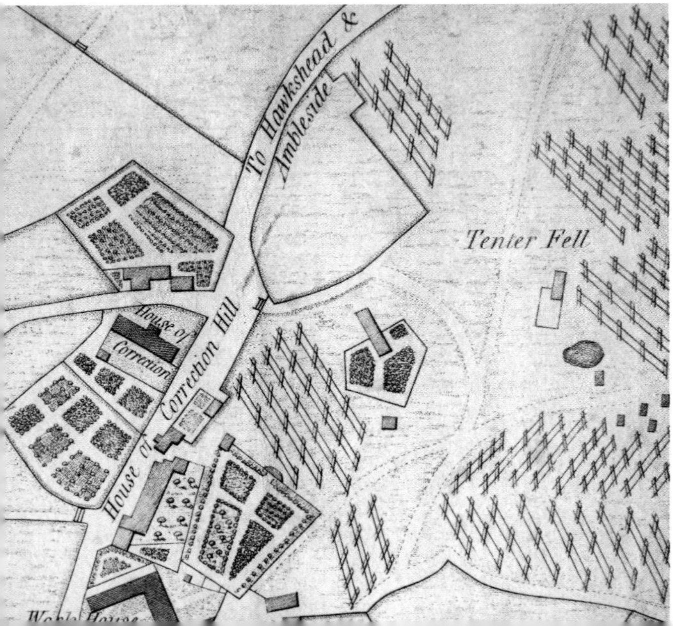

There were many stages in the cloth trade, all of them requiring specialist skills. The raw wool had to be collected from the hinterland, no mean feat in itself, then washed to remove the oils, and combed to bring the fibres into line. This was originally done with teasles but later with wire carding-combs, the latter creating other industries of wire-drawing and card-making. It was then turned into yarn and woven into cloth, which had to be fulled, tentered, dyed and trimmed. Fulling,

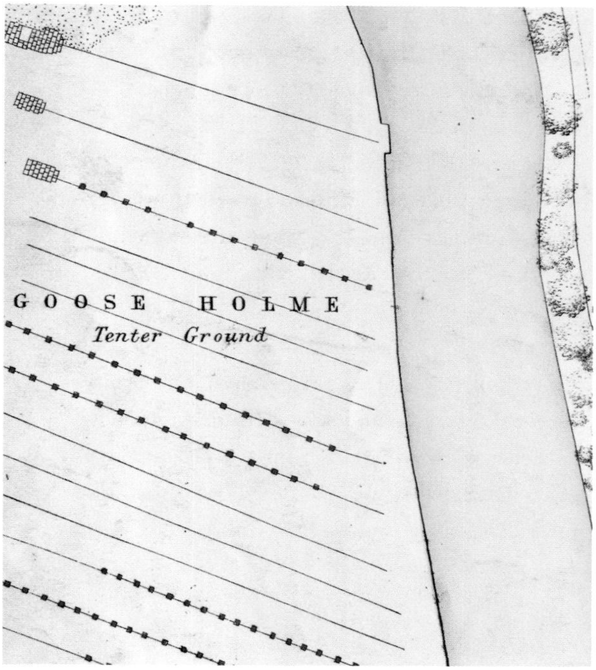

left Tenters on Goose Holme, from the 500" Ordnance Survey map of 1861.

PHOTOGRAPH CARNEGIE, FROM AN ORIGINAL HELD AT WESTMORLAND RECORD OFFICE, KENDAL

right Washing steps by the river Kent in Kirkland. A great many processes involved the river as a source of power or for cleaning. Only a few sets of steps have survived the 'tidying up' of the river banks.

which was initially carried on in specialist fulling mills, helped to strengthen the fabric by crushing and felting the fibres, as well as cleaning it further. Later this process was carried on within the larger manufactories. Tentering involved stretching the cloths, on wooden frames, in the open air on various fields and fellsides around the town. The process also helped to reduce shrinkage. The frames were furnished with many small tenterhooks, by which the fabric was held. The fields of tenter-frames were very impressive, and were often the first thing that visitors to the town noticed. As Thomas Gray noted in 1769, '... the dusk of evening coming on I enter'd Kendal almost in the dark, & could distinguish only a shadow of the Castle on a hill & tenter-grounds spread far and wide round the Town, which I mistook for houses.'[20]

When Roger Wakefield of Stricklandgate, shearman-dyer, died in 1731, his probate inventory listed tenters near his house on the west side of Stricklandgate, on Tarn Banks, and near the Kent at Stramongate Bridge.[21]

Dyeing involved local plants such as dyer's rocket and dyer's broomweed, which gave a yellow colour, as well as woad, which had to be fetched from Lincolnshire and produced a blue colour. Combined, the two gave a green shade, which is a possible explanation for the familiar term 'Kendal Green'. These vegetable dyes were fixed by using alum as a mordant. By 1600 this was being produced widely in the North Riding of Yorkshire, where alum shales could be processed along the coast north of Whitby. After dyeing the nap was raised again, using teasles or cards and the finished cloth was cropped, to lower the nap, by shearmen, using huge versions of sheep-shears.

These many processes created numerous ancillary jobs. For example, the washing and cleaning required large quantities of soap made from potash, which was produced by burning Lake District bracken. The branches of the trade were quite distinct, and recognised as such. Carding, spinning, fulling, tentering, dyeing, and cropping—each was a specialised stage in the overall process, though some entrepreneurs incorporated several stages into their work, such as the shearmen-dyers. Finally the finished goods had to be sent to market, and large numbers of packhorses were required to carry the woven cloth to London or to Southampton. We shall examine the transport requirements more fully in chapter 8.

In 1692 Thomas Machell described Kendal as

> ... a most famous town for its industry and the woollen trade, for its inhabitants sell their cottons to most parts of England ... Their trade consists of Kendal cogware, alias cottons, of Linsey wools or Kendal stuffs which are otherwise called Kidderminsters, from being sold there, and of stockings ... which at this time keeps a great many children at work ... And all these wares are sent to London every week by four Kendal carriers who set out from thence every Monday by turns.[22]

An interesting account of Kendal's manufacturing interests was given by the young American Quaker, Jabez Maud Fisher, who came here in 1775. He was partly on a pleasure tour, partly assessing fellow Quakers with whom his firm might be able to do business once the tiresome Revolutionary War was over: 'We took a walk this morning to see the different manufactories that are carried on here: Cottons, Stockings, Silk Rugs; here are Fulling Mills, Frizing Mills, Corn Mills, etc.' Fisher also lists the costs of local products:

> Isaac Wilson & Son we have hitherto dealt with...Their goods are Silk Rugs Spotted and green from 8/6 [8*s*. 6*d*.] to 18/– [18*s*.], Negro Cottons 20 yards 18/– [to] 24/–, Striped Lin[s]eys about 12, Cotton Ditto. 14d. John Wakefield is largely in the Manufactory of Kendal Cottons and Linery's [Linseys]. Thomas Crewdson would be a good hand for Stockings, if Settle was not equally convenient.[23]

At first the trade was mainly in finished cloths, to be turned into garments elsewhere, but in the later eighteenth and nineteenth centuries speciality finished items were made, such as travelling rugs, horse cloths, collar checks and carpets. The balance changed frequently. In *Bailey's Northern Directory* for 1784 the woollen trade in the town was dominated by hosiers (of whom fifteen are listed) and linsey-manufacturers (eleven manufacturers).[24] Linsey was a cloth made with a linen warp and a woollen weft. Some combined the trades, while others in the trade might be concealed behind the general title 'manufacturer'. The use of linen clearly indicates the widespread cultivation of flax in the area, with all the associated processes, some of which, especially 'retting', had very unpleasant residues and were noisome. Later on the import of Baltic flax took over, much of it from what was then Russia. The lead seals from flax bundles, with Russian merchants' marks, are often discovered by local metal-detectorists. A list of prices agreed by masters and journeymen weavers for weaving linseys and other fabrics survives for 1822 and, like the inventories discussed earlier, opens up a lost world of grograms, bombazines and Oswestrys.[25] The document relates to price-fixing, which was considered necessary to avoid undue competition within the town, and to focus such competition on the real rivals elsewhere. By 1860 Whellan could say, 'Between three and four hundred weavers are at this day employed at Kendal in the manufacture of linsey-woolseys ...'[26]

Railway rugs, trousering and carpets were also singled out for comment, and according to this source about one-third of the population was at this time engaged in woollen manufacture. But by the end of the century Kendal was no longer a principally textile town.

The most northerly of the major mills was Dockray Hall, where some buildings, including weaving sheds, survive. It was run by Messrs Gandy & Sons, and used for dyewood and woollens in the eighteenth century, and in 1794 was listed as making linseys.[27] Two disastrous fires took place there, in 1817 and 1824, destroying all the machinery.[28] It was rebuilt by Gandys, and later operated by Whitwell & Co. An associated carpet factory stood at the junction of Strickland Place and Stricklandgate. West of Stramongate Bridge were Bridge Mills and Leece Croft Mills, both of which survive though now converted into offices and apartments. Beyond the bridge was Stramongate Mill, shown on the 1861 Ordnance Survey map at the east end of New Road close to Gooseholme Bridge. It began as a fulling mill in 1755. A century later the triangular complex included an engine house, weaving shop, dye house, dye pan, drying store and three warehouses. On Hoggarth's map of 1853 it is named as 'Jno. Ireland's manufactory'.

On the opposite bank stood Castle Mills, manufacturing woollens from 1806. This site is a very ancient one, originating as the lord's manorial cornmill operating in the late twelfth century and supplied by a leat cut across the Aynam, taking water from further up river. Kirkbarrow Mill was a spinning workshop of about 1798, also water-powered and fed by the Cock Beck, which flowed out of Anchorite's Well, and is shown on Hoggarth's map of 1853. Further down were Low Mills or Wattsfield Mills, also in the woollen business, and Helsington Mills.[29]

'Prices of weaving Linseys, &c. by the piece and yard, agreed on between The Masters and Journeymen Weavers in Kendal, on the Thirteenth day of March, 1822', from the Soulby Collection.

SOULBY ZS. 1140. BY COURTESY OF BARROW ARCHIVES

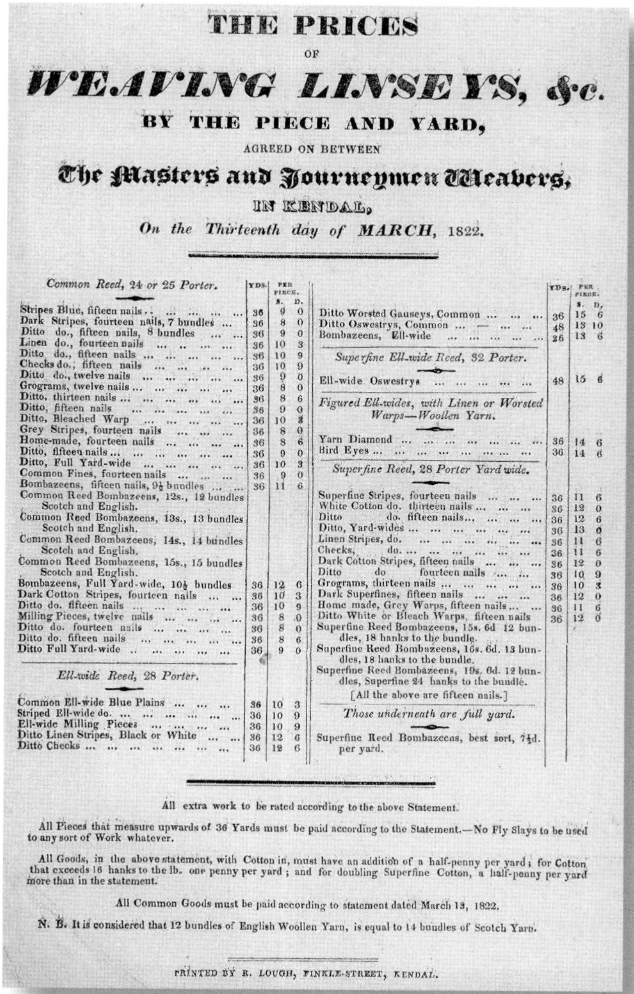

THE PRICES

OF

WEAVING LINSEYS, &c.

BY THE PIECE AND YARD,

AGREED ON BETWEEN

The Masters and Journeymen Weavers,

IN KENDAL,

On the Thirteenth day of MARCH, 1822.

Common Reed, 24 or 25 Porter.	YDS.	PER PIECE. S.	D.
Stripes Blue, fifteen nails	36	9	0
Dark Stripes, fourteen nails, 7 bundles ...	36	8	0
Ditto do., fifteen nails, 8 bundles	36	9	0
Linen do., fourteen nails	36	10	3
Ditto do., fifteen nails	36	10	9
Checks do., fifteen nails	36	10	9
Ditto do., twelve nails	36	9	0
Grograms, twelve nails	36	8	0
Ditto, thirteen nails	36	8	6
Ditto, fifteen nails	36	9	0
Ditto, Bleached Warp	36	10	3
Grey Stripes, fourteen nails	36	8	0
Home-made, fourteen nails	36	8	6
Ditto, fifteen nails	36	9	0
Ditto, Full Yard-wide	36	10	3
Common Fines, fourteen nails	36	9	0
Bombazeens, fifteen nails, 9½ bundles	36	11	6
Common Reed Bombazeens, 12s., 12 bundles Scotch and English.			
Common Reed Bombazeens, 13s., 13 bundles Scotch and English.			
Common Reed Bombazeens, 14s., 14 bundles Scotch and English.			
Common Reed Bombazeens, 15s., 15 bundles Scotch and English.			
Bombazeens, Full Yard-wide, 10½ bundles	36	12	6
Dark Cotton Stripes, fourteen nails	36	10	3
Ditto do. fifteen nails	36	10	9
Milling Pieces, twelve nails	36	8	0
Ditto do. fourteen nails	36	8	0
Ditto do. fifteen nails	36	8	6
Ditto Full Yard-wide	36	9	0
Ell-wide Reed, 28 Porter.			
Common Ell-wide Blue Plains	36	10	3
Striped Ell-wide do.	36	10	9
Ell-wide Milling Pieces	36	10	9
Ditto Linen Stripes, Black or White	36	12	6
Ditto Checks	36	12	6

	YDS.	PER PIECE. S.	D.
Ditto Worsted Gauseys, Common	36	15	6
Ditto Oswestrys, Common ... —	48	13	10
Bombazeens, Ell-wide	36	13	6
Superfine Ell-wide Reed, 32 Porter.			
Ell-wide Oswestrys	48	15	6
Figured Ell-wides, with Linen or Worsted Warps—Woollen Yarn.			
Yarn Diamond	36	14	6
Bird Eyes	36	14	6
Superfine Reed, 28 Porter Yard wide.			
Superfine Stripes, fourteen nails	36	11	6
White Cotton do. thirteen nails	36	12	0
Ditto do. fifteen nails...	36	12	6
Ditto, Yard-wides	36	13	0
Linen Stripes, do.	36	11	6
Checks, do.	36	11	6
Dark Cotton Stripes, fifteen nails	36	12	0
Ditto do fourteen nails	36	10	9
Grograms, thirteen nails	36	10	3
Dark Superfines, fifteen nails	36	12	0
Home made, Grey Warps, fifteen nails	36	11	6
Ditto White or Bleach Warps, fifteen nails	36	12	0
Superfine Reed Bombazeens, 15s. 6d 12 bundles, 18 hanks to the bundle.			
Superfine Reed Bombazeens, 16s. 6d. 13 bundles, 18 hanks to the bundle.			
Superfine Reed Bombazeens, 19s. 6d. 12 bundles, Superfine 24 hanks to the bundle.			
[All the above are fifteen nails.]			
Those underneath are full yard.			
Superfine Reed Bombazeens, best sort, 7½d. per yard.			

All extra work to be rated according to the above Statement.

All Pieces that measure upwards of 36 Yards must be paid according to the Statement.—No Fly Slays to be used to any sort of Work whatever.

All Goods, in the above statement, with Cotton in, must have an addition of a half-penny per yard; for Cotton that exceeds 16 hanks to the lb. one penny per yard; and for doubling Superfine Cotton, a half-penny per yard more than in the statement.

All Common Goods must be paid according to statement dated March 13, 1822.

N. B. It is considered that 12 bundles of English Woollen Yarn, is equal to 14 bundles of Scotch Yarn.

PRINTED BY R. LOUGH, FINKLE-STREET, KENDAL.

Dockwray Hall mill from a glass slide.

GLASS SLIDE, BY COURTESY OF KENDAL TOWN COUNCIL

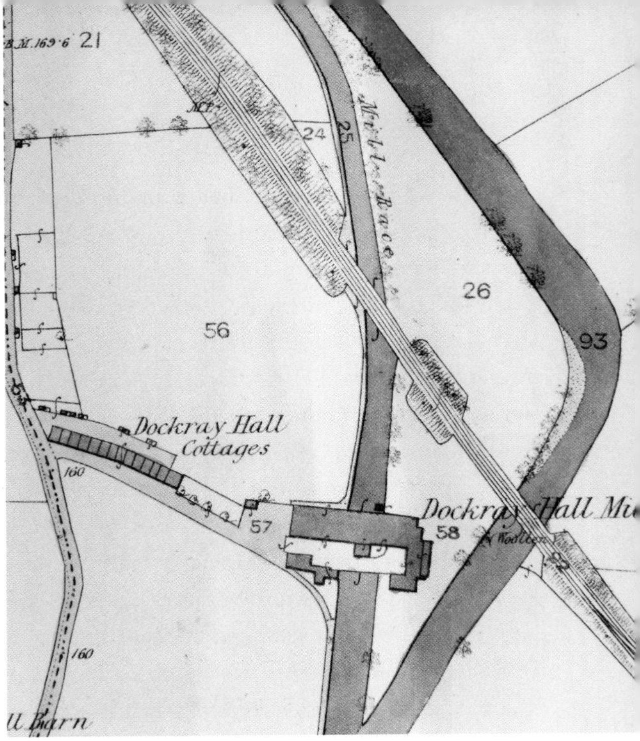

Dockwray Hall mill, from the 500" Ordnance Survey map of 1861.

PHOTOGRAPH CARNEGIE, FROM AN ORIGINAL HELD AT WESTMORLAND RECORD OFFICE, KENDAL

Carpet manufactory on Strickland Place, nearly opposite St Thomas' church, from the 500" Ordnance Survey map of 1861.

PHOTOGRAPH CARNEGIE, FROM AN ORIGINAL HELD AT WESTMORLAND RECORD OFFICE, KENDAL

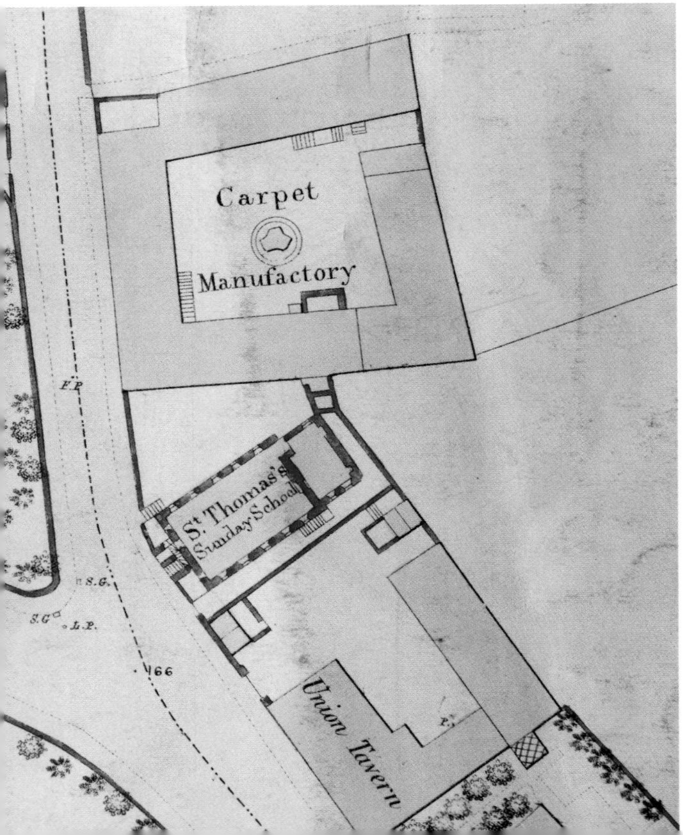

Woollen manufactory at the northern end of New Road, from the 500" Ordnance Survey map of 1861. Note also the tanning pits, bottom left.

PHOTOGRAPH CARNEGIE, FROM AN ORIGINAL HELD AT WESTMORLAND RECORD OFFICE, KENDAL

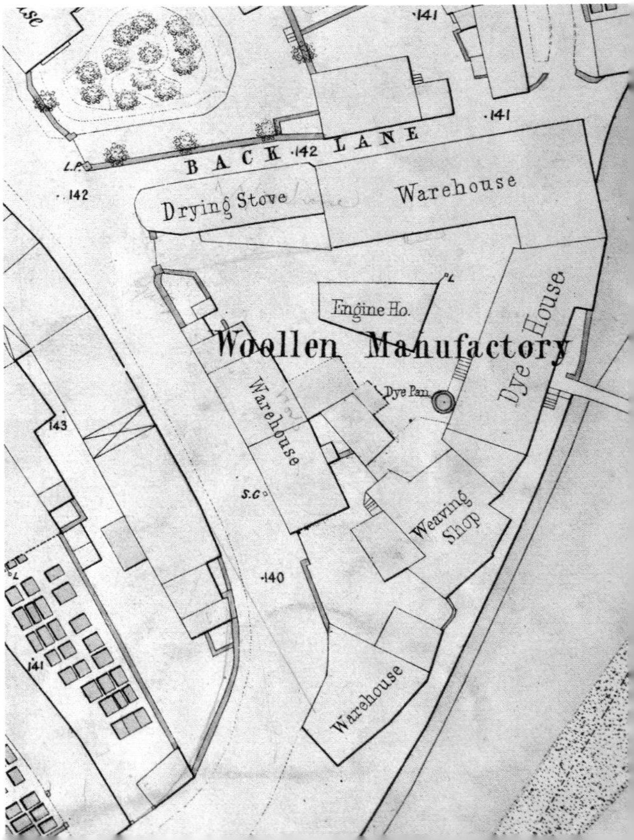

As already noted Kendal had many other trades and manufacturing interests. By 1800 all the 'Free Companies', those medieval institutions which had for centuries controlled (and restricted) trade, had passed into oblivion. There had been twelve of them, three being catch-all groupings of miscellaneous trades,[30] and their power and status were waning by the middle of the eighteenth century. By the mid-1770s a list given by Nicholson and Burn contains only seven.[31] Their disappearance did not disrupt the industrial economy of the town, and some of the traditional industries continued to flourish—not only weaving and dyeing, but also tanning and the leather trade. New industries also appeared.

Some were at the Aynam, an area opened up by the canal in 1819 and partly occupied by Canal Head. A marble works was set up by Francis Webster at Helsington Mills in 1800, and later this moved to the Aynam, just north of Castle Mills. Here, marble was cut and polished by machinery designed by Webster (limestone from Kendal Fell had been manually polished since at least 1788). Architectural details such as fireplaces, made by this process, were much in demand, and the firm had its own showroom for such goods.[32] Thomas and Margaret Braithwaite also made marble fireplaces at a workshop in Capper Lane in the early nineteenth century. Marble came from limestone quarried at Hawes Wood,[33] or from the Sizergh Castle estates.[34] In 1831 Edward Bailiff produced two fireplaces for Windsor Castle, using Kendal Fell marble.[35]

Silk was also produced in the town, from at least the mid-eighteenth century. Robert Green, 'silk man', left a very late probate inventory in 1769, with the 'utensils of trade' valued at £8 13*s*. 4*d*. and 'stock in trade on hand' at £399 1*s*. 9*d*. Even more significant were the debts owing to him—a massive £1,238, giving a total estate of over £1,800.[36] Silk was clearly a lucrative trade. Waste silk, brought from London, was worked at Stramongate Mill from the 1790s, and the yarn then sent back to London for weaving, but some weaving was carried out in Kendal, to make drugget (a half-wool, half-silk fabric), tapes for Venetian blinds, or silk stockings.[37]

Brush-making was another local trade, the wood for the handles coming from the managed coppices of the southern Lake District. The most obvious relic of this trade is the bristle 'boar' shop sign at Blackhall. The Blackhall works ran from 1869 until 1922, though production by the same firm elsewhere continued until 1963.[38]

Black boar brush sign, Blackhall Yard, Stricklandgate. Originally marking the Hodgson's brushworks, this has been kept as a survivor of once-plentiful trade signs.

Tanning was established in Kendal at an early date, and many tanyards are shown on John Todd's 1787 map of the town. Initially it was a by-product of the butcher's trade, together with the manufacture of items made of horn. Tanning was a noisome process, and involved the steeping of hides in a series of tanpits. The hides were softened in solutions of lime and dog faeces, then dehaired and defleshed using long blunt-bladed scraping knives, before the actual tanning process,

Tanpits near Stramongate Bridge, on Todd's map of 1787.

which involved soaking in solutions of oak bark, could begin. For obvious reasons the tanpits were mostly on the low ground by the river, where there was a reliable supply of water. The effluents were returned to the river, there joining sewage and all sorts of other industrial waste. Two examples serve to illustrate the problem. In 1825 fish in the Kent were killed by a leakage of waste from the tanneries, while in 1831 a boy fell into one of the tanpits in Highgate and died a couple of days later.[39] Thomas Wilson, who died in 1700, left his 'Tan House and Tanyard in Highgate' to his wife Mary, while in 1719 Brian Lancaster of Stramongate left 'Tan-house, Tan Yards and Cisterns'. In the same year another Thomas Wilson, of Stramongate, left bark-houses (where the oak-bark was kept) and skins in pits.[40] An eighteenth- and early nineteenth-century tannery site on the east side of the river was excavated recently during building work on the new K Village.[41]

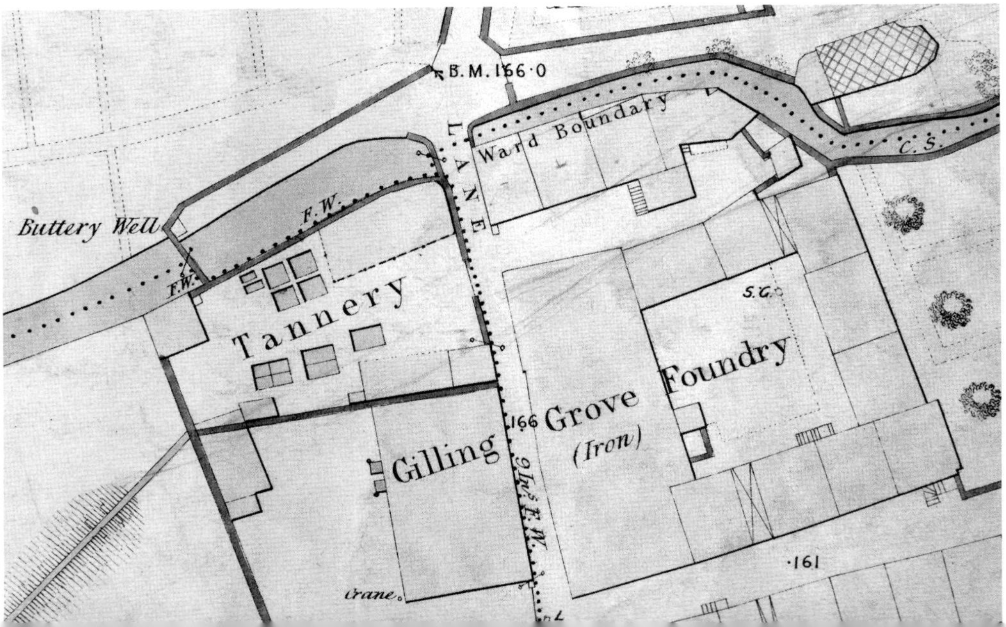

There were several tanneries in Kendal, all located near to running water. This small tannery was located on the river Blindbeck, near to the Gilling Grove Iron Foundry. (See also another section of 1861 OS map on page 56, showing tanpits near Stramongate Bridge.)

PHOTOGRAPH CARNEGIE, FROM AN ORIGINAL HELD AT WESTMORLAND RECORD OFFICE, KENDAL

Machine Room at Somervell Brothers Netherfield Works, 1862.
SCIENCE MUSEUM / SCIENCE & SOCIETY PICTURE LIBRARY

The leather was used for many purposes, the finer grades, the so-called white leather made by 'whittawers', being used for gloves. Later, boots and shoes were to form staple industries for the town. The largest manufactory was the Netherfield Works, which expanded from small beginnings after 1842, when the Somervell brothers set up at Sand Aire. They gradually created a major industry, employing some 600 people by 1900 and eventually some 20 per cent of Kendal's working population. During the First World War, despite the calling-up of most of the menfolk, the firm gained huge contracts for providing boots for British and foreign armies, including those of Russia. They also operated a chain of shops, and had several factories in other towns. The firm became a limited company in 1949 as the world-famous 'K Shoes'. Taken over in 1981 by Clarkes of Street, Somerset, the firm began to suffer from the growing world competition in inexpensive footware, and closed down in the early twenty-first century. The last production, at the firm's Natland Road factory, was in 2003. K Shoes was so closely identified with Kendal that the firm's loss was not merely material—though that was bad enough in terms of jobs—but also a bad blow to the town's self-confidence.[42]

One odd feature of Kendal associated with the tanning process was the windmill that stood on the west bank of the river east of Sandes Hospital, at the bottom end of Yard 65. It is shown on the very large-scale 1:500 Ordnance Survey dating from 1861. On the copy held by the Cumbria Record Office this is annotated 'old windmill', while Yard 65 is named 'Windmill Yard'. Its position on low ground in a river valley, and the lack of windmills elsewhere in the vicinity, means that it is somewhat incongruous. The stump of an old tower mill, it can be discerned in the background of a painting of 1819, 'Kendal from Thorny Hills' by William Brown. Windmills were not just used for grinding corn; they were also used for grinding colours for dyestuffs or, as in this case, oak bark for tanning.

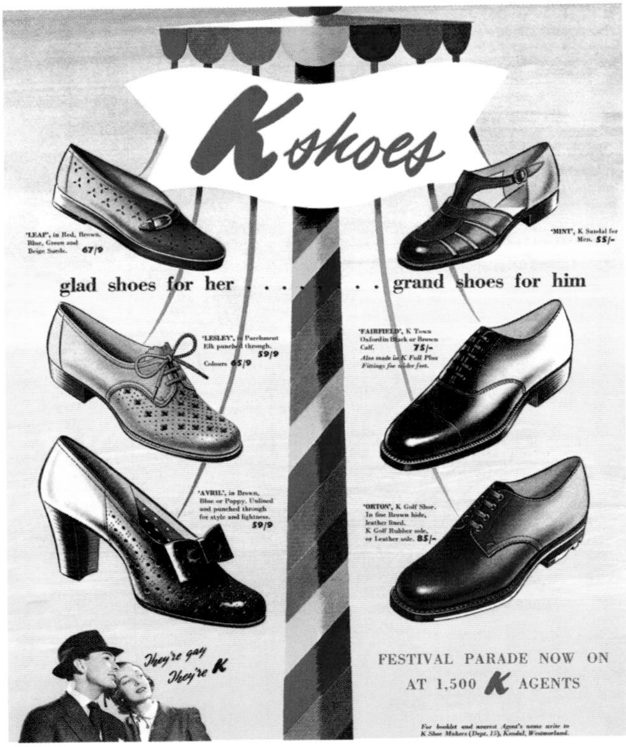

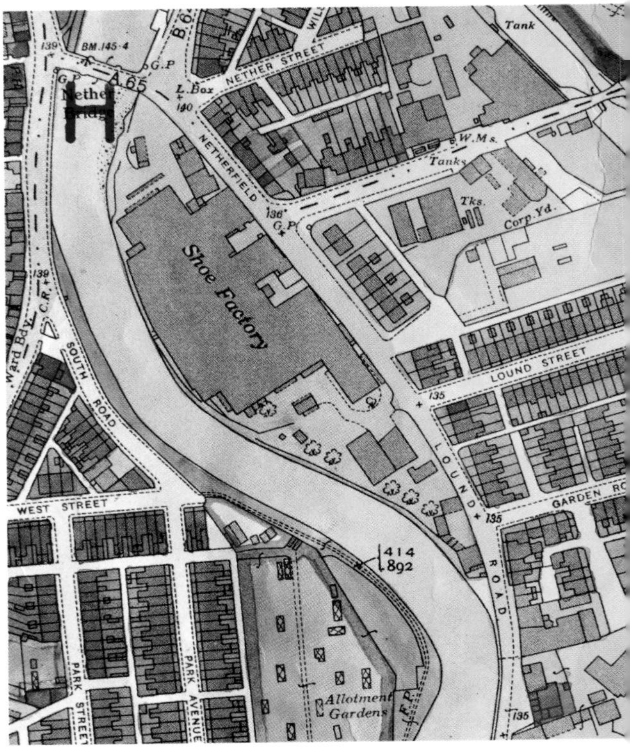

Just before the Second World War the K Shoe Company of Kendal was producing almost 900,000 pairs of shoes annually. The firm was a major employer.

Another of Kendal's distinctive industries was the working of horn, a by-product of the butchering and the tanning industry which brought cattle into the town for their meat and hides. Perhaps as a result of this an 'ivory comb manufactory' was set up in 1800 and in 1805 was operated by Berry, Clementson & Co.[43] Several comb-makers were, however, already working in the town in 1790,[44] including Richard Clementson, Richard Compston and Joseph Sison. The directory does not make clear which type of comb these were making, and some may have been manufacturing wool-combs, which were quite different and made with wire.

Paper was an important product of the southern Lake District. At Burneside, just outside the town, are two paper mills, one founded in 1750 and the other in 1833.[45] The firm that would become Croppers virtually created the village of Burneside.[46] Milnthorpe, Beetham and Kentmere also have paper mills. In the beginning water power, and the plentiful water supplies needed for the various processes, was part of the attraction of the site, but so too was the freely available waste material from the textile industries, used to make rag-paper.

A rather unexpected industry in Kendal, if only because of its degree of specialisation, was the building and repair of church organs. The organ factory was in Aynam Road, at the junction with Parr Street, and was begun by William Wilkinson in about 1839. It traded as Wilkinson & Sons after 1856, when William's son Thomas joined him, and in this period their best work was carried out. William himself had learnt his trade from an uncle in Halifax. In

1957 the firm was taken over by Rushworth & Dreaper of Liverpool. A good example of the firm's work, dating from 1883, is in St George's church.

One of the quiet success stories of Kendal has been Gilbert Gilkes & Gordon, manufacturing pumps and turbines at Canal Head. The firm originated in the agricultural implement workshop of the three brothers Williamson in 1853. Gilbert Gilkes bought the firm in 1887. Its products were exported all over the world and in particular it seems to have penetrated the Welsh woollen mills, where the firm's water turbines succeeded the use of water wheels, because they were more efficient, and only succumbed latterly to the widespread availability of mains electricity for power.[47]

Kendal has given its name to quite a few products over the centuries. The most famous of all, Kendal mintcake, is examined in another chapter, but others include Kendal Green, Kendal Brown, and Kendal Black Drop. Kendal Green, already noted above, was a dyed cloth of a green colour, and it probably takes its name from that (though note that its companion, Lincoln Green, is often said to take its name from *grain*, a type of cloth rather than a colour). Much has been said of Shakespeare's reference in *Henry IV, Part 1* to 'misbegotten knaves in Kendal Green', and this type of cloth, like the fanciful connections with Queen Katherine Parr, has filled much of Kendal's antiquarian literature. It is doubtful whether we can now have any definitive proof of just what Kendal Green actually was, although the churchwardens' accounts of Kendal indicate a very great preference for the use of green as a colour in the parish church. It does seem to have been the town's favourite colour![48]

Kendal Brown was a type of snuff. In the eighteenth century Kendal began producing snuff from the residues of tobacco and quickly established a 'niche market'. It is thought that tobacco, which was brought by packhorse from Whitehaven, was the start of the industry, because large quantities of tobacco dust and stalks were available cheaply after the shaking-up caused by the journey.[49] Thomas Harrison, the founder of the last surviving firm, went to Glasgow to learn the trade and returned to Kendal in 1792. He brought with him some second-hand machinery, believed to date from about 1750, which was at first used at Mealbank on the river Mint, north-east of the town, and still survives after several moves, at Kendal Brown House in Lowther Street. The firm was later based at Helsington, in a small mill close to the one where Websters polished their limestone. The fame of Kendal

GILKES for water power
The first Water Turbine manufactured in Kendal was built in our works in 1856. Since then the name GILKES has become famous throughout the wcrld of water power engineers. Constant research has kept our firm in the forefront of scientific water power development. Kendal is noted for individual workmanship and the high quality of its products. GILKES water turbines are built to last for generations.
We shall be pleased to show visitors over our works at any time during working hours.
These illustrations show a GILKES "Turgo" Impulse Turbine and its patented design of runner.
GILBERT GILKES & GORDON LTD · Kendal · England

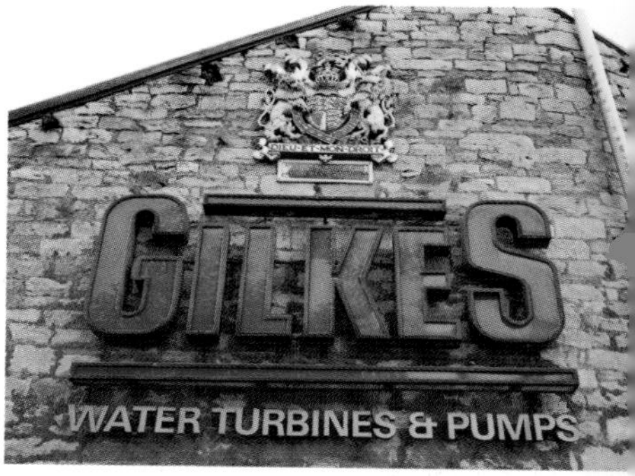

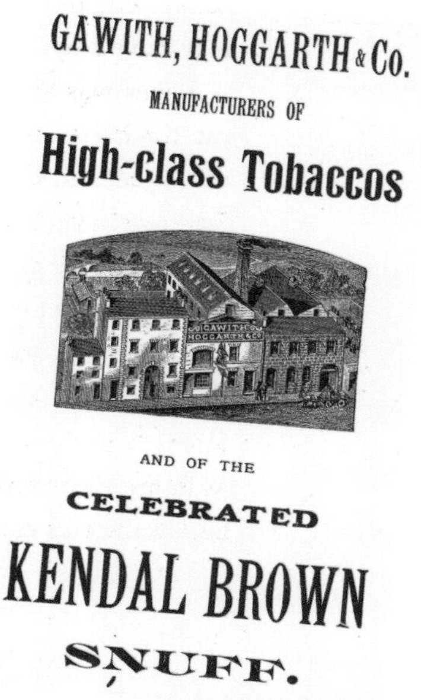
GAWITH, HOGGARTH & Co.
MANUFACTURERS OF
High-class Tobaccos
AND OF THE
CELEBRATED
KENDAL BROWN
SNUFF.

Turk trade sign at Gawith's, Lowther Street.

Brown is particularly due to the fact that Samuel Gawith, the firm that traces its origins back to Harrison, is one of the very last in the market. Another firm involved in snuff manufacture was Illingworths, working until 1983 at Aynam Mill near Castle Mills.[50]

Another very minor industry connected with tobacco was the making of clay pipes, carried out by Joseph Lyon and his son James from before 1834 to after 1873 in Stramongate and Wildman Street. Joseph was from Rainford, near St Helens, a noted centre of clay pipe production, and his son went back to Lancashire, to Blackburn, after his father's death.[51] At its peak the Kendal business employed five men, two boys and two women as pipe-finishers. This seems to have been a very localised trade, perhaps serving just local inns and tobacconists, as Kendal pipes are not found at any distance—although the absence of other makers in the Lake District and Furness may suggest that there was a market there. Before the 1830s the local supply was dominated by Lancaster and the North East, to judge from the pipes found in local archaeological excavations.

Kendal Black Drop was an opium-based medicine invented, or perfected, by the Kendal-born Lancaster surgeon, John Airey Braithwaite (died 1810), who made a considerable amount of money from it.[52] Members of his family continued to capitalise on it into the late nineteenth century. Others, such as Ann Todd and Hannah Backhouse, also made and sold versions under the same name in Kendal, albeit at a considerably cheaper price. The recipe for Lancashire Black Drop, which must have been similar, was published in the *Lonsdale Magazine* for March 1821.[53] This variant includes five ounces of purified opium, Jamaica pepper, cinnamon, saffron and Seville orange peel, and a pint of rectified spirits of wine, the whole concoction heated, strained and sweetened with sugar candy. It was reckoned to be three to four times the strength per drop compared with the conventional tincture of opium. Reader! Do not try this at home!

Opium was widely used, or misused, for all sorts of medical and recreational purposes in the eighteenth and nineteenth centuries, usually in the form of laudanum, a tincture designed to be drunk for the relief of pain. Wordsworth's friend and poetic collaborator, Samuel Taylor Coleridge, was one of its most famous addicts, as was another of his friends, Thomas de Quincey.

In the twentieth and early twenty-first centuries the large-scale industrial base of the town has declined. Paper is still made on two sites north of the town, at Burneside and Kentmere, but

Children playing in Noble's Yard, 96 Stricklandgate, in 1914. Kendal was and is renowned for its many yards, which are numbered as part of the sequence of houses etc. on the street on which they appear. (T.H.)

View in Douglas's Yard, with trade carts stacked against the wall. The building is seventeenth century in date and has 'Lake District' cylindrical chimneys. (P.H.)

A view that has changed little with the passage of time. Police Office Yard runs between the Market Place and Finkle Street and contained the town's first police station and (out of the picture to the left) the fire engine house. (T.H)

Yard 10 (Redmayne's Yard), Stricklandgate, the home of the K Cycle Works, run by Braithwaite Brothers. (P.D.)

Pack Horse Yard, Stricklandgate. The figure in the foreground is carrying an oak swill basket, of the sort made in the woodlands of the southern Lake District. (P.D.)

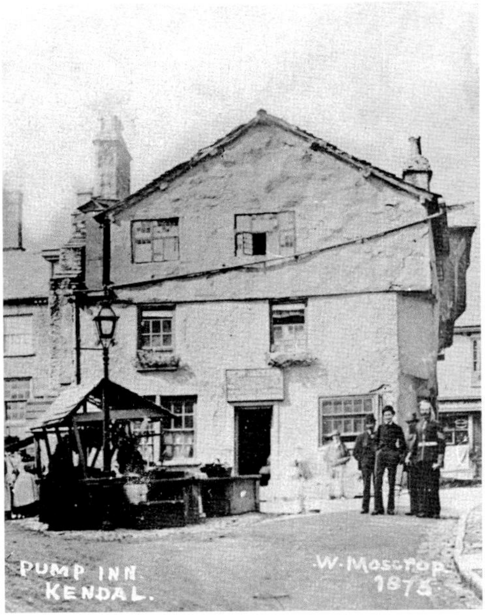

View of the rear of the Pump Inn with the Fish Market, by William Moscrop, 1875. The inn occupied a central site at the top end of Finkle Street and the Fish Market traditionally took place behind it. (P.D.)

The Fleece Inn, 14 Highgate, in 1886–92. The name is a reference to the fabled Golden Fleece sought by Jason and the Argonauts, and was a symbol of the Woolcombers' Guild. (T.H.)

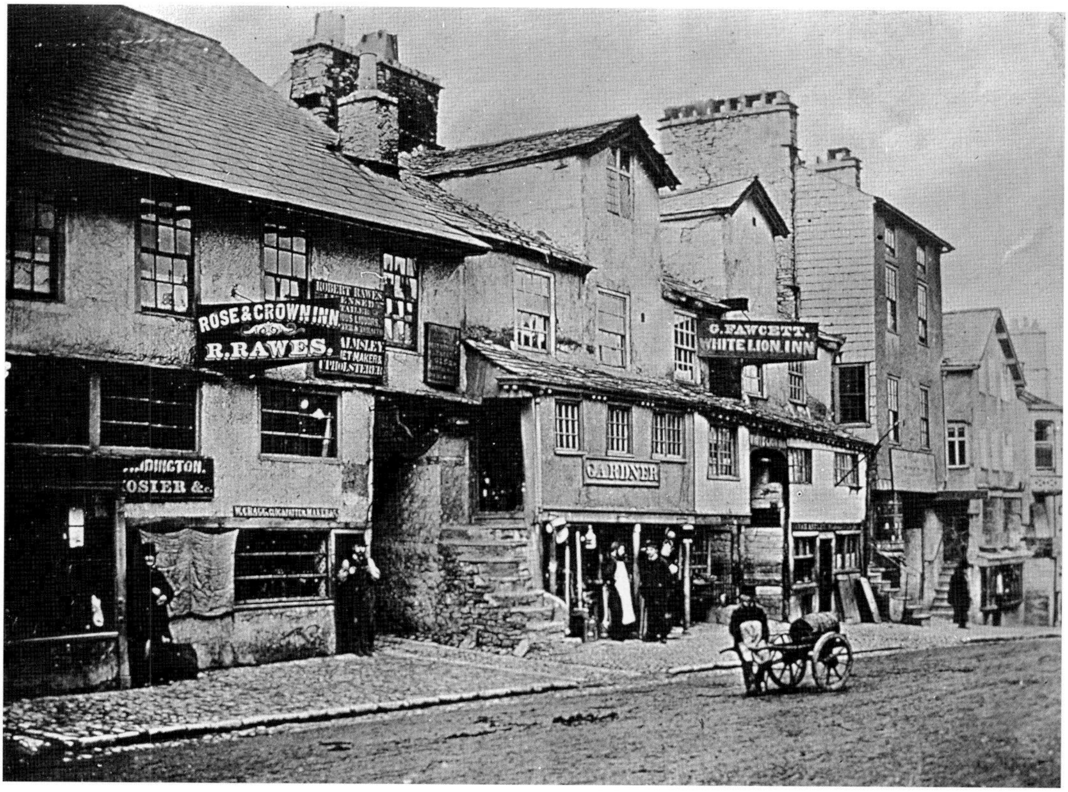

above The Rose & Crown and White Lion inns opposite the Market Place, an early photograph of the 1860s when the respective landlords were B. Rawes and G. Fawcett. (T.H.)

right the yard formerly at the rear of the Bear & Staff Inn, which lay on the north side of Captain French Lane and near the Highgate Hotel. It appears to have been divided into several properties with separate access to each. (T.H.)

opposite The King's Arms Hotel in the 1880s with a cab, or 'fly', standing outside. The hotel occupied a short frontage on the ground floor, but its bedrooms extended over the adjacent shops. (P.D.)

Portrait of Mrs Wilkinson (Aggie Bell), Fellside, with her stock-in-trade in baskets, c.1890. (P.D.)

Two Kendal tanners in their work aprons and with the tools of their trade, c.1860s. The lined and characterful faces are typical of men who had a long and physically hard working life. (P.D.)

Mrs Jane Ann Wills of Fellside, midwife. In an age before the NHS, midwives were among the most important health-care providers to poorer families, bringing experience and knowledge to anxious mothers. (P.D.)

'Dickie Stinky'. In a small town where everyone knew each other, nicknames helped to distinguish between members of large clans with identical names. Still, he must have stood out even at a time of generally poor personal hygiene. (T.H.)

Old Jimmy Quirk with a pony. Quirk is not a nickname but a common surname in the Isle of Man. (P.D.)

View of the Fish Market in Finkle Street during the 1880s, showing the temporary stalls and selling from wooden fish-boxes. An unusually informal photograph taken from pavement level. (T.H.)

Highgate fruit market 1906. Boxes and baskets of apples await a buyer, or at least a taster, such as the boy in the background, apparantly thinking hard about a purchase. (T.H.)

MARKETS

The Market Place looking west in the late nineteenth century. The scene is remarkably unchanged, apart from the costumes and the many carts that can be seen, including the upturned shafts of one in the foreground, as well as a hotel coach, ready to board. (T.H.)

The Market Hall in 1889–90, an unusually unposed and everyday view showing the goods being brought in by horse and cart. The horses would be led away to stabling, but the carts lined the streets. (T.H.)

SHOPS

Titus Wilson's shop at 28 Highgate. A well-known name in Kendal until its closure in 1988, Titus Wilson was a long-established printer, publisher and bookseller. (T.H.)

The New Shambles in 1914 looking down towards Finkle Street. This was originally built in 1803 as a row of butchers' shops. (T.H.)

Butterwith & Hunter's shop at 2 Stricklandgate. In 1885 they were grocers, provision merchants and bakers. (P.D.)

Interior of the Co-operative Store, newly fitted out c.1930, probably the Finkle Street headquarters in Waterloo House. (P.D.)

Sheep being driven through the centre of Kendal at Allhallows Lane junction, not something that would be seen these days! (P.D.)

Rear of James Bownass's shop at 72 Stricklandgate, showing shoe- and boot-making in progress, c. 1906. (P.D.)

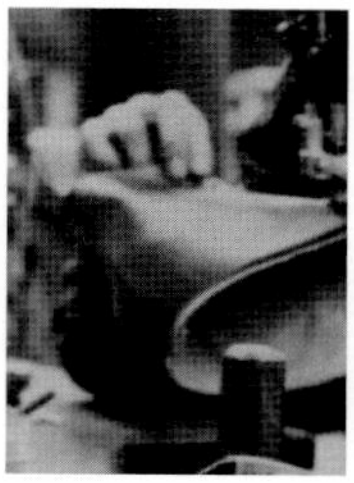

Workers at K Boot Factory, finishing by hand. (P.D.)

M. Croft & Son at 26 Wildman Street, agricultural implement makers, engineers and smiths in 1906. The whole workforce seems to be gathered outside, together with some of their products. (P.D.)

The fire brigade at the Fire Station in Aynam Road, resplendent in their best uniforms and polished helmets, ready for the Peace Celebrations on 19 July 1919. (P.D.)

left: two Crosthwaite postmen in about 1904 standing by a 'VR' monographed postbox. (P.D.)

Postmen ready for their rounds outside the Post Office in Central Buildings, Finkle Street, in about 1910. (P.D.)

Airey's Dairy Cart in about 1900. (P.D.)

Zenas Crabtree's Garage at 96–100 Kirkland in the early twentieth century. (P.D.)

Elephants being ridden by clowns outside the Co-operative store in Highgate, *c.* 1900. When the circus came to town such a parade of their wares was normal, and was intended to impress. (P.D.)

A barrel organ provides entertainment in Wildman Street, *c.* 1900. (P.D.)

the disappearance of key industries, most notably K Shoes, has not only caused major economic problems but was also a blow to the town's morale. Dairy Crest also closed its factory here in 2000. Industry has become more footloose, and is no longer carried on in large factories but in anonymous metal sheds on trading estates. Even then, it is often just an assembly or finishing process, using goods made elsewhere, increasingly in the Far East. Equally important has been the loss of local control of our own destiny, handed over to the boardrooms of international companies. This is not just relevant to manufacturing and retailing. The takeover of Provincial Insurance by AXA, and its own subsequent takeover and withdrawal from Kendal, not only led to the loss of 350 jobs but also removed from the town a previously benevolent employer with an excellent record of charitable giving and sponsorship locally. Boardrooms based elsewhere are much less likely to look with a kindly eye on requests for financial help.

The 2001 census revealed that the working population of the town was 13,867, of whom a surprising 15 per cent were engaged in manufacturing. This compares with 22 per cent in the wholesale and retail trades, almost 8 per cent in construction, over 11 per cent in health and social work, and 7 per cent in education. The categories are fairly generalised, and a superficial glance at Kendal might have suggested more managerial and white-collar positions and more people employed in service industries. Nor do the statistics reveal how many of these people actually worked in Kendal—the census looks at Kendal residents, not jobs in the town as such. How much travelling takes place to other centres, in east and south Lancashire? And how many people living outside Kendal travelled to work in the town? The rush-hour queues suggest that there are very significant numbers of these. For some the attractions of life in the town—often claimed as the best place in England to live—must help to outweigh the discomforts of commuting.[54] For others, living in beautiful countryside but reasonably close to urban jobs and amenities has a powerful advantage.

K Village Outlet, on the site of the former shoe factory. At the time of writing the shopping centre is in administration and its future is uncertain.

PHOTOGRAPH: ELLIE GODDARD

8 Road, canal and rail

Kendal's bridges

IN ANY CONSIDERATION of transport in the town and its hinterland the first theme to consider is the bridging of Kendal's shallow but unpredictable river, the Kent, which is prone to rapid rising and flooding, and very swift-flowing. Most of the town lay on the western side of the river, but important roads came in from the east, and agricultural land, the Castle estate, and the medieval cornmill all lay on the opposite bank from the town. Fording the river was perfectly feasible in good weather, but bridges were essential for year-round contact. Initially, two bridges carried the principal traffic. Nether Bridge, at the south end of the town, and Stramongate Bridge to the north-east were on the main arterial roads, with a small transpontine suburb beyond the latter. Later, Miller Bridge grew in importance, as industry developed on the east bank, and especially after the completion of the Lancaster Canal in 1819. A fourth crossing, Victoria Bridge, north of Stramongate, resulted from late-Victorian developments, while the fifth, Romney Bridge, to the south of Miller Bridge, is a recent response to the growing traffic problem within the town.

The earliest medieval references are confusing, as one cannot always be sure which bridge is being described. Some of the documents which have traditionally been interpreted as relating to Nether Bridge actually make more sense in the context of Stramongate Bridge.[1] Nether Bridge is a medieval bridge in origin. The earliest certain reference to it is in 1421, when pontage, a local tax raised to build or repair bridges, was granted 'for one year in aid of the repair of two stone bridges across the waters of Kent'.[2] It is difficult, though, to imagine that there was not a bridge here from much earlier times, and repair implies a pre-existing structure. The bridge has three arches with cutwaters and refuges for pedestrians. Evidence of two widenings can be seen underneath

Nether Bridge.

Nether Bridge ford.

GLASS PLATE NEGATIVE, BY COURTESY OF KENDAL TOWN COUNCIL

on the upstream side. The first widening was on the downstream side in 1772, but the work was washed away after only a few weeks, and so instead it was widened on the upstream side soon after. A further widening took place in 1908. In the 1530s Leland mentioned 'Nether-bridge of stone of 3 or 4 arches standynge playne este towards Yorke'.[3] The bridge lay on one of the principal roads, yet its narrowness until the last quarter of the eighteenth century tells us much about the poorly developed nature of Kendal's transport system, as only very narrow carts or pack-horses could pass over. Indeed, an ordinance of 1582 banned vehicles with more than one horse on both this and Stramongate bridge.[4]

Perhaps in consequence, the nearby ford was in use for cattle and wheeled vehicles until the nineteenth century. An accident occurred there in November 1806 when a chaise tried to ford the river a little upstream, and the driver was drowned,[5] while later in the century it was still a place to water cattle because the banks were low and access to the river easier.[6]

The other ancient bridge was Stramongate Bridge, carrying all the traffic in the direction of Shap and the north, and of Appleby, the county town. The earliest reference is a three-year grant of pontage to 'the good men of Kirkeby in Kendale' in 1376, for 'their bridge which is broken down'.[7] It was, therefore, established long enough before this time to need extensive repair, perhaps as a result of a flood? A grant of pontage merely allowed charges to be levied on

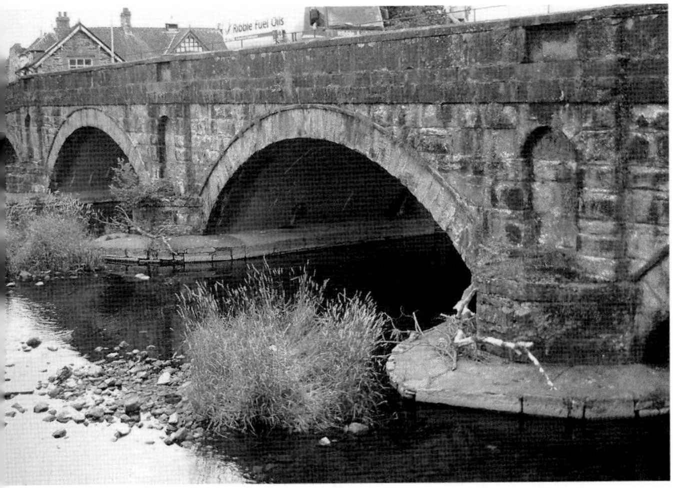

Stramongate Bridge.

certain goods passing through, and does not itself prove that anything was done. This 1376 reference is usually applied to Nether Bridge, but seems better to fit this one, as a second grant of pontage in 1379 refers to it as 'le North Brigg' (implying the existence of another, southerly one, surely Nether Bridge?) This grant was itself renewed three years later, in 1382.[8] Thomas Appleby, Bishop of Carlisle, granted indulgences in 1379 for the building of the 'ponte de Strowmondgate',[9] and in Thomas de Sandford's will of 1380,[10] when he left 13*s.* 4*d.* to the work, it is referred to as the 'new bridge' (*novo ponti*). In 1421 as we have seen both Nether Bridge and Stramongate Bridge received a pontage grant.

In the 1530s John Leland described it as 'Stramangate bridge of stone havynge 8 or 9 arches'.[11] John Speed's map of 1610 seems to show only four arches, and there are four today. If, however, we look at the topography of this crossing we can see that the bridge springs from a long ridge leading down to Sand Aire on the river's west bank across to the low ground of Wildman Street and Longpool on its east bank. Sand Aire is a place-name suggesting an island or sandbank in the river, and one might suspect that from both sides of the crossing a continuous raised causeway would be necessary over this low land, as well as other modification of the natural topography. Perhaps archaeological excavation would reveal Leland's further four or five arches buried in the roadway on one side or the other, a little like the medieval Exe Bridge in Exeter.[12]

There must have been work on the bridge in 1569–70, when Henry Kirkby of North Auckland, County Durham, bequeathed 'ten old angells of gold, that is in a brasselett, to be bestowed of Stramagatt bridge in Kendall',[13] but in 1582 a ban was imposed on large vehicles, similar to that on Nether Bridge. Although in 1706 it was ordered that the decay of Stramongate Bridge was to be repaired, little or nothing seems to have been done because of a dispute over who was responsible.[14] In 1791 the well-known architect Thomas Harrison of Lancaster, who had built Skerton Bridge over the Lune, prepared plans to demolish and replace Stramongate bridge with one of three equal arches, but the masonry resisted all attempts at destruction. The existing proportions of the arches had to be accepted, and the bridge was therefore widened on both sides in 1793–94. It now consists of four segmental arches with cutwaters and shallow *aedicules* (blank recesses) over each cutwater, all in limestone. The date 1794 is cut into panels in the parapets. The building work was undertaken by William Holme and Francis Webster of Kendal.[15] In the parish registers of Beetham the Reverend William Hutton wrote in 1794, 'Strammon Gate Bridge Kendal finish'd this Year with Stone after the fashion of cutting like my own house'. His new house is the one immediately to the north of

Miller Bridge and Romney Bridge.

the river Beela on the modern A6, and its design, as well as its sawn limestone masonry, was by Webster.[16]

The present Miller Bridge dates from the early nineteenth century, its construction being prompted by the building of the Canal Head in 1819, but it is on an earlier site. It was less important than the other two ancient bridges, as until this time it only gave local access to the Castle Mill. The first stone bridge here was built in 1743, replacing a timber bridge on stone piers that had been built in 1669. That, too, had replaced an earlier version, a timber bridge washed away in a flood in 1668. The new stone bridge of 1819 was evidently inadequate, for it was widened only three years later, in 1822. The bridge is of three arches, with round cutwaters, and is built of limestone.

Victoria Bridge forms part of the new road created in 1886 as Sandes Avenue, linking Stricklandgate with the suburbs on the east bank. The bridge is of cast iron with a flat deck and has three spans carried on triple cast columns. The parapet railings are decorative, with the Kendal coat of arm at intervals. This new bridge was opened on 13 September 1886. Romney Bridge is the most recent of the bridges over the Kent, dating only from 1990 and superseding a footbridge on the same location, south of Nether Bridge.

The footbridge, a suspension bridge, was reconstructed at Dockray Hall to the north, after campaigning by (and with financial support from) Kendal Building Preservation Trust. Goose Holme is linked to the west bank by a timber footbridge carried on three piers with steel railings. At Abbot Hall Park another footbridge of concrete and steel crosses the river on two piers. It was called 'Jennings Yard Bridge' on the Ordnance Survey map of 1911. Other bridges, once important to Kendalians, have now vanished, as the roadways have been rebuilt and the watercourses culverted beneath. These include Blind Beck Bridge, rebuilt and widened in 1823; Stock Bridge, leading from Wildman Street to Goose Holme; and the Headrace Bridge, crossing the Castle Mill leat near Miller Bridge, and designed in 1818 by Francis Webster.

Transport

Kendal produced many bulky goods, such as bolts of cloth, and from an early date it needed facilities of some sort to transport these to markets further afield. Although the town lay on the main road to the north, in the sixteenth and seventeenth centuries there was relatively little demand for transport in that direction. Most of the town's main trade lay with areas further south—Lancashire, the Midlands, London and Southampton—and its access to ports was very limited. Since outside interests did not promote transport routes to the town, this was done by Kendalians themselves using, in the medieval period and after, packhorses, which were best suited to the roads and loads of the time. This persisted throughout the seventeenth century with a loose partnership of packhorse carriers, and only began to be replaced by waggon transport from the middle of the eighteenth.

It has long been argued that the roads were so bad until 1750 (and the appearance of local turnpike trusts) that packhorses were the only practicable means of transport. However, more recently it has been demonstrated that this was not the case.[17] That wheeled traffic did exist in Kendal even in the Middle Ages is indicated, for example, by the case of the assault by Walter de Styrkeland and others upon the servants of the Abbey of St Mary, York, taking away the horses from their waggons and impounding them when they sought to collect tithes in the town in 1309.[18] Nevertheless, the reliability, speed and effectiveness of the local packhorse trains may have satisfied most needs until the wider economic picture changed and alternative methods came into favour.

The Kendal packhorses

As early as the fifteenth century Kendal cloths were being distributed to London and other cities, and even abroad, sometimes under the agency of Italian merchants. Many of the packs of cloth were carried to Southampton for export, and this work seems to have been entirely in the hands of Kendal 'chapmen'. The names of no fewer than 108 chapmen of the town are recorded in the brokage books and cloth hall accounts of Southampton between 1492 and 1584, even though there are several gaps in the records. Each of these men made at least one journey to Southampton with a train of packhorses, some of them being frequent visitors. The goods they were carrying were often Kendal cloths, 'cottons' or 'northern dozens', though not exclusively so. They sometimes carried 'kerseys', 'broad Suffolk cloths', 'Manchester cottons', and 'Welsh cottons', which they might have picked up in other towns on their way, but such names for cloth types could be generic, and some at least may have been produced in Kendal.

On their return journey northwards they frequently carried goods such as raisins and figs, produce of high value, or commodities useful in the cloth trade such as alum and dyestuffs. The double journey, perhaps via Manchester or Warrington and then through the Midlands to Oxford and Reading, seems to have taken about four weeks. The 'Kendalmen' far outnumbered other northern chapmen in Southampton.[19] There is a potential problem

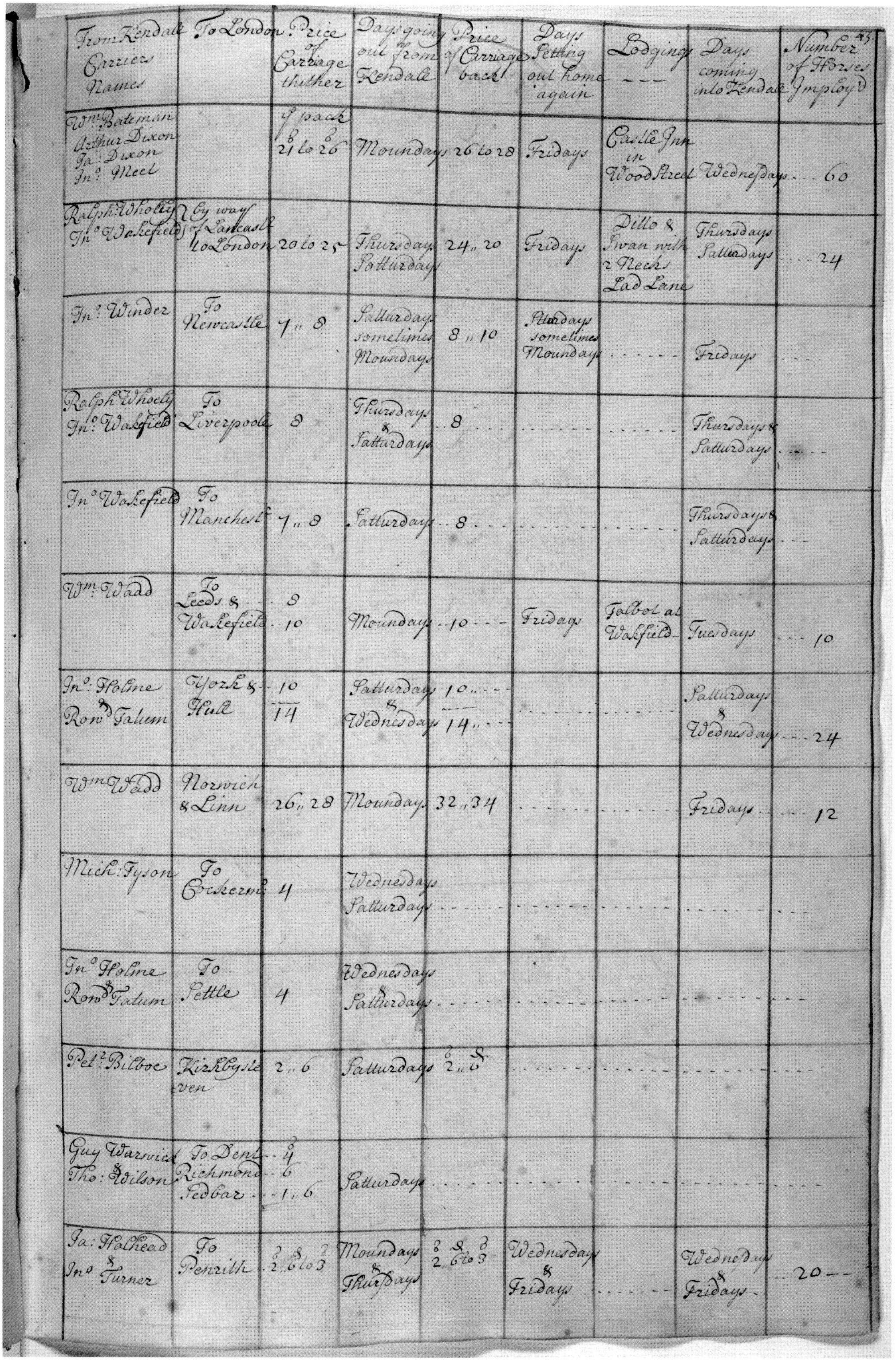

From Kendale Carriers Names	To London	Price of Carriage thither	Days going out from Kendale	Price of Carriage back	Days setting out home again	Lodgings	Days coming into Kendale	Number of Horses Imploy'd
Wm. Bateman, Arthur Dixon, Ja: Dixon, Jno. Meel		ye pack s d 21 to 26	Moundays	26 to 28	Fridays	Castle Inn in Wood Street	Wednesdays	60
Ralph Wholey, Jno. Wakefield	By way of Lancastr to London	20 to 25	Thursday, Satturday	24 „ 20	Fridays	Dillo & Swan with 2 Necks Lad Lane	Thursdays, Satturdays	24
Jno. Winder	To Newcastle	7 „ 8	Satturdays sometimes Moundays	8 „ 10	Satturdays sometimes Moundays		Fridays	
Ralph Wholey, Jno. Wakfield	To Liverpoole	8	Thursdays & Satturdays	8			Thursdays & Satturdays	
Jno. Wakefield	To Manchestr	7 „ 8	Satturdays	8			Thursdays & Satturdays	
Wm. Wadd	To Leeds & Wakefield	8 / 10	Moundays	10	Fridays	Talbot at Wakfield	Tuesdays	10
Jno. Holme & Rowd Tatum	York & Hull	10 / 14	Satturday & Wednesday	10 / 14			Satturdays & Wednesday	24
Wm. Wadd	Norwich & Linn	26 „ 28	Mounday	32 „ 34			Fridays	12
Mick: Fyson	To Cockermo	4	Wednesdays, Satturdays					
Jno. Holme & Rowd Tatum	To Settle	4	Wednesdays & Satturdays					
Petr. Bilboe	Kirkbysteven	2 „ 6	Satturdays	2 „ 6				
Guy Warwick & Tho: Wilson	To Dent / Richmond / Sedbar	4 / 6 / 1 „ 6	Satturdays					
Ja: Halhead & Jno. Turner	To Penrith	2 6 to 3	Moundays & Thursdays	2 6 to 3	Wednesday & Fridays		Wednesday & Fridays	20

List of Kendal packhorse operators in about 1700.

BY COURTESY OF CUMBRIA ARCHIVES, CARLISLE

with the term 'Kendalmen'. There was a great tendency to use generic names at this time, as witness the cloths: 'kerseys' and 'Kidderminsters' were named after their place of first origin, not necessarily the places where they were made later on. Were the 'Kendalmen' in the same way just any northern packhorsemen, bracketed together by ignorant southerners?

The tradition continued until well into the eighteenth century, with Kendal taking on a role well out of proportion to its size, and offering a service to many intermediate towns. We have good evidence in the late seventeenth century for the nationwide extent of packhorse operators.[20] Samuel and Thomas Briggs of Stainton, Richard Greenwood of Milton, and John Yeats of Holmscales (all just south of Kendal) were partners in the London carrying trade. Greenwood was robbed in 1665—probably on his way back from London—of silk, taffeta, lace and other mercers' and haberdashers' ware, perhaps bound for Kendal shops. His southbound journey had probably been with Kendal cottons. When he died in 1686 John Yeats had thirteen packhorses, so these four partners probably had at least 52 in total. In about 1700 the four main Kendal packhorse carriers had between them 60 horses. These four teams operated so that at any time one was in London, one in Kendal, and the other two on the road between. This partnership, which was very loose and more like a cooperative, continued despite the death and changes of partners for nearly a century until about 1750. In the early eighteenth century the journey to London took about ten days, covering 25 miles or so per day, and the carriers maintained a very strict timetable, so that people could meet them at intermediate points at set times. Most of their goods were from Kendal or London, but they would fill up space with part-loads en route.[21]

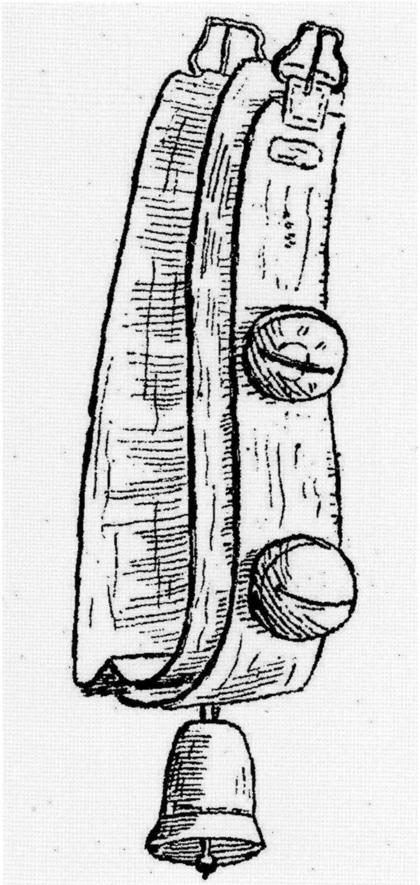

Collar for a bell-horse or leader of a packhorse train, marked 'Robert Tebay, Kendal', in Kendal Museum.

Their existence and reliability allowed further extensions to the network. In a letter to Sir Daniel Fleming at Rydal in February 1686 Sir John Lowther refers to the timing of the Kendal carriers:

> Having had a design of setting up a correspondence betwixt Kendal and Whitehaven, I have discours'd the carriers about it, and I find they constantly return from London to Kendal upon a Tuesday, and set forward for London again the Munday following, wherby I find they stay four whole dayes in the Country besides Sunday'.[22]

There is other information from the seventeenth century, suggesting that very localised needs as well were served by packhorse. In 1698 Celia Fiennes described them:

> they also use horses on which they have a sort of pannyers some close some open that they strew full of hay turff and lime and dung

and everything they would use, and the reason is plain from the narrowness of the lanes ... abundance of horses I see all about Kendall streetes with their burdens.[23]

Hugh James, steward to Colonel James Grahme of Levens Hall, regularly used the Kendal carriers to take all manner of items to his master in London. For instance, he sent a quantity of documents in six deal boxes by Preston the carrier in 1692; the frame of a dressing glass, also by Preston, in 1693; potted char from Windermere on two occasions in 1693 and 1694, both by Thomas Briggs; and three brass locks by Briggs in 1695. A coat sent to him via Briggs from London in 1694 did not arrive, and the carrier denied having ever received it.[24] Thomas Briggs of Stainton, 'London Carrier' appears in several documents dated to the 1690s.[25]

Drawing from a painting of a packhorse dated 1757, in Kendal Museum.

In 1728 a Kendal gang, or team of packhorses, was advertised thus: 'A Gang of Good Packhorses, containing eighteen in number, with their accoutrements and Business belonging to the same, being one of the ancient Gangs which have gone with Goods from York, Leeds and Wakefield to London, being the horses of Thomas Varley.'[26] Before the roads were turnpiked, after 1750, as many as 254 packhorses went weekly to and from Kendal, as well as several waggons computed to equal 100 horse loads.[27]

The packhorses worked in teams, their driver being at the rear, and the leading horse carrying bells to warn of their coming. A daily journey might be 25 miles, and their loads could be up to 260 lbs (118 kg) per horse. The load was carried on a packsaddle made of wood, being either draped over it or divided into two and placed in panniers, one on either side. It was held into place with a special rope or strap and a safe hook with which to tension it, known as a 'wanty', derived from the Old English *wamb-tige* or 'belly-band'.[28] In 1580 Thomas Tusser noted that the desirable horse-gear to have in a stable (not just for pack-horses) was 'A panel and wantey, packsaddle and ped'.[29]

A rare list of Kendal carriers in about 1700, from a document in the Cumbria Record Office in Carlisle,[30] shows not only those on the London route, but several other routes as well. A group of four men, William Bateman, Arthur Dixon, James Dixon and John Meel, operated the route to London, presumably via West Yorkshire, with 60 packhorses. Another 20 horses operated by Ralph Wholly and John Wakefield, followed a different route to London via Lancaster, also serving Liverpool and Manchester. A further 66 horses regularly ran from Kendal on other routes, according to this list.

Where appropriate, as with bundles of cloth, the load would also be fixed with long pins, and these various articles became an unofficial arms of the carriers, depicted on tokens and painted glass. There is a naïve painting of a packhorse in Kendal Museum, dated 1757 and

Daily Conveyance between Kendal & Penrith.

BETTY WALKER

RETURNS thanks to her Friends and the Public, for the many Favours already conferred, and hopes by attention to merit a continuance thereof. She begs leave to inform them that her Waggons leave Penrith every Morning, and arrive at Kendal the same Evening; and a Waggon leaves Kendal every Morning, which arrives at Penrith the same Evening; from each place Goods are forwarded by regular Carriers to the adjacent Country, and all Parts of the North and South.

Goods intended for their Conveyance may be delivered to—

JOHN HARGREAVES, White Horse, Cripple Gate, London.
JOHN LING, Birmingham.
Mr. HUNT, Sheffield.
JOHN HARGREAVES, Manchester, Rochdale, Haslingdale, Bury, Liverpool, Preston, and Lancaster.
JOHN SIMPSON, Wade Lane, Leeds.
UNION COMPANY WHARF, Liverpool, by Canal.
JOHN HARGREAVES, Glasgow, Edinburgh, Hawick, Langholm, and Carlisle.
J. BAXTER, Dumfries.

The Proprietor will not be accountable for more than Five Pounds for any Box, Package, or Parcel, of any discription if under the weight of Twenty-eight Pounds, nor more than after the rate of Twenty Pounds per Cwt. for any *Package of greater weight, unless entered of higher value, and an Insurance paid thereon, at the time of delivery.*

Kendal, March 1, 1813.

signed 'RT'. The beast is shown wearing a collar for a bell-horse or leader, which is almost exactly like the collar (also in Kendal Museum) marked with 'Robert Tebay, Kendal' on a metal plate, and also with four rumbler bells and a conventional one, two of which are marked '11/Wigan' and were perhaps made by the Scott family of bellfounders there.[31] The 1924 museum catalogue lists this item as an 'Ancient Horse Collar with Bells. Used on the leading horse of the pack train travelling 30 to 50 strong from Bleaze Hall to Lancaster and Preston'.[32] Bleaze Hall, Old Hutton, was the home of Henry Bateman, who owned the packhorses.[33]

As well as long-distance journeys, there was local work for packhorses. A team of five packhorses went each week between Kendal and Ulverston, while a team of six followed the route between Kendal and Cartmel.[34] John Parcival sought compensation in 1762 for a horse with its load which fell and drowned on the flooded road to Tebay, between Kendal and Appleby.[35] Jeremiah Sowden, carrier of Kendal, who was found dead in the snow on Shap in the harsh winter of 1744/45 was probably also using packhorses.[36] Packhorses remained in use until a surprisingly late date in parts of the Lake District, because they were well suited to the terrain, and, apart from the valley roads, routes through the mountainous interior were unsuitable for wheeled vehicles—as many are to this day. Packhorse trains continued to work between Kendal and Whitehaven into the mid-nineteenth century.[37]

Elsewhere, though, packhorse trains ceased to be a common sight on major routes in the later eighteenth century. They were gradually superseded by two different conveyances:

the stage waggons and the carriers' carts. The larger waggons, with very wide wheels to distribute their weight, and pulled by large teams of horses, were extremely slow compared with packhorses, but could carry much larger and heavier loads. In Kendal they are said to have started in either 1755 or 1757,[38] and by 1794 there were regular waggons to Whitehaven, Carlisle, Manchester and York. Thus, a waggon operated by John Jackson and Co. set off every Monday evening for the *Bull & Mouth Inn*, London, and another arrived back in Kendal every Sunday evening.[39] In 1794, too, Machell, Buxton & Co. advertised a service to Lancaster, Preston, and Manchester.[40] A later example, probably typical, was the daily service advertised in a handbill by Betty Walker in 1818, operating between Kendal and Penrith.[41]

Goods could be sent to or from London, Birmingham, Sheffield, Manchester and other Lancashire towns, and Scotland, by means of connecting services, while local carriers offered connections to smaller places nearby. In effect, the arrangement foreshadowed that of later railway networks, with main lines and branch lines. When John Hargreaves of 7 Bridge Street, Manchester, was running services in the 1820s his billheads advertised daily 'Fly Waggons' to and from Preston, Lancaster, Kendal, Carlisle, Glasgow and Edinburgh. A few of these waggon services survived the coming of the railways and continued into the early twentieth century. Despite the competition by other forms of transport, Joseph Topping was providing a daily waggon service from 67 Stramongate to London as late as 1906.[42]

Roads before the turnpikes

It has often been claimed that before the building of turnpikes the only available transport in this area was by packhorse, simply because of the narrowness and poor quality of the roads. The quality of roads was indeed a problem throughout the country, and remained so even during the turnpike era, because the surfacing and substrata were so variable. Sandy soils were best, as they drained very easily, while clay was most disliked because in wet weather it inevitably held water and clogged wheels and hooves. However, the ability to travel in all seasons was little affected, and it is clear that packhorses remained viable for so long in the North West because of their relative efficiency in all conditions, rather than because of the poor state of the roads. Doubts have been cast on the suggestion that turnpiking necessarily solved the problem of bad roads. The arguments will no doubt continue.

There were certainly adequate through roads before the turnpikes. Emmanuel Bowen's roadbook of 1720, itself heavily derivative of Ogilby's strip-maps of the late seventeenth century, shows several in Westmorland.[43] The great road that ultimately became the A6 varied only in a few stretches (most notably on the approaches to Shap) from its later turnpike alignment and indeed from the modern route. This was the route used by the Jacobite armies of 1715 and 1745 and, although they had problems on the hills with heavy supply and ammunition waggons, they were able to use this route in the months of November and December, never a particularly favourable time for travel, and particularly bad in 1745. Bowen, and thus Ogilby, also shows another route, the main road through the heart of the Lake District from

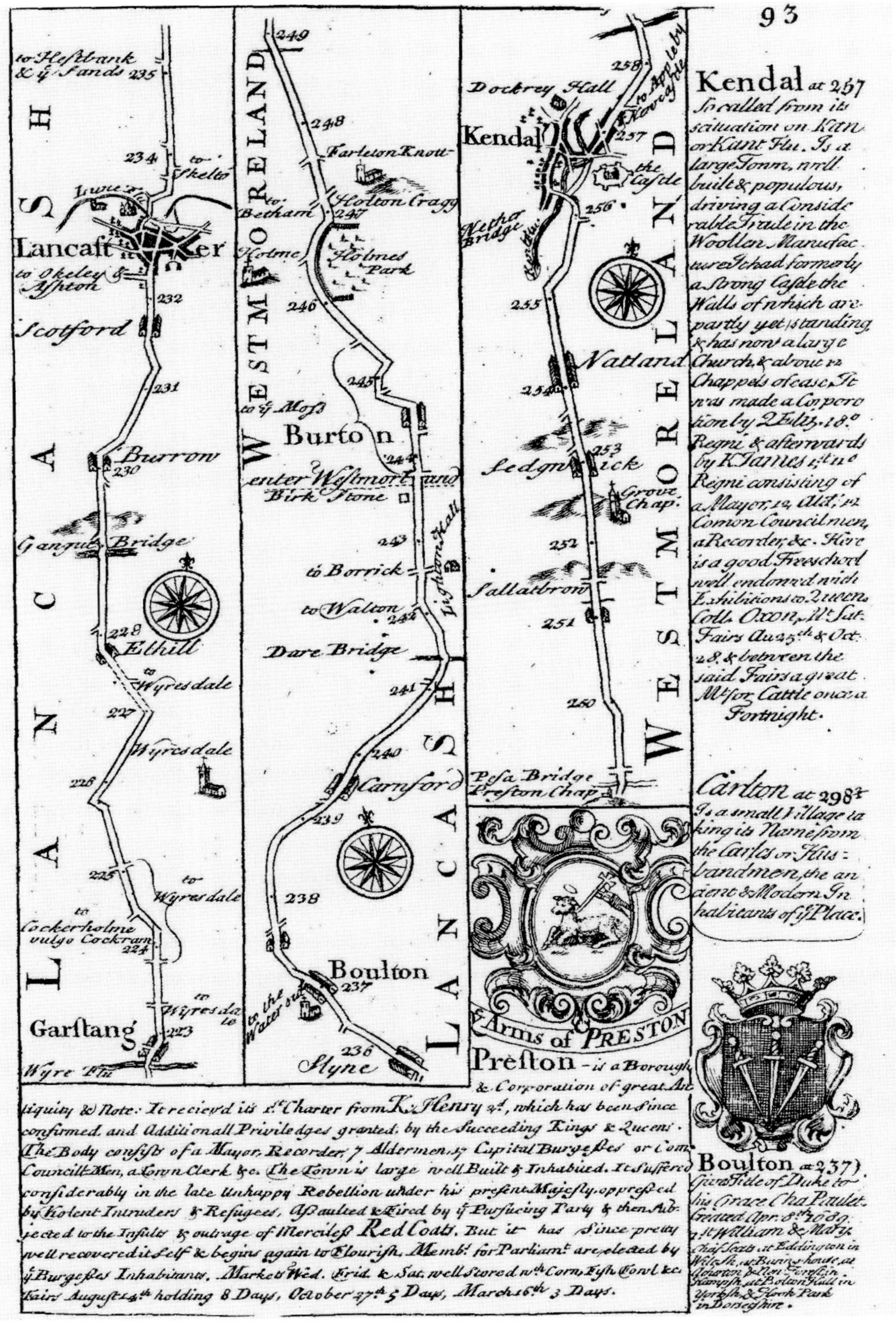

Page from Emmanuel Bowen's roadbook of 1720, showing the road from Lancaster to Kendal.

Kendal to Keswick via Staveley, Windermere and Ambleside.

On the other hand, one very early road is far from a main route. This is the narrow lane that runs from the Burton road (A65) near the Helm, and passes the *Station Inn* at Oxenholme, following the edge of the higher ground, skirting Kendal to the east, and joining the Appleby road near Meal Bank. Part of this is called 'Paddy Lane' on the Ordnance Survey. For long stretches it is followed by township boundaries, usually indicating an early feature in the landscape, and might have been an early 'bypass', allowing cattle to be driven past the town without paying tolls.

Hayclose Lane, once a drove-road bypassing Kendal to the east.

Very large herds of Scotch cattle were driven southwards towards the London markets throughout the eighteenth century and until the 1850s, when the completion of the key railway links took away the need to send cattle 'on the hoof'. No droving routes went through Kendal, because the drovers normally avoided built-up areas (the presence of large herds or flocks would cause chaos in the town). Furthermore, there was always the possibility that tolls might be levied. However another, wider, drove road runs south from the modern A684 (the Kendal to Sedbergh road) passing east of the town and going via Old Town and Kirkby Lonsdale to the Lune valley. It has distinctive wide verges for grazing and is still marked as the 'Old Scotch Road' on the Ordnance Survey map.

Turnpikes

The new turnpikes, in this area mainly dating from the 1750s onwards, were a response to the poor quality and variability of the road network. However, their initial impact was not necessarily very great. Many older roads were taken over more or less as they were and received only limited improvement as far as alignment and gradient were concerned, though more effective drainage and surfacing were invariably provided. Later, as the demands of transport increased, especially with extensive road-coach services in the 1820s, many diversions were made to avoid steep hills and sharp corners. Turnpikes were managed by trusts and authorised by Acts of Parliament. There was no overall strategy or plan, and trusts were established as and when local interests felt there was a need. Therefore the main inter-regional and long-distance routes were normally divided between a series of separate trusts. From the end of the eighteenth century there was some degree of coordination between adjoining trusts, but no statutory linkages. Thus, the present A6 north of Preston was maintained by the Preston and Heron (or Heiring) Syke Trust (1751), Heron Syke being the name of the small stream forming the county boundary just south of Burton in Kendal, while from that point northwards to the Cumberland border the road was the responsibility of the Heron Syke & Eamont Bridge Trust (1753). Another early route to be turnpiked was the modern A65, the Kendal to Keighley road, in 1751–52.[44] Within a few years the endless trains of packhorses carrying finished goods had been replaced by stage waggons, and in 1763 the 'Flying Machine' stagecoach was in operation, though the difficulty of the roads—and particularly the formidable gradients—is indicated by the fact that it required six horses.

Improvements continued to be made to the line of the turnpike north of Kendal. In 1821 the *Westmorland Gazette* reported that

> The alterations upon the road betwixt Kendal and Penrith are of such a magnitude and extent as will very soon avoid the steepest and worst parts ... the first alteration of the road takes place about 4 miles north of Kendal [and] avoids the narrow lane (Otter Bank) through the village of Gateside, passes the ravine of Bannisdale beck by an embankment and an immensely high bridge, of a single arch, and joins the old road again near Forest Hall. The new line of road will be opened to the public in the spring of 1822. A second deviation has amazingly improved the ascent from Hollowgate and the descent to High Burrow-bridge ... Soon after passing the summit a third alteration, deviating to the right, and crossing Wasdale beck by a new bridge misses the Dennings and Wasdale-bridge Mills, and, it is hoped that this deviation will be continued so as to avoid the Blea beck bridge and Wickerslack hills, and afterwards rejoin the old road near the new toll-bar.[45]

The turnpike at Sizergh also required some amendment. It was reported in 1819 that 'the Trustees are going to make immediately a very considerable improvement by deviating from the old road, for a length of 180 roods, commencing at the smith's shop on the north side of Sizergh Fell [where the *Strickland Arms* now stands], to the gate at Heaves Lodge and thereby avoiding the hill at Sizergh Fell which is an elevation of 81 feet and at a rise of three inches in the yard. The deviation will be shorter than the old road and will probably cost £1000.'[46] This deviation seems to explain the complex layout of older roads around the *Strickland Arms* and the gates to Sizergh Castle, now once more by-passed by the junction of the present A6, A590 and A591, and can still be clearly seen on the ground, and even more clearly on older Ordnance Survey maps.

Thomas Jefferys' 1770 map of Westmorland shows a number of turnpike roads radiating from Kendal.[47] Heading south, the first ran from Nether Bridge through Milnthorpe to the shores of the Kent estuary at Dixies. Part of it is now the A6. Its curious destination is explained by Kendal's need for improved access to the sea. Dixies was a local inn, and this was the nearest place where sea-going ships could call, picking up or depositing goods which travelled to or from the town by cart.[48] The Act for the Kendal via Milnthorpe to Dixies road was passed in 1759, authorising the 'repairing, amending and widening the roads from the southwest end of Nether Bridge, Kendal, by Sizergh fellside to Levens Bridge and from thence through the town of Milnthorpe to Dixies, and from the town of Milnthorpe to Hang Bridge and from thence to join the Heron Syke Turnpike Road at the guide-post near Clawthorpe Hall.' It was in effect two roads, one of which joined the Preston and Heron Syke turnpike via Holme and Burton-in-Kendal. Further Acts were obtained in 1779 and 1801.

A second road ran through Endmoor and Preston Richard towards Kirkby Lonsdale, and is now the A65. This provided an alternative to the Milnthorpe route going south, and offered a link via Crooklands to the Heron Syke road. The third route ran via Old Hutton and Old Town towards Kirkby Lonsdale, and is now the B6254. It was authorised in 1752, with further Acts in 1778 and 1800, but has all the appearance of a much older route which was given minimal treatment as a turnpike. It also connects with the 'Old Scotch Road', the former droving route discussed earlier. This route is shown in Cary's *New Itinerary* in 1798, and was an alternative to the modern A65.[49]

Cary's map, published 1811, showing turnpikes.

To the west and north-west Jefferys shows three roads. The first ran through Underbarrow and Bowland Bridge towards the foot of Windermere. Now an unclassified road, it was the Kendal to Kirkby Ireleth turnpike, authorised in 1763 and running via Newby Bridge, Bouth and Penny Bridge. According to William Pearson the old road from Kendal to Ulverston by way of Underbarrow and Cartmel-fell was originally

> a mere track, from five to six feet wide, as may yet be seen in many places, particularly below the Underbarrow toll-gate ... Improved as the road was, it still followed the old track first marked out by the pack horses; passing over two mountains, where there were long and steep declivities—Underbarrow Scaur, and Staveley Brow, near to Fell-foot ... The old and most direct road, thro' Crosthwaite, is now almost deserted; in fact, grass grows upon it on the summit of Cartmel-fell.[50]

In 1901 the Reverend F.R.C. Hutton wrote that

> The old pack-horse track from Ulverston to Kendal ran right past Witherslack Church ... you may track it from Towtop to Whitbarrow ... Subsequently to the Pack-horse time

came the mail coaches, which also came past the Church and up Towtop, the farmer at Kay Moss making quite a living by keeping horses to drag the coaches up the hill. The house just below, with its large stables, was a halting place. It was called the Spa Inn.[51]

A second turnpike ran through Crook to the Windermere Ferry. It was authorised in the same Act in 1761 as the road north-west west via Staveley to Ambleside. They were known respectively as the Plumgarth via Crook to Windermere and Ambleside to Kendal roads. To the north was a route through Skelsmergh and Selside towards Shap and Penrith, the Heron Syke, Kendal and Eamont Bridge Turnpike authorised in 1753 and joining another turnpike, authorised in the same year, which took the line on from Eamont Bridge to Carlisle. Together with the Preston and Heron Syke route this created, in a space of only three years, what was effectively a single regional or even national trunk road operated by a number of large and contiguous trusts.[52] Its line is now largely that of the modern A6.

Another road, now the A685, ran through Grayrigg and Tebay towards Appleby via Orton. It was authorised in 1761. To the east ran a road towards Sedbergh and into the North Riding, now the A684 and notable for its many bends and hills. It was the Brackenbar Gate via Garsdale and Sedbergh to Kendal road of 1762. At the Kendal end the route has been considerably altered in recent years. Most of these roads, with minor diversions to reduce hills and bends, survive and are still in heavy use today.

Road coaches

The expansion of turnpikes undoubtedly stimulated the development of road coaches. Such vehicles had existed since the sixteenth century, but they had been mostly private, the property of wealthy aristocrats who could afford the horses and servants needed to get them out of

The 'Kendal Flying Machine', a rickety old stage-waggon, as depicted by Thomas Rowlandson in 1820.

BY COURTESY OF ABBOT HALL ART GALLERY

Kendal, Penrith, and Whitehaven
POST COACHES.

THE Proprietors of the GOOD INTENT and VOLUNTEER COACHES, return their sincere thanks to their Friends and the Public, for the liberal encouragement they have hitherto received, and respectfully inform them, that the

GOOD INTENT COACHES,
FROM KENDAL TO WHITEHAVEN,

Have commenced to run DAILY (Sundays excepted) by way of Ambleside, Keswick, Cockermouth, and Workington;—leaves Kendal at Five o'clock each morning, and Whitehaven at Eight, returning by the same route to Kendal.

THE VOLUNTEER

Leaves Penrith every Monday, Wednesday, and Friday morning at eight o'clock, and arrives in time at Keswick, to take the Kendal or Whitehaven Coaches, returning the same evening to Penrith.

PROPRIETORS:
JOHN JACKSON, Kendal.
WILLIAM WILCOCK, Ambleside.
WILLIAM ATKINSON, Penrith.
JOHN I'ANSON, Keswick.
WILLIAM WOOD, Cockermouth.

The Proprietors will not be accountable for any Package or Parcel above Five Pounds value, unless entered and paid for accordingly.
February 6, 1813.

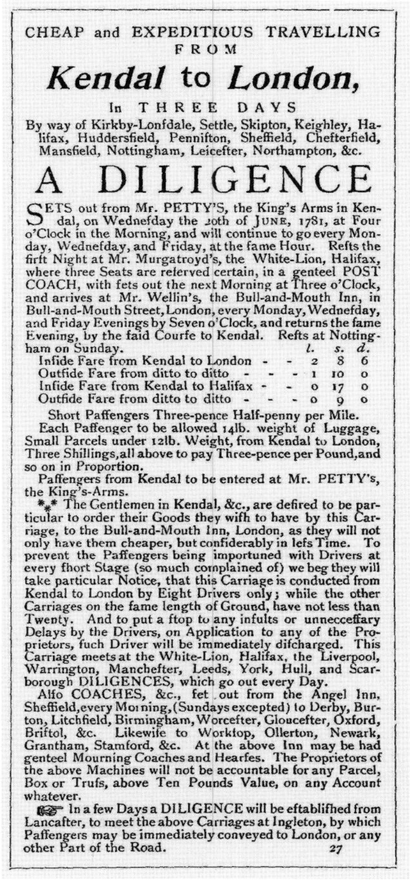

CHEAP and EXPEDITIOUS TRAVELLING FROM
***Kendal* to *London*,**
In THREE DAYS
By way of Kirkby-Lonfdale, Settle, Skipton, Keighley, Halifax, Huddersfield, Pennifton, Sheffield, Chefterfield, Mansfield, Nottingham, Leicefter, Northampton, &c.

A DILIGENCE

SETS out from Mr. PETTY'S, the King's Arms in Kendal, on Wednefday the 20th of JUNE, 1781, at Four o'Clock in the Morning, and will continue to go every Monday, Wednefday, and Friday, at the fame Hour. Refts the firft Night at Mr. Murgatroyd's, the White-Lion, Halifax, where three Seats are referved certain, in a genteel POST COACH, with fets out the next Morning at Three o'Clock, and arrives at Mr. Wellin's, the Bull-and-Mouth Inn, in Bull-and-Mouth Street, London, every Monday, Wednefday, and Friday Evenings by Seven o'Clock, and returns the fame Evening, by the faid Courfe to Kendal. Refts at Nottingham on Sunday.

	l.	*s.*	*d.*
Infide Fare from Kendal to London - -	2	8	6
Outfide Fare from ditto to ditto - - -	1	10	0
Infide Fare from Kendal to Halifax - -	0	17	0
Outfide Fare from ditto to ditto - - -	0	9	0

Short Paffengers Three-pence Half-penny per Mile.

Each Paffenger to be allowed 14lb. weight of Luggage, Small Parcels under 12lb. Weight, from Kendal to London, Three Shillings, all above to pay Three-pence per Pound, and so on in Proportion.

Paffengers from Kendal to be entered at Mr. PETTY's, the King's-Arms.

*** The Gentlemen in Kendal, &c., are defired to be particular to order their Goods they wifh to have by this Carriage, to the Bull-and-Mouth Inn, London, as they will not only have them cheaper, but confiderably in lefs Time. To prevent the Paffengers being importuned with Drivers at every fhort Stage (so much complained of) we beg they will take particular Notice, that this Carriage is conducted from Kendal to London by Eight Drivers only; while the other Carriages on the fame length of Ground, have not less than Twenty. And to put a ftop to any infults or unnecceffary Delays by the Drivers, on Application to any of the Proprietors, fuch Driver will be immediately difcharged. This Carriage meets at the White-Lion, Halifax, the Liverpool, Warrington, Manchefter, Leeds, York, Hull, and Scarborough DILIGENCES, which go out every Day.

Alfo COACHES, &c., fet out from the Angel Inn, Sheffield, every Morning, (Sundays excepted) to Derby, Burton, Litchfield, Birmingham, Worcefter, Gloucefter, Oxford, Briftol, &c. Likewife to Workfop, Ollerton, Newark, Grantham, Stamford, &c. At the above Inn may be had genteel Mourning Coaches and Hearfes. The Proprietors of the above Machines will not be accountable for any Parcel, Box or Trufs, above Ten Pounds Value, on any Account whatever.

☞ In a few Days a DILIGENCE will be eftablifhed from Lancafter, to meet the above Carriages at Ingleton, by which Paffengers may be immediately conveyed to London, or any other Part of the Road. 27

trouble, and they were most common in and around London. By the middle of the eighteenth century, though, they had become a commercial proposition, mostly being operated by co-operatives of innkeepers on the principal roads, who could accommodate and administer the teams of horses required, and who benefited most from the regular guests whom the road brought to their doors. Coach travel was very expensive, and while inside passengers, usually four or six per coach, paid most, even travel on the outside, experiencing the full rigours of the weather and the unevenness of the road, was relatively costly. It was usual to book in advance, in order to secure a place, and even at their peak the coaches carried relatively few passengers overall.

The first of these coaches to appear in Kendal was the 'Flying Machine' in 1763, arriving twice a week from London, and drawn by six horses.[53] In 1764 the coach from London to Kendal left the *Bell Inn* in Wood Street early on Monday mornings and took four days on the road, arriving in Kendal on Thursday evening. The single fare for an inside passenger was £3 7*s*. (about £300 in modern equivalent).[54] Even the relatively short journey to Liverpool took a day and a half in 1768, leaving Kendal at 4 on Friday morning and arriving in Liverpool on Saturday at 12 noon.[55] By 1781 London could be reached from Kendal via Kirkby Lonsdale and Halifax in three days at a cost of £2 8*s.* 6*d.* inside and £1 10*s.* outside, albeit by an indirect route.[56] Subsequently, the number of horses was usually reduced to four, the numbers of passengers each carried was more limited, and the speed of the coach increased greatly with the gradual improvements to the road.

Royal Mail coaches were first seen in Kendal in 1786.[57] A reorganisation of the mail in 1785 led to a new network of special coaches, operating to a new and exacting standard of turnout and time-keeping, setting off from London in all directions. These coaches, which also carried a limited number of passengers,[58] set a standard of reliability and punctuality that other coaches soon sought to emulate. In 1794 the *Universal British Directory* stated that mail coaches

The King's Arms with the departure of the *Telegraph* coach, painted by Richard Stirzaker in 1823.
BY COURTESY OF KENDAL TOWN COUNCIL

arrived in Kendal every day from both north and south, the former at about 10 a.m., the latter about 3 p.m.[59] There was also a return postal route from York via Kirkby Lonsdale three times a week. Isabella Masterson, proprietress of the *King's Arms Inn*, also operated a post coach which set out every morning for the *Swan with Two Necks* in Lad Lane, London, with a departure for Kendal every night at 11 p.m., Sundays excepted. A 'new light coach', the 'Royal Pilot', was advertised with a woodcut in the *Westmorland Gazette* in 1814.[60] It ran to Lancaster, Preston and Liverpool. A painting by Thomas Rowlandson in Abbot Hall Art Gallery satirises the *Kendal Flying Machine* in 1820 as a stage waggon.[61] Few of these coaches, apart from the Mail, ran for more than a year or two.

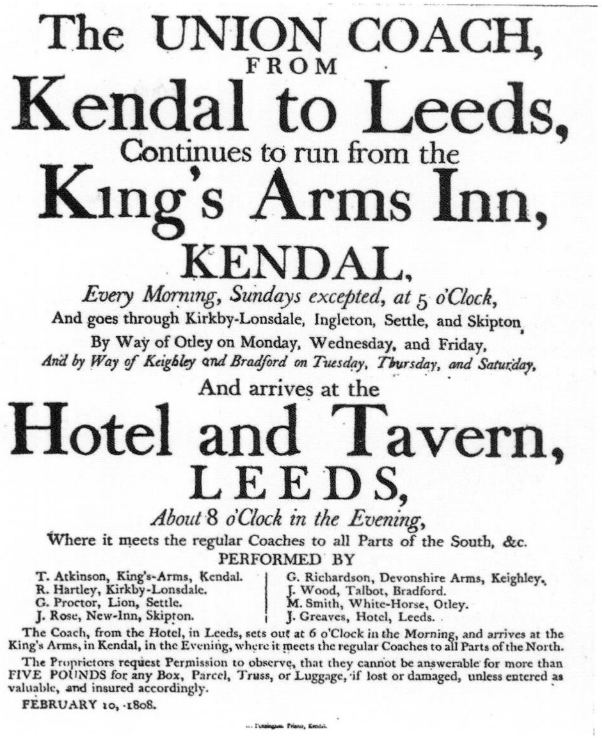

The UNION COACH,
FROM
Kendal to Leeds,
Continues to run from the
King's Arms Inn,
KENDAL,
Every Morning, Sundays excepted, at 5 o'Clock,
And goes through Kirkby-Lonsdale, Ingleton, Settle, and Skipton,
By Way of Otley on Monday, Wednesday, and Friday,
And by Way of Keighley and Bradford on Tuesday, Thursday, and Saturday.
And arrives at the
Hotel and Tavern,
LEEDS,
About 8 o'Clock in the Evening,
Where it meets the regular Coaches to all Parts of the South, &c.
PERFORMED BY

T. Atkinson, King's-Arms, Kendal.	G. Richardson, Devonshire Arms, Keighley,
R. Hartley, Kirkby-Lonsdale.	J. Wood, Talbot, Bradford.
G. Proctor, Lion, Settle.	M. Smith, White-Horse, Otley.
J. Rose, New-Inn, Skipton.	J. Greaves, Hotel, Leeds.

The Coach, from the Hotel, in Leeds, sets out at 6 o'Clock in the Morning, and arrives at the King's Arms, in Kendal, in the Evening, where it meets the regular Coaches to all Parts of the North.

The Proprietors request Permission to observe, that they cannot be answerable for more than FIVE POUNDS for any Box, Parcel, Truss, or Luggage, if lost or damaged, unless entered as valuable, and insured accordingly.

FEBRUARY 10, 1808.

Improvements in the standard of the roads from the 1820s led to a notable increase in the speed and reliability of coaches. Bends were eased, steep hills bypassed, and surfaces improved. Until about 1840 there was a brief golden age of road transport. Then the growth of the railway network, which could offer much greater speeds and cheapness, put an end to the coach services and ushered in the era of mass transport.

Parson & White's Directory for 1829 shows a great increase in coaches.[62] Royal Mail coaches arrived and departed for London, Edinburgh and Glasgow via Carlisle, and Whitehaven, whence there was a link to Ireland. Other coaches included the *New Times* and the *Telegraph* for Carlisle, Liverpool and Manchester, and the *Royal Union* for Leeds and London. These mostly ran from the *King's Arms*, but in addition the *Commercial Inn* had some services including the *Royal Bruce* to Carlisle, Liverpool and Manchester, and the *Defiance* for Whitehaven. Some services alternated between these two, while the *Dog & Duck* in Finkle Street was the starting point for the *Fair Trader*, for Liverpool and Manchester. In 1911 Richard Haresnape, recollecting the 1830s, remembered, 'especially what was called the opposition coach changing horses at Betty Dixon's, of the *Dog & Duck* in Finkle Street. There were about four other coaches so far as I can remember, then, going through Kendal daily North and South.'[63]

By 1834 the route to Carlisle was served by the *Royal Mail*, the *North Briton*, and the *Invincible*, Leeds by the *Union*, and Manchester and Liverpool by a multiplicity of services including the *Royal Liverpool*, the *Royal Mail*, the *North Briton*, *Invincible*, *Doctor* and *Telegraph*. These left from the same three inns as in 1829. A coach called, significantly, the *Lake Tourist*, served Whitehaven, presumably via the central Lake District and Keswick.[64]

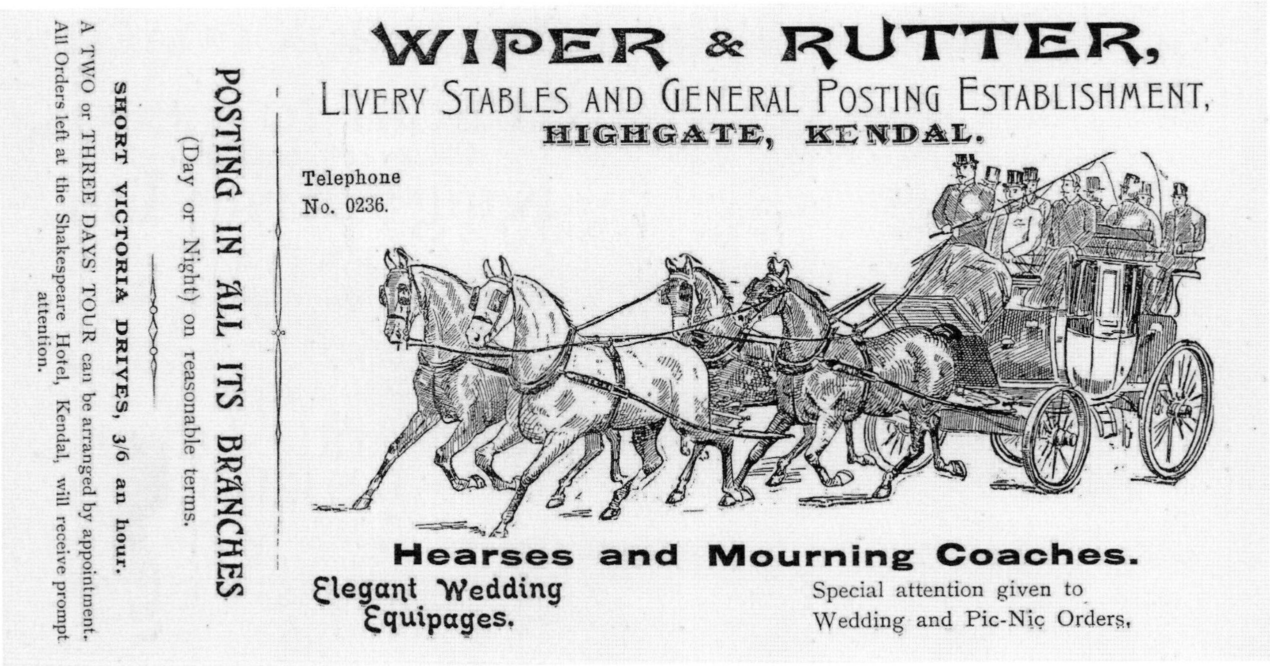
WIPER & RUTTER,
LIVERY STABLES AND GENERAL POSTING ESTABLISHMENT,
HIGHGATE, KENDAL.
Telephone No. 0236.
Hearses and Mourning Coaches.
Elegant Wedding Equipages.
Special attention given to Wedding and Pic-Nic Orders.
POSTING IN ALL ITS BRANCHES
(Day or Night) on reasonable terms.
SHORT VICTORIA DRIVES, 3/6 an hour.
A TWO or THREE DAYS' TOUR can be arranged by appointment.
All Orders left at the Shakespeare Hotel, Kendal, will receive prompt attention.

Advertisement for Wiper & Rutter, Livery Stables and General Posting Establishment, 1906.

Directories give us a snapshot of certain years, but the newspapers reveal the true complexities of name and route changes, rivalries and accidents, which were frequent and often serious—overturning was a frequent hazard. Richard Stirzaker's painting of the *King's Arms* shows a colourful scene—coaches could be booked there, and one of the booking windows is preserved in the museum. As well as the named coaches, whose titles speak of speed, reliability, strength and patriotism, there was a network of diligences, smaller, lighter coaches serving as feeders to the main centres, while post-chaises, operated by many inns as a sort of local taxi service, could be hired by individuals.

Only in those areas where the railways did not penetrate did the coaches survive beyond the mid-1840s. This included the area between Kendal, Cartmel and Furness, where the Lancaster and Ulverstone (sic) Railway was not completed until 1857. Most parts of the Lake District, with the exception of Windermere, Keswick and Coniston, were too far from railways and in unsuitable terrain, so there road coaches long continued as tourist carriers, until the arrival of practicable motor vehicles in the 1920s and 1930s.

The Lancaster Canal

The Lancaster Canal was conceived in the 1770s as a link between the coalfields of south Lancashire and the limestone resources of north Lancashire and Westmorland. Cheap coal would be carried north, to areas seriously lacking in fuel resources, while limestone, slate and agricultural produce would be moved south in return. The authorising Act of Parliament was not passed until 1792, providing for a canal almost 76 miles long, from Westhoughton, via Preston, Garstang and Lancaster, and then on to Hincaster and Kendal. Its route was designed to have the minimum number of locks, and so was somewhat circuitous—the 42 miles north of Preston would be the longest lock-free canal section in Britain.

Work began in 1793, although there were major alterations to the southern section (the canal eventually began with a junction on the Leeds and Liverpool near Chorley) and the hugely expensive engineering works, designed by John Rennie, meant that the proprietors over-reached themselves. The section from Preston as far north as Tewitfield was opened in 1797, as were the few miles from the Leeds and Liverpool to Clayton Green, but the intervening stretch across the Ribble at Preston, which was to have been carried on Britain's longest aqueduct, was never built (the link being formed instead by a horse-drawn tramway). The section from Tewitfield north to Kendal presented further difficulties, including the building of a flight of eight locks at Tewitfield, the only locks on the main line, and a tunnel under Hincaster Hill.

Joseph Budworth wrote of Kendal in 1792 that

> Coal is very dear, and they are obliged to use peat; (a species of turf) but when the intended canal between Lancashire and this place is finished, (which they are afraid will be a tedious time, from the number of locks it will require) the cheerful hearth will blaze.[65]

However, it was not until 1819 that the northernmost section was completed, and by then high inflation caused by the Napoleonic Wars, and the agricultural depression which followed the peace, had wrought havoc with the finances and the potential profitability. Nonetheless, the opening was greeted with joy in Kendal. Some of the toasts at the opening dinner have a very Georgian flavour about them: 'A bottle at night and business in the morning;' 'Old wine and young women;' 'Champagne to our real friends, and real pain to our sham friends.'[66]

Despite the precarious finances of the canal company, the opening of the waterway brought tangible benefits for Kendal. The traffic in limestone and coal proved to have been a realistic expectation, and large quantities of both commodities were carried. A new industrial suburb developed at Canal Head—the terminus of the canal—where wharves were constructed and a group of warehouses built near the ancient Castle Mill. The advent of cheaper coal supplies led to the building of the gasworks and thus to

Change Bridge on the Lancaster Canal, photographed after the canal bed had been filled in. Here for the last mile or so the towpath changed sides from west to east. The bridge allowed horses to change sides without detaching their traces.

improved street lighting.[67] From 1826, too, the building of a link between the main line of the canal and Glasson Dock, near Lancaster, at last provided Kendal with a direct route to the sea, albeit for relatively small vessels. Previously, the nearest port had been at Milnthorpe. The first vessel to use the Glasson link brought Lake District slate to Kendal, a circuitous route, but one less prone to breakages than the road alternative.

Moreover, a public passenger service was soon started on the canal between Kendal and Preston, much smoother than the road journey though not, at least until the mid-1830s, as fast. A regular service of passenger packets was put on in 1820. These were long wide boats, heavy and slow, moving only at the rate of an ambling horse—the water-borne equivalents of stage waggons. The single journey time between Preston and Kendal was some 14 hours. However, they incorporated some important ideas—notably, a degree of comfort and the serving of food and drink while on the move. Initiatives on the central Scottish canals in the 1830s were being watched with interest. It was discovered that a long light boat, pulled by powerful horses, could take advantage of what are now known as 'solitons', waves propagated along a canal of suitable width and depth, much reducing the loading of the horses and increasing the speed to some 9–12 miles per hour. A new packet, based on these ideas and named *Waterwitch*, was tried on the lockless part of the canal and in July 1833 began to run right through to Kendal. A means of quickly passing through locks and tunnel must have been worked out, probably by allocating manpower to 'setting' the locks in advance. The journey time for the whole length

A modern (2012) photograph of Canal Head.

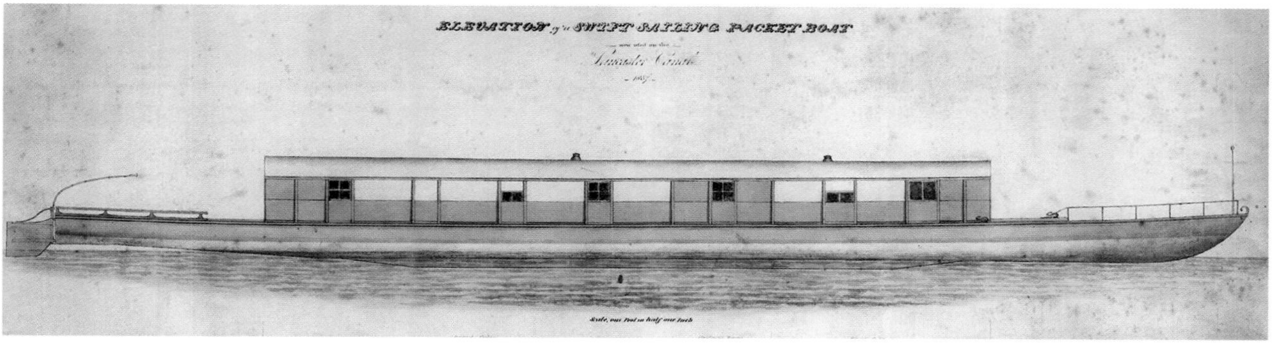

Drawing of one of the swift packet boats on the Lancaster Canal in 1837.

BY COURTESY OF LANCASHIRE LIBRARIES

between Preston and Kendal was brought down to 7 hours southwards and 7 hours 45 minutes northwards, the difference perhaps being accounted for by greater rapidity in emptying than in filling of the locks.

In the first six months of operation this one boat carried 16,000 passengers. Less than a year later, in March 1834, *Waterwitch* was joined by a second boat, *Swiftsure*. The use of two vessels allowed a more extensive timetable, which in due course was extended further by the addition of two more packets. Having a fourth boat allowed for regular repair and maintenance time for the fleet, which must have been much needed, given such intensive use. In August

Section from Wood's map of 1833, showing the early development of Canal Head.

PHOTOGRAPH CARNEGIE, FROM AN ORIGINAL HELD AT WESTMORLAND RECORD OFFICE, KENDAL

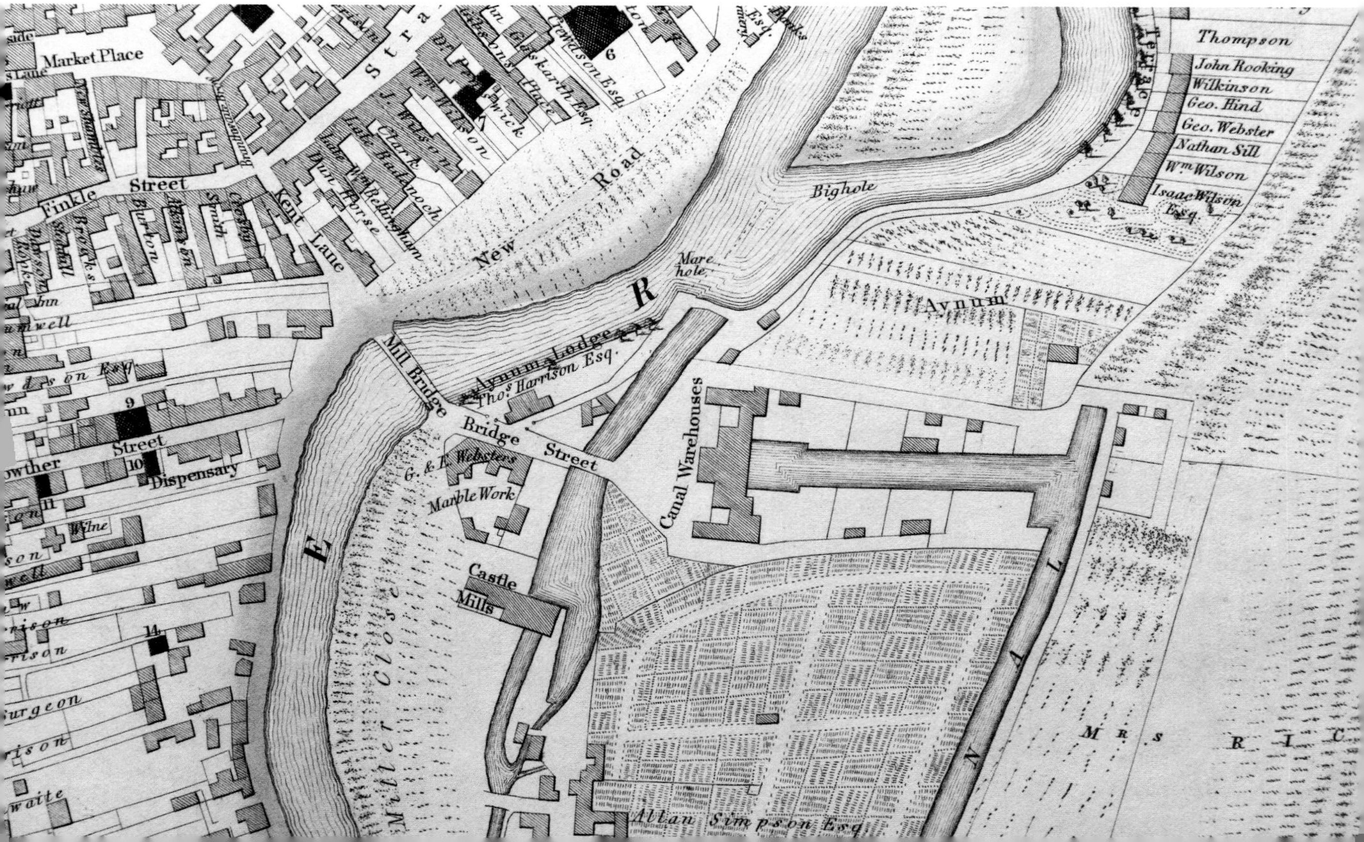

1835 *Waterwitch* and *Swiftsure* were joined by *Swallow*, of which Sir George Head wrote: 'In the meantime, the proprietors of the Preston and Kendal canal conduct operations with undiminished energy, having, besides those already described, launched a new iron boat during the present year.'[68] Finally, in the summer of 1839, *Crewdson* was acquired, named in honour of the Kendal banker, W.D. Crewdson, chairman of the Lancaster Canal Company—though she was later renamed *Waterwitch II*. Probably the best description of travel by a Lancaster Canal packet is given by John Fox, who first describes the boat:

> Sept. 21st, 1839 ... Heard of a passage boat [at Preston] by Lancaster Canal to Kendal ... And now I made the most delightful journey that ever I made in my life, starting at about half past one in the afternoon. The day was most beautiful. The boat was 72 feet long and just wide enough for two persons to sit opposite each other. It will hold about 70. Unladen it draws, I think, 5 inches of water. The head comes to the sharpest point from which 10 feet downwards, open, covered with tarpaulin, is the luggage; then 8 feet open for a boatman and about 6 passengers can sit in the open air. From this point the boat is covered with a hoop-shaped covering, watertight, and divided into three compartment—the first, fare 6s.—the middle a small sort of steward's room—the aft cabin fare 4s. The thing looked like a canoe. It ran into a covered dock.

Handbills of 1834 and 1839 for the canal packets.

SUPERIOR CONVEYANCE
BETWEEN
Manchester, Liverpool, Preston,
Lancaster, Kendal, &c. &c.

AN ADDITIONAL SWIFT
Packet Boat,
IS INTENDED TO COMMENCE SAILING
On MONDAY the 14th APRIL, 1834:—

One Boat will sail from *Kendal* to *Preston*, and return to *Lancaster* the same day—the other Boat will sail from *Lancaster* to *Preston*, and from thence to *Kendal* the same day—thereby affording two opportunities in both directions between Lancaster and Preston, and one opportunity each way between Kendal and Preston.

From KENDAL at half after Seven—from LANCASTER at half after Seven, and at a quarter before Eleven—and from PRESTON at half after Eleven, and at Three o'Clock, every Day, except Sunday.

THE HOURS OF SAILING WILL BE

FROM	FIRST BOAT.		SECOND BOAT.
KENDAL,	- - - - - -		half after Seven,
TEWITFIELD,	- - - - - -		half after Nine,
LANCASTER,	half after Seven	and	a quarter before Eleven,
GARSTANG,	a quarter before Nine	and	a quarter after Twelve,
and arrive at PRESTON at	Eleven	and	half after Two.

FROM	FIRST BOAT.		SECOND BOAT.
PRESTON,	half after Eleven	and	Three o'Clock.
GARSTANG,	a quarter after One	and	a quarter before Five.
LANCASTER,	a quarter before Three		arrives at Lancaster at half after Six.
TEWITFIELD,	half after Four,		
and arrive at KENDAL at	a quarter before Seven o'Clock.		

☞ Passengers are requested to observe that for any Place, North of Lancaster, they must take the FIRST BOAT, which sails from Preston, at half after Eleven.

*** Parcels carefully conveyed and forwarded.

Coaches meet the Packet Boats
at the Canal Wharf, *Preston*, from and to MANCHESTER, LIVERPOOL, &c.

PLACES SECURED FROM

KENDAL, LANCASTER, or PRESTON,	at the Canal Packet Boat Offices.
MANCHESTER - - - - - - -	Commercial Coach Office, Market Street.
LIVERPOOL - - - - - - -	Golden Lion Coach Office, Dale Street.
PRESTON - - - - - - -	Coach Office, Legs-of-Man Inn.

The Boats and Coaches perform the Journeys with punctuality, and at the usual very reasonable Fares.

C. CLARK, PRINTER, LANCASTER.

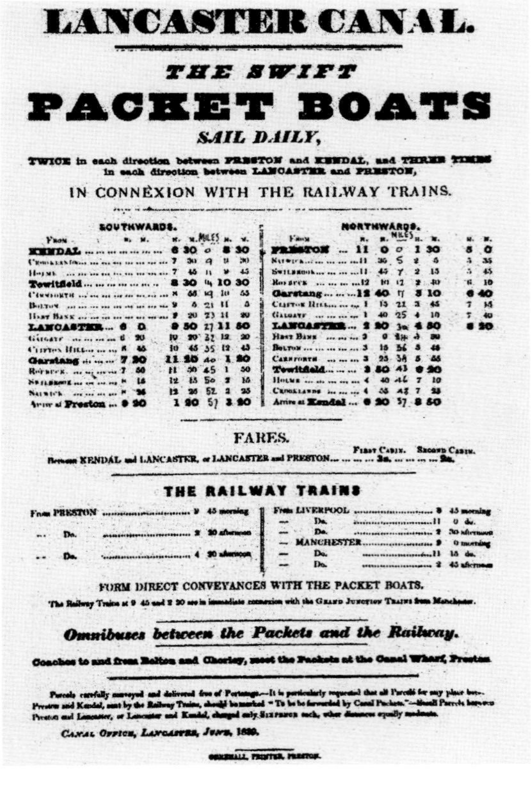

LANCASTER CANAL.
THE SWIFT
PACKET BOATS
SAIL DAILY,
TWICE in each direction between PRESTON and KENDAL, and THREE TIMES in each direction between LANCASTER and PRESTON,
IN CONNEXION WITH THE RAILWAY TRAINS.

SOUTHWARDS.

From	H. M.	H. M.	MILES	H. M.
KENDAL		6 30	0	8 30
Crooklands		7 30	9	9 30
Holme		7 45	11	9 45
Tewitfield		8 30	14	10 30
Carnforth		8 55	19	10 55
Bolton		9 5	21	11 5
Hest Bank		9 20	23	11 20
LANCASTER	6 0	9 50	27	11 50
Galgate	6 20	10 20	32	12 20
Clifton Hill	6 45	10 45	35	12 45
Garstang	7 20	11 20	40	1 20
Roebuck	7 50	11 50	45	1 50
Swillbrook	8 15	12 15	50	2 15
Salwick	8 25	12 25	52	2 25
Arrive at Preston	9 20	1 20	57	3 20

NORTHWARDS.

From	H. M.	MILES	H. M.	H. M.
PRESTON	11 0	0	1 30	5 0
Salwick	11 35	5	2 5	5 35
Swillbrook	11 45	7	2 15	5 45
Roebuck	12 10	12	2 40	6 10
Garstang	12 40	17	3 10	6 40
Clifton Hill	1 15	21	3 45	7 15
Galgate	1 40	25	4 10	7 40
LANCASTER	2 20	30	4 50	8 20
Hest Bank	3 0	34	5 30	
Bolton	3 15	36	5 45	
Carnforth	3 25	38	5 55	
Tewitfield	3 50	43	6 20	
Holme	4 40	46	7 10	
Crooklands	4 55	48	7 25	
Arrive at Kendal	6 20	57	8 50	

FARES.

	First Cabin.	Second Cabin.
Between KENDAL and LANCASTER, or LANCASTER and PRESTON	3s.	2s.

THE RAILWAY TRAINS

From PRESTON .... 9 45 morning	From LIVERPOOL .... 8 45 morning
— Do. .... 2 20 afternoon	— Do. .... 11 0 do.
— Do. .... 4 20 afternoon	— Do. .... 2 30 afternoon
	— MANCHESTER .... 9 0 morning
	— Do. .... 11 15 do.
	— Do. .... 2 45 afternoon

FORM DIRECT CONVEYANCES WITH THE PACKET BOATS.

The Railway Trains at 9 45 and 2 20 are in immediate connexion with the Grand Junction Trains from Manchester.

Omnibuses between the Packets and the Railway.

Coaches to and from Bolton and Chorley, meet the Packets at the Canal Wharf, Preston.

Parcels carefully conveyed and delivered *free of Portorage*.—It is particularly requested that all Parcels for any place between Preston and Kendal, sent by the Railway Trains, should be marked "To be forwarded by Canal Packets."—Small Parcels between Preston and Lancaster, or Lancaster and Kendal, charged only Sixpence each, other distances equally moderate.

Canal Office, Lancaster, June, 1839.

OCKERALL, PRINTER, PRESTON.

He goes on to describe the journey:

> The passengers from the north disembarked and we entered. I took a seat in the open air at the head … It was beautiful, and the manner in which we went along the water was for beauty of motion unequalled. Our boat rushed along at the rate of 9 miles an hour with a smoothness incredible. From the bow not the least wave arose but the water, unbroken, swelled gently against the bank. Two horses, one before the other, towed us in an unceasing canter. They were changed every four miles, not half a minute being taken to change. We had but two postilions for the whole way—one a boy of 19, to Lancaster from which he had but just returned so that he rode 60 miles post without stopping. I never did enjoy a journey as I did this. It was like a journey in a dream or in an Eastern tale—water, weather, scenery, motion—all was most beautiful. We were at Kendal before 9 o'clock.[69]

In 1840 the Lancaster & Preston Junction Railway opened, competing with the southern part of the route—but so badly run was the railway that it was soon in difficulties and had to be bailed out by the Canal Company! In 1842, therefore, the canal company took over

Coal barges of the Wigan Coal & Iron Co. at Canal Head in the late nineteenth century. Kendal was connected to Wigan (on the Leeds & Liverpool) and the main canal network via the Lancaster Canal's tramroad across the Ribble at Preston.

BY COURTESY OF KENDAL TOWN COUNCIL

the management of the railway, a unique episode in British railway history. It had no desire to compete with itself, so two boats were taken out of service (probably to be sold to the Bridgwater Canal), and packet boats between Lancaster and Kendal were now timed to meet the trains to and from the south. Finally with the extension of the line north beyond Lancaster, the packet boats were advertised for the last time in August 1846. In September they slipped quietly off the stage of history as the railway to Kendal and Windermere was opened.[70]

For another century the canal continued to be used for coal and other commodities, but leakage at the northern end and the very cold winter of 1940, when it froze over for a long period, sounded its death-knell. When the M6 and the Kendal Bypass were built in the late 1960s the feeder roads cut the canal which was merely culverted through their embankments. The through waterway ceased to exist, and the northern end beyond Stainton was de-watered, leaving only the bed in places and a series of rather strangely isolated overbridges. More recently plans have been put forward for reopening the northern reaches by locking up and down and parallel cuts through the road network, but whether this will now happen, after the recession, is uncertain.

Carriers

Carriers were the unsung heroes of eighteenth- and nineteenth-century transport, venturing out in all weathers to distribute goods and materials from the towns to the villages, and to rural industries. They created an informal network that covered the length and breadth of the country. John Taylor, writing in 1637, observed that:

> Others may object and say that I have not named all the towns and places that Carriers do go unto in England and Wales. To whom I yield; but yet I answer, that if a Carrier of York hath a letter or goods to deliver at any town in his way thither, he serves the turn well enough: and there are Carriers and Messengers from York to carry such goods and letters as are too be passed any ways north, broad and wide as far or farther than Berwick. So he that sends to Lancaster may from thence have what he sends conveyed to Kendal or Cockermouth.[71]

As the state of roads improved during the eighteenth century much of the small-scale redistribution of goods in the vicinity of Kendal, formerly carried out with packhorses, was refocused on the carriers' carts. The carriers generally set off for surrounding villages and towns from one of the Kendal innyards, early in the morning on several days each week, either returning the same evening on the shorter runs or the next day on longer journeys. Typically they used a light sprung two-wheeled cart with a canvas tilt (a protective hood over the goods), drawn by a single horse. Parcels and hampers of goods would be left for them at the inns, although they might also collect from manufacturers, from ships at Milnthorpe, Arnside or Sandside, or, later, from the railway stations. They could also collect items such as butter and eggs from farms along the way. The carriers used their own or others' credit to collect goods, and charged for goods plus carriage on delivery. Grocers and mercers were supplied by the carriers who collected bulk goods for them.

A well-documented example was the grocer Abraham Dent, one of the traders in the small market town of Kirkby Stephen, who was dependent on several local carriers to fetch him supplies of stock from other towns in the North West. Among those who supplied him were the carriers Thomas Pearson and Ephraim Jackson, who brought him goods from Kendal and undertook other business for Abraham which depended upon trust and goodwill.[72] While most of the carriers radiating from Kendal served a radius of no more than a dozen miles, some went much further, linking for instance with the Great North Road via Brough and Boroughbridge. Others no doubt had informal arrangements with fellow-carriers in adjacent regions to provide an inter-regional service.

The life of a carrier might have been quite idyllic at times, with the open roads, fresh air, everyone pleased to see you, a sense of performing a useful function. However, it also had its dangerous side—there was a risk of accident in lonely places; severe weather posed a major problem in the winter; and assault and theft of goods was a threat. In 1835 Thomas Varey, carrier, was found dead in the canal at Burton wharf, though whether in his own time or while at work is unrecorded. Thomas Garlick, carrier, was killed a few months later on his way to Kirkby Lonsdale. In 1837 Thomas Hunter, carrier of Orton, was shot dead on his return from Kendal. John Sisson, who worked the Appleby to Kendal route, died in the snow at Grayrigg in 1807.[73]

In the Soulby Collection at Barrow in Furness Record Office is the handbill of John Clarke of Haverthwaite, a common carrier between Kendal and Ulverston, dating from 1811.[74] It is a rare survival of what must once have been common. Carriers could set themselves up relatively easily, if they could afford a horse and cart, although some were considerable employers, with many waggons. Once established they might carry on for years, relying on word of mouth for their trade. But a new entrant into the business might well have to advertise, which may account for some handbills. Two mid-nineteenth-century firms of carriers which have been studied in detail, from records held in the Kendal Record Office, were those of Walter Berry of Milnthorpe and Thomas Ellwood of Ayside near Cartmel. The former operated between Milnthorpe and Kendal, the latter between Ulverston and Kendal.[75]

Handbill of John Clarke of Haverthwaite, common carrier, 1811.

BY COURTESY OF CUMBRIA ARCHIVES, BARROW-IN-FURNESS

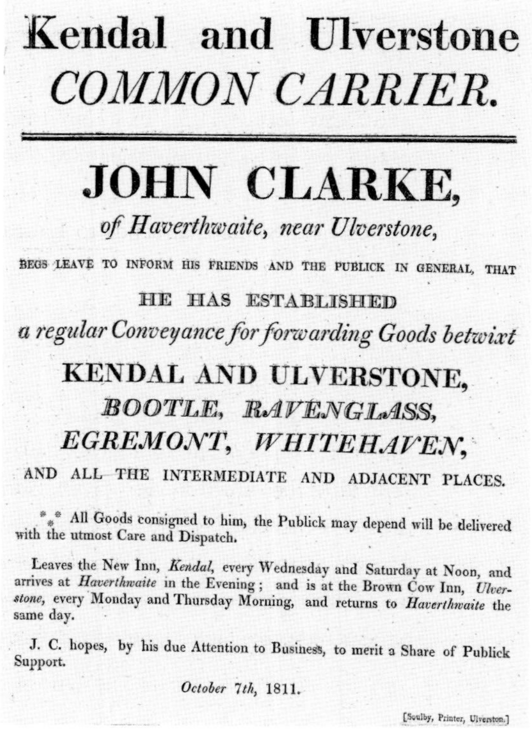

Kendal and Ulverstone
COMMON CARRIER.

JOHN CLARKE,
of Haverthwaite, near Ulverstone,

BEGS LEAVE TO INFORM HIS FRIENDS AND THE PUBLICK IN GENERAL, THAT

HE HAS ESTABLISHED
a regular Conveyance for forwarding Goods betwixt
KENDAL AND ULVERSTONE,
BOOTLE, RAVENGLASS,
EGREMONT, WHITEHAVEN,
AND ALL THE INTERMEDIATE AND ADJACENT PLACES.

*** All Goods consigned to him, the Publick may depend will be delivered with the utmost Care and Dispatch.

Leaves the New Inn, *Kendal,* every Wednesday and Saturday at Noon, and arrives at *Haverthwaite* in the Evening; and is at the Brown Cow Inn, *Ulverstone,* every Monday and Thursday Morning, and returns to *Haverthwaite* the same day.

J. C. hopes, by his due Attention to Business, to merit a Share of Publick Support.

October 7th, 1811.

[Soulby, Printer, Ulverston.]

The carrier David Burrow with Spider his horse, on the road between Kendal and Sedbergh about 1930.

It is difficult to judge the number of carriers and places served, since the individual trade directories vary so much in what detail they give, and how complete they are. In 1794, for instance, the *Universal British Directory* shows 33 carriers from Kendal, including several long-distance waggons, serving up to 32 places.[76] In 1858 there are 60 carriers, all local, serving 44 places, and this after the arrival of both railway and canal. As late as 1925 some 31 carriers were serving 39 places, but there seems to be much omission. It seems as though there is little evidence for decline until the need began to be met between the wars by relatively reliable and inexpensive motor vehicles. Competition from the railways meant that many of the later carriers ran shorter routes from railheads, or carried specialised goods to local firms, and the longer routes gradually fell out of use.

The 'last carrier out of Kendal' is said to have been David Burrow, who worked for thirty years (1910–40) between Sedbergh and Kendal, significantly a route across country with no railway competition. He was photographed on his way to Kendal in 1930 with his horse 'Spider' and spring cart. Burrow had bought the business in 1910 from Kit Metcalfe. He travelled three days a week, on Tuesdays, Thursdays and Saturdays, starting at 6 a.m., taking four hours, collecting en route, and returning about 6 p.m. He also carried specialised goods to and from Farfield Mill just beyond Sedbergh.[77]

Railways

Kendal has been unfortunate in its geographical position on at least three occasions. The first was in Roman times, when it was added only as an afterthought to the network of forts and roads guarding the southern Lake District, which had far-reaching effects for the future. The second was when the main railway line to the north bypassed it in 1846, leaving the town on no more than a branch line to Windermere, with the mainline junction station at Oxenholme. The third was when the M6 motorway bypassed it to the east, leaving the town initially clogged with Windermere traffic until the Kendal Bypass was built. At least the component of traffic headed for Shap and Carlisle was removed.

The principal railway line was the Lancaster & Carlisle, which opened late in 1846, carrying the main west-coast route through to Scotland. It ran east of the town and up through the

Ticket for the opening of the Kendal & Windermere Railway in 1847. The image of the train is a stock one held by the printer, although the locomotive is about right for its date.

NATIONAL RAILWAY MUSEUM / SCIENCE & SOCIETY PICTURE LIBRARY

Lune Gorge, with a station at Oxenholme, one and a half miles south-east of Kendal. The route of the main line had been the subject of extensive debate, and several proposals for different alignments had been put forward. The first proposal was for a line up the Lune valley from Lancaster, the railhead from 1840 until 1846, missing out Kendal altogether. The Kendal lobby, conscious of the potential financial benefits of a main line, put forward another route, by way of Kendal, Long Sleddale, a tunnel under the Gatesgarth Pass to Mardale, and thence to Penrith. A third option, canvassed by the great George Stephenson, was to avoid the uplands altogether by crossing Morecambe Bay on a great embankment, and then threading the Cumbrian coast to Carlisle.

The last option was ruled out because it was thirty miles longer; and the Long Sleddale option because of the immense cost of the huge engineering works. Even if it had been chosen, and despite the desire of the Kendal lobby for a station in the town, the topography meant that it would not have been feasible to bring the line down to the valley floor—a station at or near its present site in Oxenholme would have been required even by this scheme. In 1843 the Lancaster Canal Company offered £50,000 to the 'Caledonian Railway', that is the Lancaster & Carlisle, to follow the Lune and omit Kendal. At this time the company controlled the Lancaster & Preston Junction railway and sought to avoid any railway competition with its route to Kendal. The Lune Gorge route, heading north from Lancaster, close to Kendal and then climbing to Tebay and Shap, was eventually chosen.

From this main line at Oxenholme a branch was built to Windermere, with stations at Kendal, Burneside, Staveley and Windermere. This served the many passengers who wished to come to the Lake District by train but also, unlike most other railway lines, carried a distinctive coterie of wealthy industrialists, who lived on the shores of Windermere, to their businesses in Manchester, Bradford and elsewhere. The naming of Windermere is an example of railway sleight of hand. A stranger might expect to arrive on the shores of the lake of that name, rather than a mile and a half away and 250 feet higher. The main settlement on the lake was Bowness, where the ancient parish church stands. Windermere station (actually in Birthwaite) for a time stood alone, apart from a railway hotel.[78]

It is a great irony that William Wordsworth, by then an old man, vehemently opposed the building of this railway, sending a stream of letters to the press in 1844. Had he lived a century or so later he would undoubtedly have been one of those intent on saving the line from closure. The two letters to the *Morning Post* were published by R. Branthwaite & Son of Kendal in 1844, with a sonnet which begins:

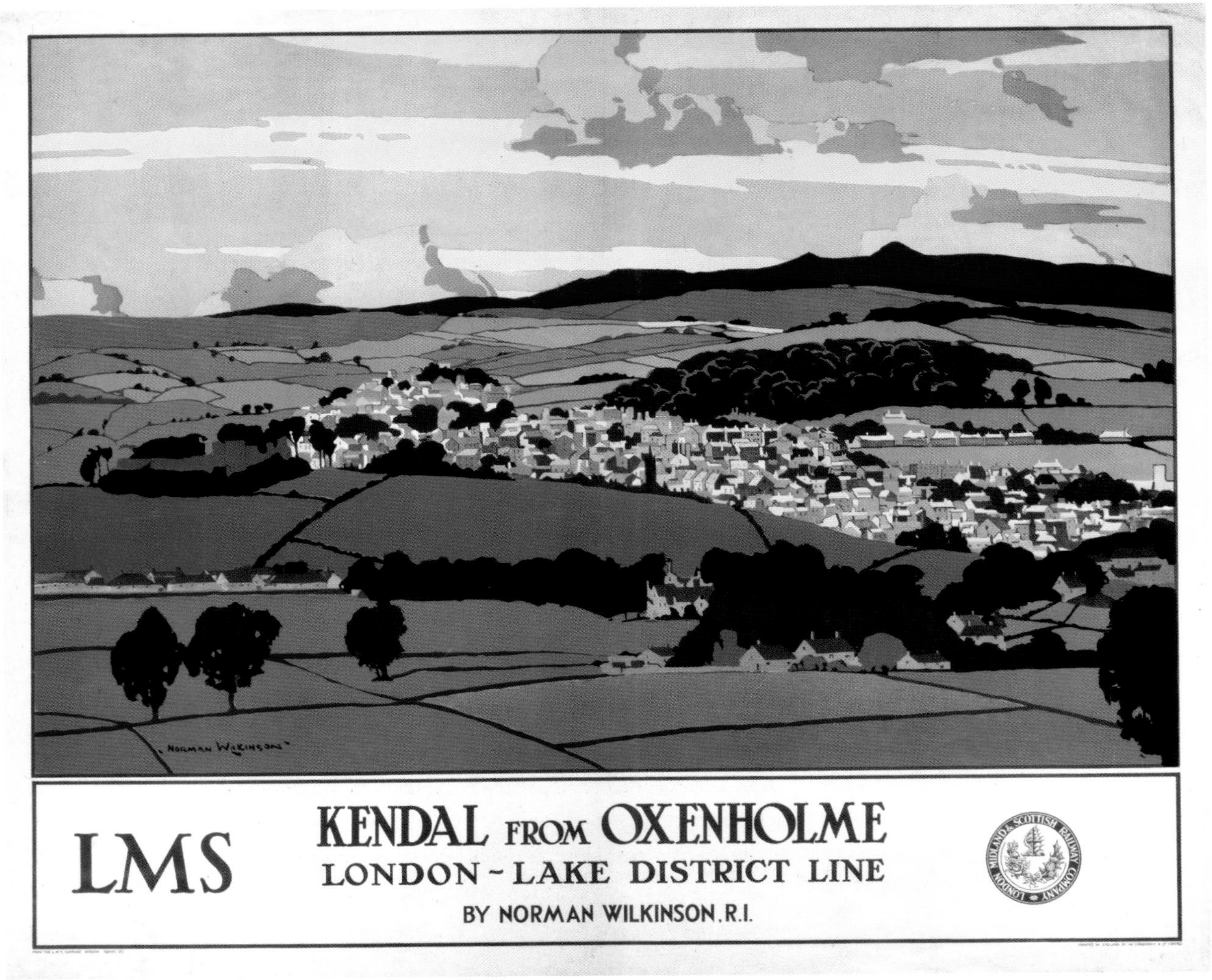

Kendal from Oxenholme, a railway poster for the LMS designed by Norman Wilkinson in the 1920s..

NATIONAL RAILWAY MUSEUM / SCIENCE & SOCIETY PICTURE LIBRARY

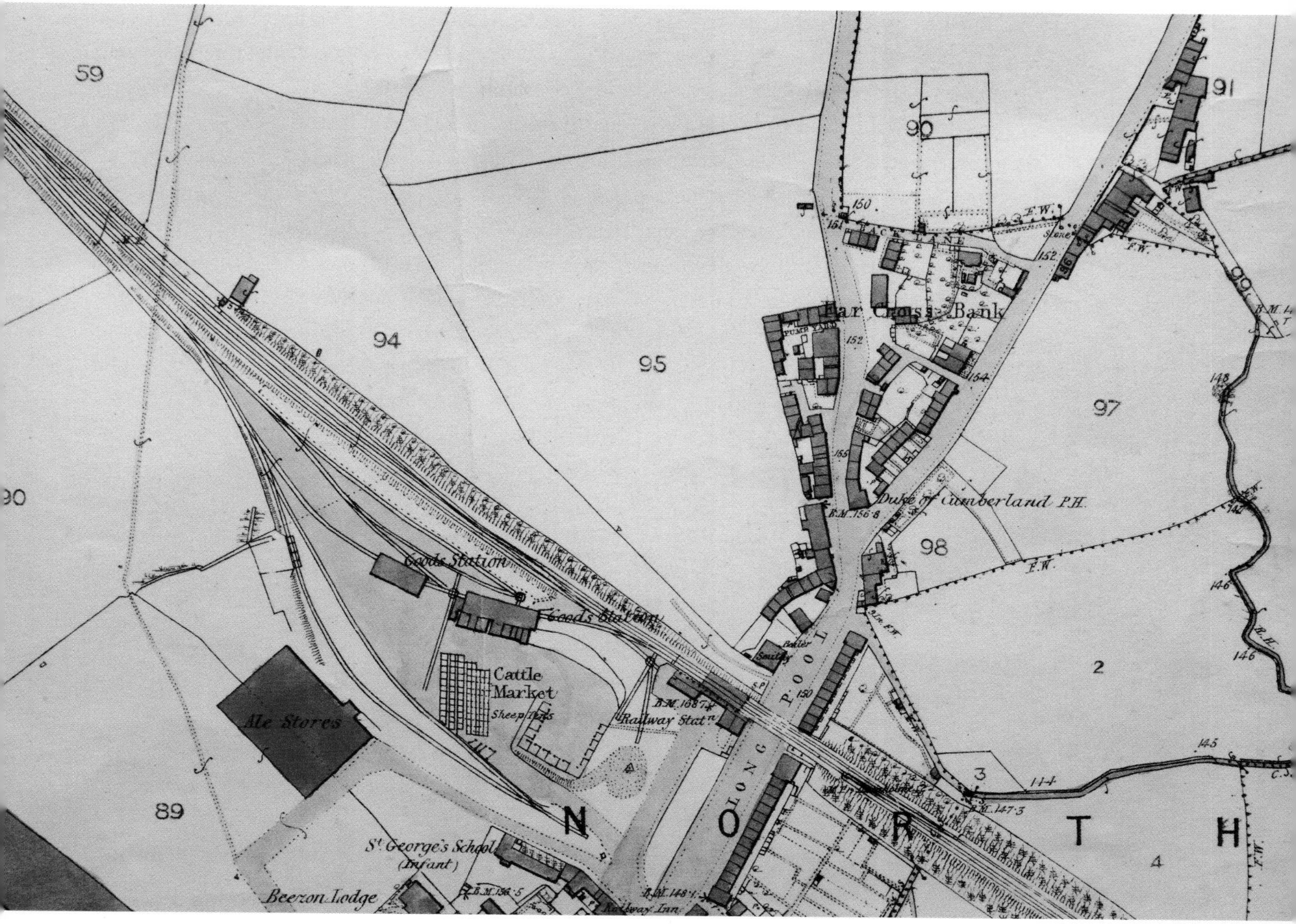

Railway passenger and goods stations at Kendal, from the large-scale Ordnance Survey map of 1861.

PHOTOGRAPH CARNEGIE, FROM AN ORIGINAL HELD AT WESTMORLAND RECORD OFFICE, KENDAL

Is then no nook of English ground secure
From rash assault? Schemes of retirement sown
In youth, and 'mid the busy world kept pure
As when their earliest flowers of hope were blown,
Must perish.

The first letter argues that 'Summer TOURISTS (and the very word precludes the notion of a railway) it has in abundance,' so that 'Surely that good is not to be obtained by transferring at once uneducated persons in large bodies to particular spots.' We can ridicule his views as being merely the reactionary sentiments of an old man (which they were), but a glance at Windermere or Bowness at a busy holiday period would quickly convince one of the essential correctness of his vision. The Lake District would never be the same place again.[79]

Notwithstanding such opposition, the railway was authorised by Parliament in June 1845 and was opened in stages as the work progressed. The section from Oxenholme to Kendal, coinciding with the completion of the southern section of the Lancaster & Carlisle, was opened to the public on 22 September 1846. Kendal now had a railway connection to London, and the canal company took the opportunity of discontinuing its fast packet boats in the face of the new competition. The remainder of the line to Windermere was opened on 20 April 1847.

The line was leased to the Lancaster & Carlisle in 1858 and both railways were leased in turn to the London and North Western Railway in the following year. Twenty years later the Kendal & Windermere Railway Company was formally dissolved and absorbed within the LNWR. In 1881 Oxenholme Station was rebuilt and three years later Kendal Station was enlarged by the provision of an 'up' platform. In 1895 Windermere froze over, and special excursion tickets were available 'as long as the frost shall last'. Another occasion in the early 1930s when this happened is captured for ever in Arthur Ransome's *Winter Holiday*. In 1905 the 'Club' train was added to the timetable, providing luxurious travel for captains of industry between Windermere and Manchester and surviving, astonishingly, until 1966. From the mid-1960s, although it escaped the Beeching Axe (despite being originally included in plans for closure), the branch was drastically reduced in status. It was single-tracked, and new stations with minimal facilities were built at Windermere and Kendal in 1986 and 1991, the former station at Windermere being sold to Booth's supermarket.[80] But it survived, which is in itself an achievement, and since the late 1990s has undergone something of a

The assembled buses and drivers of the Kendal Motor Bus Company in the late 1920s. The company was begun by a group of ex-servicemen.

BY COURTESY OF KENDAL TOWN COUNCIL

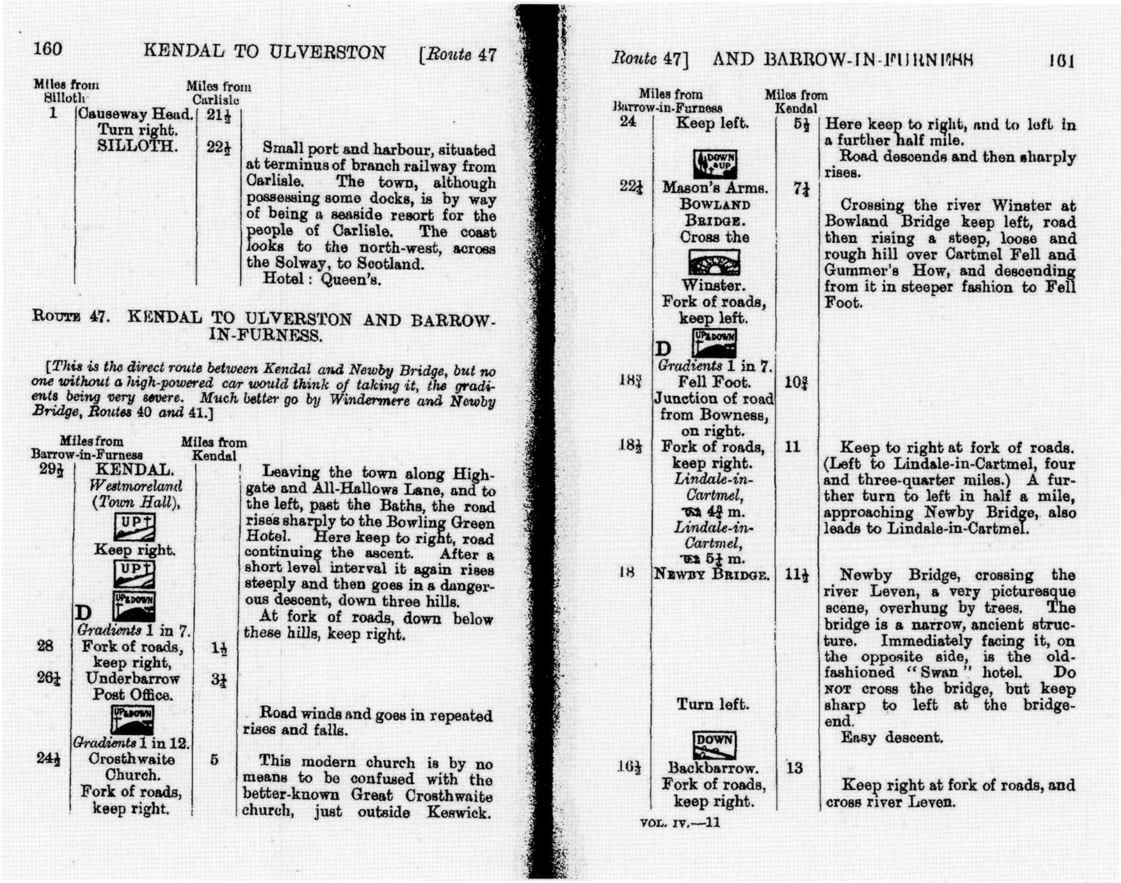

160 KENDAL TO ULVERSTON [*Route* 47

Miles from Silloth		Miles from Carlisle	
1	Causeway Head. Turn right.	21½	
	SILLOTH.	22½	Small port and harbour, situated at terminus of branch railway from Carlisle. The town, although possessing some docks, is by way of being a seaside resort for the people of Carlisle. The coast looks to the north-west, across the Solway, to Scotland. Hotel: Queen's.

ROUTE 47. KENDAL TO ULVERSTON AND BARROW-IN-FURNESS.

[*This is the direct route between Kendal and Newby Bridge, but no one without a high-powered car would think of taking it, the gradients being very severe. Much better go by Windermere and Newby Bridge, Routes* 40 *and* 41.]

Miles from Barrow-in-Furness		Miles from Kendal	
29½	KENDAL. *Westmoreland* (*Town Hall*), UP. Keep right. UP. UP&DOWN. D *Gradients* 1 in 7.		Leaving the town along Highgate and All-Hallows Lane, and to the left, past the Baths, the road rises sharply to the Bowling Green Hotel. Here keep to right, road continuing the ascent. After a short level interval it again rises steeply and then goes in a dangerous descent, down three hills. At fork of roads, down below these hills, keep right.
28	Fork of roads, keep right,	1½	
26½	Underbarrow Post Office. UP&DOWN. *Gradients* 1 in 12.	3½	Road winds and goes in repeated rises and falls.
24½	Crosthwaite Church. Fork of roads, keep right.	5	This modern church is by no means to be confused with the better-known Great Crosthwaite church, just outside Keswick.

Route 47] AND BARROW-IN-FURNESS 161

Miles from Barrow-in-Furness		Miles from Kendal	
24	Keep left. DOWN & UP.	5½	Here keep to right, and to left in a further half mile. Road descends and then sharply rises.
22½	Mason's Arms. BOWLAND BRIDGE. Cross the Winster. Fork of roads, keep left. UP&DOWN. D *Gradients* 1 in 7.	7½	Crossing the river Winster at Bowland Bridge keep left, road then rising a steep, loose and rough hill over Cartmel Fell and Gummer's How, and descending from it in steeper fashion to Fell Foot.
18¾	Fell Foot. Junction of road from Bowness, on right.	10¾	
18½	Fork of roads, keep right. *Lindale-in-Cartmel*, 4¾ m. *Lindale-in-Cartmel*, 5¼ m.	11	Keep to right at fork of roads. (Left to Lindale-in-Cartmel, four and three-quarter miles.) A further turn to left in half a mile, approaching Newby Bridge, also leads to Lindale-in-Cartmel.
18	NEWBY BRIDGE. Turn left. DOWN.	11½	Newby Bridge, crossing the river Leven, a very picturesque scene, overhung by trees. The bridge is a narrow, ancient structure. Immediately facing it, on the opposite side, is the old-fashioned "Swan" hotel. Do NOT cross the bridge, but keep sharp to left at the bridge-end. Easy descent.
16½	Backbarrow. Fork of roads, keep right.	13	Keep right at fork of roads, and cross river Leven.

VOL. IV.—11

The road from Kendal to Barrow-in-Furness from the Autocar Road Book of 1913. As one might expect in the early days of motoring, there is great emphasis on gradients, bends and road surfacing.

renaissance, with regular through trains to Manchester Airport, and the possibility that it may eventually be electrified.

The railway brought with it another crossing of the river Kent, near Dockray Hall Mill, and a nucleus of businesses close to the station and dependent upon the freight services provided. The 1914 Ordnance Survey 25-inch map shows in detail the layout of Kendal station, including the separate goods station, timber and coal yards, cattle pens, ale and wool stores, and a bonded warehouse, all reminders of the indirect economic benefits that a railway could bring with it.

M6 and Kendal Bypass

In the 1930s there was increasing pressure upon the government to plan and build a network of new high-speed roads, as the Germans were doing with their autobahn network. A major lobbying force was Lancashire County Council, which recognised the problems that poor road communications created for economic recovery. Just before the Second World War the government accepted in principle the idea of a motorway network, and after the war, in 1949, a formal plan was drawn up, to which Lancashire's highway engineer, Sir James Drake, made a major contribution. The plan envisaged, among others, a trunk motorway from London, via the West Midlands and south Lancashire, to the Scottish border at Carlisle.

Work on this, the M6, began in 1955 and the first section (Britain's first motorway) was opened in 1958, bypassing Preston. This was followed by the Lancaster bypass section (1960), and by 1965 there was continuous motorway from London to Carnforth. Work on the challenging northward extension began in 1967, and in 1970 the M6 was opened to Penrith and Carlisle. This section was highly sensitive because it passed through important and beautiful landscapes. There was talk of putting sections of the road in tunnels, but that option was never part of serious government thinking. Eventually the road wove its way through the Lune Gorge, its visual impact being much reduced by vertical separation of the carriageways, terracing them into the very steep hillside—that was in any case essential, as there was not enough flat ground on which to build a full-width motorway. This route has been a great success in landscape terms, and lessons learned here were put to use elsewhere.[81]

In a strange parallel to the railway situation of over a century before, Kendal was too far from the route of the new motorway to gain all the benefits immediately, although the motorway had a blessed effect on the town by taking out the traffic heading north over Shap. Can anybody who experienced them ever forget the awfulness of the permanent traffic jams on all the towns along the road, and the endless processions of lorries crawling up the A6 past the Jungle Café and over Shap summit? Suddenly the A6 was almost deserted, although after perhaps five years or so traffic began to creep back. The M6 had no effect on the traffic heading for Windermere, and initially Kendal retained its congestion, but the Kendal bypass, opened soon after, was an integral part of the same overall strategy. It was intended to channel the holiday and commercial traffic from the M6 along a high-quality dual-carriageway and out towards Windermere. It opened in 1970, though apart from the short Staveley bypass none of the other 'improvements' originally proposed, such as bypasses at Windermere and Ambleside, has ever materialised. The new bypass had a salutary effect, since most through traffic could now avoid Kendal to east or west.

Again, for a few years Kendal seemed almost deserted by traffic, but the extraordinary growth in car use since 1970 means that the period between road improvement and a return of congestion seems to shorten inexorably. By the mid-1990s the town's roads were again subject to regular gridlock. More recent changes have therefore taken place, with the creation of a one-way system and, most recently, a block to northbound traffic so that for the first time Kendal's distinctive spine, from Kirkland via Highgate to Stricklandgate, is not a through road—except for happy pedestrians!

Health and welfare | 9

EVIDENCE of care for the poor and sick in Kendal goes back to the Middle Ages. Neither operated in the way we would recognise today, but the needs of at least some of the people received attention, although the overall level of poverty and deprivation would undoubtedly seem shocking to us.

The earliest hospital in Kendal was the leper hospital of St Leonard at Scalthwaiterigg, apparently founded in the time of William de Lancaster III, in the second quarter of the thirteenth century.[1] As a matter of deliberate policy it was sited outside the town, for leprosy was much feared and thought to be contagious. To contemporaries the only solution to this frightening condition was isolation, to protect the healthy from infection—though we now know that it is not seriously contagious and about 95 per cent of the population have natural immunity to the disease. Like most medieval hospitals the leper hospital was not concerned with cures, for medical treatment of leprosy was not possible until the twentieth century. The best that an inmate could expect was regular food, warmth and shelter, all of which were in short supply in the world outside, and particularly so for anyone with a sickness or disability. Its position on a main road was not fortuitous either, for the hospital no doubt benefited from the alms of travellers on the Appleby road, who shuddered, contributed and passed on. In 1310 it was noted as having a master, in the gift of William de Ros, with two chaplains and four lepers dwelling there.[2] This seems to have been its full complement.

Leper hospitals flourished in the early Middle Ages when leprosy, which at one time was thought to have been brought back from the Holy Land by returning Crusaders, seemed to represent a serious threat. In fact the disease existed even in Roman Britain and was probably endemic. In the later fourteenth century, however, the disease seems to have started to disappear from this country, by mechanisms as yet unknown, and before long hospitals that had provided for lepers began to take in the poor or old people instead (or, too often, the able-bodied friends and clients of local landowners). They enjoyed a reasonable level of comfort and diet in these circumstances, but the charitable foundations were wide open to misuse and abuse, and their revenues and property were jealously watched by those who would willingly snatch some part.[3]

In the case of Kendal's Hospital of St Leonard, the advowson (the right to appoint the priest) was transferred to Conishead Priory in 1246, and thereafter it was held to be in a

Spital Farm, on the raod from Kendal to Appleby, site of a medieval leper hospital.

loose way subordinate to the mother house. The hospital managed to survive the dissolution of Conishead in 1537, but nine years later fell victim to the dissolution of chantries in 1545–46. In 1548 or 1549 the newly dissolved hospital was bought by Alan Wilson and Alan Bellingham.[4] Its value was small, two alternative figures putting it at £6 4*s*. 3*d*. in 1535 and £11 10*s*. 3*d*. in 1545–46. Apart from private rooms and a common hall of some sort, the hospital had a chapel, probably houses for the master and priest, and a watermill that provided income towards its upkeep. The site is marked today by the substantial farm called Spital (meaning 'hospital') on the Appleby road, now just outside the built-up area. In 1836 a number of rather haphazardly arranged burials was found there, but despite Nicholson's view that these may have been victims of the Pilgrimage of Grace of 1536–37 it seems much more likely that they were the burials of inmates.[5] It was no doubt difficult to find anyone to bury a leper, because of the irrational fear the disease engendered.

Benefactions

Among the many benefactions left by Kendal people, most were for education or the care of the old. Sometimes these schemes came together, as at the Sandes Hospital where a school was combined with accommodation for poor widows. It is hard for us today to appreciate how easy it was in times past to fall from sufficiency and respectability, and how hard to recover from such an event. Some people of course started with all the disadvantages of poverty, while others came to it through accidental processes. Old age, chronic illness or the death of the family breadwinner could all be causes. Later on we shall see how harshly the Poor Law treated such people. Widows were least able to recoup their position, so it was to them, and unmarried old women (the 'old maids') that a great deal of the charity was directed.

There were private charities, such as those that supported the three sets of almshouses in Kendal, and later there was also the Poor Law, which provided a basic level of support from a levy on the ratepayers, first as 'outdoor relief', allowing people to stay in their homes, and then after 1834 in the dreaded workhouse. It was never popular with those who had to pay, and that unpopularity grew in hard years, when bread prices were high and casual employment hard to find, with a consequent rise in the number of claimants. While the Poor Law which existed from 1601 onwards was relatively flexible and pragmatic, and could allow a degree of humanity and benevolence, there was a growing pressure to create a system with a philosophy of making the charity as cold as possible, thereby rendering it deeply unattractive to potential claimants. This was particularly enshrined in the Poor Law Amendment Act, which was passed in 1834. In Kendal, from 1767 onwards, the Kendal Fell Trustees (whom we met in chapter 2) administered the local Poor Law and maintained the workhouse.

What is notable about the private charities that supported almshouses is the quality and quantity of accommodation provided, compared with that of people who rented or owned their property. For instance, each of the inmates of Dowker's Almshouses had three rooms, while those at Sleddall's had four each. In both cases the density of occupation was much less than usual, with no more than two people in each unit in the first, and no more than three in the second. Sandes Hospital may have provided less space originally, but its accommodation was rebuilt to a more generous scale in 1852, with a large and a small room for each inmate, plus a shared porch and other facilities. Of course, these catered for a tiny proportion of the elderly poor, and should not be seen as typical of overall conditions.

Sandes Hospital

The oldest almshouses in Kendal are those in Highgate, established in 1670 by Thomas Sandes, a successful merchant in Kendal Cottons, and known as 'Sandes Hospital'. (Sandes himself lived at a house now known as Grandy Nook, then on the western edge of the town, which still retains his datestone upon the rear wing.) A long building with an entrance on the frontage forms a gatehouse to the hospital, with the date 1659 and the initials of Sandes and

Sandes Hospital in Highgate, founded by Thomas Sandes in 1670.

his wife Katherine (T. K/S) and the arms of the Shearmen Dyers Company over the door. This has been altered since Thomas Machell saw and drew it in the late seventeenth century.[6] The gatehouse served as lodging for the schoolmaster, with a schoolroom and library in a chamber over. There is an almost-contemporary description of this foundation by Sir Daniel Fleming in 1671:

> and that of Mr. Thomas Sands (yet living in this town), is the most considerable, for he hath lately upon his own charge built a large house, wherein eight antient widows, skilled in wool work, have each of them a convenient lodging-room, and a room for work, and 4 marks a year in money towards their relief. There is also a room for a school-master to read prayers to them, and to teach the poor children of the town … and lastly, there is a large room for a library.[7]

The Hospital housed eight poor widows, selected from each of the main streets of Kendal and a couple of its out-townships, and also accommodated the Blue-Coat School for poor children, both girls and boys. The original layout had a quadrangle accessed through the gatehouse, with the widows' cottages in two rows, one on each side. The 1841 census listed the schoolmaster, James Whitaker, and his young family, as well as eight women aged between 60 and 80, and a variety of daughters and grandchildren, a total of nineteen people including the Whitaker family.

Today, behind the gatehouse on the northerly side, is a row of eight single-storey cottages erected in 1852 for the poor widows, set in two groups of four and divided by a taller library building. The library had formed a part of the original charitable endowment. In 1861,[8] after the almshouses were rebuilt, the houses were occupied by:

Arms of the Shearmen Dyers Company over the door of Sandes Hospital.

The rebuilt rear of Sandes Hospital with library and cottages.

Agnes Gibson	78	born Kendal
and her daughter		
Hannah Atkinson	70	born Christchurch, Hampshire
and her daughter		
Ann Watson	68	born Kendal
Elizabeth Chamley	71	born Penrith, Cumberland
and her daughter		
Agnes Story	67	born Farleton
and her grand-daughter		
Ann Gibson	73	born Kendal
Ann Ridley	71	born Old Hutton
and her daughter		
Hannah Dawson	79	born Thursby, Cumberland
and her daughter		

In 1861 the schoolmaster James Whitaker was still living there, with his wife and six children. The school endowment was merged with the Kendal Grammar School in 1886 and since 1980 has formed part of Kirkbie-Kendal School, although the building itself has long since ceased to be used for the purpose. In the entrance passage is a stone alms-box reading 'REMEMBER THE POORE' at the top in raised lettering of the seventeenth century and below it 'Remember the Poor Widows' in a later script.

Almsbox at Sandes Hospital.

Dowker's Almshouses

Dowker's, or 'the Old Maids' Hospital', was endowed by Miss Dorothy Dowker with over £3,000 when she died in 1831 aged 82. She was the last surviving child of James Dowker Esq., and given her rank and single status a charity for poor single women would have been considered most appropriate at that time. The hospital subsequently received a further bequest of £1,000 from a Miss Maria Wilson in 1839 and another £1,097 on her death in 1863. The buildings themselves cost £400 and stood at the very bottom of Highgate on its east side, just a little to the north of the Blind Beck. They were demolished in the 1950s to make Dowker's Lane, with access to backland in the area. The foundation was for six women 'of good and chaste character' over the age of fifty and unmarried.[9] A detailed plan of the buildings is provided by the 1861 Ordnance Survey 1:500 scale map, which shows that there were two houses on the street frontage in a gothick style, backing on to two more, with two further houses a little way up the yard. In 1891 the following were in residence:[10]

left Dowker's Almshouses in Highgate, now demolished.

right Inmates of Dowker's Almshouses.

BY COURTESY OF KENDAL TOWN COUNCIL

Elizabeth Newby	s	62		born Westmorland, Kendal
Dorothy Oddy	s	81		born Westmorland, Kendal
Sarah Ridley	s	67	Retired nurse	born Westmorland, Kendal
Mary Ridley (sister)	s	80		born Lancashire, Liverpool
Isabella Bateman	s	78		born Westmorland, Kendal
Dinah Thompson	s	64	Living on her own means	born Westmorland, Kendal
Fanny Braithwaite	s	68		born Westmorland, Kendal

[In this table s stands for 'single']

Sleddall's Almshouses

On the east bank of the Kent in Aynam Road stands an impressive memorial to Victorian philanthropy, the Sleddall Almshouses or, to give them their full title, the 'Sleddall Victoria Jubilee Almshouses'. In 1887 John Sleddall built a row of twelve substantial gabled stone cottages, in pairs, with barge-boarded porches, with its own chapel, converted into two further houses in 1986. The buildings cost £4,250 and Sleddall also gave a generous endowment to the scheme. The architect of the buildings was E. Cox.[11] William was a successful wine and spirit merchant and claimed as an ancestor Thomas Sleddal, first Mayor of Kendal in 1636. Other Sleddalls had provided such things as the Green Coat School and a Bible Charity. John Sleddall and his brother William (another wine-merchant) were born at Hutton-in-the-Hay and both seem to have remained unmarried. In his latter days John is described as 'landed proprietor'. It was not uncommon for unmarried or childless people at that time to leave large sums to charitable purposes. Unlike the two other sets of almshouses these ones catered for men as well as women. In 1901 the following were in residence:[12]

1	Elizabeth Johnson (widow)	57	Inmate of almshouse	b. Burton & Holme
2	Jane Thompson (widow)	74	Inmate of almshouse	b. Kendal
	Sarah Airey (widow) (visitor)	50	Domestic housekeeper	b. Grayrigg
3	George Hodgson	63	Inmate of almshouse	b. Kirkby Lonsdale
	Annie Maria (daughter)	32	Housekeeper	b. Kendal
4	John Hayes	76	Inmate of almshouse	b. Lambrigg
	Mary (wife)	67		b. Newchurch, Lancs
5	Thomas Heap	79	Retired tailor/ I of almshouse.	b. Kendal
	Betsy (wife)	77		b. Scalthwaitrigg
	Charles (son)	54	Tailor	b. Kendal
6	George Jennings (widower)	83	Inmate of almshouse	b. Kendal
	Jane (daughter)	55	Housemaid domestic	b. Kendal
	Elizabeth (daughter)	42	Housekeeper for father	b. Kendal
7	Colin McLiesh	78	Inmate of almshouse	b. Scotland

left
Plaque on the wall of Sleddall's Almshouses.

right
Sleddall's Almshouses and former chapel.

	Isabella (wife)	76		b. Scotland
8	Thomas Stables	80	Retired carpenter & joiner/inmate of almshouse	b. Kendal
9	William Paine	73	Retired carpenter/ Inmate of almshouse	b. Burton Overy, Leics
	Mary (wife)	71		b. Midgeley, Yorks
10	James Capstick	72	Retired railway lab./ Inmate of almshouse	b.Killington
	Matild (wife)	68	Seamstress, shirt	b. Sawrey, Lancs
11	Margaret Dodgson (widow)	80	Inmate of almshouse	b. Shap
	Ann Kilner (widow)	70	Domestic nurse	b. Cockermouth
12	Jane Cowherd (widow)	64	Inmate of almshouse	b. Farleton, Lancs

Childbirth

A midwife was indispensable to the health of the community in the early modern period. Unusually the diary of Mrs Elizabeth Thompson of Kendal, midwife, covering the period 1669–75 has survived.[13] It is particularly valuable in that it covers a period when the parish records are missing. The diary is very basic, naming only the child, the father (and sometimes his occupation), the time of birth, and the area or house of the family, but it does give an authentic flavour of the period. Mrs Thompson was reasonably prosperous—the probate inventory made at her death in 1675 shows a house with six rooms including a little parlour, a high parlour and a new parlour, as well as a cellar, lofts and stable, and goods to the value of £156. She belonged to the age when the management of childbirth had not yet been taken

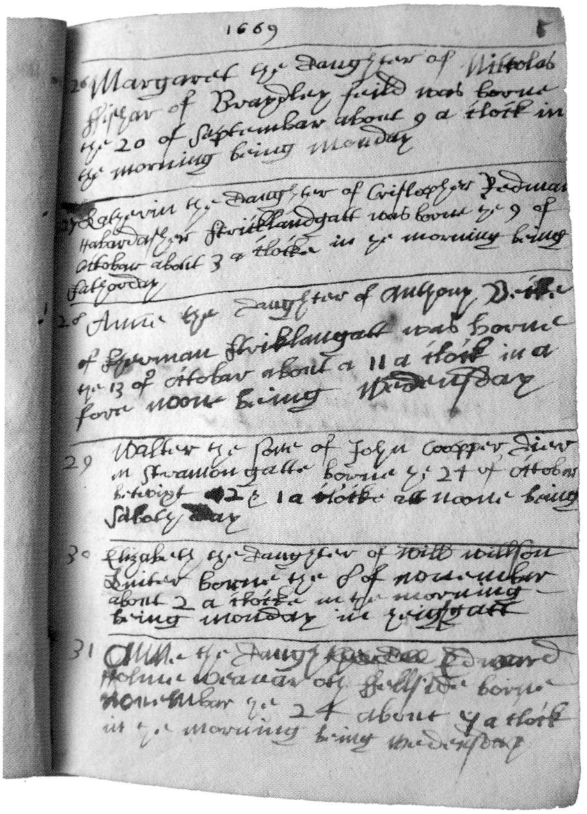

left
Certificate in midwifery issued to William Coward, surgeon, in 1781.

right
Pages from the midwifery notebook of Elizabeth Thompson, dated 1669.

over by the male-dominated medical profession, and her diary may have been kept lest she needed to clear herself or provide proof of what had happened and when. Sadly, it does not tell us the fate of the children whose birth she attended, but quite a few appear without names, as though stillborn or not expected to live, and other records come to our aid to show that they did not survive.

The 1767 return of papists records two Catholic midwives, Widow Russell aged 60 and Mrs Yapes aged 80. The latter had been in Kendal about forty years, so her working life perhaps went back to the 1720s. They both lived in Highgate. Whether they only served the Catholics or the population at large remains unrecorded.[14]

By the eighteenth century there was growing pressure to have midwifery included among the skills of a doctor, and a long battle ensued between the male and female practitioners. This resulted in a victory for the males, at least until the twentieth century. One man who trained in midwifery, by a course of lectures and actual experience, was William Coward of Kendal, whose certificate of 1781 survives in the record office.[15]

Concerns about public health

Until the nineteenth century the environment of Kendal was neither better nor worse than most small industrial towns of its kind. Its industries did not cause significant pollution; there was abundant fresh air; and the open country was only minutes away from most houses and places of work. But problems began to develop as a result of an increasing density of population, a direct result of the intensive building within the congested yards, and the deteriorating quality of water supply and sanitation. In that the geography of the town was a problem, for gravity and the various watercourses brought filth and rubbish downhill towards the river from the yards on the west side of Highgate and Stricklandgate, together with the effluent from the butchers' shambles. With no overall management of the problem, one person's answer became the next person's problem. Such conditions allowed the emergence and rapid spread of diseases, and those difficulties could not to be solved until mains water and proper sewerage systems were provided, and the reduction in the density of population in central area yards became possible.

It is easy to form the impression that Kendal was a terrible place to live in the nineteenth century, but in spite of clear and serious problems over water and drainage, which were by no means uncommon at that time, the town was clearly by no means the worst even in Cumbria, not least because it was of limited geographical extent, and the population was small. In the early 1840s the government established a Royal Commission to investigate the health of towns and this, together with a national panic over a major cholera epidemic in 1847, led to a crucial piece of legislation, the Public Health Act of 1848. The story of first fumblings and gathering of detailed evidence in Kendal is well seen in *Cleaning up Kendal: a century of sanitary history*, which contains the reports of Thomas Proudfoot in 1822, of George Clark in 1849 and of David Page in 1875, linking health (or its lack) with water supply, overcrowding, drainage and sewerage in the town.[16]

Doctors

The first medical man to appear in Kendal's records is Israel Walth or Walts, who is noted in the parish register in 1583. The first occasion was the christening of a son of 'Mr Israell Walth, surgener of Highgate in Kendall'. The use of the title 'Mr' shows that he was a man of some status. His name occurs twice again that year, on both occasions when someone died at his house in Stricklandgate, presumably during or as a result of surgery.[17] This might be bad news for a medical practitioner, not to mention the patient, but in the 1580s surgery was crude, with no knowledge of antisepsis, and only attempted on very serious conditions, so blame does not necessarily attach to him. The next record of a medical practitioner is over a hundred years later, in 1695; Anthony Askew, of Highgate, who appears in the list analysed in chapter 6. There were several successive generations of Askews, who retained the medical talent. Other names are recorded by gravestones in the parish church, such as John Archer, doctor of physick, who died 1735. In 1765 Dr James Ainslie, a Jedburgh man who had studied at Edinburgh, set up in practice in Kendal, living and working at Highgate House for many years. His portrait, with that of his wife Margaret, who died very soon after their arrival as a result of complications in childbirth, was painted by Romney.[18]

Until well into the nineteenth century, the role of surgeon was much less regarded than that of physician (to this day, indeed, surgeons are known as Mr, while physicians are Dr). The former carried out surgical procedures, while the latter used only medicine and non-interventional processes. One reason was the origin of surgeons among the barber-surgeons, whose principal medical activity was the letting of blood. In Kendal the 'Twelve Severall Companies' listed in 1578 include 'Surgons, Scryveners, Barbors, Glovers, Skynners, Parchement and Poyntemakers'. This was perhaps as miscellaneous a group as one could hope to find. The company could choose two wardens each year, one of whom had to be a glover, suggesting that they were in a majority in the company.[19] Training for surgeons and physicians was quite basic: they qualified either by attendance at one of the recognised universities, such as Edinburgh, or by a form of apprenticeship to an established doctor, or by a combination of the two. The result was a very variable set of standards and procedures.

Another group associated with medicine was that of the apothecaries, later chemists. The three groups had long had an uneasy relationship over status, function and training. All were of course in private practice, and so were essentially orientated towards paying patients. Only with the appearance of the dispensaries, and later of the hospitals, was medicine available to a wider public, but on a far more limited scale than that provided after 1948 and the advent of the National Health Service. Poorer people often did without, unless they could find a 'respectable' sponsor who could get them into the dispensary, or else they went to one of the many quacks who peddled dubious or even dangerous remedies. One of these was undoubtedly the famous 'Kendal Black Drop', an opium-based preparation which we have already encountered in chapter 7. However, in many places some basic forms of medical care were usually available to the poor under arrangements and contracts between the overseers of the poor and medical practitioners.

One Kendal surgeon of whom quite a lot is known was one James Towers, for the unfortunate reason that he shot his wife in December 1821 while in a fit of insanity, or possibly *delirium tremens*. The defence of insanity saved him from execution for murder. He had practised in Kendal since leaving Edinburgh University in about 1808, and had taken at least three apprentices.[20] Several of his colleagues lived nearby and attended the tragedy, including Dr Thomas Proudfoot, the only one of the eighteenth- and nineteenth-century physicians in the town who attained the formal status of MD. A pompous and somewhat self-satisfied man, who clearly thought more highly of his own attainments than others did, he nevertheless understood the place of environment in the study of disease, as can be seen from his analysis of the town's medical geography in his study 'Topographical Pathology of Kendal and its Neighbourhood' of 1822.[21]

Doctors and other medical men listed in eighteenth- and nineteenth-century directories

Universal British Directory, 1790

Brookbank, John	Chymist & druggist
Claxton, John	Surgeon
Coward, William	Surgeon
Fell & Gaugh	Surgeons
Kitching, Thomas	Surgeon
Mason, George	Surgeon
Newton, —	Surgeon
Smith, John	Surgeon
Tatham, Edmund	Surgeon
Tobey, John	Master of the Dispensary

Holden, 1805

Claxton, John	surgeon	Branthwaite Brow
Harrison, Thomas	surgeon	Stramongate
Tatham, Edmund	surgeon	Highgate

Parson & White, 1829

Cragg, Robert	surgeon	Highgate
Forrest, George	surgeon	Stramongate
Gawthorp, Matt.	surgeon	Dispensary, Lowther St
Harrison, Thomas	surgeon	Bridge St
Holden, James Fawcett	surgeon	Highgate
Longmire, William	surgeon	Highgate
Noble, James	surgeon	Stricklandgate
Proudfoot, Thomas MD	surgeon	Highgate
Tatham, Edmund & Son	surgeon	Stramongate

Pigot & Co., 1834

Baird, James Watson	Physician	Highgate
Harrison, Thomas	Physician	Aynam Lodge
Proudfoot, Thomas	Physician	Lowther St
Atkinson, Thomas	Surgeon	Highgate
Forrest, George	Surgeon	Highgate
Gawthorp, Matt	Surgeon	Highgate
Harrison, Thomas (jun.)	Surgeon	Aynam Cottage
Kay, John C	Surgeon	Dispensary, Lowther St
Longmire, William	Surgeon	Finkle St
Noble, James	Surgeon	Stricklandgate
Read, William Miles	Surgeon	Staveley
Singleton, William	Surgeon	Highgate
Tatham, Edmond	Surgeon	Stramongate

The Dispensary and hospitals

Kendal's first formal medical institution was the Dispensary, operating between 1783 and 1848, when it failed through lack of funds. It was situated in Lowther Street, at one time known as New Street. In the third quarter of the eighteenth century the idea of dispensaries, which were intended to provide medical care to the poor and operated on a charitable basis, became popular nationally. In Kendal and Lancaster dispensaries were opened in 1783, these being among the first in the North West. Prosperous individuals could subscribe sums of money for the upkeep of the dispensary, and in return were allocated tickets which they could hand out to what they perceived to be deserving cases. These individuals would then receive the ministrations of a doctor, who was attached to the dispensary as well as pursuing private practice. The Kendal Dispensary was open between 10 and 12 each morning, and again between 6 and 7 in the evening in the days of Dr Gawthorp in the 1820s and 1830s.[22] It consisted of a waiting room, a consulting room, and a place for making up the medicines. Apart from the numbers of people who attended, and this was the only source of medical help available to the poor, it must have recognisably resembled a modern GP's surgery. Like most dispensaries this also had a small hospital for fever cases.

The Dispensary was followed by Kendal Memorial Hospital (1870–1908) which stood in Captain French Lane. It was founded by James Cropper, proprietor of the Burneside paper mills, in memory of his wife, Fanny. In 1908 this in turn was replaced by Westmorland County Hospital, a substantial building on the north side of Captain French Lane,[23] built by public

Westmorland County Hospital, built in 1908 on the north side of Captain French Lane.

BY COURTESY OF KENDAL TOWN COUNCIL

subscription to extend the work of the older institution. It was taken over by the National Health Service in 1948, until which event it had been entirely dependent on public subscriptions and gifts. This in turn stood until 1991 when the new Westmorland General Hospital was built on an entirely new site to the south of the town on Burton Road.[24] This hospital now forms part of a larger Trust with hospitals and facilities at Kendal, Barrow in Furness and Lancaster.

In recent years the removal of certain services from this hospital, such as Accident & Emergency or the Cardiac Unit, to the other hospitals of the trust has produced robust opposition. It serves to emphasise the national tendency for services, and decision-making, to migrate elsewhere and to be centralised in larger cities. A recent decision on ambulance services for Kendal betrayed an appalling lack of understanding about the local traffic issues, particularly the time taken for an ambulance to reach hospital from the furthest limit of its catchment area, especially when the situation is exacerbated by tourist traffic.

The poor

Over the centuries provision for the poor took many forms. While many believed it was their Christian duty to support the old, sick or poor, particularly in cold winters or at times of bad harvests, there were limits to generosity. There was always a lurking suspicion that among those claiming support were strangers from elsewhere, or those who ought to be supported by their own families, or 'sturdy beggars' who were too idle to work. Much time and effort was spent in making sure that people from other places did not become chargeable on the local area, and indeed parish officers were empowered to 'move on' those who they thought did not belong. Although provision for relief of poverty has changed greatly, the anecdotes relating to street beggars, and attitudes to 'scroungers', remain remarkably similar today.

The cornerstone of the Old Poor Law, before 1834, was the Act of 1601. This placed a duty on local communities to assist their own poor, to pay for that from the rates, and to appoint an overseer of the poor each year to manage the system. After 1662 everybody had a 'legal place of settlement', which meant that a particular parish or township was liable to support them should they become a pauper. The criteria for settlement included not only birth and family connections, but also factors such as apprenticeship, employment, occupying property above a certain value, and uninterrupted residence. This extended to agricultural labourers and accounts at least in part for the customary 'six months hire' practised by northern farmers, thus avoiding the labourer gaining a settlement. Those who, having been examined by the overseer and magistrates, did not satisfy the criteria for settlement in their place of residence might be removed to another place where they were deemed to be legally settled. Two examples from 1734 illustrate the point. William Harrison, tailor, was given a removal order by the quarter sessions court, requiring him to be sent from Strickland Roger to Kirkland, while Elizabeth Satterthwaite and her two infant sons were removed from Kendal to Kirkland, her husband having left her.[25] Simply having been born in a place, or living in a place, were not regarded as sufficient criteria to obtain settlement.

In 1759 there was the sad case of Ellenor Warrener, 50, who with her daughter Jane aged 10 was apprehended at Brough under Stainmore. She was the widow of James Warrener, late of Kendal, weaver, who had died some weeks earlier, having served his time (that is, been apprenticed) there. His wife and child had headed off 'into the Bishopric' (in other words, County Durham) to do casual harvest work there and on their return had fallen ill at Brough. They were to be returned to Kendal, as James had had his settlement there because he had served an apprenticeship in the town. Married women always took their husband's place of settlement, and legitimate children inherited that of their father—so to Kendal they had to go, whether or not that was their choice.[26]

Poor relief started at parish or township level, providing so-called 'outdoor relief', but during the eighteenth century in some parts of the country the idea of 'unions', groups of parishes which combined for Poor Law purposes, began to emerge. After 1723, too, the option of providing a workhouse was also available. From 1834 a national system of Poor Law Unions was established, and each union was required to build a large central workhouse. The notoriety of this system, with workhouses regarded as places of dread, where human dignity was lost, long-married couples separated, food was sparse and work hard and dreary, particularly emerged after 1834. It matched changes in the prison system as custodial sentences began to take over from the death sentence for a wide range of offences after 1832, and grimness and inhumanity became institutionalised.

Kendal Workhouse

The Kendal Workhouse was built in 1769 under the provisions of a local Act of Parliament passed in 1767. It was at the northern end of Stricklandgate and its name, the Kendal Union Workhouse, later led to the naming of the Union Building Society and one of the adjacent streets in the new Liberal development which is discussed in chapter 5. A wing was added in 1776, both new wing and original building being to the design of Richard Pedder.

Eden, writing in 1797, describes the workhouse thus:

> The Poor are either relieved at home or maintained in a Workhouse, which is a commodious building, in an airy situation, and kept with great neatness and propriety. It contains 55 rooms, 35 of which are lodging rooms, very judiciously distributed. A garden supplies vegetables. Beans and cabbages are occasionally substituted for potatoes, and bacon for beef, but the usual rotation is: Breakfast—Every day, hasty pudding and milk, or milk boiled with oatmeal. Dinner—Sunday, Wednesday, Friday, milk pottage and bread; Monday, Thursday, Saturday, broth, boiled beef, potatoes and bread; Tuesday, hough stewed, potatoes and bread. Supper—every day same as breakfast. The allowance of bread is very plentiful. On beef days each person is allowed half-a-pound of beef without any distinction being paid to age or sex.

He goes on to say

> There were in the house on 4th April, 1795, 136 persons, viz., 57 males, 79 females, of which 38 were under 10, 26 between 10 and 20, 12 between 20 and 30, 8 between 30 and 40, 15 between 40 and 50, 4 between 50 and 60, 17 between 60 and 70, 10 between 70 and 80, 6 between 80 and 90. Their employments are various. Men are generally employed out of the house; women spin and make Kendal cottons, etc.; children are generally sent to the different manufactories, where they earn about 1*s*. a week each. Encouragement money is paid to the industrious, viz., 1*d*. for every shilling earned ... The deaths in the house were: 1791, 33 (a fever prevailed); 1792, 15; 1793, 15; 1794, 10. Weekly pensions amounting to £2 0*s*. 2*d*. for the week 3rd April are paid to a number of casual Poor, mostly for children, but the average for the previous ten weeks was £5 12*s*. 9*d*. The weekly pensions to regular Out-Poor amounted to £6 2*s*. 7*d*. The weekly charge for bastards out of the house was 17*s*. 6*d*., and for the families of militia men £1 11*s*. 0*d*.[27]

It is salutary to find the punishment accorded to one Poor Law official who did not carry out his duty to the poor. In 1799 William Alderson, overseer of the poor for Natland, was found guilty at the quarter sessions of not sufficiently relieving the poverty of Elizabeth and Eve Atkinson. His severe punishment was to spend three months in a solitary cell at the House

A view within the courtyard of the Workhouse, looking towards the Male Ward, early twentieth century.

BY COURTESY OF KENDAL TOWN COUNCIL

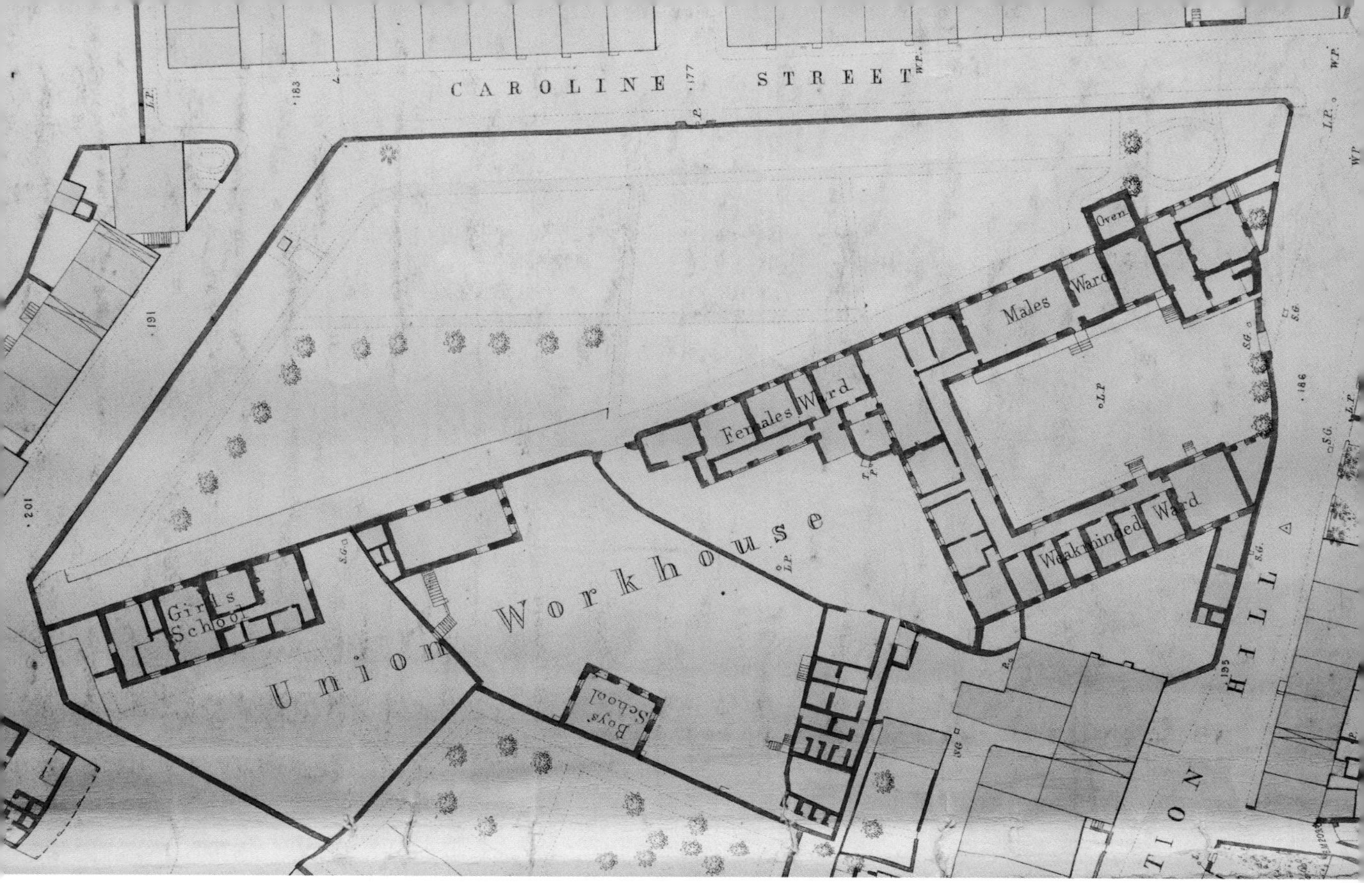

The Workhouse complex, as seen on the large-scale Ordnance Survey map of 1861.

PHOTOGRAPH CARNEGIE, FROM AN ORIGINAL HELD AT WESTMORLAND RECORD OFFICE, KENDAL

of Correction and to stand in the pillory for one hour on 8 November, presumably to make his public humiliation complete.[28]

Following the 1834 Act, which among other purposes intended to make workhouses so unpleasant that people would prefer to find work and 'stand on their own two feet', the Kendal Poor Law Union came into being as a grouping of 57 local townships, based upon Kendal but supported financially by a very wide swathe of territory, from Ambleside and Grasmere in the north to Kirkby Lonsdale in the south. It was managed by a Board of Guardians of the Poor, with 67 members representing the constituent places. The new Poor Law Union retained the existing workhouses at Kendal and at Milnthorpe, but henceforth used them for different categories of inmate, such as able-bodied women and unmarried mothers at Milnthorpe. In 1849 the Kendal Workhouse had accommodation for 335 people, and that at Milnthorpe held 300. The 1841 census gives the names of 209 people then living in Kendal Workhouse, including the master and family and some members of staff. In 1861 Nicholson described the workhouse:

> a large, uniform building, two stories high, occupying three sides of a quadrangle, the fourth, which is the entrance, being open to the street. It contains, for the purposes of the paupers, one large general dining-room, kitchens, store-rooms, sick-rooms, &c. on the first floor; and on the second floor thirty-five well-ventilated lodging-rooms, which contain eighty-nine good beds, supplied with sufficient comfortable clothing, and capable

> of accommodating two hundred persons; together with suitable apartments appropriated to the use of the governor and his family. In the yard behind the Workhouse stands a commodious School-room for boys, and the contiguous building, which was formerly the harden manufactory, is, the lower part of it, appropriated as a play-ground, and the upper part is used for dormitories. What was formerly the Fever Ward is now occupied partly as a schoolroom for girls, and partly as girls' dormitories, with apartments for the schoolmistress. A productive garden is attached to the Workhouse, cultivated by the labour of the inmates.[29]

Confirming this the Ordnance Survey 1:500 map of 1861 shows five divisions in the workhouse: a male ward, female ward, boys' school, girls' school, and 'weakminded ward'. The latter reminds us how little other provision there was for those suffering from mental illness, especially among the poor. (Private asylums had long existed for the well-to-do.) In the 1881 census no fewer than 15 of the 151 inmates of Kendal Workhouse were listed as 'imbecile'.[30] The reference to the 'harden manufactory' reminds us that hard labour, in this case the weaving of a coarse woollen fabric for sale, was one of the purposes of the workhouse, and had been recorded from at least the early nineteenth century until the 1840s.[31]

The character of the workhouse changed over the years, with subdivision into a number of units and in response to changing conditions. After the First World War the increase in 'tramps', defined as men with no fixed abode, moving around the country, meant a greater demand for accommodation in the 'casual ward', while by then separate orphanages had been set up. The 1929 National Assistance Act formally abolished the Poor Law, repealing the 1834 Act, and the workhouses for a time were officially known as 'Public Assistance Institutions' (though of course everybody still called them 'the workhouse'). In 1948, with the creation of the National Health Service, the Poor Law finally passed into history, and the concept of the workhouse came to an end. The local institution became the Kendal Green Hospital for the Elderly,[32] and was later demolished. The site is now occupied by houses.

Population

We know a good deal about the people of Kendal in the past because of the survival of a series of lists and surveys, drawn up for particular contemporary purposes but giving information about population and households. The earliest list appears in *The Boke of Recorde* in 1576, which seems to record those who had contributed to the costs of acquiring the new charter in the previous year. The names of 713 men and women appear, together with those of 146 young unmarried men, not yet householders. As was customary with Kendal records they are listed by the names of the main streets, which tacitly include the smaller lanes and localities. Those who contributed were eligible for freedom of the borough, but the list also contains many names of those who did not contribute, so can be seen as a roll of householders (and others) of that date. While we cannot tell how many people were omitted (for example, the very poor are unlikely to have been included), or how many actual households this represents, this is a remarkable survey of the inhabitants of Kendal, and few other places in England have any comparable listing.[33] This survey has been analysed more recently and a population figure of perhaps 3,200 for the town has been proposed.[34]

There was a major catastrophe in Cumbria in the late summer and autumn of 1598, when the area was 'visited by plague'. A carving in Penrith church used to record the death by plague of 2,500 people in Kendal, 2,200 in Richmond, 2,266 in Penrith, and 1,196 in Carlisle in that year. The figures seem so fantastic in relation to the likely total population that we would probably dismiss them out of hand. However, in all cases they refer to the deaneries of those names, each of which included a very large rural area. The figures for Kendal have recently been backed up by contemporary documentary evidence showing that 500 died in Highgate, 326 in Stricklandgate and Marketstead, 400 in Stramongate, 'wherof beyond the bridge [in Longpool and Farcrossbank] 160', and 245 in Kirkland.[35] Some of the figures are suspiciously round, but the total would be 1,471. This is a staggering mortality rate. If the total population in 1576 was about 3,200, then the death rate would be some 45%, even higher than that postulated for the Black Death of the fourteenth century. The effect on morale can be imagined, and those who could afford to would undoubtedly have fled the town. One person's loss, however, can be another's opportunity, and it is likely that by 1600 many people had moved in from the countryside to try their luck and to fill some of the vacancies. Nonetheless the shattering of trade and the loss of skills must have been disastrous, regardless of the precise percentages of mortality.

Very recently the Hearth Tax Survey of 1674–75 for Westmorland has been published.[36] As the name suggests, this was a tax upon hearths, and therefore is both reasonably comprehensive and shows some social gradation; the returns reveal houses in Kendal possessing between none and nine hearths. The greatest number, nine, belonged to Wm Potter of Highgate. Of these four were 'new'. Although as usual there was a column for 'po', representing 'poor', in the case of Kendal this was not used. The survey proceeds from Highgate to Stricklandgate, then 'Stramondgate' and 'Churchland'. A final section lists 'exemptions'. What is clear is that in Westmorland (and some other adjacent counties) the possession of one hearth concealed a wide range of wealth, largely because of differing traditions in building and way of life. So, while larger numbers of hearths might well show conspicuous consumption in their owners, the smaller numbers do not necessarily indicate abject poverty. There is also the question of how many people occupied a whole house, and how subdivision was accounted for. Typically at this period widows and single men, in particular, occupied a room or two in a shared house, and the allocation of hearths might be quite random.

Another seemingly comprehensive list of the people of Kendal dating from 1695 is considered in detail in chapter 6, as it provides useful information on the trades of the town. It also gives us a raw population figure for Highgate of 776, Stramongate of 668 and Stricklandgate of 738 (Kirkland has no statistics), totalling 2,182. To this we should add a figure for Kirkland and for the surrounding out-of-town areas, to give us a figure somewhat in excess of 3,000.

If this is to be trusted it shows no great change in population from the late sixteenth century. Unusually the survey lists men and women and servants by name, and children by number, so is not just a list of heads of households. The degree of omission, if any, is unknown. Clearly the collectors of the information had difficulty with some of their entries.[37]

Several more lists were produced towards the end of the eighteenth century. In 1784 the parish clerk, Joseph Garnett, surveyed the townspeople and calculated the total population as 7,571. Three years later came the 'census' of Westmorland,[38] but unfortunately in Kendal Ward only the return for Stricklandgate has survived. In 1793 Garnett made a second survey and at that time stated that the population of the town was 8,080.[39] Trade directories begin to appear in the late eighteenth century, but are extremely variable in their inclusivity. They are useful for employers, but do not claim to be comprehensive listings of ordinary citizens. However, from 1801 we have the national census every ten years, giving much more reliable evidence and, for 1841–1911, the detailed returns of individual households. (The raw data of the census is kept confidential for one hundred years, except, oddly, that of 1911.) Ironically, therefore, we often know more about the people of mid-nineteenth-century Kendal than we do of their descendants a hundred years later.

The 1801 census recorded a total of 7,978 people in the borough of Kendal together with Kirkland, so that Garnett's figure of just over 8,000 in 1793 was probably a slight over-estimate. Thereafter the figures for the borough plus Kirkland (and the Nether Graveship from 1821) are as in the following table:

1801	7,978
1811	8,759
1821	10,362
1831	11,613
1841	11,770
1851	11,829
1861	12,028
1871	13,446
1881	13,696
1891	14,430
1901	14,183
1911	14,033
1921	14,146
1931	16,316
1941	*no census because of war*
1951	18,541
1961	18,599
1971	21,596
1981	23,550
1991	24,500
2001	28,031

The figures for late eighteenth- and early nineteenth-century Kendal are by no means small by national standards. Some 75 towns and cities were more populous than Kendal in 1801, but it was at that time still of a respectable size, comparatively. There were large discrepancies throughout the late eighteenth and early nineteenth centuries between numbers of men and women, often between 500 and 1,000 on a total population of 7,500–12,000.[40] This was not uncommon in towns and at that time, being perhaps accounted for by a higher survival rate among girls than boys, more employment for women servants, and more men away in the armed services, especially during the Napoleonic Wars up to 1815. Young men might also have been drawn to larger towns and cities, such as Lancaster and Liverpool, with their greater prospects.

We should also look at population in relation to the space available for growth. This is the key to many of the health problems of the nineteenth century, and Kendal was not alone in discovering the dangers and problems that occur when the population doubles within essentially the same area, because of the lack of building ground available beyond the existing limits, especially for the poorer townsfolk. The building up of the yards, with no extra provision for water or drainage, was to cause serious outbreaks of infectious diseases in the early part of the nineteenth century.

Today, with a population of approaching 30,000, Kendal is a medium-sized country market town, but its commercial and social catchment area is very wide, stretching across many square miles of thinly populated countryside and including smaller towns such as Milnthorpe and Windermere. The simple population statistics therefore mislead to some extent, for Kendal has a relative importance far beyond its size.

The 2001 census reveals another intriguing fact about Kendal: its remarkable lack of ethnic diversity. This is also true of Cumbria as a whole. The population enumerated a decade ago was 98.05% of British and Irish origin, with 1.01% 'other white', and the remainder, 1.19% (the figures are not exact because of rounding) covering all other origins. That means that there were only some 22 black people of all origins in the town, and 39 people of Asian origin, mostly from the Indian sub-continent, with about the same number of ethnic Chinese. The figures can be confusing, because most second-generation immigrants disappear from the count, so there is a bias to recording new immigrants, but the significance of these figures is very clear, and is very much at variance with the profile of most large cities and former textile towns.[41]

Since 2001 the biggest change has been the influx of people from eastern Europe seeking work, of whom the Poles are the largest and most easily identified group. There is no clear idea of numbers, but the commonplace sound of Polish spoken on the streets of Kendal suggests that Poles have quickly become one of the largest minorities. That situation could change again, as the international labour market itself changes, and indeed, the spacing of the censuses is wide enough to miss such trends altogether, a risk we have in the interpretation of all lists and statistics.

10 Church and chapel

As we have already seen, the antiquity of Kendal parish church of Holy Trinity is demonstrated by the fact that it stands outside the medieval borough boundary in what became the suburb of Kirkland, which predates the creation of the borough in the thirteenth century. In the vast parishes of northern England the 'church-town' or 'Kirkby' often lay more or less central to the many townships which made them up, so we must often look at the larger picture to understand the relationship between settlement and church. However, in Kendal's case the position in relation to the borough is very significant.

For centuries the parish church was the dominant religious site in the town. Although Allhallows chapel was established on the edge of Fellside by the fifteenth century, and functioned as a chapel-of-ease, Holy Trinity controlled a huge parish that extended from the high fells at the top of Kentmere and Long Sleddale in the north to Old Hutton in the south, and included not only Kendal but also such places as Winster, Grayrigg and Staveley. Indeed, there is some evidence to suggest that the parishes of Grasmere and Windermere, both of which were themselves very extensive, were in the distant past part of an even larger Kendal parish. From the sixteenth century at least, the parish of Kendal was served by no fewer than 33 churchwardens (most 'conventional' parishes made do with two), of whom ten represented the township of Kendal and one was from Kirkland, the remaining 22 being appointed from the other townships that made up the parish. The numbers gradually decreased as the parish was carved up into smaller units, in the eighteenth and nineteenth centuries, eventually leaving just four churchwardens by 1994.[1]

It should not be forgotten that for centuries the ecclesiastical role of the parish was paralleled by a variety of functions that we would now consider entirely civil in character, including control of pastures, straying cattle, some law enforcement, and the relief of the poor. Another odd responsibility was the payment of bounties for the bodies of vermin brought in. In 1729 the churchwardens decided that henceforth they would only give bounty on foxes, otters and ravens, although they had previously paid out on more exotic creatures such as wildcat.[2]

In the time of William II (r. 1087–1100) the rights over the parish church were given by Ivo Taillebois to St Mary's Abbey in York. It was very common for monastic houses to acquire control of parish churches, and St Mary's at York was particularly adept at securing such assets, which were valuable. One result was the building of the first Abbot Hall, a manorial site that

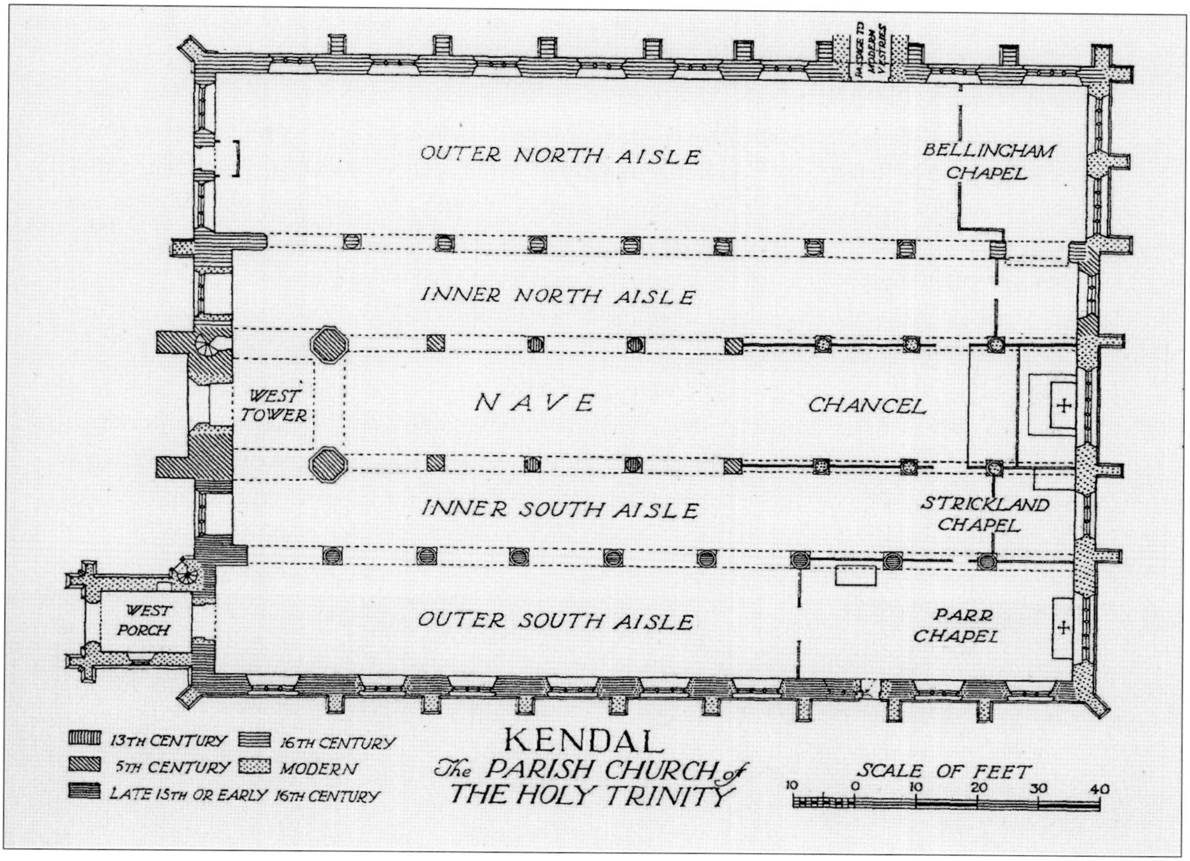

Plan of Kendal parish church, from the RCHM Westmorland survey of 1936.

served as the base from which monastic officials could oversee their new property. By 1302 the abbey had gained a licence to appropriate the church (that is to take it entirely into their own hands and serve it with their own clergy, keeping all the revenues), except its chapels, under pretext of the abbey's impoverishment.[3] The abbey was in reality extremely wealthy, but this procedure had become quite widespread among monasteries seeking additional sources of income when gifts of land dried up in the late thirteenth century, after the Statute of Mortmain. A few years later, in 1309, Walter de Styrkeland and others were accused of assaulting the abbey's servants and hindering them from collecting tithe corn and hay.[4] Clearly all was not well in the abbey's public relations. The connection of the church with York was to be long-lived, ending only with the dissolution of St Mary's Abbey in 1539. In 1553 Queen Mary gave the living to Trinity College, Cambridge, which is still the patron.

The parish church is both very large and very plain. At its core can be seen the original nave of the thirteenth century, flanked by two aisles, which in turn are flanked by two further aisles of the fourteenth and sixteenth centuries, and terminate at the east end in a series of chapels. The west tower and the chancel are also incorporated within the main footprint of the building, which is therefore essentially a large rectangle in plan. The result is one of the widest parish churches in England, filled with a forest of pillars, and its original layout is not at all apparent at first glance. The plainness is partly created by the largely clear glass of the windows, which renders the building quite light inside. Nevertheless, the whole still has a medieval appearance, since there was no large-scale Victorian rebuild or 'restoration' of the sort that rewrote history in so many other parish churches across the land. The work that was undertaken in 1829 and 1853 was very limited in scope, involving simply the removal of the ancient plaster and the seventeenth-century decorative scheme, and a rearrangement of the interior.

Until then the church interior must have presented a very unusual impression, not just because of its width but also because the decoration was so extremely florid—most of the furnishings were painted green, or were in green fabric. That decorative scheme originated in 1684, when James Addison of Hornby, Lancashire, contracted to redecorate the church for £30—subsequently increased to £36, with some additional work, so pleased were the churchwardens with the result. Curiously, no other example of his work is yet known, although

Interior of the parish church, looking west down the inner north aisle.

Brass memorial to Alan Bellingham Esquire, dated 1577, with two sets of arms, in the Bellingham chapel of the parish church.

it is hardly likely that he came untried to Kendal. When complete it was described as 'sundry fat cherubim and seraphim, green hissing serpents and flying dragons, which, with texts of scripture written in black letters within oval and other shaped compartments ornamented in green, yellow and black, occupied nearly every available space on the interior of the walls of the church'.[5] This all sounds like a classic Roccoco design. The exterior of the church was roughcast at least as far back as 1658. In 1679 Edward Shepherd was buried at the church's expense after he was killed, presumably by a fall from the scaffolding, while rough-casting the 'steeple' (i.e. the tower).[6]

Rev. Benjamin Newton visited the church in 1818 and described how

> We got an excellent breakfast at Kendal, walked a great deal about the town and among other places to the Church where there happened to be assembled a numerous body of the clergy and a sermon was preaching for the benefit of poor clergymen and the widows

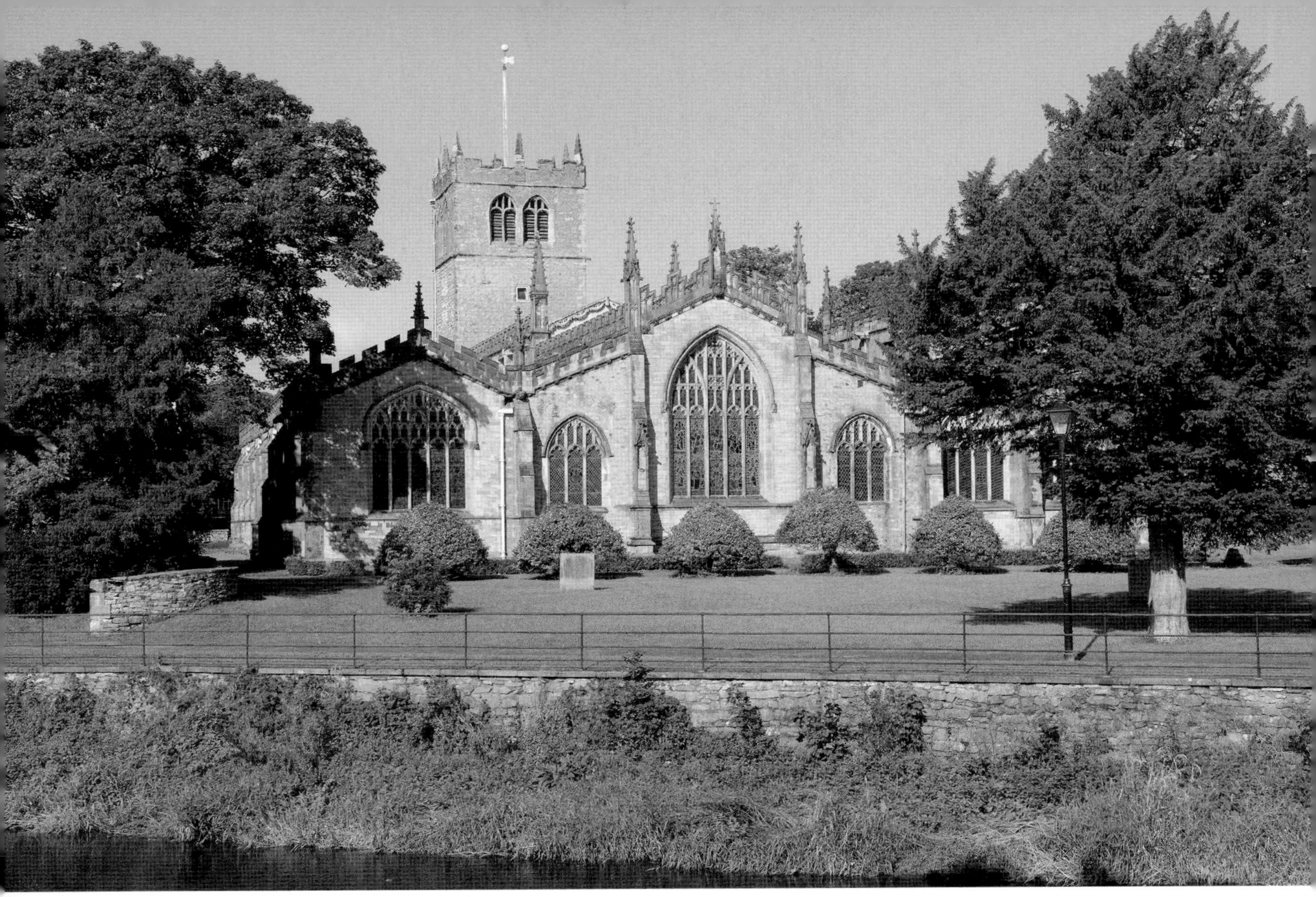

Kendal parish church seen from the east across the river Kent, showing its great width.

and orphans of the clergy by a gentleman who had one of the most powerful voices I ever heard and a very good delivery, making some allowance for a North Country dialect … I forgot to mention that the church at Kendal is very handsome and the lightest within that I ever saw.[7]

The chapels of the parish church

Kendal has a notable range of chapels within the church. They are ranged across the east end, and today they are, starting from the north:

1 The Bellingham chapel, containing the brass of Alan Bellingham, 1577 and the Victorian recreations of those to Sir Roger and Margaret his wife, of 1555;
2 The Chambre or Beckett chapel, now a Regimental chapel to the Border Regiment; (The chancel)
3 The Strickland chapel, with monuments to the Strickland of Sizergh Castle, who remained Catholic;
4 The Parr chapel, named after the final medieval and Tudor owners of the castle.

Funerary armour in the north chapel of the parish church: a basket-hilted sword and a 'Spanish' morion, now detached from the tomb above which it originally hung. It is (wrongly) associated with the legend of 'Robin the Devil' (Robert Philipson).

Chantries

Formerly there were several other chapels partitioned off from the body of the church, which were used as chantries in the late Middle Ages. Chantries had become popular in that period, and were established so that a priest could sing regular masses at the altar for the soul of a named (and usually wealthy) individual who was buried there, and sometimes for his whole family. The chantries were endowed with land and property to create an income, and each generally had its own chantry priest. These priests sometimes lived in a shared hall and, being educated men, often had secondary tasks such as teaching a school. The chantries outlived the dissolution of the monasteries and the Reformation by a few years, but were abolished by order of parliament in the late 1540s. In the case of Kendal the following chantry chapels are known to have existed:

1. St Christopher, founded by Elizabeth Sadler, widow, in the early sixteenth century, and endowed with property mostly in Kendal.
2. St William (probably St William of York), founded by Thomas Strickland and William and Thomas Stainbank, in the early sixteenth century. Much of the endowment was in the form of land in Lancaster and district. Some of the income

of this chantry was later diverted to the fledgling grammar school.

3 St Anthony, founded in 1543 by William Harrison and William Shepherd. It was very short-lived, lasting for only five years. Even Shepherd, in the terms of his will, seems to have foreseen the end of the chantries (no great act of prescience to those who had just witnessed the dissolution of the monasteries). Most of the land forming its endowment lay in Furness.

4 Guild of the Trinity, founded by Thomas Wright, some time after 1389. Unlike the individual chantries set up by rich men, this was presumably for people of the middling sort, who belonged to the religious guild of the Trinity. Its endowment land seems to have lain within Kendal, in Kirkland and Stramongate.

The old sign from the Ring of Bells inn, now in the Parish Church. It shows the ten ringers at their bell-ropes in 1816 or soon after. Many of the ringers can be identified by name.

5 St Thomas a Becket's chapel, founded by Sir Thomas Ros, holder of the Marquis Fee, who died in 1390. Its lands were mostly in Kendal.

6 'Tholde Warke', called St Mary, in the parish church, founded by the vicar, Roger de Kirkeby, in 1321. It presumably gained its name from being the oldest of the chantries, which probably meant that it stood in one of the inner aisles, but recreating the topography of the medieval church is by no means easy. Its endowment was a pension of £5 per year from St Mary's Abbey, York, which had recently acquired the church.

7 St Katherine, which can be identified with the surviving Strickland chapel at the eastern end of the inner south aisle: this is known because it was where Thomas Strickland was buried in 1516, and Sir Walter Strickland in 1528.

8 'The altar of Jesus in the parish church' is recorded in a chantry certificate of 1547. It had a small endowment worth 20 shillings per year, and was founded by Matthew, William and Rowland Phillipson.

Board in the belfry of the parish church commemorating a bell-ringing event in 1765.

The free grammar school of Kendal was set up as a joint foundation, together with a chantry, by Adam Penyngton of Boston in 1525. A master (who had to be a priest) was to teach the school and also to pray for the souls of Adam, his wife and parents. We will return to the history of the grammar school in the next chapter.[8]

Bells and organ

An outward sign of its prosperity was that the parish church possessed a significant peal of bells and an early example of an organ. The tower had five bells from at least the mid-sixteenth century and from 1695 had six, with a tenor (the largest bell) of unusual size. This bell, named 'St Michael', was said to weigh 35 hundredweight (approx. 1.75 tonnes), but it does not survive. An unusual feature of the churchyard was the so-called 'bell house', rented by various bellfounders between the 1680s and the early eighteenth century to cast bells for Kendal and other churches in the area, including Beetham (1684), Ravenstonedale and Kendal itself (1695), and for Kendal, Killington, Orton, Staveley, Brigham, Aldingham and Urswick (1711), all made by the founder Abraham Rudhall of Gloucester. Kendal was remote from the principal bellfounders in England, and it was difficult to transport huge and heavy objects such as bells to the area, so it was more feasible to set up a 'branch operation' here whenever demand made it worthwhile.[9]

According to a board in the tower of the parish church, the first extent of 120 changes was rung on these bells in 1765 by William Brough, John Wilson, Richard Carter, William Simpson, William Teasdale and Paul Holme. Given the weight of the peal, this was an extraordinary achievement. Nine years later two more bells were added, and in 1816 the existing eight were augmented to ten, an unusual number at this time outside the major cities.[10] All was not sweetness and harmony, however, for the ringers struck over wages twice in the early nineteenth century, once for nearly a year in 1834–35 and again in 1838.[11] A group of ten ringers (the numbering meaning that it must be after 1816) was portrayed on the old inn sign of the *Ring of Bells* next to the church. It is now kept in the church itself, and the inn has a newer sign.

Unusually the parish church also seems to have had an organ of some sort from at least 1637, when 'organ pypes' are referred to in the churchwardens' accounts. It acquired a 'Father Smith' organ in 1703.[12] Most churches at this time (and indeed until the late eighteenth century) had 'west gallery' choirs and bands to play the metrical psalms. The organist became an important person in the church organisation, usually training and controlling a choir. In 1822 an organist named Scarisbrick, aged only 17, was appointed following a competition. On the Corn Rent map of the 1830s two fields in the Park Lands, nos 79 and 80, are marked as 'Organ Close', because the rent income derived from letting them out to tenants paid part of the organist's salary, the rest being made up from the sale or rent of pews and from voluntary contributions.[13] The organ was replaced by a new instrument by Willis of London in 1877, and rebuilt in 1904.[14]

In the Middle Ages Kendal had no monastic house or friary, which is perhaps a sign of its small size and relative poverty at that time, although it could merely indicate that the principal landlords had never been moved to found such an institution. Monasteries needed land as a basis of survival, but friaries generally held no property and relied entirely on alms, either from townsfolk or from travellers passing through on the principal roads. Warrington, Preston, Lancaster, Penrith and Carlisle all had friaries, but not Kendal. There was, however, the leper hospital of St Leonard, north-east of the town in Scalthwaiterigg, a quasi-monastic institution that was discussed in the previous chapter.

The Reformation

In northern England there is little evidence for Lollardy, a sort of proto-Protestantism that flourished in the Midlands in the years around 1400. The northern counties remained strongly attached to Catholicism, adhering to traditional forms or worship and belief, but inevitably the Reformation led to changes in worship itself, and to the imposition of a new 'official' faith. Although there was a brief Catholic revival under Queen Mary in the 1550s, for the next 250 years Catholics suffered significant, and sometimes extreme, penalties. Exactly how the nature of English religion in general changed between the mid-sixteenth and mid-seventeenth centuries, and how it was altered in particular geographic areas, is the subject of extensive debate among historians, and there are many conflicting and contradictory views. For many ordinary people, and especially country folk, not a great deal may have changed in the initial period after the Reformation. The year was still punctuated by saints' days, while piety and concern for religious absolution remained high. One way in which people continued to show their traditional views was in the making of their last will and testament. Whatever else they might do in their lifetime, the fear of purgatory and hell continued to exercise the minds of dying people, and influenced the wording of their testament. In the 1520s and 1530s wills were likely to contain instructions about bequests to the church and its works, for trentals of masses (cycles of thirty) to be said by priests, and the bequest of the testator's soul.

Among Kendal men whose wills have such clauses were Henry Jenkinson (1532), John Slater (1537) and Thomas Wilkinson (1531). The absence of references to saints, to the statues, altars and candles in the church, and to Our Lady, is often held to be a sign of Protestantism. Examples of the latter sort are the wills of Thomas Wilson (1553) and his namesake of 1559. However, there is some middle ground, only to be expected, by those who were genuinely uncertain or who wished to hedge their bets in the hereafter (or who followed the safe politically correct line in the wording of the document, whatever their private views might have been). And of course the attorneys, priests or schoolmasters who helped to draw up these wills may well have had some influence on the particular wording.

So how effective was the Reformation in Kendal and surrounding areas? Margaret Clark has argued that, from a background of a normal late Catholic piety in the 1520s and 1530s, Kendal became determinedly Protestant and even Puritan in its ministers and its administration during the later sixteenth and early seventeenth centuries.[15] This contrasts with many other parts of the North West (and especially west and south-west Lancashire) where Catholicism survived quietly or even quite openly.

The answer is equivocal. We tend to see Catholic and Protestant as absolute opposites, doomed in Elizabethan and Jacobean times to fight to the death. This ignores the way in which neighbours of apparently opposing creeds co-existed quite peaceably in many parts of the North, where even members of the same family could conform or not depending upon other circumstances. It probably took several generations for people living far from the centres of power and decision-making, down in London and the South East, to move wholeheartedly to espouse the new ways, and naturally quite a few never did so.

One possible reason for the apparent absence of large numbers of Catholics in Kendal is the relative lack of Catholic gentry in the vicinity. As the experience of south-west Lancashire demonstrates, local Catholic gentry offered economic, political and spiritual support and shelter, and often employed a priest, thus making a congregation viable. Of those gentry families in south Westmorland who did do this, the Leyburns of Cunswick and the Stricklands of Sizergh were the most important. Although there were Catholics in post-Reformation Kendal, some nearby villages had more significant numbers: Skelsmergh alone produced three 'Tyburn martyrs'.[16]

Even after the Reformation, and into the last years of the sixteenth century, the various trade guilds continued to perform their Corpus Christi plays, very much in the tradition of the old medieval mystery plays. As late as 1644, an old man at Cartmel Fell assured his Puritan minister, John Shaw, that he had indeed 'heard of that man you speak of [Jesus Christ] once at a play at Kendall, called Corpus Christi play, where there was a man on a tree, and blood ran down'.[17]

New Anglican churches

As we have seen, before the Reformation the only place of worship in the town, apart from the parish church, was the chapel of Allhallows that stood on the road leading to Fellside

left
Allhallows chapel..

right
St George's chapel in the Market Place, 1754–1855.

St Thomas's church from the west.

St George's church, still with its western turrets, now reduced in height.

BY COURTESY OF KENDAL TOWN COUNCIL

(Allhallows Lane is named after it). Very little is known about its origins, though it certainly went back to at least the late fifteenth century. It was rebuilt as a mission church in 1864, but closed in 2002. Other churches only started to appear in the town much later, with a reawakening of piety, a need to accommodate the growing population, and the recognition by the Church of England that if it was to compete effectively with other denominations it had to provide plenty of new places for worship.

The first new chapel was that of St George, which was built in 1754 in one of the entrances to the Market Place. The chapel itself, with a rather elegant Georgian classical design, occupied the first floor of the building, while the lower floor was used for commercial purposes as a butter market. It was a strange combination, rendered more so by the fact that the structure also included the town lock-up, used for holding prisoners (usually those of low status) until they could appear in court. The chapel of 1754 survived until 1855, although a new church of St George had been opened over the river, near Stramongate Bridge, in 1840. The parish of the new St George's reflects the location of the old chapel, in that it included the market place. The building of the new St George's church, and its contemporary, St Thomas's, resulted from the great growth of population in the early nineteenth century, particularly in the northern and eastern parts of the town, furthest from the parish church. Both were accompanied by the creation of new parishes, with rights of burial, which helped to relieve pressure on the old churchyard pending the opening of the new municipal cemetery.

The church of St Thomas, in Stricklandgate, was designed by George Webster. Work began on the new building in August 1835 and the dedication took place in July 1837. Although built by the Websters, its design is quite conventional, in the 'lancet' style favoured at the time. The oddest feature is its back-to-front orientation, with the 'west' tower at the east end and the sanctuary to the west, caused by difficulties with the site. Its substantial tower has pinnacles at the corners, much reduced in size in 1970–71 for safety reasons. A dedication slab can be seen inside. There are stairs up to the west or organ gallery, while other galleries once stood against the north and south walls. At the liturgical east (geographical west) is a small chancel. The pews are of pitch-pine, with low backs, and form a central block without an aisle, flanked by two side aisles. A hall was built in about 1978 to the north of the church.[18] From the outset, St Thomas's provided a place of worship for the more evangelically minded churchgoers, as it still does.

St George, in Castle Street, stands on the far bank of the Kent in an area where high-quality houses had been built not long before—among the local residents was George Webster himself, and it was he who designed the building. Constructed in 1839–40, it too has the then-fashionable 'lancet style', providing the maximum number of seats with the clearest view and audibility, representing the requirements of the age. Originally it had a west gallery and two side galleries, offering greatly more accommodation than it does today.[19] The design gives a sense of great width, with open trusses spanning the whole space. The original chancel was extremely small, but it was replaced in 1910–11 by Paley & Austin of Lancaster, who added a quite complex east end, with choir stalls, vestries and organ chamber.[20] The original west end was unusual, to say the least—a pair of western turrets carried spires, while an internal lobby gave access to stairs to the galleries, in the eighteenth-century tradition. The western turrets dominated the design, but were cut down and their spires removed in the late twentieth century, reducing the overall height by about one-third. Subsequently the west front was extended outward, providing extra space but giving a degree of incoherence to the external appearance. Internally the whole of the western part, including the former west gallery, has been separated off for meeting rooms, so that the church is much shortened.

Nonconformists and dissenters

The Toleration Act of 1689 granted freedom of worship to Protestant Dissenters, the nonconformists, and allowed them to open their own chapels (provided that they registered these with the authorities). There had been dissenters in the town since the early seventeenth century, but they were never particularly prominent, and the Anglicans were numerically much the most important denomination. According to the *Notitia Cestriensis*, a survey commissioned by Bishop Gastrell of Chester in the early eighteenth century, there were only two dissenters' meetings in 1714–25, one of them Presbyterian and the other Quaker.[21] The Presbyterian (later Unitarian) Chapel in Branthwaite Brow, facing the Market Place, was established in 1720. Known as the 'Protestant Dissenting Congregation of Presbyterians', this congregation had been founded in 1687, and owed its existence to the Reverend Richard Frankland, an Anglican who was ejected as perpetual curate of St Andrew Auckland in County Durham, and established various congregations during his journeyings in Yorkshire and Westmorland. Old pew ends preserved in the present vestry, and dating from the 1690s, suggest that an earlier chapel had existed, but where it stood is unknown.

In 1720 money was raised by subscription to purchase the ground and build a chapel on the present site, and despite considerable alterations to the building and especially to its interior in about 1845 and again in 1881–82, this is essentially the chapel that survives today. The former galleries have gone, and the pulpit was moved to a new position against the north-east wall. The date AD/1720 can be seen on the rainwater heads. The chapel stands back from the Market Place, with gardens in front and behind (the latter used as a graveyard) and is accessed via iron gates through an archway under the former parsonage house of 1777.

Although founded as a Presbyterian congregation the chapel became openly Unitarian in the 1820s. It evaded attempts in 1838 to convert it, and its endowments, to the orthodox Calvinist Presbyterians, and as a Unitarian and Free Christian Chapel it has survived. Its founding minister was the Reverend Caleb Rotheram, who died in 1752 and was succeeded by his son, Caleb junior. The latter ministered to the congregation for over forty years, and died in 1796. Their joint ministry of over 75 years must have set the tone of the chapel for several generations—it was strongly supported by the merchant community, forming an alternative focus to the Anglicans, not just for religious attitudes but also for social activities. The congregation was also known for its anti-slavery attitudes and was a powerful voice in

above
The Unitarian chapel in Branthwaite Brow.

below
Quaker tombstone of George and Hannah Backhouse, in the burial ground off Sepulchre Lane.

above
Entrance to the Unitarian chapel in Branthwaite Brow.

below
Tombstone of Rev Caleb Rotheram, who died in 1752 and is buried in the grounds of the Unitarian chapel.

the town.[22] Various Presbyterian groups later broke away and established their own chapels, including those in Beast Banks; Zion Chapel off Highgate; Lowther Street; and the former theatre in Woolpack Yard. What was afterwards called the 'Scotch Burial Ground' for Presbyterians was in Beast Banks, in use between 1760 and 1855 and still so marked on a sign outside.

The Quakers (or Society of Friends) established themselves in Kendal during the Commonwealth period, in 1656. In that year, even before they had a meeting-house, they bought land in Sepulchre Lane from Roger Backhouse to be used as a burial ground. This was eventually closed in 1855 and is now in part an area of public open space, but there are three tombstones still visible, notable for the Quaker form of expressing the days and months ('first day', 'second month') without the use of what were considered pagan names.

The Quakers were notable in their rejection of the whole structure of the Anglican Church. Originating as rebels and radicals, they were persecuted in their early years, often for unauthorised meetings or for non-payment of tithes or church rates. In time they became regarded as the most law-abiding and self-regulating of all denominations, although they still encountered many disadvantages because of their refusal to swear oaths, which barred them from office-holding and many other positions of responsibility. This helped to push them into trade, where many prospered greatly. Their organisational structure was completely outside the parochial and diocesan structure of the Established Church, being based upon monthly and yearly meetings, as well as the day-to-day operation of individual meeting-houses. (Kendal was also the location for a monthly meeting.) There were no ministers, their egalitarian principles only stretching to the creation of 'elders' who administered the system. This distinctive group, rendered more so by their sober and old-fashioned dress and by their pacifism, held themselves largely aloof from 'worldly' pursuits and pleasures and retained a separate identity by their

Friends' Meeting House in Stramongate.
PHOTOGRAPH ELLIE GODDARD

refusal to 'marry out' into other groups. The trading links and international connections between Quakers were also very close. When a young American Quaker visited Kendal during the Wars of Independence, he could be sure of a most friendly and open reception from the local Quaker community, and not only because he was on the Loyalist side![23]

The Friends' Meeting House in Stramongate was begun in 1688 on land purchased by Thomas Wilson, adjacent to his house and tanyards. In 1816 it was replaced by the present, much larger building, designed by Francis Webster. The clerk of works, William Fisher, was a Quaker joiner who was probably responsible for the woodwork. The meeting-house could hold 850 people and is an elegant and beautifully simple structure.[24] It now houses the Quaker Tapestry, a history and explanation of Quakerism in needlework, produced between 1981 and 1996.[25] The Quakers became very numerous and influential in Kendal, forming some 10 per cent or more of the population in the early nineteenth century, until an obscure and today meaningless controversy, the 'Beaconite controversy', prompted by the publication in 1835 of a book by Kendal-born Isaac Crewdson, split them and reduced them to insignificance for several generations. A number of the more prominent Quakers became Anglicans at this time. The Manchester Meeting was also badly affected.[26]

Kendal had several other chapels and meeting-houses, as we have seen. The Presbyterian Zion Chapel, standing at the end of New Inn Yard off Highgate, was built in 1771 and is now disused. It was replaced by the United Reformed Church, set back behind buildings off Highgate, and dated 1896. The Inghamite Chapel, in High Beast Banks, was built in 1844, but stands on the site of the original chapel, converted from Pear Tree Barn in 1756. In the 1780s there were only some 43 members of this denomination in the town.[27] The chapel was converted into a residence in 1985. It is of limestone rubble, quite large (five bays by two) with windows in two tiers, the lower ones small and the upper ones long with round heads, reflecting no doubt the original layout with an all-round gallery. The eaves are very deep, in the style of the 1840s.

The Wesleyan Chapel is in Windermere Road. The present building dates from 1882–83, but succeeds others on different sites (from 1787, the old playhouse in Woolpack Yard; 1802–08, the Fold, Stricklandgate; and 1808–82 a predecessor on the present site). The Methodists were particularly riven by divisions and this led to a number of separate congregations, such as the Primitive Methodists, until the diminution of the overall numbers encouraged reconsolidation. The Windermere Road chapel is substantial and has elaborate detailing and imposing architecture, reflecting the gradual rapprochement in styles between the nonconformist churches and the Established Church that was apparent by the mid-nineteenth century. Its scale also reveals the comparative prosperity of the Methodists by the

Wesleyan chapel in Windermere Road.

1880s. A central façade of three bays, with round-headed doors and windows, is flanked by a pair of tower-like structures, the whole frontage topped by urns. On the upper part of the frontage is a tablet inscribed 'Wesley Chapel 1882'.

Roman Catholics

During the long years when to be a Catholic was always dangerous and potentially very costly a small congregation survived in the Kendal area, supported particularly by the Strickland family of Sizergh, the nearest Catholic gentry. Bishop Gastrell's *Notitia* records 72 papists in 1714–25, while in 1767 a return of papists in the diocese of Chester listed in the order of 150 in the town alone, without including the rural townships such as Skelsmergh or Helsington where there were other groups.[28] This figure was confirmed by Bishop Porteus in 1779.[29]

The Roman Catholic church of Holy Trinity and St George in New Road.

There was no single place for Catholic worship, since it was both illegal and potentially dangerous, although local Catholic landowners provided priests and secret mass centres. The *Hie Comber* Inn beyond Nether Bridge; Horncup Hall; and a house in the yard of 27 Stramongate were all used as more-or-less secret mass centres in penal times,[30] but from the 1760s tolerance gradually increased and the penal laws were less likely to be enforced, so Catholics could worship openly with growing confidence. However, as late as 1780 there was an extremist Protestant plot to burn down Sizergh Castle, influenced no doubt by the anti-Catholic Gordon Riots in London.[31] On the whole, despite official intolerance, relations with local Anglicans were good. However, the Catholics had to wait quite a time for their first purpose-built post-Reformation church. Holy Trinity and St George, on New Road, was built in 1835–37 to the designs of George Webster of Kendal, quite close to the site of the Stramongate Yard chapel. In architectural terms it is perhaps the most successful of the three churches the Websters built in Kendal in that decade, and, like their St Thomas's, it has a false orientation because of its position.

Religion in Kendal since the 1850s

In 1851 we can at last identify more clearly the various religious groups in the town, because a national religious census was held on 30 March that year with a view to finding the capacity and actual usage of places of worship. For this area the figures are only given for the Kendal

Ward of Westmorland, with a total population of 36,572 and therefore extending far beyond the town itself (which had then a population of 11,829). It includes many churches and chapels situated in other parts of the district. Of 68 places of worship in total, 42 were Anglican; they accounted for 14,624 sittings out of 21,226. There were 7 Wesleyan Methodist chapels, 5 Independents, and 4 'undefined'. We can clearly identify the Quaker (Society of Friends) meeting as being that in the town, since only one is listed, with 850 sittings but a pitiful combined morning and afternoon attendance of 149. This was after the 'Beaconite' schism, as a result of which attendances were at a notably low level. The two Catholic churches had a healthy combined morning and evening attendance of 675. The seven Wesleyan Methodist chapels between them had approximately 16% of the numbers that the 42 Anglican churches managed. However, as some of these churches were in small hamlets the comparisons are not very helpful. What is perhaps most surprising is that in a period which we tend to think of as one when people were most devout and most likely to attend a place of worship, only 47% of the ward population at most actually did so on the Sunday in question.[32]

All the churches and chapels in Kendal acted as centres for specific communities of people within the wider town community. They provided a focus for social life, help for the poor or sick, and opportunities to find marriage partners and business contacts for their members. To a great extent townsfolk in the past were identified and labelled by their religious allegiances, while groups such as the Unitarians and the Quakers became very significant in business. In the twentieth century, however, church- and chapel-going declined markedly. The effects were felt first by smaller chapels, which had no large financial backers to support them—a problem most had always experienced. They had survived by virtue of the regular attendance of their members, but once that enthusiasm began to wane they were increasingly vulnerable. These were the chapels and churches that disappeared, having combined with others and often seeing their buildings sold and converted to other uses. The main denominations have all seen retrenchments, but in Kendal, unusually, there have been no closures or redundancies as yet.

In many towns of north-west England the increasingly complex ethnic mix of the last half-century has given rise to a wide variety of non-Christian places of worship, in some cases taking over disused churches. In Kendal, however, the disappearance in the earlier part of the twentieth century of the textile trade, which elsewhere attracted immigrants from the Indian sub-continent, means that the town's ethnic diversity is unusually small. There are therefore comparatively few Moslems or Hindus (the 2001 census recorded only 20 and 14 respectively) and consequently an absence of temples and mosques. Likewise there are only some 62 Buddhists and 14 Jews, while the majority of those who claimed a religion (22,301) were Christians (denomination unstated). Given the average attendance at churches of all sorts at the present day, this must be regarded as a pious hope rather than any statement of reality.[33]

Education, leisure, culture and the arts | 11

Schools

AT THE END OF THE MIDDLE AGES Kendal, like most market towns, began to emerge as a centre for education. The Church had been responsible for most of the relatively limited educational provision in the medieval period, but locally there is almost no record of this. It is possible that one or two of the priests of the parish church, such as the chantry priests, provided some form of private schooling, but if so we do not hear about it. The recorded history of schooling in the town begins with the creation of the grammar school in 1525. This was one of the earliest such foundations in Cumbria: the grammar schools at, for example, Penrith, Kirkby Stephen, Keswick, Blencow, St Bees, Kirkby Lonsdale, Stainmore and Dean were all established later, being founded between 1564 and 1596. Only the grammar school at Appleby, the county town, was earlier—it was of medieval foundation, although it was refounded with a new charter in 1574.[1]

Kendal's Free Grammar School was established shortly before the Reformation by Adam Penyngton of Boston, Lincolnshire, jointly with a chantry in the parish church. A prominent Boston merchant, trading with Europe at a time when that town was at its commercial zenith, Penyngton nevertheless came from a family that originated in this area (probably, as his surname implies, from Furness). He gave the sum of £10 a year for 98 years to pay the wage of a schoolmaster, who was also to be the chantry priest. It is not certain where the school stood in its early days, but many grammar schools were held in churches and, indeed, were often taught by minor priests. At Kendal one of the former chantry priests, Adam Shepherd, was the master in 1548, receiving not just this wage but also a pension from his former chantry.[2]

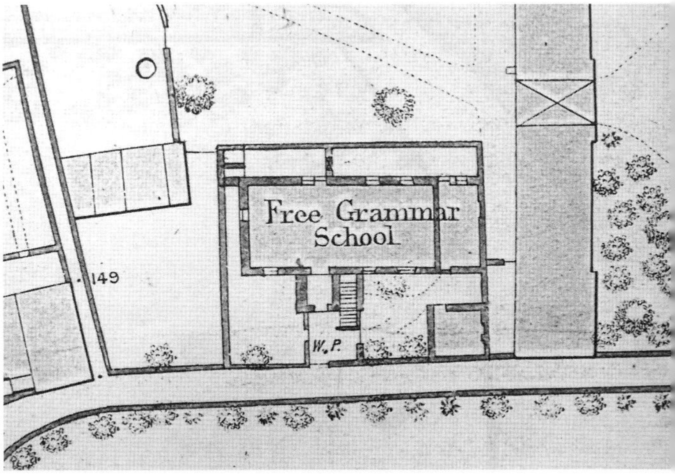

The Free Grammar School, from the large-scale Ordnance Survey of 1861.

PHOTOGRAPH CARNEGIE, FROM AN ORIGINAL HELD AT WESTMORLAND RECORD OFFICE, KENDAL

Bluecoat School girls in their distinctive uniforms.

BY COURTESY OF KENDAL TOWN COUNCIL

Kirkbie-Kendal School.

In 1588 a new building was established just to the rear of what is now Abbot Hall, on land granted by Miles Phillipson. This building is shown in plan on the 1861 OS large-scale map, and was clearly quite small. Typically a master took the upper school, an usher the lower school, and various part-time assistant taught grammar or writing. The teaching of Latin and Greek grammar distinguished these schools from others which, while perhaps less formal and less illustrious, often taught a wider and more commercial syllabus. In early schools such as this, taught by only one or two masters, much depended upon the character of the staff as well as on the quality of their teaching. A mediocre teacher could blight the chances of a whole generation, while a charismatic master could make their fortunes. With long tenures among the staff commonplace, it is not surprising that some schools were in high demand while others remained in the doldrums. At the beginning of the eighteenth century Cowan noted that, 'Near the Church is a free school, endow'd with good Exhibitions for poor scholars who remove from hence to Queens Colledge in Oxford'.[3] Such scholarships (there were others to St John's College, Cambridge) gave further advancement to promising but impoverished boys.

The school continued to be governed largely by its Tudor constitution until 1886 when, not without considerable disagreement, it was joined with the Blue Coat School behind Sandes Hospital.[4] Three years later it moved to a new site on the other side of the river, with new buildings and more space to expand. In 1980, as part of the reorganisation of secondary education in Kendal, it was combined with the former High School for Girls (of which more below) to become Kirkbie-Kendal School.[5]

Slate plaque from the National School for Boys, Beast Banks.

The Society of Friends also had its own school. The Quaker Academy flourished from 1698 until 1932. It is likely that it originally stood near the meeting house, but by 1772 a new building had been erected on land belonging to Bryan Lancaster. Nicholson and Burn, writing in 1777, record that, 'The quakers also have lately built an elegant school-house for the instruction of youth'.[6] The school stood behind the north-west side of Stramongate, accessible via a yard from the street, just opposite the end of New Road (originally Rosemary Lane). The Friends considered education to be particularly important, a virtuous route out of poverty and towards self-improvement. However, they could not attend those schools controlled by the Established Church (including most of the old grammar schools) and so ran many of their own across the country. In 1787 the cost of a full education here, including board and teaching, but excluding washing (shades of Lewis Carroll!) would amount to £20 12*s.* per annum. The caning exploits of Thomas Rebanks, master of the Quaker Academy for fifty years from 1715, are preserved in a verse:[7]

Lord ha' mercy upon us
Save us from Rebanks Thomas
For if he comes
He'll tickle our [thumbs]
And ha' na mercy upon us.

When it was written down by Whitwell in 1866 he placed 'thumbs' in square brackets, obviously in place of 'bums'! If it was true, such behaviour was very unquakerly, but it was matched by the chastisement meted out by the young scientist John Dalton who came here as master, with his brother Jonathan, in 1785. Dalton is best known for his later work at the Dissenters' College in Manchester, where he gained his name as founder of the atomic theory of matter and a father of modern chemistry.[8] A 1787 advertisement in the *Cumberland Pacquet* newspaper states that:[9]

> The School House is a large and elegant Building purposely erected for the Accommodation of Youth, in an agreeable and airy Situation, and has belonging to it a very valuable Library of Books, chiefly on ancient and modern History, Mathematics, and Natural Philosophy, also an Air Pump, Globes, and several other Philosophical, Mathematical, and Optical Instruments.

The Friends' School showed much early promise, but after the mid-nineteenth century it gradually fell behind as educational improvements were made in the wider world, and as universal schooling was gradually introduced. It closed in 1932. Kendal Museum has a case of old uniforms from this school. The Society of Friends was not the only dissenting body with its own school. The Reverend Caleb Rotheram ran an academy from what is now the Unitarian Chapel in the Market Place from 1733, albeit on a very small scale, teaching a total of some 176 pupils.[10]

The School of Industry had the most places to offer, giving essentially practical instruction. It was founded in 1799 behind Whitehall by nonconformist philanthropists such as the Quaker Crewdsons and had room for about 130 children, under the care of one master and two mistresses.[11] It balanced a small amount of conventional teaching with practical skills. According to its rules of 1811 it taught sewing, knitting, plaiting and reading to the girls, with card-making for boys. The latter skill involving setting hundreds of wires into bases, to make the 'cards' that were used for preparing wool for the spinning trade. The boys received, in return, a pittance—it clearly was exploitation.[12] However, the products of the pupils must have covered some of the costs, and it was an education of sorts for those who might not otherwise have had one at all.

A charity school was founded as part of Sandes Hospital in 1670 and conveyed with the rest of the benefaction to the mayor and aldermen of Kendal. John Jefferson, schoolmaster, listed among the inhabitants of Highgate in 1695, was almost certainly the master of the school. The 'Blue Coat' element of the name, derived from the uniform common to many charity schools, was not introduced until 1714. In 1720 Cox gave the following description: 'Kendal, where there is one school for sixteen Boys and ten Girls, all clothed and taught, but whether by Contributions, or a settled Revenue, we know not'.[13] In general, until the nineteenth century, education was not offered to girls, except in practical subjects such as textiles and domestic work, but the Blue Coat School did teach a few girls—nine were being taught there by Isabel Fisher in 1714—and in 1789 there were thirty girls at the school. Up to 1838 there was provision for forty boys to be educated, but this was subsequently increased when new endowments were obtained.[14] In 1886 the school foundation was combined with that of the grammar school, its buildings closed, and its revenues taken for the new school.

In Beast Banks there still stands the building of the former National School for Boys, founded in 1818 by public subscription and with an endowment of £2,000 left by Matthew Pyper, a rich but unpopular Quaker of Whitehaven. Not only did he leave a substantial sum of money, but also stipulated that his body was to be buried in the middle of the school! This detail was honoured by the trustees in 1821, and he was there until 1987, when his body was moved to the Quaker cemetery before the school was made into flats. According to the *Westmorland Gazette*, 'As he lived without respect, so he died without regret, and was buried without solemnity'.[15] A Girls' National School followed in 1823. In 1829 the two schools took 150 and 120 pupils respectively.[16] There was also a British School in Castle Street, run on Lancasterian principles (with pupil-teachers), and a number of Church and Sunday schools, including St Thomas's, a Catholic School, and a Wesleyan School, which provided an education of sorts to a considerable number of children (in 1860 at least 3,433 in total). Among them was the Green Coat Sunday School, established under the will of William Sleddall, who died in 1813. In 1829 it provided places (and uniforms) for 35 boys and 12 girls.[17] In contrast the Grammar and Blue Coat Schools educated only 72 between them in the same year, according to Nicholson.[18]

Private schools came and went. A poor but educated man, or one with some disability that prevented him from taking on a trade, might open a school with very little ceremony. Clergymen, in particular, often taught a small school to supplement their income. Widows and unmarried ladies often did the same, as it was one of few 'respectable' openings available to them. The overheads were usually very low, the space requirements small, and the school would probably not outlive its teacher. While the grammar school taught Greek and Latin, the private schools usually offered a more commercial education, with subjects such as mathematics, surveying or book-keeping. Thomas Selby, schoolmaster, and his family, are listed among the inhabitants of Stricklandgate in 1787.[19] The trade directories reveal some of the diversity of private schools. That of 1829 lists seventeen 'academies' in addition to the Grammar School, Blue Coat School and other more 'official' establishments. These ranged from Henry Bacher (French) in Kirkland, via Sarah Brocklebank and Jane King (ladies') in Market Place and Stramongate respectively, to Samuel Marshall (gentlemen's boarding) also in Stramongate.[20]

By 1849 there were twelve private schools and a couple of infant schools in Castle Street and Jennings Yard. Three of the private schools, all for girls and all run by respectable ladies, were boarding establishments.[21] By 1858 the existing schools had been joined by one for Fell Side, run by Miss Ann Jennings.[22] Girls' schools, for that minority of girls before the Education Acts who were given any education at all, were usually run on the familiar principles of the private sector, managed and taught by unmarried ladies or widows. They offered boarding facilities and taught manners and deportment as well as academic subjects, and were seen as a safe place to store girls until matrimony, often until they were nineteen or twenty years old. Although there were earlier private schools for young ladies, and some studied at the Blue

Kendal Green British School infants, photographed early in the twentieth century.

BY COURTESY OF KENDAL TOWN COUNCIL

Coat School, the High School for Girls was not established until 1887 at Ellerbank, moving in 1903 to a pair of elegant houses at 10–11 Thorny Hills.[23]

By 1914 the pattern of education provision revealed major changes. In 1903 an education committee of the borough council had been set up to administer the eleven or so 'public elementary schools', some of which were old foundations—for example, the Boys' and Girls' National Schools, which were now renamed 'Central'. A number of the others were what we would call church primary schools, such as Holy Trinity, St George's, St Thomas's, and the Catholic Dean Gibson Memorial School, as well as a few in new areas such as Kendal Green.[24] Under the auspices of the borough council, and later of Westmorland County Council and Cumbria County Council, education provision was extended and standardised, culminating in the total reorganisation of secondary education in the area in 1980. At that date the High School for Girls was combined with the Grammar School to form Kirkbie-Kendal School, one of the two 11–18 comprehensive schools in the new arrangement. The other was Queen Katherine School, which stands on a new site in Appleby Road and is named after Kendal's heroine, Katherine Parr, sixth and last wife of Henry VIII.

Kendal's artists

During the eighteenth and early nineteenth centuries Kendal produced, or was closely associated with, a remarkable group of outstanding artists, who specialised in portrait painting: Christopher Steele (1733–67), George Romney (1734–1802), Daniel Gardner (1750–1805) and Thomas Stewardson (1781–1859). Steele, the earliest, established himself in Redman's or Redmayne's Yard in Highgate. Gardner and Stewardson were Kendal-born, but Steele was

Portrait of Alderman Thomas Wilson, by George Romney.

BY COURTESY OF KENDAL TOWN COUNCIL

from Egremont and Romney from Dalton-in-Furness. Romney and Gardner were pupils of Steele, while Stewardson had some training from Romney in his final years.[25]

The most famous of the group was Romney, who became a society portrait painter in London. He used generally to be placed in the second rank, behind Reynolds, but contemporary opinion regarded him more highly. Romney painted over 2,000 portraits, but today he is principally known for his many sketches of Emma Hart, who married Sir William Hamilton, and was later Nelson's mistress. Finding her the ideal model, he painted her in a series of 'Attitudes'. Romney married quite young, but his wife remained in Kendal until he returned from London in 1799, and she nursed him through his final illness. Many of his northern subjects were painted on his brief visits to the area in 1765 and 1767. A rather cross response by his son John to a review of his work in the *Lonsdale Magazine* for 1822 reveals the dates of several local portraits: Walter Strickland and his lady, painted when he was two years out of his indentures (*c.*1759); Mrs Cecilia Strickland, three or four years later; Charles Strickland, fishing, in 1762; and the Rev. William Strickland in about 1765.[26] Later research has established that the portrait of Colonel George Wilson, builder of Abbot Hall, was painted in 1759 and that of his brother, Rev. Daniel Wilson, in 1760. There is some doubt over the date of the portrait of Mrs Anne Wilson and her daughter Sibyll, the family of Colonel George of Abbot Hall, since Sibyll's picture may be posthumous.[27] Undoubtedly the most memorable of Romney's paintings in Abbot Hall is that of the Leveson-Gower children (usually known as the 'Gower Family') dating from about 1777. It has been compared with Poussin's 'A Dance to the Music of Time'.[28]

Daniel Gardner specialised in a rather novel system of painting in gouache and tempera, on hand-made paper. His mixture often included brandy. The colours had to be laid on quickly, and the results were often vivid, but a nightmare for modern conservators, due to the tendency to flake and fragment, and the unpredictable nature of his materials.[29] There are memorials to Stewardson and to Romney in the north-west corner of the parish church, beside the west door, and examples of the work of all four artists can be found in Abbot Hall Art Gallery.

Richard Stirzaker was born in Lancaster in 1791 but came to Kendal at the age of twenty, working for some time as a draughtsman in the office of George Webster. He later set up as a drawing-master.[30] A number of his paintings survive, including 'Lowther's Entry into Kendal' (1820), the 'King's Arms Hotel' (1823), two entitled 'Interior of the Parish Church', 'The Conflagration at Dockwray Hall Mills' (1824) and 'The Old Shambles' (1825).[31] There are also several paintings by Stirzaker of places outside the town, such as Underley and Burrow Halls.

The sculptress Josefina de Vasconcellos (1904–2005) provides a small footnote to Kendal's artistic history. She was born near London, but spent many years in the Lake District and knew Beatrix Potter. As well as her work being shown in Kendal, with examples in Abbot Hall and at the parish church, she spent some time at the very end of her very long life in a tiny flat at the rear of the so-called Bonnie Prince Charlie's house, 95 Stricklandgate, with a small studio and gallery. She died in Blackpool shortly after her 100th birthday, in 2005.

Literary associations

William Wordsworth can hardly be claimed for Kendal as he lived in Cockermouth as a child and later, as an established poet, in Grasmere and at Rydal, but he was a great influence on the area. Kendal was a natural centre for transport and commerce, and he is chiefly remembered here for his extremely reactionary resistance to the building of the Kendal & Windermere Railway in the 1840s. His successor at Dove Cottage in Grasmere was Thomas de Quincey, a man of wide but uneven literary distinction. He should be better known in Kendal as possibly the worst choice of editor of a provincial newspaper ever made, with his brief period of tenure at the *Westmorland Gazette* between 1818 and 1819. Nobody less suitable for a rather staid and determinedly agricultural area could have been found, his only redeeming feature to contemporary readers being that he had high Tory views. He inflicted on his readership a diet of German philosophy and interest in the whole world (indeed, almost anywhere except their own locality), and it found few enthusiasts.[32]

A very unlikely bedfellow to the Lake Poets, albeit one much later in time, is Postman Pat, who emerged as a hero of children's literature in 1978. His creator, John Cunliffe, spent six years in Kendal, basing Pat and his round on local postal services in the area—Greendale is modelled on the nearby valley of Long Sleddale. The books were transferred to children's television in 1981 and quickly became world-famous. Ironically, the local post office in Greenside, on which the stories are based, was closed in 2003. Another well-known Kendal author, of a completely different variety, was Alfred Wainwright, born in Blackburn in 1907. He became borough treasurer of Kendal in 1948, but is remembered for his series of books entitled 'Pictorial Guides to the Lakeland Fells', completed between 1955 and 1966 and published by the *Westmorland Gazette*. Their meticulous detail has made them beloved of fell-walkers, and early editions have become very collectable. His name is commemorated in Wainwright's Yard, a new shopping development off Stricklandgate.

above
Postman Pat.

below
The former Greenside Post Office, centre of Postman Pat's Greendale world.

The town has attracted several able historians. The earliest to give form to its history was Cornelius Nicholson, whose *Annals of Kendal* appeared in two editions of 1832 and 1861.[33] Despite its title the book is not an annal (literally, a year-by-year history) at all, unlike the anonymous *Kendal Chronology*, published in 1865.[34] The latter is based upon the two nineteenth-century newspapers and their predecessors. This was followed in 1900 by John Curwen's *Kirkby-Kendal*. This is an idiosyncratic volume, containing vast amounts of information but arranged in a house-by-house order along the main streets.[35] In the twentieth century there have been several slim volumes of no very great account and a very substantial volume by Roger Bingham, *Kendal—A Social History*, published in 1995 but now unfortunately out of print.[36] Many articles by Dr John Marshall, and books and articles such as *Kendal on Tenterhooks* by Dr Satchell have added much to the corpus of knowledge.[37] Recently there have been various books based upon old photographs, many of them from the Margaret and Percy Duff Collection. An excellent initiative of recent years has been the marking by Kendal Civic Society of important buildings, or buildings with important associations, with explanatory plaques. This has been splendidly backed up by Trevor Hughes, who in 2005 produced a boxed set of illustrated cards providing more information on all these sites.

Newspapers

The town has a long tradition of local newspapers, beginning with the *Kendal Courant* in 1732, followed by the *Weekly Mercury* in 1735. Both contained principally national news and were short-lived.[38] The *Westmorland Gazette & Kendal Advertiser* (1818–1920) and its successor, the *Westmorland Gazette* (1920–) have had a particularly long run. It is not so many years ago that the *Gazette* presented a front cover to the world which would have been quite at home in the eighteenth century, with advertisements and fatstock prices prominently displayed and the news being safely hidden within. Even today one or two newspapers maintain this tradition, but it is fast disappearing, the most recent casualty being the *Craven Herald*. In the early nineteenth century the *Westmorland Chronicle* (founded 1811) and the *Westmorland Gazette* (founded 1818) maintained a sort of bare-fist fight, attacking each other, and their respective editors and proprietors, in the most scandalous terms. This was especially so during and after the contested election of 1818, which polarised the town between the Tory Lowther supporters and the Whig Brougham supporters. The *Chronicle* was a liberal and even radical paper, the *Gazette* a very traditional and reactionary one. Their political differences led to a significantly contrasting choice of stories, as they tended to ignore events which were in any way connected with the opposition.

The *Gazette*'s old adversary was also long-lived, with several name-changes: the *Westmorland Advertiser & Kendal Chronicle* (1811–34), the *Kendal Mercury & Westmorland/Northern Advertiser* (1834–80), and the *Kendal (Mercury &) Times* (1880–1920). There were also two shorter-lived papers serving the locality: the *Kendal News* (1820–23?) and the *Kendal Times* (1864–80). Copies of all the local newspapers, on microfilm, may be read in Kendal Library.

Music and theatre

The parish church was a centre for music from the seventeenth century. It certainly had an organ by 1637, and its organists were respected citizens. There was a choir from 1601, and a robed choir from 1850 (despite allegations that this was tantamount to popery)! Musical and choral performances took place in the church which was, here as elsewhere, one of the largest public meeting places in the town, and was of course acoustically and spiritually appropriate as a venue. The Mary Wakefield Festival, one of the very earliest anywhere in Britain, began in 1885 (the first event was held to raise funds for the refurbishment of Crosscrake church). It took place in the grounds of Mary Wakefield's own residence, Sedgwick House. A keen amateur musician, born in Kendal in 1853, she wanted to pursue a professional singing career, but this was socially unacceptable to her family. She was, therefore, particularly enthusiastic

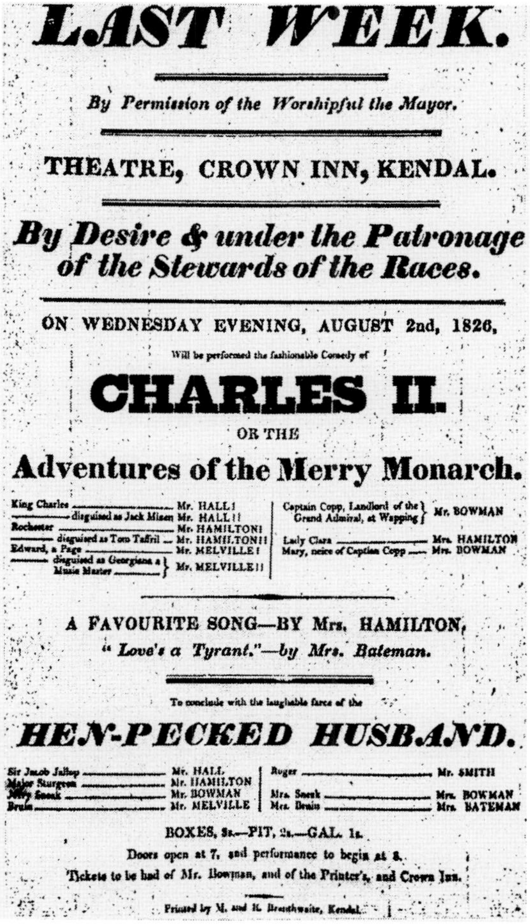

LAST WEEK.

By Permission of the Worshipful the Mayor.

THEATRE, CROWN INN, KENDAL.

By Desire & under the Patronage of the Stewards of the Races.

ON WEDNESDAY EVENING, AUGUST 2nd, 1826,

Will be performed the fashionable Comedy of

CHARLES II.

OR THE

Adventures of the Merry Monarch.

King Charles — Mr. HALL!
— disguised as Jack Mizen Mr. HALL!!
Rochester — Mr. HAMILTON!
— disguised as Tom Taffril — Mr. HAMILTON!!
Edward, a Page — Mr. MELVILLE!
— disguised as Georgiana a Music Master — Mr. MELVILLE!!
Captain Copp, Landlord of the Grand Admiral, at Wapping — Mr. BOWMAN
Lady Clara — Mrs. HAMILTON
Mary, neice of Captian Copp — Mrs. BOWMAN

A FAVOURITE SONG—BY Mrs. HAMILTON,
"Love's a Tyrant."—by Mrs. Bateman.

To conclude with the laughable farce of the

HEN-PECKED HUSBAND.

Sir Jacob Jallop — Mr. HALL
Major Sturgeon — Mr. HAMILTON
Jerry Sneak — Mr. BOWMAN
Bruin — Mr. MELVILLE
Roger — Mr. SMITH
Mrs. Sneak — Mrs. BOWMAN
Mrs. Bruin — Mrs. BATEMAN

BOXES, 3s.—PIT, 2s.—GAL. 1s.

Doors open at 7, and performance to begin at 8.

Tickets to be had of Mr. Bowman, and of the Printer's, and Crown Inn.

Printed by M. and R. Branthwaite, Kendal.

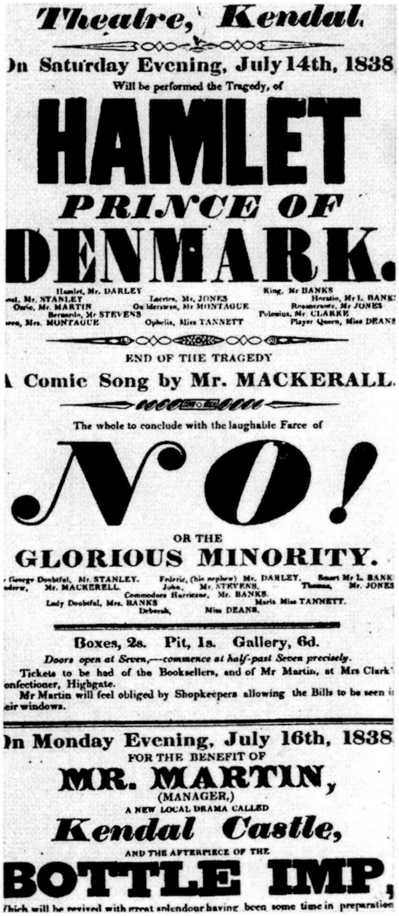

Theatre, Kendal.

On Saturday Evening, July 14th, 1838,

Will be performed the Tragedy, of

HAMLET PRINCE OF DENMARK.

Hamlet, Mr. DARLEY — Laertes, Mr. JONES — King, Mr BANKS
Ghost, Mr. STANLEY — Horatio, Mr L. BANKS
Osric, Mr. MARTIN — Guilderstern, Mr MONTAGUE — Rosencrantz, Mr JONES
Bernardo, Mr STEVENS — Polonius, Mr. CLARKE
Queen, Mrs. MONTAGUE — Ophelia, Miss TANNETT — Player Queen, Miss DEANS

END OF THE TRAGEDY

A Comic Song by Mr. MACKERALL.

The whole to conclude with the laughable Farce of

NO! OR THE GLORIOUS MINORITY.

Sir George Doubtful, Mr. STANLEY. — Frederic, (his nephew) Mr. DARLEY. — Smart Mr L. BANKS
Widow, Mr. MACKERELL. — John, Mr. STEVENS. — Thomas, Mr. JONES
Commodore Hurricane, Mr. BANKS.
Lady Doubtful, Mrs. BANKS — Maria Miss TANNETT.
Deborah, Miss DEANS.

Boxes, 2s. Pit, 1s. Gallery, 6d.

Doors open at Seven,—commence at half-past Seven precisely.

Tickets to be had of the Booksellers, and of Mr Martin, at Mrs Clark's Confectioner, Highgate.

Mr Martin will feel obliged by Shopkeepers allowing the Bills to be seen in their windows.

On Monday Evening, July 16th, 1838,

FOR THE BENEFIT OF

MR. MARTIN, (MANAGER,)

A NEW LOCAL DRAMA CALLED

Kendal Castle,

AND THE AFTERPIECE OF THE

BOTTLE IMP,

Which will be revived with great splendour having been some time in preparation

Handbills for Kendal Theatre.

The former theatre building in Woolpack Yard.

in her support of choral singing—indeed, this was without doubt the first music festival in the country to focus on that aspect of performance. She died in 1910, but the Festival to which she gave her name lives on. It is biennial, with an emphasis on choral music, and includes workshop and presentation days for primary and secondary schools, adjudicated classes for vocalists and instrumentalists of all age groups, and other events such as 'Bring and Sing' concerts. Entry as a competitor is open to all inhabitants of the former county of Westmorland or to people within 25 miles of Kendal.

Because there were relatively few visiting or resident gentry, Kendal lacked some of the amenities that might have contributed to make it a more prominent cultural centre. However, there seems to have been a long-standing interest in the theatre, and the town is exceptionally well provided with the surviving theatre buildings. Until the middle of the eighteenth century all the theatres were in buildings originally for other purposes, pressed into temporary service for performances. From that time on, however, no fewer than four successive theatres survive: in the north-east corner of the Market Place (1758), in Wool-pack Yard (1777), in the Old

The former theatre building in the yard of the *Shakespeare* inn.

Shambles (1828) and a new building behind the Shakespeare Inn (also 1828).[39] The Woolpack Yard theatre afterwards became the chapel of the Scottish Presbyterians. A single example must suffice to illustrate the type of programme given in the early nineteenth century. In April 1815 the townspeople were treated to 'Jane Shore', 'Harlequin Sun Dial', 'Timour the Tartar', 'The Sultan', a dance by Miss Butler and 'The Black Forest or the Robbers of the Cave'.

From 1785 until 1811 the Kendal Theatre was one of a circuit run by Samuel Butler, an actor-manager, and his company, and after his death his widow continued the operation for a few years. Most provincial theatres could not sustain a continuous programme, and performances were therefore focused on a couple of weeks in the year. The company moved from theatre to theatre, often on foot, rehearsing new plays as they went and performing a very wide repertoire. An evening's performance might include three or four items. Other theatres in this circuit included those at Richmond, Ulverston, Beverley, Harrogate and Whitby, and the company might spend a week or so at each, twice a year.[40] A set of twenty-seven playbills for the year 1807 can be seen in Kendal Museum.

A pastiche playbill, put up in 1823 at the behest of a clergyman, the Reverend William Whitelock of St George's Chapel, offered, 'The Great and Terrible Day of the Lord ... Tickets for the Pit are sold at every place of Temptation, Tickets for the Gallery may be had gratis at the Fountain open for Sin and for Uncleanness'. It was this kind of religious disapproval that destroyed the theatre in Kendal, as it did in so many towns in the early nineteenth century.[41] By the 1840s, therefore, it was mostly travelling 'raree' shows and entertainments that were the antecedents of the music hall which came to the town. These less intellectual events are less well documented, but the roads and county towns of Georgian, Regency and early Victorian Britain saw a succession of 'raree' shows such as General Tom Thumb;[42] the Hottentot Woman; the Learned Pig; and Gustavus Katerfelto, the Prussian quack who rode around in a coach full of black cats.[43] Typical of this interest was the showing in Kendal in 1787 of 'the two Irish Giants': a handbill survives from their visit.[44] Polito's Menagerie called in 1817,[45] Tussaud's travelling show in 1828,[46] and Wombwell's Menagerie in 1822 and in 1832, stopping in New Road and advertised with the woodcut of an elephant.[47] The same year saw the ascent of Mr Green, the aeronaut, in his balloon, from the gasworks (he required large quantities of highly explosive coal gas as a lifting agent).[48]

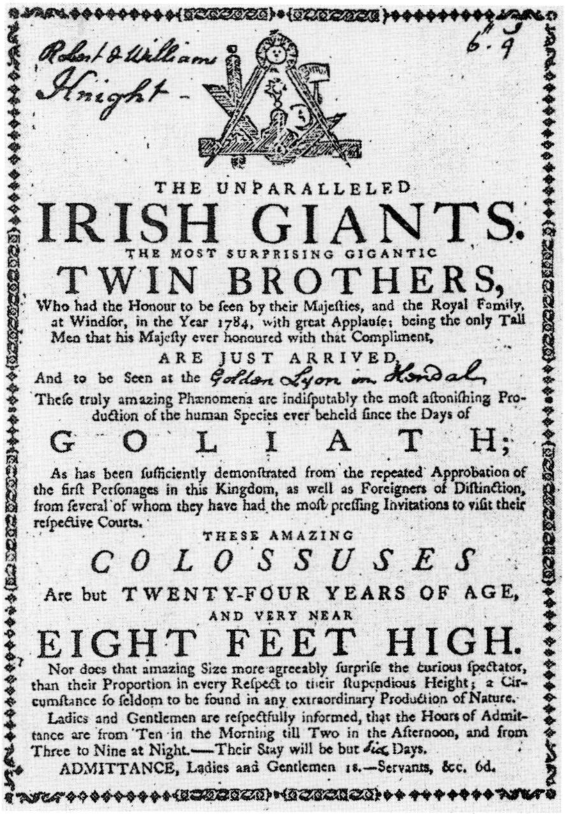

Robert & William Knight - 6.9

THE UNPARALLELED

IRISH GIANTS.

THE MOST SURPRISING GIGANTIC

TWIN BROTHERS,

Who had the Honour to be ſeen by their Majeſties, and the Royal Family, at Windſor, in the Year 1784, with great Applauſe; being the only Tall Men that his Majeſty ever honoured with that Compliment,

ARE JUST ARRIVED,

And to be Seen at the Golden Lyon in Kendal

Theſe truly amazing Phænomena are indiſputably the moſt aſtoniſhing Production of the human Species ever beheld ſince the Days of

G O L I A T H;

As has been ſufficiently demonſtrated from the repeated Approbation of the firſt Perſonages in this Kingdom, as well as Foreigners of Diſtinction, from ſeveral of whom they have had the moſt preſſing Invitations to viſit their reſpective Courts.

THESE AMAZING

COLOSSUSES

Are but TWENTY-FOUR YEARS OF AGE,

AND VERY NEAR

EIGHT FEET HIGH.

Nor does that amazing Size more agreeably ſurpriſe the curious ſpectator, than their Proportion in every Reſpect to their ſtupendious Height; a Circumſtance ſo ſeldom to be found in any extraordinary Production of Nature.

Ladies and Gentlemen are reſpectfully informed, that the Hours of Admittance are from Ten in the Morning till Two in the Afternoon, and from Three to Nine at Night.—Their Stay will be but Six Days.

ADMITTANCE, Ladies and Gentlemen 1s.—Servants, &c. 6d.

Handbill for the showing of the two 'Irish Giants' in 1787 at the Golden Lion inn, Kendal. If the annotation is correct they were far from 8 feet in height, and at 6 feet 9 inches would hardly be considered 'giants' today.

Libraries

From 1794 there had been a subscription library in New Street. In 1854 it moved to Stricklandgate House under the auspices of the Kendal Literary and Scientific Society. This was only available to its subscribers, and out of reach of most Kendalians. The first public library in Kendal was set up under the 1891 Public Libraries Act in a building, at the entrance to the Market Place, which had been used as a covered market until the new market hall was opened in 1887. It stood upon the site of St George's chapel (1754–1855). When the new Carnegie Library was opened in 1909 in Stricklandgate the former library building was demolished but its façade re-erected in Sandes Avenue. For the first time in some two centuries this entrance to the Market Place was unimpeded—but not for long, as the war memorial was placed on the same spot in 1921. The Carnegie Library is a splendid building with red sandstone dressings and cost nearly £10,000, of which Andrew Carnegie, a Scottish-American millionaire and philanthropist, paid just over half. The library still has many of its original fittings and decorations. One of the few changes has been the transfer of the local collection from the front upstairs to new premises over the Elephant Yard shopping centre next door.

Carnegie Library, Stricklandgate.
BY COURTESY OF KENDAL TOWN COUNCIL

Museum of the Kendal Natural History & Science Society in Stricklandgate House.

BY COURTESY OF KENDAL TOWN COUNCIL

Museums

One of the unusual features of the Lake Counties in the eighteenth century was the existence of three commercial museums, relying for their business on the thriving tourist trade.[49] Two, Crosthwaite's and Hutton's, were in Keswick, and the third, run by William Todhunter, in Kendal. It was opened in Kirkland at the former *Seven Stars* public house in 1796 and moved in about 1800 to the corner of the fish market. Its collections were most varied. One or two handbills survive, as well as the eventual auction list in the local newspapers. William Gell, a tourist who came in 1797, was extremely unimpressed: 'We arrived at Kendal about six in the evening and saw there a miserable museum a most wretched imitation of Crosthwaite's.'[50] In fairness to Todhunter, it must be said that he had at that time only recently set up his museum. Its collections grew substantially over the years and eventually included much of local interest. Parson & White's directory of 1829 says of the museum that it had 'existed upwards of 30 years, during which time the proprietor has gathered together, at great labour and expense, a very large and interesting collection'.[51]

When Todhunter died in 1834 there was no successor, and the collections were sold at auction in 1835.[52] Some objects were acquired for the Museum of the Kendal Natural History & Science Society, established soon after in Stricklandgate House, and they have eventually reached the Kendal Borough Museum, established in 1910 in a former wool warehouse.[53] Among the specialities of both Crosthwaite's and Todhunter's museums were spectacular stone xylophones, Todhunter's using a hard limestone collected from Kendal Fell. This stone rings out surprisingly when hit by a wooden mallet. It appears that smaller versions were sold to visitors, while large multi-octave sets were used for performances by the Till and Richardson families, who must therefore be given their due recognition as two of the earliest 'rock bands'!

The borough museum was joined in 1962 by Abbot Hall Art Gallery, which not only has an excellent permanent collection of paintings and decorative arts, but also puts on substantial exhibitions of contemporary artists. The house, a family home until the late nineteenth century, was given to the Corporation in 1897, and its grounds became a public park. However, plans to make the hall a centre for the arts came to nothing and the building mouldered and decayed for over fifty years. Eventually in the 1950s a preservation trust was formed and the Lake District

Interior of the Museum.

BY COURTESY OF KENDAL TOWN COUNCIL

Abbot Hall, from a vignette on Todd's map of 1787.

The Brewery Arts Centre, occupying the former brewery of Whitwell, Mark & Co.

Art Gallery Trust, whose successor trust still runs it, restored it and set up the art gallery. It was opened officially in 1962. A later addition to the complex, in the former stable-block, was the opening in 1971 of the Museum of Lakeland Life and Industry. The Museum shows the artefacts illustrating the life and traditions of the Lake District, as well as the work of some of its famous authors such as Alfred Wainwright and Arthur Ransome.

Among Kendal's more memorable cultural assets is The Brewery, the arts centre that occupies the former Whitwell Mark & Co. Brewery buildings at the top of Highgate. The buildings were bought by the Lake District Theatre Trust Limited in 1970, and in May 1972 the Brewery Arts and Community Centre was opened. At that time it had only a small theatre and two other rooms. Today there is the 350-seat Malt Room for music events, a photographic gallery, the warehouse gallery for visual arts, a drama studio, art and crafts workshops, darkroom facilities, playgroup and meeting rooms, restaurant, Vats Bar, and an enlarged theatre seating 250, opened in 1993. Further improvements were made in 1998–2000 with Arts Council support, including two new cinema screens with 192 and 115 seats respectively.

Leisure

It is difficult for us to appreciate how little leisure time earlier generations had. The well-to-do, of course, had most control over their time, but many of that so-called 'leisured class' took on social, administrative and legal duties which today would represent paid employment. For the working people there was little or no time off during the week, the working day occupying most of the usable light. There were only occasional holidays, mostly of a religious nature, and no paid holiday at all until quite recent times. Of course the young and the active would still try to engage in leisure activities whenever and wherever they could, but officialdom took a dim view of many of their sports and pastimes and regarded them as either criminal or at least a nuisance, because of the noise or damage caused. Games played in churchyards were frowned upon because of where they took place, even more so if it was on Sunday. There were few areas of open space available for games because of the crowded nature of the town, and nothing that we would recognise as recreation grounds until the nineteenth century, so play almost inevitably led to damage and then to a ban … as perhaps it still does.

The prototypes of many games were loud and rough, with a fair chance of collateral damage. It was only with time and with respectability—some of the games were played in more sedate fashion, or at least according to sets of rules developed in the public schools—that there emerged a middle class that indulged in sport. It was a long time before any respectability was attached to working-class sports. But by the late nineteenth century employers and churches began to encourage 'wholesome' and 'healthy' sports as a means of occupying leisure time in a positive manner, keeping young men off the streets and out of the pubs. The first requirements were time in which to play, somewhere to play that did not offend the burghers, and finally the money for equipment and team uniforms.

Leisure and entertainment were therefore in short supply to medieval Kendalians. We hear little of either, although religious holidays and processions, as well as the markets and fairs, must have provided a little colour and variety in an otherwise monotonous diet, with an occasional outstanding event such as the Guild Merchant, held every twenty-one years. By the sixteenth century we see a little more evidence. Archery was not only popular but was actively encouraged as it was held to produce a nation capable of defending itself and offered 'manly' exercise. Generally our only information on popular pastimes in the past comes from when the authorities tried to ban or at least regulate them. That, too, carries on—think of the alarm over skate-boarding a few years ago—and so it was in 1657 with the sport of Kattstick and Bullyett, which was outlawed from the streets of Kendal for all inhabitants over twelve years old on pain of fine or imprisonment. The game was probably a form of 'knurr and spel', a sort of poor man's golf still practised in Yorkshire.[54]

A rough form of football was probably carried on from an early date. In 1641 it was ordered by the Corporation that 'whosoever do play at Football in the street and break any windows shall forfeit ... the sum of 12*d.* for every time every party and 3*s.* 4*d.* for every window by the same broken'.[55] Such draconian measures undoubtedly failed in their intent—and the fines were so large that no youth could afford them. The sport must have continued, unrecorded, but most references to football date from the early nineteenth century onwards. The form of football played until the later Victorian period was the ancestor of both football and rugby, and was traditionally played on Shrove Tuesday or another local festival time. It involved the younger male population of several villages and required the ball, or some other object, to be got by main force into the opponents' goal, with a large and ill-defined 'pitch', often covering a number of villages. There were few rules and many injuries, while property was frequently damaged by the scrimmage, so it became highly unpopular with the authorities. In 1819 the men of Killington, Natland and Hutton competed in such a game and the area of damage extended into Kendal itself.[56] Another such match took place in the same year at the *Beehive Inn*, between Kendal and its surrounding countryside.[57] The original football from one of these games is said to have been preserved at the *Football Inn* in the Market Place.[58] The game was carried on in several Cumbrian villages.[59] A few examples of this rougher kind of football still survive, despite generations of the frowns and tuts from both church and state. They include, among others, the Haxey Hood in Lincolnshire, bottle-kicking at Hallaton, Leicestershire, and football at Ashbourne, Derbyshire and Workington, Cumbria.[60]

Wrestling was also a popular sport, in a particular version still known as Cumberland and Westmorland wrestling, but probably at one time much more widespread. In this version the opponents, both wearing rather gorgeous costumes, would 'come to grips' within a ring and attempt to throw each other out or down. The main difference is that both would hold on to each other, rather than letting go to establish a better grip. This version of the sport seems to be extremely ancient, and a Norman font at Cowlam in East Yorkshire shows a pair of wrestlers gripping each other. This sport can now be seen mainly at Lakeland shows, such as Grasmere Sports, but once it was commonplace, usually as a side-event at races or other events such as the Doodleshire Races in Far Cross Bank. Bare-fist fighting became popular

Sunday School outing to Levens Park by canal barge. On Whit Tuesdays many children were sent out of the town thus to avoid Kendal Races and their associated evils.

BY COURTESY OF KENDAL TOWN COUNCIL

and widespread in the early nineteenth century, with many a brutal contest leading to serious injuries and large wagers on the outcome. There was a fight on Castle Hill as early as 1777 between Egerton Smith, a Kendal apprentice, and Adam Dodd.[61]

Horse-races took place at Kendal between 1820 and 1830. There were races here in the eighteenth century but little is known about them, or even where they were held. They were revived in 1820 when a temporary course was set up at Ladyford, near Burneside Hall. The next year the races moved onto the fell west of the town, at Scout Scar, and in due course a grandstand was constructed.[62] Even in its best years, though, the local press bemoaned the lack of support by local gentry, and like many other race-meetings Kendal's eventually fell victim to a combination of the Victorian religious reaction (as did the theatre) and to the social reaction against the betting, cheating, drinking and lawlessness that were generally associated with such events. Races were seen as attracting many 'bad lots' into the area, and said to have a corrupting effect on the poorer members of the populace. The wild behaviour of various members of the gentry could be safely overlooked.

Cock-fighting was closely associated with races and was held more or less clandestinely, although many of the gentry joined in. A match between Westmorland and Lancashire, known as a 'Welsh Main', took place at the Kendal races in 1828. It was held in a 'covered pit', which suggests some degree of permanence and therefore regularity about the sport.[63] It is said that the strange structure on the roof of 21 Highgate was originally used as a cockpit, but it seems more likely that it was a lantern to light the stairs.

While racing and cock-fighting were sports enjoyed both by the gentry and the unrespectable poor, there was little sporting outlet for the respectable working class or the growing middle class. Until the early nineteenth century neither had much spare time or inclination, but by the 1820s and 1830s time and enthusiasm were more readily available. Cricket and rugby were both regarded as 'respectable' sports, because of their association with the public schools. Teams were socially selective, but any activity that required special clothing or some sort of uniform inevitably tended to rule the majority out. In time some of the larger local firms saw the benefit of sport and sobriety in their workers, and started to sponsor equipment, grounds and clothing. Cricket was established in the town in 1829 with the founding of the Kendal Union Cricket

Rugby on Maude's meadow in the 1930s.

BY COURTESY OF KENDAL TOWN COUNCIL

Club.[64] Wood's map of 1833 shows a cricket ground on the east bank of the river just beyond the canal and opposite Abbot Hall. The club played a country match at Milnthorpe in 1834.[65] It became a founder member of the North Lancashire League in 1892 and of the Northern League in 1952. Its ground is now at Shap Road.

Rugby arrived much later, but by the late 1880s the town supported no fewer than three teams: the Hornets, Cardinals and Excelsiors. In 1888 a Maori touring side played in Kendal as part of a national visit. With the formation of Kendal RFC there has been a continuous tradition since 1905. The venue has, however, changed several times, from Mints Feet in 1905 to Maudes Meadow in 1906–07, then after the First World War to Mint Bridge off the Shap road.[66]

What we would recognise as football (as opposed to its rough predecessor considered earlier) began in Kendal in the 1890s—by 1894 there was a Kendal Association Football Club, with Arthur G. Brotherhood as its secretary. This was a relatively early beginning for organised football in a country market town, away from the heartland of the fast-rising game in the new industrial centres. Netherfield AFC dates from this time, and was associated with K Shoes which owned its ground and no doubt fostered the sport in other ways, as did so many large employers. The club became Kendal Netherfield FC after the severing of links with K Shoes in 1999.

Quieter forms of leisure included walking and picnicking on the high ground to the west of the town. In 1824 a group of 39 subscribers gave work to unemployed workers during

Serpentine Walk.
BY COURTESY OF KENDAL TOWN COUNCIL

left The former Croft's Victory Cycle Works at Stramongate Bridge.

right Enamelled sign for K Cycles, still to be seen in Redmayne's Yard, Stricklandgate.

a stagnation in trade, using their labour to create the Serpentine Walk over the fell, with woodland and a cottage to accommodate tea parties.[67] After mixed fortunes the area was thrown open to the public free of charge in 1847, and has been ever since. Cycling became a popular sport in the last quarter of the nineteenth century, with young men vying for speed and endurance on 'ordinary' (i.e. 'penny-farthing') bicycles. With the development of the safety bicycle the sport was opened up to women as well, becoming an important factor in female emancipation, since it allowed women to travel and to take part in events previously closed to them. Kendal had a Bicycle Club (William Bower, secretary) in 1894 and could also boast its own cycle manufacturers—Braithwaite Brothers, in New Inn Yard, Highgate, made 'K' Cycles, and there were also a number of agents and dealers for other makes. Askew Cycles on Wildman Street claims to be the oldest-established such firm in the town.

Food

Kendal had in the past many distinctive local foodstuffs, some of which have survived despite the growing uniformity of modern life. Many early visitors to the town mentioned clapbread, an oaten bread that was almost universal in the north of England, where wheat and consequently wheaten bread was scarce because of the wet climate. It was made in a number of ways, which led to differences in hardness, size and keeping ability.[68] Many people, not just the poorest, used it as a staple form of carbohydrate, breaking it up in soups and possets, or serving it with meat or cheese. The indefatigable lady traveller Celia Fiennes described its manufacture in Kendal in 1698:

> Here it was I saw the oat Clap bread made: they mix their flour with water so soft as to rowle it in their hands into a ball, and then they have a board made round and something

'Woman making oat cakes', from *The Costume of Yorkshire*, 1814.

hollow in the middle riseing by degrees all round to the edge a little higher, but so little as one would take it to be only a board warp'd, this is to cast out the cake thinn and so they clap it round and drive it to the edge in a due proportion till drove as thinn as a paper, and still they clap it and drive it round, and then they have a plaite of iron same size with their clap board and so shove off the cake on it and so set it on coales and bake it; when enough on one side they slide it off and put the other side; if their iron plaite is smooth and they take care their coales or embers are not too hot but just to make it looke yellow, it will bake and be as crisp and pleasant to eate as any thing you can imagine; but as we say of all sorts of bread there is a vast deale of difference in what is housewifely made and what is ill made ...[69]

We have already come across reference to a baker of 'Kendal Wigs', a yeasted bun flavoured with caraway seeds or currants. These were popular in the late eighteenth and early nineteenth centuries, when other cereals and hence wheaten flour began to be available in the area, and when the use of imported fruits and spices began to spread. However, Mrs Ann Martindale, who died in 1835 aged 86, was celebrated as a baker of rye bread, a dark, heavy and somewhat glutinous foodstuff which most people would have willingly given up had anything lighter been available.[70]

It is difficult to find evidence of what ordinary people ate in the past. Most evidence comes from the middling sorts or the well-to-do, and thus is not characteristic of the majority of local society. However, in 1797 Eden wrote of this area of Westmorland that,

> Oat-cake is the principal bread used by the labouring classes: the men generally eat hasty-pudding, or boiled milk, twice a day: the women live much on tea, but have, of late, discontinued the use of sugar. Potatoes are a very general article for dinner: they are sometimes eaten with a little butter, and sometimes with meat; and not infrequently without either.[71]

In his memoir of life in the 1820s and 1830s in Kendal Richard Haresnape gives a snapshot of the food offered in those days to apprentices, which sounds quite generous, although of course the work was physical and the hours were long:

> in the morning a basin of porridge, bread and cheese and milk; dinner was always a solid meal of meat and potatoes, frequently followed by a pudding; in the afternoon the younger apprentices had a gill of beer with bread and butter; the elder ones tea instead of beer; at night again a basin of porridge.[72]

Potted char, a particular local delicacy, was known much further afield as it was preserved and so would travel well. The only source of the fish (*salmo savelinus*), a relation of the trout, was Windermere. Celia Fiennes commented in 1698:

> At the Kings Arms one Mrs. Rowlandson she does pott up the charr fish the best of any in the country, I was curious to have some and so bespoke some of her, and also was as curious to see the great water [Windermere] which is the only place that fish is to be found in ... Charr fish being out of season could not easily be taken so I saw none alive...the season of the Charrfish is between Michaelmas and Christmas, at that tyme I have had of them which they pott with sweete spices, they are as big as a small trout rather slenderer and the skinn full of spotts some redish, and part of the whole skinn and the finn and taile is red like the finns of a perch, and the inside flesh looks as red as any salmon; if they are in season their taste is very rich and fatt tho' not so strong or clogging as the lamprys are, but its as fatt and rich a food.[73]

In the 1720s Daniel Defoe referred to char as 'a curious fish [which] as a dainty, is potted, and sent far and near, as presents to best friends'.[74] The practice was perhaps begun, or at least most enthusiastically carried on, by Sir Daniel Fleming of Rydal in the last quarter of the seventeenth century.[75] In 1816 60 dozen of char were caught near Miller Ground, on Windermere,[76] but by this time they were being over-fished. Account books for the sale of char between 1821 and 1836 survive among the papers of William Garnett, fishmonger of Bowness.[77] Kendal became a centre for their sale and potting.

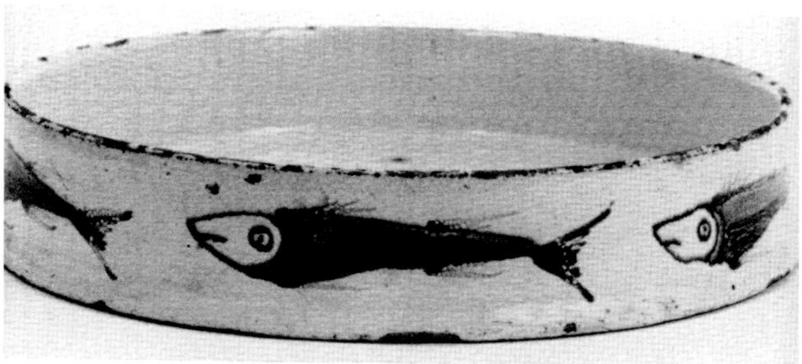

Delft ware char pot, probably made in Liverpool or Lancaster.

They were generally potted in shallow vertical-sided dishes with lids (or possibly paper covers). Many examples survive, the vertical sides having naively painted fish swimming around them. The pots were made in the Liverpool delftware and creamware potteries, and as we now know, also in delftware at Lancaster.[78] The practice seems similar to that still used for potting Morecambe Bay shrimps, in spiced butter.

Although not a manufactured foodstuff, damsons grown locally (and in particular of course in the Lyth Valley) were an important staple of Kendal's trade, justifying a special fair called 'Damson Saturday' in late September.[79] In 1938 as much as 250 tons of damsons was sold in Westmorland, mostly through Kendal. The coming of war in 1939 effectively killed off the trade, which had largely been to jam factories in Lancashire and Yorkshire, because of the lack of sugar supplies. The woodlands of the Lake District also produced nuts in profusion, and these, too, were often sold through Kendal.

A dinner held for the Commercial Travellers' Association on Christmas Eve 1841 at the *King's Arms* inn was graced by a huge pie seven feet in circumference, ten inches in depth, and weighing 5 stone 8 pounds (in metric terms, 2.13 metres × 25.4 cm, 35.5 kg). It contained two fat geese, two large turkeys, four fowls, two pheasants, four grouse, two hares, four prize rabbits, three tongues, beefsteak and ham.[80] Surprisingly, perhaps, it seems not to have created an epidemic of food-poisoning, a common hazard with such spectacularly large but often seriously under-cooked pies. Perhaps that was at the end of a long tradition of extra-large

Pure Home-made Confectionery.
DANIEL QUIGGIN,
WHOLESALE CONFECTIONER,
AND SUGAR BOILER,
86, Stricklandgate, & 25, Allhallows Lane,
KENDAL.
All Sweets are Guaranteed Pure and are sold at the lowest prices.
Mint Rock, Butter Drops, and Butter Toffee—a Speciality.
Our Cream and Treacle Toffee is Delicious.
TRY QUIGGIN'S "MONA" DROPS for Winter Use.
SHOPS SUPPLIED ON THE BEST TERMS.

left
Advertisment for Daniel Quiggin, 1906.

right
Quiggin's shop, 44 Highgate.

BY COURTESY OF KENDAL TOWN COUNCIL

Christmas pies in Kendal, matching that of the Yorkshire Christmas pies with hot-water crust and varied contents which are described by Peter Brears.[81] Another enormous pie had passed through Kendal in January 1763 on its way from Lowther to London, where it was to be a present for Lord Bute from James Lowther, his son-in-law. Mrs Maude of Highgate remembered it travelling in its own waggon, pulled by two horses.[82]

Quite the most famous modern product of the town is Kendal Mintcake, a glucose-based sweet tablet invented by Joseph Wiper in about 1869 while he was trying to make a clear glacier mint. It is extremely simple in composition, being made of sugar, water, peppermint oil and, in some recipes, a little milk.[83] Joseph himself emigrated to Canada, but the recipe was bought in 1919 by George Romney Ltd, then a wholesale confectionery supplier, which started making it in a yard in Highgate and has been making it ever since (and bought out Wipers in the 1980s). Mintcake gained its special international fame from being taken on the successful ascent of Everest in 1953: as Sir Edmund Hillary remembered, he and Sherpa Tenzing 'made seats for ourselves in the snow, and sitting there in reasonable comfort we ate with relish a bar of mintcake'. Since then, with that accolade, Kendal mintcake has filled the pockets and rucksacks of many thousands of walkers and climbers. Today three local firms, Quiggins, Romneys, and Wilsons, all make versions of mintcake, increasingly in 'exotic' forms such as chocolate covered or rum-and-butter flavour, or in gift boxes. Romneys took over Wipers' business in 1987 but still retain the brand. As an energy-source mintcake is very convenient and compact, but rarely can something so simple have made such an impact, and carried the name of its home town around the world.

Customs

On Easter Monday in the nineteenth century up to 1,500 children used to come to Kendal Castle for the egg-rolling ceremony, when eggs were trundled against each other by pairs of children. The loser's egg (the one whose shell was first to break) was forfeit to the winner, who ate it then and there.[84] Characteristic of the rougher customs of earlier times was that of 'barring out'. It was carried out by the scholars of the grammar school against their master, and involved keeping him out of the school by all means fair and foul until he agreed to a holiday, or holidays. The practice was not unique to Kendal, and often included food bribes which the poorer schoolmasters found hard to resist. The practice led to one schoolmaster, the Reverend John Towers, losing an eye in an incident in about 1740.[85]

This practice of 'barring out' was also associated with Sergeant Monday, the occasion each October when children would scramble or 'scraffle' for apples. The bellman, wearing his full regalia, would lead a large group of boys who had escaped their studies to the town hall,[86] where the new mayor was elected. The mayor's sergeants would then throw large quantities of apples or nuts out of the windows of the town hall and the boys scrambled for them. It matched the lavish feasting that would take place at the beginning and end of the mayoral year. The custom came to an end with the new Corporation in 1835.[87]

As we have already seen, Corpus Christi plays were put on by the various trade companies until the beginning of the seventeenth century. These were clearly used as an excuse for excessive consumption of food or drink (or at least the Corporation thought so). A ban on this is among the orders written in the 1575 *Boke off Recorde*, while some dispute about the authorising of these plays appears in 1586.[88] Evidently excess consumption was only part of the problem, for the authorities worried about the gathering of large numbers of people, where (they feared) treason or subversion might be fomented. Tudor authority was very jumpy about such things. The source reveals that 'Shotings in long bows' as well as the planning of the Corpus Christi plays was a reason (or pretext) for such gatherings.

The same record reveals the existence of 'merye nyghts' and 'Nutcasts', as well as 'Applecasts', all of them occasional sources of entertainment for local people in the late sixteenth century. 'Merye nyghts' were a well-known part of the social calendar in the northern counties, being an informal mixture of singing, dancing, story-telling, eating and drinking, roughly equivalent to a *ceilidh*.[89] 'Nutcasts' were equated by the editor of the *Boke off Recorde* with Nutcrack Night on All Hallows' Eve, although in the context it looks like a more frequent event, and the word 'nutcasts' seems to indicate more a distribution of nuts, similar to the apples of Sergeant Monday.[90] And Kendal also had its maypole, standing in Kirkland near the parish church and a little to the north of the *Wheatsheaf Inn*.[91] It was removed in the 1780s, but its base was rediscovered in 1903 and is now in the museum.[92]

Crime and punishment | 12

IN A TOWN SUCH AS KENDAL, where for centuries most people knew each other, where strangers were very noticeable, and where much of everyone's business was known, there was, historically, not a great deal of crime. Of course, people still got drunk, fell out with each other, or tried to obtain some small advantage, but it would have been difficult to get away with more serious crime, a state of affairs that persisted until rapid and cheap transport threatened to change the position radically. Even today the level of crime, whatever local perceptions might be, is low. For centuries the peace, such as it was, was kept in the town by constables appointed by the corporation. They had manifold duties other than attending to law and order issues, and even on occasion had to form the thin blue line between the corporation's junketing and the angry populace: an anonymous diarist records that on 25 September 1815, when there was a mayoral feast, 'the Constables all got a beating a pretty shine'.[1]

Police Office and Fire Engine House from the large-scale Ordnance Survey of 1861.

PHOTOGRAPH CARNEGIE, FROM AN ORIGINAL HELD AT WESTMORLAND RECORD OFFICE, KENDAL

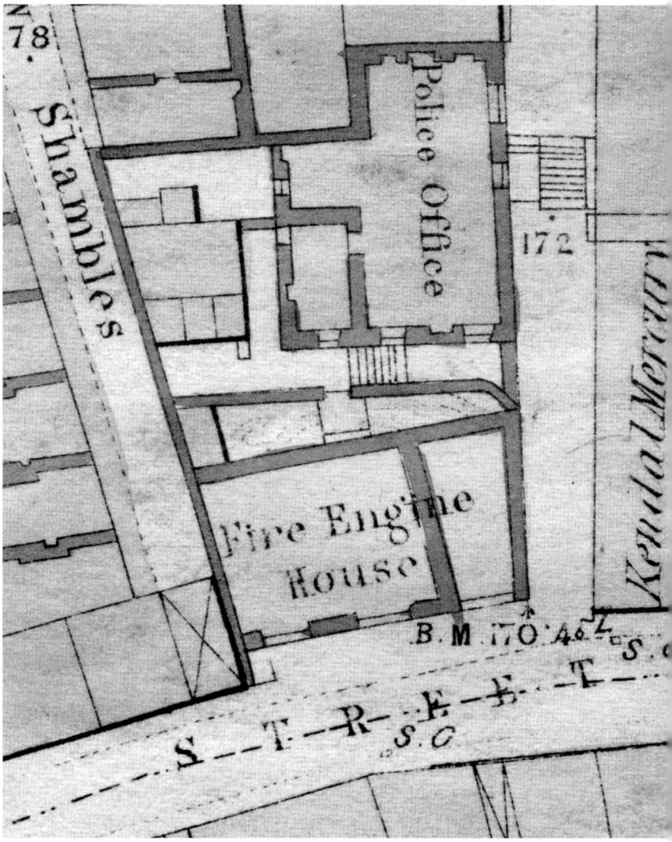

Before the creation of the police force the town had a 'watch', which operated only in the winter months (when darkness made it easier to get away with committing crime). In 1831, under the name of the 'Patrol', it in theory consisted of two men for Kirkland and ten for Kendal, under the overall control of Mr Unsworth, the police officer.[2] However, Richard Haresnape states that in 1830, when he first came to Kendal, there were only two (Thomas Barrow and Dan Ellwood).[3] Kendal's police force was established in 1836, following the reform of municipal corporations. The Commission on Municipal Corporations report of 1837 states, 'there is no watch or police now, but the one Constable appointed by the Rate Payers', but this must surely refer to some interim position.[4] After the Westmorland County Constabulary was formed in 1856 the borough force was administered by the chief constable of the county, until in 1876 it acquired its own chief constable. As a small force which paid only modest salaries it was normally unable to retain the services of its chief constables for very long. The government's Inspector of Constabulary made annual inspections and reports on all the police forces in the country, and those for Kendal are summarised in the table below.

Inspectors of Constabulary reports for Kendal Borough Police

1892–93
14 in force
Chief Constable also runs fire brigade, all policemen
1 Chief Constable (salary £260)
3 Sergeants (30 shillings per week)
10 Constables (28–23 shillings per week)

1899–1900
16 in force
4 Chief Constables in five years; the last just left to be Chief Constable of York (James Burrow) and his replacement is Charles Harriss [he did not last long either; in 1902 he became Chief Constable of Lancaster]

Superintendent Notman of the Westmorland County Police and his wife with a pony and trap.
BY COURTESY OF KENDAL TOWN COUNCIL

Chief Constable also runs Fire Brigade, all policemen
1 Chief Constable (salary £160)
1 Inspector (salary £91)
2 Sergeants (30 shillings per week)
12 Constables (26–23 shillings per week)

1900–1901
16 in force
1 Chief Constable (salary £160)
1 Inspector (salary £91)
2 Sergeants (30 shillings per week)
12 Constables (29–23 shillings per week)[5]

The methods of policing progressed relatively little in the early twentieth century, and almost all aspects of the work still depended upon officers on the beat, observation and a network of information. The individual policemen communicated by means of a wooden rattle, and later by whistle. Another means of getting attention was to rap the kerb with their truncheon, a sound that could carry over considerable distances. Sergeants and senior officers met their constables at pre-arranged times and places to maintain a finger on the pulse of law-keeping. There were few technical aids until cars became reliable (and necessary, since a main road passed through the town).

The emergency nationalisation and combining of police and fire services during the Second World War showed the benefits of co-operative working (which really meant amalgamation) in both fire brigades and police forces. In 1947 the Kendal force was amalgamated with the Westmorland County Constabulary, which itself later combined with Cumberland, and then also with parts of Lancashire to form the Cumbria Police in 1974. Recently it appeared that the force would once again amalgamate, this time with Lancashire, to create a regional force. For the time being this idea is in abeyance, but the inexorable trend seems to be towards larger and larger units in order to afford the wide range of specialised services needed by a modern police force. The creation of a regional force surely cannot be far in the future.

Chief Constables of the Kendal Borough Police

1876–1882	Joseph Wilkinson
1881–1890	Thomas Cotton
1890–1895	Luke Talbot
1895–1899	George Hardy
1899–1900	James Burrows
1900–1902	Charles E. Harriss
1902–1908	A.M. Berry
1908–1923	I. Joseph Smith
1923–1947	Patrick O'Neill

Imprisonment

The county gaol was at Appleby, where the privileges of a county town were jealously guarded. The House of Correction, however, was Kendal's prison, standing beyond the northern end of Stricklandgate on what was to become House of Correction Hill. The following description was written in 1829:

> The House of Correction at the north end of the town, serves both for the borough and the county, and was built in 1786, but was greatly enlarged and altered in 1828 and 1829, so that it now contains 35 sleeping rooms, and 15 day rooms, with a Governor's house, commanding a view of the whole prison, which is circumscribed by a strong wall, enclosing a triangular area nearly 240 yards in circumference. Mr. James Fawcett is the present Governor.[6]

There had been an earlier House of Correction, probably on the same site. Evidence points to its existence (and disrepair) in the early eighteenth century, and in 1731 its master, Miles Atkinson, reported that it was 'ruinnous and very likely to fall down'.[7] About £400 was spent in 1786 on the construction of the new Kendal House of Correction, and a further £5,500 between 1817 and 1832 on extending it.[8] It was closed as a civil prison in 1894 but used for

left The grim outline of the House of Correction on House of Correction Hill.

right Interior of the House of Correction, built in 'porridge' or Pentonville fashion, with landings.

BY COURTESY OF KENDAL TOWN COUNCIL

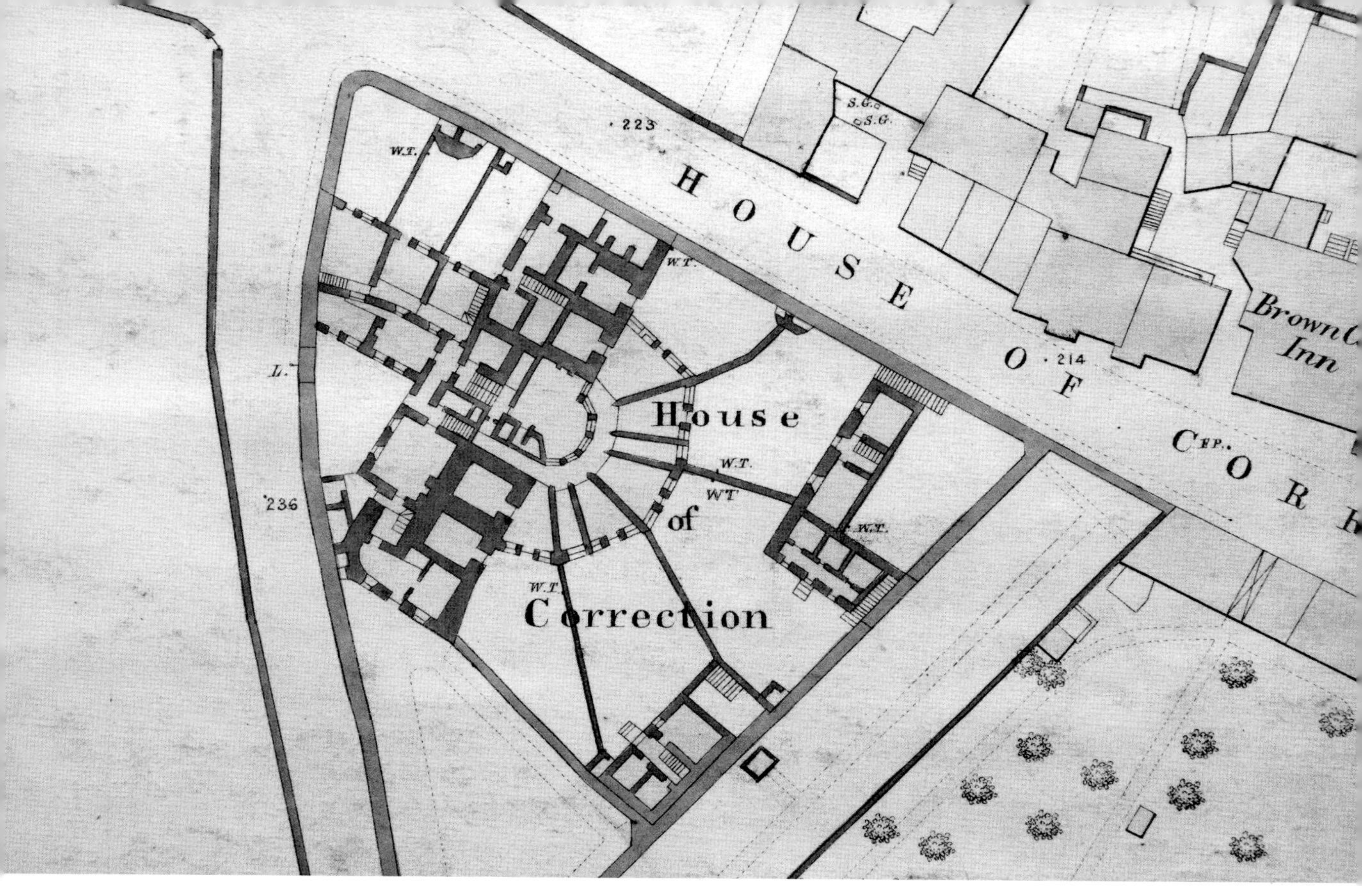

Plan of the House of Correction showing the radiating exercise yards, from the large-scale Ordnance Survey of 1861.

PHOTOGRAPH CARNEGIE, FROM AN ORIGINAL HELD AT WESTMORLAND RECORD OFFICE, KENDAL

military prisoners until after the Boer War (1899–1902).[9] Photographs of the interior show that at some stage the main block was adapted to the classic 'porridge' or Pentonville model, with a series of landings opening off a open central well, and cells opening off each of these.[10] House of Correction or not, this was a prison in the usually understood sense of the word.

Kendal had its own borough court, the Court of Conscience, from 1764. It was used by townspeople to settle disputes (usually of a financial nature). Many found it useful to have an official record of their disputes and settlements, in case of later repercussions. More serious cases might be dealt with by the county quarter sessions, held at both Appleby and Kendal, but many cases from Kendal town were clearly heard at the borough court, since much of the business of the quarter sessions was from surrounding villages and Kirkland, outside the borough's jurisdiction. The quarter sessions, where the county magistrates or justices of the peace sat, covered a very wide range of business, including the civil administration of the county. As well as criminal offences, they also dealt with bastardy orders, petitions for poor relief, other aspects of Poor Law business, approving people serving parish and ward offices, civil defence and the militia, and roads and bridges. This last role, which they exercised under the Highways Act of 1555, was used to enforce work on roads and bridges which had not had adequate repairs, or were sub-standard. An example is the presentment of 'Braidleyfield Laine' in 1733 for being out of repair.[11]

Petty theft was a common reason for appearance at the quarter sessions. For example in 1735

Martin Wilson of Dillicar, yeoman, was accused of stealing two half-pounds of combed wool from John Atkinson in Kendal, one drab-coloured, the other light blue, with a leather bag. The case was thrown out, but reappeared a year later.[12] William Towers, late of Kendal, butcher, appeared in 1755 on a charge of stealing back a promissory note for £1 19*s.* 4*d.* from John Jackson and then destroying it. He, too, was found not guilty.[13] Disputes between neighbours were not uncommon. In 1757 Abigail Horn missed some silver teaspoons inscribed 'HJA' (the initials of her husband and herself). Later she was invited to tea by Isabel Canny, a widow, of Kirkland. Imagine her surprise when she saw a teaspoon marked just the same! Isabel was taken to court for theft—her defence was that she had bought it from a Jewish pedlar in Kirkland some years before, and whether or not that was true the court threw the case out. Isabel would have had to be rather stupid in any case to invite in a neighbour if she had in fact stolen the spoon from her.[14] In 1795 it was alleged that Benjamin Hamley of Kirkland, a blacksmith, had stolen three pairs of stockings worth sixpence from the yard adjoining the house of George Hastwell. The court found him guilty and sentenced him to confinement for six weeks in a single cell in the House of Correction. This might seem an excessive punishment but he was perhaps lucky—theft of goods with just a little more value could have seen him hanged or transported.[15]

A good deal of the juvenile crime recorded between the sixteenth and eighteenth centuries involved being caught playing games in unsuitable places or on the Sabbath. However, there seems to be evidence for a more serious crime, that of the persecution of John Allen, a Kirkland hosier, by eight apprentices of neighbouring hosiers in 1764. Their masters had to find recognisances for their future good behaviour.[16]

Much of the punishment meted out by local courts in the seventeenth and eighteenth centuries was of a summary nature, designed to act as a warning and an example to others. Pending trial, prisoners were held in a cell in the town hall or later in the 'Black Hole' under St George's Chapel. A cuckstool was set up in 1589 for drunkards and scolds—a device for ducking the unfortunate victim in the river, no doubt a very frightening and quite possibly fatal experience.[17] As late as 1810 an anonymous Kendal diarist records, 'Ducking the whores in the mill Dam', which sounds like a late, less formal extension of the older practice.[18] Many others, both men and women, were whipped, either through the streets at the tail of a cart, or at a fixed point such as the whipping post. Robert Dickenson was sentenced to be whipped from the Cold Stone to Newbiggin for theft in 1717,[19] and James Addyson at the whipping post for petty larceny in 1720,[20] while Richard Smith was whipped from the Cold Stone to the barn at Nether Bridge End in 1723.[21] As late as 1776, Isobel Lowis was to be whipped to the maypole in Kirkland for theft.[22] The stocks were also used, both in the borough near St George's Chapel and in Kirkland, as a means of public humiliation, generally for offences such as drunken behaviour.[23] Thus one Nathan Sandwich was sentenced for being drunk in 1816 to sit in Kirkland stocks for six hours on several Sundays.[24]

Prison was little used as a punishment for petty offences at this time. The prison cells were mainly used for holding prisoners until another sentence, rarely custodial, was established. In

Victorian times, however, there was a considerable change, following the drastic reduction in the range of crimes that carried the death penalty, a process beginning in the 1830s. There was a new move towards custodial sentences under a highly oppressive prison regime. This included hard labour, which ranged from sewing mailbags to less useful exercises, such as carrying heavy weights, or to the treadmill, henceforth a standard item in prisons. The more wearisome and pointless the labour, the more it was approved by the authorities. This paralleled the move to make workhouses as distasteful an experience as was humanly possible.

We know relatively little of Kendal's malefactors, apart from those recorded as whipped or pilloried, but Duncan's *Reminiscences* (1890) hints darkly at some early nineteenth-century 'bad women' who lived, and plied their trade, in the lower part of the town—they included Mal Madge and May Monkhouse.[25] We also know of an export, Margaret Heaton alias 'Kendale Peg', who kept a disorderly house in Lancaster in the 1760s.[26] There was little chance of any of these prostitutes or their clients remaining discreet or unseen in a town where everyone knew each other's business. Then, as today, there was an uneasy mixture of official turning of a blind eye, tempered with occasional exemplary punishment.

More serious cases, both criminal and civil, were referred to the assizes, which were held twice a year in the county town, Appleby. This was part of the higher court system that had been established in the twelfth century, whereby the justice of the King's Bench was administered throughout the land, by judges travelling in pairs on six 'circuits': Westmorland formed part of the northern circuit. From the early sixteenth century it was accepted that only assize judges had the power to impose the death penalty. A few early Kendal victims of the gallows, after the assizes at Appleby, have burial entries in the parish registers: Thomas Waltam in August 1617, Edward Moore and William Curwen in August 1618, and Peter Rowlandson in 1630.[27] With its small population and relative peacefulness the county did not produce arduous business for the judges. Indeed it was said in 1813 that only one Westmorland man had been executed in the county for a century, even against a background of a savage and to our eyes excessive and over-reactive law code.

A few Kendal cases tried at Appleby give a flavour of the whole. A case of stabbing at the *Elephant Inn* in Kendal led to a 'not guilty' verdict in 1820,[28] but in 1822 Dr Towers, who had shot dead his wife and then attempted to shoot himself, was declared insane and detained at Appleby. A few months later he helped to foil the escape of another prisoner.[29] In 1828 John Wells was found guilty of knocking down and robbing Henry Mattinson in the *Nag's Head* yard, and was transported to Australia for seven years.[30] In the following year a servant girl, Agnes Cornthwaite, returning home to Kendal through Kendal Parks, was brutally raped by three men. One turned king's evidence and one was only 16 years old, but William Jennings, aged 17, was executed at Appleby soon after the trial.[31]

One notorious Kendal man accused at the assizes in the 1820s was Solomon Carradice, an inveterate poacher. He was found guilty of trespass in Levens Park, but only in damages of the sum of one farthing. However, as he could not pay legal costs he was imprisoned at Appleby for eighteen months. Little over a year after emerging from prison he was back, this time for a year, for an assault on a gamekeeper at Levens. Such punishment tended towards a vicious circle of poverty and crime.[32] In this period the game laws were most brutally enforced, many landowners using spring-guns and man-traps to maim poachers, or invoking the full force of the law to deal with them if they persisted. As these landowners were often also the magistrates it was a very one-sided affair. Coinciding with the end of the Napoleonic wars in 1815, with many former soldiers and sailors seeking work in vain, and a series of disastrous harvests (such as the so-called 'year without a summer' of 1816) this decade was a hungry one for many families. Brutality inspired brutality, and poachers and gamekeepers had many a running battle, with wrong on both sides.

On the whole, though, Kendal has always been a peaceful and largely crime-free area, apart from occasional election-related or drink-induced fights and fracases. It has had little to show in the way of major crimes or famous criminals. Long may that continue!

War and other troubles | 13

For most Kendalians throughout history life must have been relatively peaceful. The overall calm of life in the town was disrupted only by occasional mob activity (especially at elections), and the workforce was generally industrious and serious-minded. However, there were from time to time events that left their mark on ordinary people and with which their personal history was punctuated. In more recent times the Second World War was one such, leading to memories of 'before the war'. In many towns these events included extensive fires, leading to dramatic rebuilding. Fire was an ever-present danger in towns of timber-framed buildings, but Kendal has been comparatively lucky in that respect, with no serious fires except perhaps in the mid-fourteenth century and definitely in 1698. A petition to the king, asking him to reduce taxation on the town after a great fire which occurred about a month after Michaelmas [that is, at the end of October], suggests a major disaster—its date is unknown, but circumstantial evidence suggests that it was sent in about 1360.[1]

In 1698, after a serious fire, the overseers of the poor raised over £8 in contributions from the three wards of the borough. However, only four householders were compensated, which suggests that the event was small beer by the standards of town fires elsewhere. The absence of an organised fire service and the general use of timber and thatch made such problems an everyday risk, and a small fire might easily spread. The absence of major fires has helped Kendal to retain to a high degree its medieval street pattern and the wide variety of date and style of its buildings. On 11 July 1788, though, there was a destructive fire on the west side of Stricklandgate following a gunpowder explosion.[2]

The main road passing through Kendal, the key western route to Scotland, did however bring unwelcome visitors—hostile armies from Scotland or, hardly more welcome, English armies chasing the Scots back again. There were several such destructive episodes in Kendal's medieval history, which may have contributed to the early loss of medieval buildings—though that was not unusual in northern towns. The first recorded episode was in 1322, after the rebellion of Thomas, earl of Lancaster against his cousin, Edward II. During the subsequent power-vacuum the Scots invaded northern England, dividing their army into two halves. One of these, under the Earl of Moray and Lord James Douglas, headed south by Shap and Kendal and then joined further south with the other half, under King Robert Bruce, which had come via the Solway fords, the Cumberland coast and over the sands of Morecambe Bay.[3]

In common with other towns in the path of the invading armies, Kendal suffered considerable destruction by the Scots. There is no direct evidence for the damage, but when the lord of the Richmond Fee, Ingram de Gynes, died in 1324 it was recorded that the burgage rents had fallen in value from 40 shillings to 6 shillings, the proceeds of the court and stallage (fines for trading as a non-burgess) from 26*s.* 8*d.* to nothing, and the fishery in the water of Kent was halved in value from £4. Evidence from elsewhere suggests that such reductions in values were the consequence of the burning of property and theft of livestock and goods.[4] There may have been a Scottish raid in 1389 in the aftermath the battle of Otterburn (Northumberland), when neighbouring Lancaster certainly suffered and petitioned the king for aid. It is hardly likely that Lancaster alone would have experienced difficulties, since Kendal was on the same strategic road, and nearer to Scotland.[5]

The Civil War of the 1640s had little direct effect on Kendal, which was not the scene of any battle or siege, but the economic impact was undoubtedly felt, and the fear and uncertainty which was ubiquitous during wartime. The town was not a strategic prize of any value to either side, but during the Second Civil War in August 1648 a huge Scots army, numbering between 18,000 and 24,000 men under the Duke of Hamilton, passed through Kendal on its way south—it was soon after defeated by Cromwell at Preston. History does not record the impressions of Kendalians, but even the comparatively peaceful passage of such an army would leave a deep impression on those who watched it. Judging by the better-documented visit by the Jacobite forces in 1745, such an army would take days to pass through the town, and would demand considerable resources of food and drink, as well as horses and wagons, which it was unwise to refuse. The same was no doubt true of the Scots army led by General Leslie in support of Prince Charles Stuart (later King Charles II) which came through Kendal in August 1651, before its defeat at Worcester. The new king was proclaimed at market crosses on the way, including that of Kendal, but in reality he to wait another nine years before actually taking the throne.

Sixty-four years later, in 1715, there was another commotion as the Jacobite army passed through the town on its way to defeat, again at Preston. The rebellion was the result of the succession of George I of Hanover to the throne, which offended many Protestants as well as Catholics. The rebels marched in the name of the Old Pretender, James III, the son of James II who had been deposed (or abdicated, depending on your political perspective) in 1688. The Jacobites appeared in Kendal on 5 November and the mayor, Thomas Scarisbrick, was able to gain sufficient intelligence on their numbers and disposition to materially assist the government army to defeat them a few days later. According to Peter Clarke, a witness, they made a poor show in the town: 'their horse and their footmen did not draw their swords, nor shew their Colours, neither did any drums beat. Onely six highland bagpipes played,' and 'it rained very hard here this day.' That might have had some impact, for the Kendal weather can be very disheartening at times.[6] The Jacobite army of 1715 was quite small (only about 1,600 men) and made up of Scots and disaffected northerners, some of whom later paid the price of rebellion. After the defeat many were executed and a larger number imprisoned—400 at Lancaster alone—in such deplorable conditions that of over 200 prisoners held longer than the first month, one in five died of gaol fever, along with a number of their gaolers and guards.[7]

Thirty years later another Jacobite army marched through Kendal. Those of 1745 were very different in many ways—better led, more organised, and in greater numbers. However, they failed to attract much local support as they passed through northern England, many potential sympathisers no doubt dissuaded by the memory of what had happened in 1715. The country had in any case become more at peace with itself, and the lack of general support here was matched by a failure even of many Scots to join the rebellion. This time those that did marched with the Young Pretender, Prince Charles Edward, in the name of his father, James. The army was about 6,000 strong, mainly Highland Scots with a number of Irish professional officers who had seen service in Europe. Their leadership, principally that of Lord George Murray, was excellent, and they maintained discipline and good order in the most trying circumstances, especially the winter weather.

The advance guard of the army, Lord Elcho and his Lifeguards, arrived in Kendal on 20 November: 'all brave men, poorly mounted and in good spirits. ... They are dressed with two pistols on each side, a musket slung over their shoulder and a broadsword. They have plenty of money, principally French guineas.'[8] These men arranged billeting for the main body of the army which followed them on 22–23 November, among them the prince himself. Tradition states that he stayed in the house at 95 Stricklandgate. By now some four-fifths of the army was gathered in Kendal, and the advance guard moved on. Even an army of 6,000 took several days to pass through a town, the vanguard and rearguard being some miles apart, unless imminent attack was expected. The stringing-out of the army aided the feeding and billeting requirements, spreading the burden which, for the entire army, would have been overwhelming.

On 24 November the prince was still in Kendal, and was proclaimed regent for his father by the army.[9] The Jacobites then moved on into Lancashire and ultimately to Derby where, because of the failure to attract sufficient English recruits, the decision was taken to return to Scotland. It was a bitter blow for the prince, for the government armies were neither well led nor well motivated, and there is a very real chance that the Jacobites could have broken through to London and victory. Even in retreat they maintained the initiative, and on several occasions turned about and inflicted serious damage on their pursuers, notably at Clifton, just south of Penrith, usually claimed to be the last battle on English soil.

The advance guard of the retreating army came back into Kendal on 14 December in very different circumstances. The townsfolk were in a dangerous mood, and it was market day. They stoned the horsemen of the Duke of Perth as they rode through Finkle Street, and a shot was fired at them. His men returned fire on the crowd and three townsmen were killed, but five Scots were captured including the duke's cook, who later died of his wounds. The parish registers record the burial on 15 December of two men, Richard Toulman and Archibald Armstronge of Highgate, 'kil'd by ye Rebbels', and of two more, John Slack of New

above
'Charlie's Café Bar' in Bonnie Prince Charlie's House (95 Stricklandgate).
PHOTOGRAPH: ELLIE GODDARD

below
The Duke of Cumberland inn, Far Cross Bank.

Hutton 'kil'd by ye Scotts' and a 'Scotch reball his name not known' (perhaps Perth's cook?) on the following day.[10] Perth's men retreated northwards from the town and on the next day the main army arrived. Some of Lord George Murray's horses were stolen, and the hitherto disciplined Highlanders reacted by looting and causing other damage, which was eventually controlled. On 16 December the army moved forwards towards Shap in appalling weather conditions. The rearguard patrolled the roads to the south beyond Nether Bridge and the *Cock & Dolphin* inn until the main body was safely out of the town, as the pursuers were coming ever closer.

That same day the advance guard of the Hanoverian forces arrived in Kendal, and on the following day, 17 December, the Duke of Cumberland himself arrived, staying, by tradition, in the same house in Stricklandgate so recently relinquished by Bonnie Prince Charlie.[11] The retreat into Scotland and eventual defeat of the Jacobites at Culloden in 1746 is another story. One tiny Kendal footnote to this event is the death in 1817 of Elizabeth Clark, aged 90, who in 1745 had charged the rebels the outrageous price of 3½*d.* per pound of butter. She must have dined out often on this heroic story.[12]

From its position on the fast-flowing river Kent the town also suffered more than its fair share of inundations, which punctuate its history at irregular intervals until flood prevention work reduced the incidence. The river has a large catchment in the high fells to the north of the town, so that heavy rain or snowmelt can quickly result in the rapid rise of the river, and its powerful destructive force being unleashed. Most of the early floods are now forgotten—they must have been frequent, and not in any sense remarkable, and in any case the built-up area of the town had not yet extended onto the lower ground. But in the

Floods at Victoria Bridge in 1898.

BY COURTESY OF KENDAL TOWN COUNCIL

nineteenth and twentieth centuries there was a series of severe and destructive floods which are recorded in the newspapers and on markers by the river. Their significance was now that they threatened both houses and industry, because of the spread of both into vulnerable areas. Some of the worst recorded were in 1635, 1671, 1771, 1772, 1890 and 1968, but a marker on the riverbank near the foot of Lowther Street records the height of some of the principal floods—those in 1831, 1861, 1927, 1954 and, the highest of all, 1898.[13] Modern flooding is more destructive to houses because of their construction and their electrical and drainage systems. Until at least the mid-nineteenth century solid floors and absence of such systems rendered flooding a nuisance rather than a menace, unless people were actually swept away.

Luckily for Kendal the disastrous Cumbrian floods of 2009 had little effect here, the epicentre of the heaviest rainfall lying in the north-west of the Lake District. The building of flood defences through Kendal and the better management of the flow after 1972 have reduced the risk considerably. However, as the case of Lowther Park area of the town in 1999 shows, knowing that an area is liable to flood can not necessarily be used as a defence by the planning authority against rash building. It sometimes takes actual flooding of that area after building has taken place to force some retrospective action. In this case the action was the Stock Beck Flood Alleviation Scheme, a notable case of locking the stable door after the horse had bolted.[14] Despite the apparent success of the improvements to the river-flow of the Kent in recent years it would be unwise to claim that the risk has been entirely eradicated!

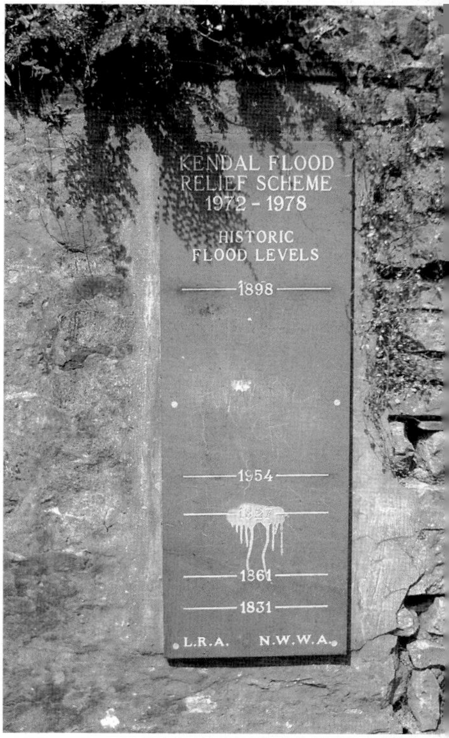

Flood marker near the foot of Lowther Street.

Notes and references

Chapter 1: Origins

1 E. Ekwall, *English River Names* (OUP: Oxford, 1928), 226–8; E. Ekwall, *Concise Oxford Dictionary of English Place-Names* (OUP: Oxford, 1960), 272.

2 D. Whaley, *A Dictionary of Lake District Place-Names* (English Place-Name Society: Nottingham, 2006), 194.

3 Ekwall, *English Place Names* (1960), 271–2, 328, 435.

4 J.M. Ewbank, *Antiquary on Horseback: the first publication of the collections of the Rev. Thos. Machell chaplain to King Charles II towards a history of the Barony of Kendal* (CWAAS Extra Series, Vol. XIX, Titus Wilson: Kendal, 1963), 12–13.

5 J.J. Cartwright (ed.), *The Travels Through England of Dr Richard Pococke* (Camden Society, London, Vol. 1, 1888), 43.

6 D. Shotter, *Romans and Britons in North-West England* (CNWRS, Lancaster University: Lancaster, 3rd edn, 2004), 68.

7 A.L.F. Rivet and C. Smith, *The Place-Names of Roman Britain* (Book Club Associates: London, 1981), 135, 170–2, 223, 244, 310, 328; D. Shotter, *Romans and Britons*, 2004, 67f.

8 O.H. North, 'The Roman Station at Watercrook', *CW2*, XXXII (1932), 116–23; O.H. North, 'Finds from the Roman Station at Watercrook', *CW2*, XXXIV (1934), 35–40; O.H. North and E.J.W. Hildyard, 'Excavations at the Roman fort at Watercrook 1944', *CW2*, XLV (1945), 148–62; E.B. Birley, 'The Roman fort at Watercrook', *CW2*, LVII (1957), 13–17; T.W. Potter, *Romans in North-West England; excavations at the Roman forts of Ravenglass, Watercrook and Bowness on Solway* (CWAAS Research Series, Vol. I, Titus Wilson: Kendal, 1979), esp. 139–314.

9 Potter, *Romans in North-West England* (1979), 221–3 and Fig. 88, nos 106–11.

10 D.C.A. Shotter, 'The Roman Conquest of the North-West', *CW2*, C (2000), 33–53; F. Wild, 'The Development of the Roman Road System in the North-West: the Evidence of the Samian Ware', *Britannia*, XXXIII (2002), 271.

11 P. Graystone, *Walking Roman Roads in Lonsdale and the Eden Valley* (CNWRS, University of Lancaster, Occasional Paper, 2002), 45–54; I.D. Margary, *Roman Roads in Britain*, 2 vols (Phoenix House: London, 1957), Vol. 2, map and 91, 114–5, 119.

12 R.G. Collingwood and R.P. Wright, *Roman Inscriptions in Britain, Vol. 1, Inscriptions on stone* (OUP: Oxford, 1965), 752, 753 and 754; E. Birley, 'A Roman Inscription from Watercrook', *CW2*, LV (1955), 46–53.

13 D. Shotter, 'The Roman Fort at Watercrook (Kendal)', *Contrebis* (Journal of the Lancaster Archaeological & Historical Society), XXV (2000), 6–10.

14 N. Higham, *A Regional History of England: The Northern Counties to 1000 AD* (Longman, London, 1986), 253, 271, fig. 6.2; A. Breeze, 'The Kingdom and Name of Elvet', *Northern History*, 39 (2002), 169.

15 W.G. Collingwood, 'An Anglian Cross-fragment at Kendal', *CW2*, IV (1904), 330–3.

16 R.N. Bailey and R. Cramp, *Corpus of Anglo-Saxon Stone Sculpture, Vol. 2, Cumberland, Westmorland & Lancashire North of the Sands* (OUP/British Academy: London, 1988), 120.

17 Ewbank, *Antiquary on Horseback* (1963), 7.

18 J. Marsh, 'The Anchorite Well, Kendal—recent changes', *CW2* (1991), 295.

19 P. Davies, *Sacred Springs; In Search of the Holy Wells and Spas of Wales* (Blorenge Books: Abergavenny, 2003).

20 J.F. Curwen, *Records relating to the Barony of Kendale, Vol. III* (CWAAS/Westmorland County Council: Kendal, 1926), 82.

21 University of Edinburgh, Centre for Archaeology, *Report* No. 2 (1992–93), 11.

22 R.J. Whitwell, 'Chantries in Kendal and Lonsdale Wards, 1546', *CW2*, VIII (1908), 124–35, 128–34.
23 M.L. Faull and M. Stinson (eds), *Domesday Book, Yorkshire*, 2 vols (Phillimore: Chichester, 1986), 302a.
24 D. Roffe, *Domesday the Inquest and the Book* (OUP, Oxford, 2000), 119.

Chapter 2: The borough and town government

1 A. Crosby, 'The Towns of Medieval Lancashire: an Overview', *Lancaster University Centre for North-West Regional Studies, Bulletin*, 8 (1994), 7–18.
2 M.W. Beresford and H.P.R. Finberg, *English Medieval Boroughs: a handlist* (David & Charles: Newton Abbot, 1973), 176.
3 J. Munby, 'Medieval Kendal: the First Borough Charter and its Connexions', *CW2*, LXXXV (1985), 95–114.
4 J.F. Curwen, *Records relating to the Barony of Kendale, Vol. III* (CWAAS/Westmorland County Council: Kendal, 1926), 83.
5 J. Somervell, *Some Westmorland Wills, 1686–1738* (Titus Wilson: Kendal, 1928), 9, 67.
6 W. Farrer (J.F. Curwen (ed.)), *Records Relating to the Barony of Kendale* (CWAAS Record Series, Vol. IV, Titus Wilson: Kendal, 1923), 40n.
7 A.J.L. Winchester, *Landscape and Society in Medieval Cumbria* (John Donald: Edinburgh, 1987), 31–2.
8 W. Parson and W. White, *History, Directory and Gazetteer of the counties of Cumberland & Westmorland, 1829* (repr. M. Moon: Beckermet, 1976), 649, 650, 654.
9 Munby, 'Medieval Kendal: the First Borough Charter', *CW2*, LXXXV (1985), 95–114, 106–10; CRO, Kendal, Kendal Corn Rent Map, WQ/R/C/8.
10 R.S. Ferguson (ed.), *The Boke off Recorde of the Burgh of Kirkby Kendal* (CWAAS Extra Series, Vol. VII, Titus Wilson: Kendal, 1892).
11 R. Bingham, *Kendal—A Social History* (Cicerone Press: Milnthorpe, 1995), 263.
12 C. Kightly, *The Customs and Ceremonies of Britain* (Thames & Hudson: London, 1986), 166–7.
13 Bingham, *Kendal* (1995), 428–9.
14 Act of 1907 CRO, Kendal, WD RG/419/1/4.
15 Ferguson, *Boke off Recorde* (1892), 110–11.
16 Bro. Rev. H. Poole, *Some Notes on the Trade Companies of Kendal in the 16th and 17th centuries* (no publication data, n.d.).
17 R.S. Ferguson, *A History of Westmorland* (Elliot Stock: London, 1894), 171.
18 Anon. (Editors of the Kendal Mercury and Westmorland Gazette), *Local Chronology, being notes of the principal events published in the Kendal Newspapers since their establishment* (Hamilton Adams & Co.: London, 1865), xxix.
19 Ferguson, *Boke off Recorde* (1892), 258–73.
20 CRO, Kendal, WD RG/1524/1.
21 CRO, Kendal, WSMB/K 1.7.
22 J.D. Marshall, *Old Lakeland; some Cumbrian Social History* (David & Charles: Newton Abbot, 1971), 159.
23 Bingham, *Kendal* (1995), 357.
24 Bingham, *Kendal* (1995), 365–6.
25 J. Satchell and O. Wilson, *Christopher Wilson of Kendal; an eighteenth-century hosier and banker* (Kendal Civic Society/Frank Peters: Kendal, 1988), 2–4.
26 E. de Selincourt (ed.), *The Letters of William and Dorothy Wordsworth; III, The Middle Years, Part 2, 1812–1820* (Clarendon Press: Oxford, 1970), 453–4.
27 (H.W. Duncan) D.K.K., *Reminiscences of people and places in Kendal, sixty years ago* (Titus Wilson: Kendal, 1890), 25–28, 72; J.F. Curwen, *Kirkby-Kendall: Fragments collected relating to its ancient streets and yards; church and castle; houses and inns* (Titus Wilson: Kendal, 1900), 370.
28 C. Nicholson, *Annals of Kendal, being a historical and descriptive account of Kendal and the neighbourhood with biographical sketches of many eminent personages connected with the town*, 2nd edn (Whitaker & Co.: London, 1861), 275.
29 R. Homan, 'The Kendal Union Building Societies', *CW2*, LXXXII (1982), 183–90.
30 J.D. Marshall and J.K. Walton, *The Lake Counties from 1830 to the mid-twentieth century. A Study in Regional Change* (MUP: Manchester, 1981), 110.
31 Bingham, *Kendal* (1995), 283–4.

Chapter 3: Kendal's castles

1 W.G. Collingwood, 'Three more ancient castles of Kendal', *CW2*, VIII (1908), 97–112, 97–102; J. Munby, 'Medieval Kendal: the First Borough Charter and its Connexions', *CW2*, LXXXV (1985), 95–114, 107f.; J.F. Curwen, *The Castles and Fortified Towers of Cumberland, Westmorland, and Lancashire North-of-the-Sands* (CWAAS, Extra Series, Vol. XIII, Kendal, 1913), 30–1.
2 C.M.L. Bouch, *Prelates and People of the Lake Counties; A History of the Diocese of Carlisle, 1133–1933* (Titus

Wilson: Kendal, 1948), facing 137; Machell MSS, CRO, Carlisle, ii, 71.

3 W. Farrer (J.F. Curwen (ed.)), *Records Relating to the Barony of Kendale* (CWAAS Record Series, Vol. IV, Titus Wilson: Kendal, 1923), 37.

4 *Cal. Pat. Rolls*, 1431, 144.

5 *CW2*, LI (1951), 185–6.

6 B. Harbottle, 'Excavations at Kendal Castle, Westmorland, 1967', *Quarto*, 5/4 (Abbot Hall Art Gallery: Kendal, 1968); B. Harbottle, 'Excavations at Kendal Castle, Westmorland, 1968, *Quarto*, 6 (Abbot Hall Art Gallery: Kendal, 1969); B. Harbottle, 'Excavations at Kendal Castle, Westmorland, 1969', *Quarto*, 7/4 (Abbot Hall Art Gallery: Kendal, 1970), 13–18; B. Harbottle, 'Excavations at Kendal Castle, Westmorland, 1971', *Quarto*, 10/1 (Abbot Hall Art Gallery: Kendal, 1972), 12–16.

7 C. Howard-Davis, *Kendal Castle; a guide* (South Lakeland District Council: Kendal, 2000); D.R. Perriam and J. Robinson, *The Medieval Fortified Buildings of Cumbria; an Illustrated Gazetteer and Research Guide* (CWAAS Extra Series, Vol. XXIX, 1998), 348–9. I am also grateful to Rachel Newman for discussing these excavations with me.

8 Farrer, *Barony of Kendale* (1923), 37.

9 *Cal. Close Rolls*, 1272, 4, 40.

10 Farrer, *Barony of Kendale* (1923), 17–18.

11 Farrer, *Barony of Kendale* (1923), 53.

12 Farrer, *Barony of Kendale* (1923), 56.

13 G.F. Duckett (ed.), *Description of the County of Westmorland by Sir Daniel Fleming of Rydal AD 1671* (CWAAS Tract Series, Vol. I, Quaritch: London, 1882), 9.

14 J.M. Ewbank, *Antiquary on Horseback: the first publication of the collections of the Rev. Thos. Machell chaplain to King Charles II towards a history of the Barony of Kendal* (CWAAS Extra Series, Vol. XIX, Titus Wilson: Kendal, 1963), 64–5.

15 S.E. James, 'Queen Kateryn Parr (1512–1548)', *CW2*, LXXXVIII (1988), 107–19; S.E. James, 'Parr memorials in Kendal Parish Church', *CW2*, XCII (1992), 99–103; S.E. James, 'Sir William Parr of Kendal: Part I, 1434–1471', *CW2*, XCIII (1993), 99–114; S.E. James, 'Sir John Parr of Kendal, 1437–1475', *CW2*, XCVI (1996), 71–86; S.E. James, 'Sir William Parr of Kendal: Part II, 1471–1483, *CW2*, XCIV (1994), 105–20.

16 C. Nicholson, *Annals of Kendal, being a historical and descriptive account of Kendal and the neighbourhood with biographical sketches of many eminent personages connected with the town*, 2nd edn (Whitaker & Co.: London, 1861), 95.

17 Curwen, *Castles and Fortified Towers* (1913), 147.

18 Pers. comm. Rachel Newman.

19 Ewbank, *Antiquary on Horseback* (1963), 64.

20 van A. Burd and J.S. Dearden, *A Tour to the Lakes in Cumberland: John Ruskin's Diary for 1830* (Scolar Press: Aldershot, 1990), 49.

Chapter 4: Kendal on the map

1 P. Hindle, *Maps for Historians* (Phillimore: Chichester, 1998), 54–9; A. Hawkyard and N. Nicholson, *The Counties of Britain; A Tudor Atlas by John Speed* (Pavilion Books/Michael Joseph Ltd, London, 1988), 181–4; S. Bendall, 'Draft Town Maps for John Speed's theatre of the empire of great Britaine', *Imago Mundi* (The International Journal for the History of Cartography), 54 (2002), 30–45.

2 P. Hindle, *Thomas Jefferys Historic Map of Westmorland 1770, reproduced in four sections from the original engravings* (CWAAS, Record Series, Kendal, Vol. XIV, 2001).

3 P. Hindle, 'The first large scale county maps of Cumberland and Westmorland in the 1770s', *CW3*, I (2001), 139–53.

4 D. Smith, *Maps and Plans for the Local Historian and Collector* (Batsford: London, 1988), 171.

5 E. Evans, 'A nineteenth-century Tithe Dispute and its significance; the Case of Kendal', *CW2*, LXXIV (1974), 159–85.

6 R.J.P. Kain and H.C. Prince, *Tithe Surveys for Historians* (Phillimore, Chichester, 2000); CRO, Kendal, Kendal Corn Rent Map, WQ/R/C/8.

7 See the website of Portsmouth University's Geography Dept, [www.geog.port.ac.uk/webmap/the lakes/].

8 C. Nicholson, *Annals of Kendal, being a historical and descriptive account of Kendal and the neighbourhood with biographical sketches of many eminent personages connected with the town*, 2nd edn (Whitaker & Co.: London, 1861).

9 J. West, *Town Records* (Phillimore: Chichester, 1983), 150–65.

10 CRO, Kendal, OS Map 1861 1:500 scale, WSMB/K [Folder 8].

11 Anon., *A Description of the Ordnance Survey Large Scale Plans* (Ordnance Survey: Chessington, 1954), 11.

Chapter 5: House and home

1 R. Newman, 'Archaeology in Kendal, 1987/88', *Contrebis* (Journal of the Lancaster Archaeological & Historical Society), XIV (1988), 45–50.

2 N. Jennings, *Clay Dabbins: Vernacular Buildings of the Solway Plain* (CWAAS: Carlisle, 2003).

3 M. Brennand (ed.), *The Archaeology of North West England. An Archaeological research Framework for North West England. Vol. 1, Resource Assessment* (Council for British Archaeology North West, Manchester, 2006), Fig. 5.11.

4 *CW3*, V (2005), 283, 284, 285; Brennand (ed.), *Archaeology of North West England* (2006), 126; *CW3*, VII (2007), 260; *CW3*, VIII (2008), 278; *CW3*, IX (2009), 255–6.

5 British Library 005 ADD 00004202; Royal Commission on Historic Monuments (England), *An Inventory of the Historical Monuments in Westmorland* (HMSO: London, 1936), 125.

6 J.H. Palmer (rev. & ed. W.T. McIntire), *Historic Farmhouses in and around Westmorland* (Westmorland Gazette: Kendal, 1952), 36.

7 J.M. Ewbank, *Antiquary on Horseback: the first publication of the collections of the Rev. Thos. Machell chaplain to King Charles II towards a history of the Barony of Kendal* (CWAAS Extra Series, Vol. XIX, Titus Wilson: Kendal, 1963), 60, 65–6.

8 Ewbank, *Antiquary on Horseback* (1963), 101.

9 D.R. Perriam and J. Robinson, *The Medieval Fortified Buildings of Cumbria; an Illustrated Gazetteer and Research Guide* (CWAAS Extra Series, Vol. XXIX, 1998), 330; Palmer, *Historic Farmhouses* (1952), 22.

10 Perriam and Robinson, *Medieval Fortified Buildings of Cumbria* (1998), 346; Palmer, *Historic Farmhouses* (1952), 56.

11 J.M. Robinson, *A Guide to the Country Houses of the North West* (Constable: London, 1991), 275–6, 286–8.

12 Perriam and Robinson, *Medieval Fortified Buildings of Cumbria* (1998), 346; Palmer, *Historic Farmhouses* (1952), 30.

13 RCHM (E), *An Inventory of the Historical Monuments in Westmorland* (1936), 124.

14 Palmer, *Historic Farmhouses* (1952), 18.

15 A. Clifton Taylor, *The Pattern of English Building* (Faber & Faber: London, 1972), 98, 153, 161, 185, 187; R.W. Brunskill, *Vernacular Architecture of the Lake Counties; a field handbook* (Faber & Faber: London, 1974), passim.

16 CRO, Kendal, WD/Ry Box 32.

17 LRO WRW/K/1675.

18 LRO WRW/K/1688.

19 LRO WRW/K/1700.

20 LRO WRW/K/1769.

21 W. Stukeley, *Itinerarium Curiosum, Or, An Account of the Antiquitys and Remarkable Curiositys in Nature or Art, Observ'd in Travels thro' Great Brittan. Centuria II* (London, 1776), 40.

22 W. Roberts (ed.), *Thomas Gray's Journal of his Visit to the Lake District in October 1769* (LUP: Liverpool, 2001), 89.

23 C. Nicholson, *Annals of Kendal, being a historical and descriptive account of Kendal and the neighbourhood with biographical sketches of many eminent personages connected with the town*, 2nd edn (Whitaker & Co.: London, 1861), 126.

24 Deeds in CRO, Kendal, WSMB/K7/2/T1.

25 J. Whitwell, *The Old Houses of Kendal, or the Local Perambulator* (Kendal Literary & Scientific Association/ Thos Atkinson: Kendal, 1866), 17 and 23.

26 A. Brown (ed.), *The Rows of Chester: The Chester Rows Project*, English Heritage Archaeological Report 16 (1999), 59.

27 pers. comm. Jonathan Ratter.

28 A. Sedgwick, *A Memorial by the Trustees of Cowgill Chapel* (1868).

29 S. Denyer, *Traditional Buildings & Life in the Lake District* (National Trust/Victor Gollancz/Peter Crawley: London, 1991), 87–8, 125–8, 141–3; A. White, *The Buildings of Georgian Whitby* (Keele UP; Keele, 1995), 10–12, 35.

30 P. Allen, *The Old Galleries of Cumbria and the early wool trade* (Abbot Hall: Kendal, n.d. but 1984).

31 J. Briggs (ed.), *The Lonsdale Magazine or Provincial Repository*, Vol. II (J. Foster: Kirkby Lonsdale, 1821), 2–5.

32 Anon. (Editors of the Kendal Mercury and Westmorland Gazette), *Local Chronology, being notes of the principal events published in the Kendal Newspapers since their establishment* (Hamilton Adams & Co.: London, 1865), 53.

33 On land formerly known as Hubbersty Close; Deeds in CRO, Kendal, WD RG/303/T1–2.

34 R. Homan, 'The Kendal Union Building Societies', *CW2*, LXXXII (1982), 183–90.

35 L. Ashcroft (ed.), *Vital Statistics; the Westmorland 'Census' of 1787* (Curwen Archives Trust: Kendal, 1992).

36 H.M. Colvin, *A Biographical Dictionary of British Architects 1600–1840*, 3rd edn (Yale University Press: New Haven, 1995), 1032–1035; A. Taylor (ed. J. Martin), *The Websters of Kendal. A North-Western*

Architectural Dynasty (CWAAS Record Series, Vol. XVII, Titus Wilson: Kendal, 2004).

37 Taylor, *The Websters of Kendal* (2004), 30.

38 J.F. Curwen, *Kirkby-Kendall: Fragments collected relating to its ancient streets and yards; church and castle; houses and inns* (Titus Wilson: Kendal, 1900), 319–21.

39 J. Holloway, *The Oxford Book of Local Verses* (OUP: Oxford, 1987), 266.

40 Colvin, *Biographical Dictionary of British Architects* (1995), 468, 811; Taylor, *The Websters of Kendal* (2004), 9.

41 CRO, Kendal, WD AG/BOX 159/2/1.

42 CRO, Kendal, WD RG/419/2/4.

43 CRO, Kendal, WD RG/PLANS/6.

44 J. and J. Coopey, *Kendal Green. A Georgian Wasteland Transformed* (Helm Press: Kendal, 2002).

45 W. Hitchmough, *C.F.A. Voysey* (Phaidon: London, 1995), 201–3, 212–13; E. Davidson, *The Simpsons of Kendal, Craftsmen in Wood 1885–1952* (Visual Arts Centre, Lancaster University: Lancaster, 1978), 39–41, figs 109–111.

46 D.M. Butler, *Summer Houses of Kendal* (Abbot Hall: Kendal, 1982).

47 English Heritage 'Images of England' website (www.imagesofengland.org.uk).

48 Deeds in CRO, Kendal, WD W/Box11/9/1–4.

49 1861 Census: enumerators' returns; TNA RG 9/3971, ff. 36–42.

50 *Post Office Directory of Westmorland & Cumberland* (Kelly & Co.: London, 1858).

51 L. Ashcroft, Cleaning up Kendal: a century of sanitary history (Curwen Archives Trust; Kendal, 2006), 46.

52 R. Hughes, 'Social Housing: Local Authority and Housing Society providers in 1930s Kendal', MA dissertation (Open University, 2000).

53 R. Bingham, *Kendal: A Social History* (Cicerone: Milnthorpe, 1995), 316–18.

Chapter 6: Shops and businesses

1 W. Farrer (J.F. Curwen (ed.)), *Records Relating to the Barony of Kendale* (CWAAS Record Series, Vol. IV, Titus Wilson: Kendal, 1923), 2; C. Nicholson, *Annals of Kendal, being a historical and descriptive account of Kendal and the neighbourhood with biographical sketches of many eminent personages connected with the town*, 2nd edn (Whitaker & Co.: London, 1861), 250; R.H. Britnell, 'Boroughs, markets and trade in northern England, 1000–1216' in R.H. Britnell, R.H. Hatcher (eds), *Progress and Problems in Medieval England* (CUP: Cambridge, 1996), 65.

2 *Cal. Ch. Rolls*, 1300–26, 130.

3 Nicholson, *Annals of Kendal* (1861), 122–4; J.F. Curwen, *Kirkby-Kendall: Fragments collected relating to its ancient streets and yards; church and castle; houses and inns* (Titus Wilson: Kendal, 1900), 29–31.

4 R.S. Ferguson (ed.), *The Boke off Recorde of the Burgh of Kirkby Kendal* (CWAAS Extra Series, Vol. VII, Titus Wilson: Kendal, 1892), 108–9.

5 W. Parson and W. White, *History, Directory and Gazetteer of the counties of Cumberland & Westmorland, 1829* (repr. M. Moon: Beckermet, 1976), 640.

6 Nicholson, *Annals of Kendal* (1861), 157.

7 Curwen, *Kirkby-Kendall* (1900), 299.

8 G.H. Martin, 'The Town as Palimpsest', 155–69 in H.J. Dyos (ed.), *The Study of Urban History* (Edward Arnold: London, 1971), 166 and pls 17–19.

9 *Westmorland Gazette* 12 November 1870.

10 J.D. Marshall, *Old Lakeland; some Cumbrian Social History* (David & Charles: Newton Abbot, 1971), 58–9, 91; J. Catt, *Northern Hiring Fairs* (Countryside Publications: Brinscall, 1986), 62.

11 J.D. Marshall, 'Kendal in the late seventeenth and eighteenth centuries', *CW2*, LXXV (1975), 188–257, 194–5.

12 Deeds in CRO, Kendal, WD RG/405/12.

13 Anon. (Editors of the *Kendal Mercury* and *Westmorland Gazette*), *Local Chronology, being notes of the principal events published in the Kendal Newspapers since their establishment* (Hamilton Adams & Co.: London, 1865), 78.

14 P. Clark, *The English Alehouse: A Social History, 1200–1830* (Longman: London, 1983), 96.

15 W. Cowan (ed.), *A Journey to Edenborough in Scotland by Joseph Taylor, Late of the Inner Temple, 1705* (W. Brown: Edinburgh, 1903), 160.

16 Ferguson (ed.), *Boke off Recorde* (1892), 111.

17 Marshall, 'Kendal in the late seventeenth and eighteenth centuries', *CW2*, LXXV (1975), 188–257, 194–5.

18 Clark, *The English Alehouse* (1983), 208; B. Tyson (ed.), *The Estate and Household Accounts of Sir Daniel Fleming of Rydal Hall, Westmorland, 1688–1701*, C & W Record Series, vol. XIII (Kendal, 2001), 224.

19 LRO, WRW/K/1678.

20 LRO, WRW/K/1742.

21 A. Hillman (transcr.), *The Rake's Diary: The Journal of George Hilton* (Curwen Archives Trust: Kendal, 1994), 2, 9, 11, 16, 20, 48, 66.

22 F.M. Eden, *The State of the Poor*, 3 vols, 1797 (repr. Cass: London, 1966), 753.

23 CRO, Kendal, WD RG/419/2/1.

24 *Holden's Triennial Directory for 1805, 1806, 1807* (Holden: London, 1805).

25 CRO, Kendal, WD/Ry Box 32.

26 E.S. Worrall, *Returns of Papists 1767 Diocese of Chester* (Catholic Record Society: London, Occasional Paper No. I, 1980), 155.

27 L. Ashcroft (ed.), *Vital Statistics; the Westmorland 'Census' of 1787* (Curwen Archives Trust: Kendal, 1992), 281–344.

28 Nicholson, *Annals of Kendal* (1861), 124.

29 Anon., *The Tradesmen's Tokens issued during the 17th Century in the County of Westmorland* (no publisher cited, Kendal, 1855); G.C. Williamson, *Boyne's Trade Tokens issued in the Seventeenth Century in England, Wales and Ireland*, 1889–91 (repr. Seaby: London, 1967).

30 B. Loomes, *Westmorland Clocks and Clockmakers* (David & Charles: Newton Abbot, 1974), 116; S.E. Stuart, *Biographical List of Clockmakers, North Lancashire and South Westmorland, 1680–1900* (CNWRS, Lancaster University, 1996), 85–107.

31 D. Davis, *A History of Shopping* (Routledge & Kegan Paul: London, 1966), 138.

32 N. Penney (ed.), *The Household Account Book of Sarah Fell, 1673–78* (CUP: Cambridge, 1920), 123.

33 S.D. Smith, *'An Exact and Industrious Tradesman': The Letter Book of Joseph Symson of Kendal 1711–1720* (Records of Social and Economic History, new series, Vol. 34, 2002).

34 W. Bailey, *Northern Directory* (Bailey: Warrington, 1784), 554.

35 T. Fitzgibbon, *A Taste of the Lake District in Food and Pictures* (Ward Lock: London, 1980), 67.

36 J. Whitwell, *The Old Houses of Kendal, or the Local Perambulator* (Kendal Literary & Scientific Association/Thos Atkinson: Kendal, 1866), 11.

37 T. Hughes, Historic Kendal: A comprehensive guide to Kendal Civic Society's commemorative plaques displayed on historic buildings in and around Kendal (Kendal Civic Society: Kendal, 2005), cards 19 and 24.

38 George Smith's MS diary (private possession) for 13 February 1826.

Chapter 7: 'Pannus mihi Panis'—Cloth is bread to me

1 J. Nicholson and R. Burn, *The History and Antiquities of the Counties of Westmorland and Cumberland*, 2 vols, 1777 (repr. EP Publishing: East Ardsley, 1976), vol. 1, 66.

2 J. Satchell, *Kendal on Tenterhooks* (Kendal Civic Society/Frank Peters: Kendal, 1984); J. Satchell, *The Kendal Weaver* (Kendal Civic Society/Frank Peters: Kendal, 1986).

3 C. Nicholson, *Annals of Kendal, being a historical and descriptive account of Kendal and the neighbourhood with biographical sketches of many eminent personages connected with the town*, 2nd edn (Whitaker & Co.: London, 1861), 235–6.

4 M. Davies-Shiel, *Wool is my Bread, or, the Early Woollen Industry of Kendal from c.975–1575 AD* (Frank Peters: Kendal, 1975), 26–8.

5 Satchell, *Kendal on Tenterhooks* (1984); Satchell, *The Kendal Weaver* (1986); Davies-Shiel, *Wool is my Bread* (1975).

6 Davies-Shiel, *Wool is my Bread* (1975), 33.

7 CRO, Kendal, WD/Ry Box 32.

8 LRO, WRW/K/1688.

9 CRO, Kendal, Microfilm GL95.

10 *Ibid.*

11 *Ibid.*

12 LRO WRW/K/1730.

13 LRO, WRW/K/1738.

14 M. Hartley and J. Ingilby, *The Old Hand Knitters of the Dales* (Dalesman: Clapham, 1951); P.C.D. Brears, 'The Knitting Sheath', *Folk Life*, vol. 20 (1981–82), 16–40.

15 (J. Budworth), *'A Rambler', A Fortnight's Ramble to the Lakes 1792* (Preston Publishing: Upper Basildon, repr. 1990), 12.

16 Satchell, *The Kendal Weaver* (1986), 43, 61; J. Somervell, *Some Westmorland Wills, 1686–1738* (Titus Wilson: Kendal, 1928), 45f., 87f.

17 W.G. Stevens, 'Old-Time Links between Cambridge and the Lake District; pt. 1 Stourbridge Fair and the cloth merchants of Kendal', typescript (1968); 'pt. 2 The Knights Hospitallers and the Docwra family', typescript (1966). I am grateful to Miss A.R. Plint for showing me these sources.

18 J.J. Cartwright (ed.), *The Travels Through England of Dr Richard Pococke* (Camden Society, London, vol. 2, 1889), 2.

19 A.Young, *A Six Months Tour through the North of England*, 4 vols, vol. III (London, 1771), 134.

20 W. Roberts (ed.), *Thomas Gray's Journal of his Visit to the Lake District in October 1769* (LUP: Liverpool, 2001), 89.

21 Somervell, *Some Westmorland Wills* (1928), 89.

22 J.M. Ewbank, *Antiquary on Horseback: the first publication*

of the collections of the Rev. Thos. Machell chaplain to King Charles II towards a history of the Barony of Kendal (CWAAS Extra Series, vol. XIX, Titus Wilson: Kendal, 1963), 60–1.

23 K. Morgan (ed.), *An American Quaker in the British Isles: the Travel Journals of Jabez Maud Fisher, 1775–1779* (OUP: Oxford for the British Academy, 1992), 291.

24 W. Bailey, *Northern Directory* (Bailey: Warrington, 1784), 554–6.

25 CRO, Barrow-in-Furness, ZS1140.

26 W. Whellan, *The History, Topography & Directory of the Counties of Cumberland and Westmorland* (W. Whellan & Co.: London, 1860), 844.

27 *Universal British Directory of Trade & Commerce* (4 vols) vol. 3 (1794), 473–6.

28 Anon. (Editors of the *Kendal Mercury* and *Westmorland Gazette*), *Local Chronology, being notes of the principal events published in the Kendal Newspapers since their establishment* (Hamilton Adams & Co.: London, 1865), 58.

29 J. Somervell, *Water-Power Mills of South Westmorland on the Kent, Bela and Gilpin and their Tributaries* (Titus Wilson: Kendal, 1930), 56–70; M. Davies-Shiel and J.D. Marshall, *Industrial Archaeology of the Lake Counties* (David & Charles: Newton Abbot, 1969), 245–7.

30 R.S. Ferguson (ed.), *The Boke off Recorde of the Burgh of Kirkby Kendal* (CWAAS Extra Series, vol. VII, Titus Wilson: Kendal, 1892), 110ff.

31 Nicholson and Burn, *The History of Westmorland and Cumberland*, 1777 (1976), vol. I, 72.

32 W. Parson and W. White, *History, Directory and Gazetteer of the counties of Cumberland & Westmorland, 1829* (repr. M. Moon: Beckermet, 1976), 638–9.

33 J. Martin, 'Mislet, the Braithwaites, and the Black Drop', *CW3*, II (2002), 201–7, 206n.

34 pers. comm. Dick White.

35 Anon., *Local Chronology* (1865), 82.

36 LRO, WRW/K/1769.

37 Satchell, *Kendal on Tenterhooks* (1984), 38–9.

38 W. Rollinson, *Life and Tradition in the Lake District* (Dalesman Books: Clapham, 1981), 148.

39 Anon., *Local Chronology* (1865), 62, 84.

40 Somervell, *Some Westmorland Wills* (1928), 8, 64, 68–9.

41 M. Railton, *The Excavation of the Remains of an eighteenth century Tannery on Land at Riverside Place, K-Village, Kendal* (Kendal Civic Society: Kendal, 2009).

42 S. Crookenden, *K Shoes—the First 150 Years, 1842–1992* (K Shoes: Kendal, 1992).

43 *Holden's Triennial Directory for 1805, 1806, 1807* (Holden: London, 1805), 168.

44 *Universal British Directory* Vol. 3 (1794), 473–6.

45 Davies-Shiel and Marshall, *Industrial Archaeology of the Lake Counties* (1969), 229.

46 M. Cropper, *'The Leaves we Write on'; James Cropper; a History in Paper-Making* (Ellergreen Press: London, 2004).

47 CRO, Kendal, WDB 29/1924/1.

48 G. Rushforth, 'Churchwardens' Accounts, Kendal', *CW1*, IX (1887–8), 269–83.

49 Davies-Shiel & Marshall, *Industrial Archaeology of the Lake Counties* (1969), 101.

50 J.W. Dunderdale (ed. A. Bonney), *Kendal Brown; the History of Kendal's Tobacco and Snuff Industry* (Helm Press: Natland, 2003); J. Satchell, *Kendal's Canal: History, Industry and People* (Kendal Civic Society: Kendal, 2000), 42–5, 103–6.

51 Census Enumerator's Returns, Kendal, 1841–71; Habergham Eaves, 1881.

52 Martin, 'Mislet, the Braithwaites, and the Black Drop', *CW3*, II (2002), 201–7.

53 J. Briggs (ed.), *The Lonsdale Magazine or Provincial Repository*, vol. II (J. Foster: Kirkby Lonsdale, 1821), 95.

54 *Census 2001; Key Statistics for urban areas in England and Wales* (Office of National Statistics: London, 2004), KS 11a, 173.

Chapter 8: Road, canal and rail

1 E. Jervoise, *The Ancient Bridges of the North of England* (The Architectural Press: London, 1931), 125–6; J.F. Curwen, *Kirkby-Kendall: Fragments collected relating to its ancient streets and yards; church and castle; houses and inns* (Titus Wilson: Kendal, 1900), 196, 353, 380, 409.

2 *Cal. Pat. Rolls*, 1421, 399.

3 L. Toulmin Smith (ed.), *The Itinerary of John Leland in or about the years 1535–1543*, 5 vols (repr. Centaur Press: Fontwell, 1964), vol. 5, 47.

4 J.F. Curwen, *Records relating to the Barony of Kendale, Vol. III* (CWAAS/Westmorland County Council: Kendal, 1926), 84.

5 *Lancaster Gazette* 29 November 1806.

6 J. O'Connor, *Memories of Old Kendal; recollections and pictures of people of bygone Kendal, and the town and times they lived in*, 3rd edn (Westmorland Gazette: Kendal, 1962), 132; J. Marsh, *Images of Westmorland* (Sutton: Thrupp, 2002), 156.

7 *Cal. Pat. Rolls*, 1376, 237.
8 *Cal. Pat. Rolls*, 1379, 314.
9 Curwen, *Barony of Kendale* (1926), 82.
10 *Ibid.*
11 Toulmin Smith (ed.), *The Itinerary of John Leland* (1964), vol. 5, 47.
12 W.G. Hoskins, *Two Thousand Years in Exeter* (Phillimore: Chichester, 1969), 28–31.
13 J.C. Hodgson (ed.), *Wills & Inventories from the Registry at Durham, pt III*, Surtees Society, Vol. 112 (1906),
50–1.
14 Curwen, *Barony of Kendale* (1926), 88.
15 A.C. Taylor, 'Thomas Harrison and Stramongate Bridge, Kendal', *CW2*, LXIX (1969), 275–9.
16 C.D. Bishop (transcr.), Beetham Parish registers, 1754–1812 (1993), CRO, Kendal, WPR 43/3.
17 D. Gerhold, *Carriers and Coachmasters: trade and travel before the Turnpikes* (Phillimore: Chichester, 2005), xi.
18 Curwen, *Barony of Kendale* (1926), 1.
19 B.C. Jones, 'Westmorland Pack-horse Men in Southampton', *CW2*, LIX (1959), 65–84.
20 T. Delaune, *The Present State of London* … (London, 1681 and 1690), appendix on carriers.
21 Gerhold, *Carriers and Coachmasters* (2005), 5–6, 183.
22 M.L. Armitt (ed. W.F. Rawnsley), *Rydal* (Titus Wilson: Kendal,1916), 451.
23 C. Morris (ed.), *The Illustrated Journeys of Celia Fiennes c.1682–c.1712* (Macdonald & Co.: London, 1982), 166.
24 A. Bagot and J. Munby (eds), *'All Things is Well Here; letters from Hugh James of Levens to James Grahme, 1692–95* (CWAAS Record Series, Vol. X, Kendal, 1988), 13, 48, 68, 71f, 136, 128f.
25 CRO, Kendal, WD U/Box 19/3a9, 10 & 11.
26 D. Hey, *Packmen, Carriers & Packhorse Roads: trade and communications in North Derbyshire and South Yorkshire*, 2nd edn (Landmark: Ashbourne, 2001), 65.
27 J. Nicholson and R. Burn, *The History and Antiquities of the Counties of Westmorland and Cumberland*, 2 vols, 1777 (repr. EP Publishing: East Ardsley, 1976), vol. I, 66.
28 J. Wright (ed.), *English Dialect Dictionary*, 6 vols (Frowde & Amen Corner: London, 1898).
29 T. Tusser, *Five Hundred Points of Good Husbandry, 1580* (OUP: Oxford, 1984), ch. 15.
30 CRO, Carlisle, D/Lons/W1/34.
31 H. Swainson Cowper, 'On some obsolete and semi-obsolete appliances', *CW1*, XIII (1895), 86–102, 102–2, Pl.XIII.
32 Anon., *Official Handbook and Catalogue to the Kendal Borough Museum* (Titus Wilson: Kendal, 1924), 10.
33 J.H. Palmer (rev. & ed. W.T. McIntire), *Historic Farmhouses in and around Westmorland* (Westmorland Gazette: Kendal, 1952), 8–9.
34 J.L. Hobbs, 'The Turnpike Roads of North Lonsdale', *CW2*, LV (1955), 250–92, 251, 267.
35 CRO, Kendal, WQ/SR/233/22.
36 CRO, Kendal, WD MM/Box 9/Bundle 6.
37 W. Rollinson, *Life and Tradition in the Lake District* (Dalesman Books: Clapham, 1981), 193.
38 Anon. (Editors of the *Kendal Mercury* and *Westmorland Gazette*), *Local Chronology, being notes of the principal events published in the Kendal Newspapers since their establishment* (Hamilton Adams & Co.: London, 1865), xxix, 52.
39 *Universal British Directory of Trade & Commerce* (4 vols) vol. 3 (1794), 472.
40 Anon., *Local Chronology* (1865), 28.
41 Curwen, *Kirkby-Kendall* (1900), 324.
42 T. Bulmer & Co., *History, Topography & Directory of Westmorland* (Bulmer: London, 1906), 438.
43 E. Bowen, *Britannia Depicta or Ogilby Improv'd; Road Atlas of Britain, 1720* (Frank Graham: Newcastle upon Tyne, repr. 1970).
44 Curwen, *Barony of Kendale* (1926), 9–13.
45 *Westmorland Gazette*, 10 November 1821.
46 *Westmorland Gazette*, 31 December 1819.
47 P. Hindle, *Thomas Jefferys Historic Map of Westmorland 1770, reproduced in four sections from the original engravings* (CWAAS, Record Series, Kendal, Vol. XIV, 2001); Curwen, *Barony of Kendale* (1926), 9–13; W. Albert, *The Turnpike Road System in England 1663–1840* (CUP: Cambridge, 1972), 205–11.
48 L. Smith, *Kendal's Port. A Maritime History of the Creek of Milnthorpe* (Lensden Publishing: Kendal, 2009).
49 J. Cary, *Cary's New Itinerary* (J. Cary: London, 1798), 339.
50 Curwen, *Barony of Kendale* (1926), 1–20.
51 F.R.C. Hutton, 'Witherslack Church and Manor', *CW2*, I (1901), 186–93, 192; Curwen, *Barony of Kendale* (1926), 1–20; Hobbs, 'The Turnpike Roads of North Lonsdale', *CW2*, LV (1955), 250–92.
52 J. Woods, *The North Road. A Brief History of the Kendal to Shap Road* (p.p., 2001).
53 Anon., *Local Chronology* (1865), xxix–xxx.
54 R. Bingham, *Kendal—A Social History* (Cicerone Press: Milnthorpe, 1995), 105.
55 Curwen, *Kirkby-Kendall* (1900), 276.
56 *Cumberland Pacquet* 3 July 1781.
57 Anon., *Local Chronology* (1865), xxx.
58 E. Vale, *The Mail-Coach Men of the late Eighteenth Century* (Cassell: London, 1960).

59 *Universal British Directory* vol. 3 (1794), 471.
60 *Westmorland Gazette*, 10 December 1814.
61 Abbot Hall acc. no. AH1648/77.
62 W. Parson and W. White, *History, Directory and Gazetteer of the counties of Cumberland & Westmorland, 1829* (repr. M. Moon: Beckermet, 1976), 657.
63 *Westmorland Gazette*, 23 December 1911.
64 *Pigot & Co.'s National Directory of the counties of Chester, Cumberland, Durham, Lancaster, Northumberland, Westmoreland & York* (J.Pigot: London, 1834), 652.
65 (J. Budworth) *'A Rambler', A Fortnight's Ramble to the Lakes 1792* (Preston Publishing: Upper Basildon, repr. 1990), 12.
66 P.N. Wilson, 'Canal Head, Kendal', *CW2*, LXIX (1969), 132–50, 132n.
67 J. Satchell, *Kendal's Canal: History, Industry and People* (Kendal Civic Society: Kendal, 2000).
68 Sir G. Head, *A Home Tour through the Manufacturing Districts of England in the Summer of 1835* (A.M. Kelley: New York, repr. 1968), 428.
69 L.T.C. Rolt, *The Inland Waterways of England* (George Allen & Unwin: London, 1950), 146–7.
70 A. White, 'Fast Packet Boats to Kendal', *CW3*, VI (2006), 145–62.
71 J. Taylor, *The Carriers' Cosmography* (A.G.: London, 1637).
72 T.S. Willan, *An Eighteenth Century Shopkeeper, Abraham Dent of Kirkby Stephen* (MUP: Manchester, 1970), 41–3.
73 Anon., *Local Chronology* (1865), 101, 102, 105, 118.
74 CRO, Barrow-in-Furness, ZS539.
75 R. Vickers, 'Country Carriers in Victorian Lakeland', *CW2*, XCVIII (1998), 277–86; CRO, Kendal, WDB1 and WDB84.
76 *Universal British Directory* vol. 3 (1794), 471–2.
77 M. Hartley and J. Ingilby, *Life and Tradition in the Yorkshire Dales* (Dalesman Books: Clapham, 1981), 198.
78 R. Smith, *The Kendal & Windermere Railway* (Cumbrian Railways Association: Barrow in Furness, 2002).
79 E. de Selincourt (ed.), *William Wordsworth's Guide to the Lakes, 5th Edn (1835)* (OUP: Oxford, 1977), 146–66.
80 A. Frater, *Stopping-Train Britain; a Railway Odyssey* (Hodder & Stoughton: London, 1985), 13–22.
81 H.L. Yeadon, *The Motorway Achievement. Building the Network: The North West of England* (Motorway Archive Trust/Phillimore: Chichester, 2005), 41–6.

Chapter 9: Health and welfare

1 W.G. Wiseman, 'The Medieval Hospitals of Cumbria', *CW2*, LXXXVII (1987), 83–100, 90–2.
2 *Cal. Inq.*, v, 118.
3 W. Farrer (J.F. Curwen (ed.), *Records Relating to the Barony of Kendale* (CWAAS Record Series, Vol. IV, Titus Wilson: Kendal, 1923), 176–82; C. Rawcliffe, *Leprosy in Medieval England* (Boydell & Brewer: London, 2006).
4 Farrer, *Barony of Kendale* (1923), 87–9.
5 C. Nicholson, *Annals of Kendal, being a historical and descriptive account of Kendal and the neighbourhood with biographical sketches of many eminent personages connected with the town*, 2nd edn (Whitaker & Co.: London, 1861), 81–2.
6 J.M. Ewbank, *Antiquary on Horseback: the first publication of the collections of the Rev. Thos. Machell chaplain to King Charles II towards a history of the Barony of Kendal* (CWAAS Extra Series, vol. XIX, Titus Wilson: Kendal, 1963), 64.
7 G.F. Duckett (ed.), *Description of the County of Westmorland by Sir Daniel Fleming of Rydal AD 1671* (CWAAS Tract Series, vol. I, Quaritch: London, 1882), 10.
8 TNA, RG 9/3971 (Census Enumerator's Returns, Kendal, 1861).
9 Nicholson, *Annals of Kendal* (1861), 228–9.
10 TNA, RG 12/4332 (Census Enumerator's Returns, Kendal, 1891).
11 Plans etc. for the proposed twelve almshouses and mission chapel are in the CRO, Kendal, WSMB/K11/Book 4/665.
12 TNA, RG 13/4913 (Census Enumerator's Returns, Kendal, 1901).
13 L. Ashcroft (ed.), *The Diary of a Kendal Midwife, 1669–1675* (Curwen Archives Trust: Kendal, 2002).
14 E.S. Worrall, *Returns of Papists 1767 Diocese of Chester* (Catholic Record Society: London, Occasional Paper No. I, 1980), 155.
15 CRO, Kendal, WDX 354/1.
16 L. Ashcroft (ed.), *Cleaning up Kendal; a century of sanitary history* (Curwen Archives Trust: Kendal, 2006).
17 H. Brierley, *The Registers of Kendal 1558–1587*, 2 vols (Titus Wilson: Kendal, 1921 and 1922), 71, 207, 209.
18 A. Kidson, *George Romney, 1734–1802* (NPG: London, 2002), 44–5, 56–7.
19 R.S. Ferguson (ed.), *The Boke off Recorde of the Burgh of Kirkby Kendal* (CWAAS Extra Series, Vol. VII, Titus Wilson: Kendal, 1892), 110–111.
20 B. Tyson, 'James Towers, a Kendal surgeon (1785–1846) and some of his medical colleagues', *CW2*,

XCIII (1993), 197–213.

21 (H.W. Duncan) D.K.K., *Reminiscences of people and places in Kendal, sixty years ago* (Titus Wilson: Kendal, 1890), 148–9; Ashcroft (ed.), *Cleaning up Kendal* (2006), 1–32.

22 CW2, XCVII (1997), 243; (Duncan), *Reminiscences of people and places in Kendal* (1890), 145–8.

23 CRO, Kendal, WT/HOS/1.

24 E. Bingham, *A History of Kendal Memorial Hospital and Westmorland County Hospital 1870–1991* (p.p.: Kendal, 1991).

25 CRO, Kendal, WQ/SR/57/1–2.

26 CRO, Kendal, WQ/SR/286/13–14.

27 F.M. Eden, *The State of the Poor*, 3 Vols, 1797 (repr. Cass: London, 1966), 750–71.

28 CRO, Kendal, WQ/SR/561/14–16.

29 Nicholson, *Annals of Kendal* (1861), 188.

30 TNA, RG 11/5214 (Census Enumerator's Returns, Kendal, 1881).

31 CRO, K, WC/W/1/10; WC/W/1/14b.

32 R. Bingham, *Kendal—A Social History* (Cicerone Press: Milnthorpe,1995), 302.

33 Ferguson (ed.), *Boke off Recorde* (1892), 1–17.

34 C.B. Phillips, 'The population of the borough of Kendal in 1576,' *CW2*, LXXXI (1981), 57–62.

35 C.B. Phillips, 'The Plague in Kendal in 1598: some new evidence', *CW2*, XCIV (1994), 135–42.

36 C. Phillips, C. Ferguson & A. Wareham (eds), *Westmorland Hearth Tax Michaelmas 1670 and Surveys 1674–75* (xxx, London, 2009), 2–7, 85–9, 265–302.

37 CRO, Kendal, WD/Ry Box 32.

38 L. Ashcroft (ed.), *Vital Statistics; the Westmorland 'Census' of 1787* (Curwen Archives Trust: Kendal, 1992).

39 Eden, *The State of the Poor* 1797 (1966), 750, 751.

40 Nicholson, *Annals of Kendal* (1861), 274–5.

41 *Census 2001; Key Statistics for urban areas in England and Wales* (Office of National Statistics: London, 2004), KS06, 89.

Chapter 10: Church and chapel

1 J. Hodgkinson, *The Greater Parish of Kendal, 1553–2002, during the patronage of Trinity College, Cambridge* (Little Trinity Publishing: Levens, 2002), 87–8.

2 Anon. (Editors of the *Kendal Mercury* and *Westmorland Gazette*), *Local Chronology, being notes of the principal events published in the Kendal Newspapers since their establishment* (Hamilton Adams & Co.: London, 1865), 116.

3 *Cal. Pat. Rolls*, 1302, 20.

4 *Cal. Pat. Rolls*, 1309, 129.

5 G. Rushforth, 'Churchwardens' Accounts, Kendal', *CW1*, IX (1887–88), 269–83, 275–6.

6 G. Rushforth, 'Churchwardens' Accounts, Kendal', *CW1*, IX (1887–88), 269–83, 274.

7 C.P. Fendall and E.A. Crutchley, *The Diary of Benjamin Newton, Rector of Wath, 1816–1818* (CUP: Cambridge, 1933), 169–70.

8 R.L. Storey, 'The Chantries of Cumberland and Westmorland, pt II', *CW2*, LXII (1962), 155–70; W. Farrer (J.F. Curwen (ed.)), *Records Relating to the Barony of Kendale* (CWAAS Record Series, vol. IV, Titus Wilson: Kendal, 1923), 57, 85–7, 152.

9 B.L. Thompson, 'Westmorland Church Bells', *CW2*, LXX (1970), 51–68, 64.

10 D.J. Handley, *Notes on Furness Branch Bells* (The Reminder Press: Ulverston, 1983), 13–14.

11 Anon., *Local Chronology* (1865), 98, 101, 103, 106.

12 Hodgkinson, *Greater Parish of Kendal* (2002), 113–21.

13 CRO, Kendal, WQ/R/C/8; J. Nicholson and R. Burn, *The History and Antiquities of the Counties of Westmorland and Cumberland*, 2 vols, 1777 (repr. EP Publishing: East Ardsley, 1976), 78.

14 Hodgkinson, *Greater Parish of Kendal* (2002), 117–18.

15 M.A. Clark, 'Kendal, The Protestant Exception', *CW2*, XCV (1995), 137–52.

16 M.B. Rowlands (ed.), *Catholics of Parish and Town, 1558–1778* (Catholic Record Society: London, Monograph 5, 1999), 190.

17 P. Edwards, '"Blood Ran Down"; Early Drama in Kendal', in *A History of Kendal*, vol. 4 (Lectures by CWAAS and Kendal Civic Society, Kendal, 2000), 1–6; Rowlands, *Catholics of Parish and Town* (1999), 120–1.

18 http://www.churchplansonline.com.

19 *Ibid.*

20 *Ibid.*

21 L.A.S. Butler (ed.), *The Cumbria Parishes 1714–1725 from Bishop Gastrell's Notitia with additions by Bishop Porteus 1778–1779* (CWAAS Record Series, vol. XII, Kendal, 1998), 115.

22 F. Nicholson and E. Axon, *The Older Nonconformity in Kendal: A History of the Unitarian Chapel in the Market Place* (Titus Wilson: Kendal, 1915); C. Stell, *Royal Commission on Historical Monuments (England): An Inventory of Nonconformist Chapels and Meeting-Houses in the North of England* (HMSO: London, 1994), 176–7.

23 K. Morgan (ed.), *An American Quaker in the British Isles: the Travel Journals of Jabez Maud Fisher, 1775–1779*

(OUP: Oxford for the British Academy, 1992), 78–80.

24 D.M. Butler, *The Quaker Meeting Houses of Britain* (2 vols) (Friends Historical Society: London, 1999), vol. 2, 654–60.

25 O. Greenwood, *The Quaker Tapestry; a celebration of insights* (Impact Books: London, 1990).

26 R. Mingins, 'The Beacon Controversy and Challenges to British Quaker Tradition in the Early Nineteenth Century', *Quaker Studies*, vol. 6 (2004).

27 J.D. Marshall, 'Kendal in the late seventeenth and eighteenth centuries', *CW2*, LXXV (1975), 188–257, 241.

28 E.S. Worrall, *Returns of Papists 1767 Diocese of Chester* (Catholic Record Society: London, Occasional Paper No. I, 1980), 155–6.

29 Butler, *Bishop Gastrell's Notitia* (1998), 203.

30 Rowlands, *Catholics of Parish and Town* (1999), 191.

31 R. White, '"Sizergh to be burnt within two days". Sizergh Castle and the Gordon Riots', *CW3*, VI (2006), 103–112.

32 *1851 Census Great Britain Report and Tables on Religious Worship England and Wales (1852–53)* (Irish University Press Series of British Parliamentary Papers, Population 10, 1970), 119; the figures do not allow us to determine how many of those attending did so more than once on the same day.

33 *Census 2001; Key Statistics for urban areas in England and Wales* (Office of National Statistics: London, 2004), Tables KS06, 89, and KS07, 107.

Chapter 11: Education, leisure, culture and the arts

1 W. Rollinson, *A History of Cumberland and Westmorland*, 2nd edn (Phillimore: Chichester, 1996), 64.

2 R.L. Storey, 'The Chantries of Cumberland and Westmorland, pt. II', *CW2*, LXII (1962), 155–70; W. Farrer (J.F. Curwen (ed.)), *Records Relating to the Barony of Kendale* (CWAAS Record Series, vol. IV, Titus Wilson: Kendal, 1923), 57, 85–7, 152.

3 W. Cowan (ed.), *A Journey to Edenborough in Scotland by Joseph Taylor, Late of the Inner Temple, 1705* (W. Brown: Edinburgh, 1903), 160.

4 R. Bingham, *Kendal—A Social History* (Cicerone Press: Milnthorpe, 1995), 399–400.

5 J. Cochrane, *Kendal Grammar School, 1525–1975* (Westmorland Gazette: Kendal, 1975).

6 J. Nicholson and R. Burn, *The History and Antiquities of the Counties of Westmorland and Cumberland*, 2 vols, 1777 (repr. EP Publishing: East Ardsley, 1976), 80.

7 J. Whitwell, *The Old Houses of Kendal, or the Local Perambulator* (Kendal Literary & Scientific Association/ Thos Atkinson: Kendal, 1866), 27.

8 A. Raistrick, *Quakers in Science and Industry*, 1950 (repr. Wm Sessions: York, 1993), 270–1; P. Wood (ed.), *Science & Dissent in England, 1688–1945* (Ashgate Publishing: Aldershot, 2004), 73–4.

9 *Cumberland Pacquet* 24 January 1787.

10 Wood, *Science and Dissent in England* (2004), 73–4.

11 W. Parson and W. White, *History, Directory and Gazetteer of the counties of Cumberland & Westmorland, 1829* (repr. M. Moon: Beckermet, 1976), 643.

12 Anon., *Rules for the Government of the School of Industry, Kendal, 1811* (W. Pennington: Kendal, 1811).

13 T. Cox, *Magna Britannia et Hibernia, vol. 6, Westmorland* (London, 1720), 39.

14 C. Nicholson, *Annals of Kendal, being a historical and descriptive account of Kendal and the neighbourhood with biographical sketches of many eminent personages connected with the town*, 2nd edn (Whitaker & Co.: London, 1861), 195–202.

15 *Westmorland Gazette*, 9 November 1820.

16 Parson & White, *Directory ... of the counties of Cumberland & Westmorland, 1829* (1976), 643.

17 Parson & White, *Directory ... of the counties of Cumberland & Westmorland, 1829* (1976), 644.

18 Nicholson, *Annals of Kendal* (1861), 209.

19 L. Ashcroft (ed.), *Vital Statistics; the Westmorland 'Census' of 1787* (Curwen Archives Trust: Kendal, 1992), 309.

20 Parson & White, *Directory...of the counties of Cumberland & Westmorland, 1829* (1976), 660.

21 P.J. Mannex, *Directory of Westmorland and Lonsdale North of the Sands in Lancashire* (Simpkin, Marshall & Co.: London, 1849), 318.

22 *Post Office Directory of Westmorland & Cumberland* (Kelly & Co.: London, 1858), 34.

23 M.S. Morris, *An Honourable History: the story of Kendal High School* (p.p.: Kendal, 1991).

24 *Kelly's Directory of Cumberland & Westmorland* (Kelly's: London, 1914), 77.

25 M.E. Burkett, *Four Kendal Portrait Painters* (Abbot Hall: Kendal, 1973); *Treasures from Abbot Hall, an exhibition at the Leger Galleries, London, and Abbot Hall, Kendal* (Titus Wilson: Kendal, 1989).

26 J. Briggs (ed.), *The Lonsdale Magazine and Kendal Repository*, vol. III (J. Foster: Kirkby Lonsdale, 1822), 183; D. Piper, *The English Face* (NPG: London, 1992), 146, 162–3, 190.

27 A. Kidson, *George Romney, 1734–1802* (NPG: London, 2002), 44–5, 108–9.
28 Kidson, *George Romney* (2002), 115–17.
29 Piper, *The English Face* (1992), 186.
30 J.F. Curwen, *Kirkby-Kendall: Fragments collected relating to its ancient streets and yards; church and castle; houses and inns* (Titus Wilson: Kendal, 1900), 34.
31 J. Satchell, *Old Kendal: A Selection of Paintings, Drawings and Prints from the Collection of Kendal Town Council* (Kendal Civic Society: Kendal, 2003), 22–3, 25.
32 R. Caseby, *The Opium-eating Editor Thomas de Quincey and the Westmorland Gazette* (Westmorland Gazette: Kendal, 1985).
33 Nicholson, *Annals of Kendal* (1st edn 1832, 2nd edn 1861).
34 Anon. (Editors of the *Kendal Mercury* and *Westmorland Gazette*), *Local Chronology, being notes of the principal events published in the Kendal Newspapers since their establishment* (Hamilton Adams & Co.: London, 1865).
35 Curwen, *Kirkby-Kendall* (1900).
36 Bingham, *Kendal* (1995).
37 J. Satchell, *Kendal on Tenterhooks* (Kendal Civic Society/Frank Peters: Kendal, 1984).
38 F. Barnes and J.L. Hobbs, *Handlist of newspapers published in Cumberland, Westmorland,and North Lancashire* (CWAAS Tract Series, Vol. XIV, Titus Wilson: Kendal, 1951); J.S.W. Gibson, *Local Newspapers 1750–1920 England and Wales, Channel Islands, Isle of Man. A Select Location List* (Federation of Family History Societies: Birmingham, 1987); Parson & White, *Directory ... of the counties of Cumberland & Westmorland, 1829* (1976), 645.
39 M. Eddershaw, *Grand Fashionable Nights: Kendal Theatre, 1575–1985* (CNWRS, University of Lancaster, Occasional Paper No.17, 1989).
40 S. Rosenfeld, *The Georgian Theatre of Richmond Yorkshire and its circuit: Beverley, Harrogate, Kendal, Northallerton, Ulverston and Whitby* (Society for Theatre Research/Wm Sessions: York, 1984); W. Rollinson, *Life and Tradition in the Lake District* (Dalesman Books: Clapham, 1981), pls 164–9.
41 Eddershaw, *Grand Fashionable Nights* (1989), 23–4.
42 Eddershaw, *Grand Fashionable Nights* (1989), 33.
43 R. Bayne-Powell, *Travellers in Eighteenth-century England* (John Murray: London, 1951), 189–98.
44 Rollinson, *Life and Tradition in the Lake District* (1981), pl. 164.
45 Anon., *Local Chronology* (1865), 16.
46 Anon., *Local Chronology* (1865), 75.
47 *Westmorland Gazette*, 2 June 1832.
48 *Westmorland Gazette*, 7 July 1832.
49 A.J. White, 'Early Museums in Lakeland', *CW2*, LXXXIX (1989), 269–75.
50 W. Rollinson (ed.), *A Tour in the Lakes in 1797 by William Gell* (Smith Settle: Otley, 2000), 72.
51 Parson & White, *Directory ... of the counties of Cumberland & Westmorland, 1829* (1976), 645.
52 *Lancaster Guardian*, 11 July 1835.
53 Anon., *Official Handbook and Catalogue to the Kendal Borough Museum* (Titus Wilson: Kendal, 1924).
54 R.S. Ferguson (ed.), *The Boke off Recorde of the Burgh of Kirkby Kendal* (CWAAS Extra Series, vol. VII, Titus Wilson: Kendal, 1892), 174; M. Hartley and J. Ingilby, *Life and Tradition in the Yorkshire Dales* (Dalesman Books: Clapham, 1981), 199.
55 Ferguson, *Boke off Recorde* (1892), 170–1.
56 Anon., *Local Chronology* (1865), 34.
57 Anon., *Local Chronology* (1865), 121.
58 Curwen, *Kirkby-Kendall* (1900), 304.
59 L. Murfin, *Popular Leisure in the Lake Counties* (MUP: Manchester, 1990).
60 C. Kightly, *The Customs and Ceremonies of Britain* (Thames & Hudson: London, 1986), 56, 136, 205.
61 Anon., *Local Chronology* (1865), xxx.
62 Anon., *Local Chronology* (1865), 42, 44, 47–8, 77, 98.
63 Anon., *Local Chronology* (1865), 74–5.
64 Anon., *Local Chronology* (1865), 77–8; J. Clarke, *History of Cricket in Kendal from 1836 to 1905* (Thompson Bros.: Kendal, 1906).
65 Anon., *Local Chronology* (1865), 98.
66 D. Kingwell and the Centenary Seven, *A Northern Stronghold—The History of Kendal Rugby Union Football Club 1905–2005* (Kendal RUFC: Kendal, 2005).
67 Parson & White, *Directory...of the counties of Cumberland & Westmorland, 1829* (1976), 646.
68 P. Brears, *Traditional Food in Yorkshire* (John Donald: Edinburgh, 1987), 59–73; C.A. Wilson (ed.), *Traditional Food East and West of the Pennines* (Alan Sutton: Stroud, 1991), 88–90.
69 C. Morris (ed.), *The Illustrated Journeys of Celia Fiennes c.1682–c.1712* (Macdonald & Co.: London, 1982), 167.
70 Anon., *Local Chronology* (1865), 101.
71 F.M. Eden, *The State of the Poor*, 3 vols, 1797 (repr. Cass: London, 1966), 753.
72 *Westmorland Gazette*, 23 December 1911.
73 Morris (ed.), *Celia Fiennes* (1982), 166.
74 P. Rogers (ed.), *Daniel Defoe, A Tour through the Whole Island of Britain* (Penguin Books: Harmondsworth, 1973), 550.
75 Rollinson, *Life and Tradition in the Lake District* (1981), pl. 45; B. Tyson (ed.), *The Estate and Household Accounts of Sir Daniel Fleming of Rydal Hall, Westmorland,*

1688–1701 (C & W Record Series vol. XIII: Kendal, 2001), 122.

76 Anon., *Local Chronology* (1865), 12.

77 CRO, Kendal, GB/NNAF/C106444.

78 Rollinson, *Life and Tradition in the Lake District* (1981), pl. 28; M. Towne, North Pennine Archaeological Trust, pers. comm.

79 Satchell, *Old Kendal* (2003), 30.

80 Curwen, *Kirkby-Kendall* (1900), 281.

81 Brears, *Traditional Food in Yorkshire* (1987), 178–9.

82 *Westmorland Gazette*, 4 February 1826.

83 C. Gregory, *Favourite Lakeland Recipes* (Salmon: Sevenoaks, n.d.), 43.

84 Wilson (ed.), *Traditional Food East and West of the Pennines* (1991), 100.

85 (H.W. Duncan) D.K.K, *Reminiscences of people and places in Kendal, sixty years ago* (Titus Wilson: Kendal, 1890), 47; E.M. Wilson, 'Some Extinct Kendal Customs', *CW2*, XXXVIII (1938), 164–79; Bingham, *Kendal* (1995), 398–9.

86 Duncan, *Reminiscences* (1890), 47.

87 Anon., *Local Chronology* (1865), 103; Wilson (ed.), *Traditional Food East and West of the Pennines* (1991), 109; Wilson, 'Some Extinct Kendal Customs', *CW2*, XXXVIII (1938), 164–79, 167–70.

88 Ferguson, *Boke off Recorde* (1892), 91, 137.

89 N. Nicholson, *The Lake District; an anthology* (Penguin Books: Harmondsworth, 1978), 356–7.

90 Ferguson, *Boke off Recorde* (1892), 91.

91 Duncan, *Reminiscences* (1890), 57.

92 Anon., *Local Chronology* (1865), 121; anon., *Handbook and Catalogue to Kendal Museum* (1924), 10.

Chapter 12: Crime and punishment

1 J.D. Marshall, *Old Lakeland; some Cumbrian Social History* (David & Charles: Newton Abbot, 1971), 101.

2 Anon. (Editors of the *Kendal Mercury* and *Westmorland Gazette*), *Local Chronology, being notes of the principal events published in the Kendal Newspapers since their establishment* (Hamilton Adams & Co.: London, 1865), 85; (H.W. Duncan) D.K.K, *Reminiscences of people and places in Kendal, sixty years ago* (Titus Wilson: Kendal, 1890), 37–8.

3 *Westmorland Gazette*, 23 December 1911.

4 Commission on Municipal Corporations, England & Wales, *Municipal Corporation Boundaries; Kendal* (1837).

5 *Inspectors of Constabulary Reports* (HMSO: London, 1894), 127; (1901), 148; (1902), 116.

6 W. Parson and W. White, *History, Directory and Gazetteer of the counties of Cumberland & Westmorland, 1829* (repr. M. Moon: Beckermet, 1976), 637.

7 R. Bingham, *Kendal—A Social History* (Cicerone Press: Milnthorpe, 1995), 332; CRO, Kendal, WQ/SR/27/1.

8 C. Chalklin, *English Counties and Public Building, 1650–1830* (Hambledon Press: London, 1998), 167, 188.

9 J. O'Connor, *Memories of Old Kendal; recollections and pictures of people of bygone Kendal, and the town and times they lived in*, 3rd edn (Westmorland Gazette: Kendal, 1962), 34.

10 M. and P. Duff, *Kendal in Old Photographs* (Alan Sutton: Stroud, 1992), 62–3.

11 CRO, Kendal, WQ/SR/42/5.

12 CRO, Kendal, WQ/SR/67/7.

13 CRO, Kendal, WQ/SR/248/3.

14 CRO, Kendal, WQ/SR/263/26–7.

15 CRO, Kendal, WQ/SR/536/6–8.

16 CRO, Kendal, WQ/SR/313/5–12.

17 J.F. Curwen, *Records relating to the Barony of Kendale, Vol. III* (CWAAS/Westmorland County Council: Kendal, 1926), 84–5; R.S. Ferguson (ed.), *The Boke off Recorde of the Burgh of Kirkby Kendal* (CWAAS Extra Series, Vol. VII, Titus Wilson: Kendal, 1892), 159.

18 Marshall, *Old Lakeland* (1971), 101.

19 Curwen, *Barony of Kendale, Vol. III* (1926), 89.

20 Curwen, *Barony of Kendale, Vol. III* (1926), 90.

21 *Ibid.*

22 Curwen, *Barony of Kendale, Vol. III* (1926), 93.

23 (Duncan) *Reminiscences* (1890), 39.

24 Anon., *Local Chronology* (1865), 13.

25 (Duncan) *Reminiscences* (1890), 138.

26 A. White, *Life in Georgian Lancaster* (Carnegie: Lancaster, 2004), 75.

27 Bingham, *Kendal* (1995), 68.

28 Anon., *Local Chronology* (1865), 46.

29 Anon., *Local Chronology* (1865), 49.

30 Anon., *Local Chronology* (1865), 73.

31 Anon., *Local Chronology* (1865), 76.

32 Anon., *Local Chronology* (1865), 75, 79.

Chapter 13: War and other troubles

1 *CW2*, III (1903), 418.

2 Anon. (Editors of the Kendal Mercury and Westmorland Gazette), *Local Chronology, being notes of the principal events published in the Kendal Newspapers since their establishment* (Hamilton Adams & Co.: London, 1865), xxx.

3 J. Johnson *et al.*, *Holinshed's Chronicles of England, Scotland and Ireland in Six Volumes*, 1808 (repr. AMS Press Inc., 1965), V, 355.

4 W. Farrer (J.F. Curwen (ed.)), *Records Relating to the Barony of Kendale* (CWAAS Record Series, Vol. IV, Titus Wilson: Kendal, 1923), 17.

5 A. White, *Lancaster a History* (Phillimore: Chichester, 2003), 116.

6 R.C. Jarvis, *The Jacobite Risings of 1715 and 1745* (Cumberland County Council: Carlisle, 1954), 24–5.

7 White, *Lancaster a History* (2003), 120–1.

8 F. McLynn, *The Jacobite Army in England 1745; the Final Campaign* (John Donald: Edinburgh, 1998), 69.

9 Historical Manuscripts Commission, *Report on MSS in Various Collections*, VIII (HMSO: London, 1913), 133.

10 CRO, Kendal, Kendal Parish Registers, sd 1745.

11 J.D. Oates, *The Jacobite Invasion of 1745 in North West England* (CNWRS, Lancaster University, Occasional Paper, 2006), *passim*; McLynn, *The Jacobite Army in England 1745* (1998), esp. 63–70, 173–5.

12 Anon., *Local Chronology* (1865), 14.

13 S. Watkin and I. Whyte, *Floods in North-West England, c.1600–2008* (CNWRS, Lancaster University, Occasional Paper, 2009), 27, 95–98.

14 Watkin and Whyte, *Floods in North-West England* (2009), 50–2.

Select bibliography

Documents

NB This is not an exhaustive list

Bodleian Library, Oxford

William Stukeley prospect of Church and Castle from Kirkbarrow Hill, 1725, MS. Top. gen. d.14, f.20
Gough Map of Britain, *c.* 1360

CRO, Kendal

Kendal Corn Rent Map, WQ/R/C/8
OS Map 1861 1:500 scale, WSMB/K [Folder 8]
1695 'census', WD/Ry Box 32
Microfilms of wills and inventories proved at Richmond
Quarter Sessions depositions WQ/SR

CRO, Carlisle

List of Kendal Carriers, c1700, CRO Carlisle, D/Lons/W1/34
Castle reconstruction, Machell MSS, CRO Carlisle, ii, 71

CRO, Barrow-in-Furness

Soulby Collection of handbills etc., class ZS

LRO, (Lancashire Record Office), Preston

Wills and inventories proved at Richmond, WRW/K etc.

British Library

Drawing of Castle Dairy, BL 005 ADD 00004202

Books and articles

Abbreviations

p.p.	privately published
CNWRS	Centre for North West Regional Studies, at Lancaster University
CW	*Transactions of the Cumberland & Westmorland Antiquarian & Archaeological Society* 1, 2 and 3 being the respective series.
CWAAS	Cumberland & Westmorland Antiquarian & Archaeological Society
CUP	Cambridge University Press
LUP	Liverpool University Press
MUP	Manchester University Press
OUP	Oxford University Press
NPG	National Portrait Gallery

Note: 'Westmorland Gazette' is used for all quotations from that newspaper and its predecessors, regardless of their changing title.

Albert, W., *The Turnpike Road System in England 1663–1840* (CUP: Cambridge, 1972)

Allen, P., *The Old Galleries of Cumbria and the early wool trade* (Abbot Hall: Kendal, n.d., but 1984)

Anon., *Rules for the Government of the School of Industry, Kendal, 1811* (W. Pennington: Kendal, 1811)

Anon., *The Tradesmen's Tokens issued during the 17th Century in the County of Westmorland* (no publisher cited, Kendal, 1855)

Anon. (Editors of the *Kendal Mercury* and *Westmorland Gazette*), *Local Chronology, being notes of the principal events published in the Kendal Newspapers since their establishment* (Hamilton Adams & Co.: London, 1865)

Anon., *Official Handbook and Catalogue to the Kendal Borough Museum* (Titus Wilson: Kendal, 1924)

Anon., *A Description of the Ordnance Survey Large Scale Plans* (Ordnance Survey: Chessington, 1954)

Armitt, M.L. (ed. W.F. Rawnsley), *Rydal* (Titus Wilson: Kendal, 1916)

Ashcroft, L. (ed.), *Vital Statistics; the Westmorland 'Census' of 1787* (Curwen Archives Trust: Kendal, 1992)

Ashcroft L. (ed.), *The Diary of a Kendal Midwife 1669–1675* (Curwen Archives Trust: Kendal, 2002)

Ashcroft, L. (ed.), *Cleaning up Kendal; a century of sanitary history* (Curwen Archives Trust: Kendal, 2006)

Bagot, A. and J. Munby (eds), *'All Things is Well Here; letters from Hugh James of Levens to James Grahme, 1692–95* (CWAAS Record Series, vol. X, Kendal, 1988)

Bailey, W., *Northern Directory* (Bailey: Warrington, 1784)

Bailey, R.N. and R. Cramp, *Corpus of Anglo-Saxon Stone Sculpture, vol. 2, Cumberland, Westmorland & Lancashire North of the Sands* (OUP/British Academy: London, 1988)

Barnes, F. and J.L. Hobbs, *Handlist of newspapers published in Cumberland, Westmorland, and North Lancashire* (CWAAS Tract Series, vol. XIV, Titus Wilson: Kendal, 1951)

Bayne-Powell, R., *Travellers in Eighteenth-century England* (John Murray: London, 1951)

Beresford, M.W. and H.P.R. Finberg, *English Medieval Boroughs: a handlist* (David & Charles: Newton Abbot, 1973)

Bingham, E., *A History of Kendal Memorial Hospital and Westmorland County Hospital 1870–1991* (pp: Kendal, 1991)

Bingham, R., *Kendal—A Social History* (Cicerone Press: Milnthorpe, 1995)

Birley, E., 'A Roman Inscription from Watercrook', *CW2*, LV (1955), 46–53

Birley, E.B., 'The Roman fort at Watercrook', *CW2*, LVII (1957) 13–17

Bouch, C.M.L., *Prelates and People of the Lake Counties; A History of the Diocese of Carlisle, 1133–1933* (Titus Wilson: Kendal, 1948)

Bowen, E., *Britannia Depicta or Ogilby Improv'd; Road Atlas of Britain, 1720* (Frank Graham: Newcastle upon Tyne, repr. 1970)

Brears, P., *Traditional Food in Yorkshire* (John Donald: Edinburgh, 1987)

Brierley, H., *The Registers of Kendal, 1558–1587*, 2 vols (Titus Wilson: Kendal, 1921 and 1922)

Briggs, J. (ed.), *The Lonsdale Magazine or Provincial Repository*, Vol. II (J. Foster: Kirkby Lonsdale, 1821)

Briggs, J. (ed.), *The Lonsdale Magazine and Kendal Repository*, Vol. III (J. Foster: Kirkby Lonsdale, 1822)

Britnell, R.H., 'Boroughs, markets and trade in northern

England, 1000–1216' in Britnell, R.H. and R.H. Hatcher (eds), *Progress and Problems in Medieval England* (CUP: Cambridge, 1996)

Brunskill, R.W., *Vernacular Architecture of the Lake Counties; a field handbook* (Faber & Faber: London, 1974)

(Budworth, J.), *'A Rambler', A Fortnight's Ramble to the Lakes 1792* (Preston Publishing: Upper Basildon, repr. 1990)

Bulmer, T. & Co., *History, Topography & Directory of Westmorland* (Bulmer: London, 1906)

van Burd A. and J.S. Dearden, *A Tour to the Lakes in Cumberland: John Ruskin's Diary for 1830* (Scolar Press: Aldershot, 1990)

Burkett, M.E., *Four Kendal Portrait Painters* (Abbot Hall: Kendal, 1973)

Butler, D.M., *Summer Houses of Kendal* (Abbot Hall: Kendal, 1982)

Butler, D.M., *The Quaker Meeting Houses of Britain*, 2 vols (Friends Historical Society: London, 1999)

Butler L.A.S. (ed.), *The Cumbria Parishes, 1714–1725, from Bishop Gastrell's Notitia with additions by Bishop Porteus 1778–1779* (CWAAS Record Series, Vol. XII, Kendal, 1998)

Cartwright, J.J. (ed.), *The Travels Through England of Dr Richard Pococke* (Camden Society, London, vol. 1, 1888; vol. 2, 1889)

Cary, J., *Cary's New Itinerary* (J. Cary: London, 1798)

Caseby, R., *The Opium-eating Editor Thomas de Quincey and the Westmorland Gazette* (Westmorland Gazette: Kendal, 1985)

Catt, J. *Northern Hiring Fairs* (Countryside Publications: Brinscall, 1986)

1851 Census Great Britain Report and Tables on Religious Worship England and Wales (1852–53),(Irish University Press Series of British Parliamentary Papers, Population 10, 1970)

Census 2001; Key Statistics for urban areas in England and Wales, (Office of National Statistics: London, 2004)

Chalklin, C., *English Counties and Public Building, 1650–1830* (Hambledon Press: London, 1998)

Clark, P., *The English Alehouse: A Social History, 1200–1830* (Longman: London, 1983)

Clark, M.A., 'Kendal, The Protestant Exception', *CW2*, XCV (1995), 137–52

Clarke, J., *History of Cricket in Kendal from 1836 to 1905* (Thompson Bros.: Kendal, 1906)

Clifton Taylor, A., *The Pattern of English Building* (Faber & Faber: London, 1972)

Cochrane, J., *Kendal Grammar School, 1525–1975* (Westmorland Gazette: Kendal, 1975)

Collingwood, R.G. and R.P. Wright, *Roman Inscriptions in Britain, Vol. 1., Inscriptions on stone* (OUP: Oxford, 1965)

Collingwood, W.G., 'An Anglian Cross-fragment at Kendal', *CW2*, IV (1904), 330–3

Collingwood, W.G., 'Three more ancient castles of Kendal', *CW2*, VIII (1908), 97–112

Colvin, H.M., *A Biographical Dictionary of British Architects, 1600–1840*, 3rd edn (Yale University Press: New Haven, 1995)

Cowan W. (ed.), *A Journey to Edenborough in Scotland by Joseph Taylor, Late of the Inner Temple, 1705* (W. Brown: Edinburgh, 1903)

Cox, T., *Magna Britannia et Hibernia, vol. 6, Westmorland* (London, 1720)

Crookenden, S., *K Shoes—the First 150 Years, 1842–1992* (K Shoes: Kendal, 1992)

Cropper, M., *'The Leaves we Write on'; James Cropper; a History in Paper-Making* (Ellergreen Press: London, 2004)

Crosby, A., 'The Towns of Medieval Lancashire: an Overview', *Lancaster University Centre for North West Regional Studies Bulletin*, 8 (1994), 7–18

Curwen J.F., *Kirkby-Kendall: Fragments collected relating to its ancient streets and yards; church and castle; houses and inns* (Titus Wilson: Kendal, 1900)

Curwen, J.F., *The Castles and Fortified Towers of Cumberland, Westmorland, and Lancashire North-of-the-Sands*, (CWAAS, Extra Series, vol. XIII, Kendal, 1913)

Curwen, J.F., *Records relating to the Barony of Kendale, Vol. III* (CWAAS/Westmorland County Council: Kendal, 1926)

Davies-Shiel, M. and J.D. Marshall, *Industrial Archaeology of the Lake Counties* (David & Charles: Newton Abbot, 1969)

Davies-Shiel, M., *Wool is my Bread, or, the Early Woollen Industry of Kendal from c.975–1575 AD* (Frank Peters: Kendal, 1975)

Davis, D., *A History of Shopping* (Routledge & Kegan Paul: London, 1966)

Denyer, S., *Traditional Buildings and Life in the Lake District* (National Trust/Victor Gollancz/Peter Crawley: London, 1991)

de Selincourt, E. (ed.), *The Letters of William and Dorothy Wordsworth; III, The Middle Years, Part 2, 1812–1820* (Clarendon Press: Oxford, 1970)

de Selincourt, E. (ed.), *William Wordsworth Guide to the Lakes, 5th edn (1835)* (OUP: Oxford, 1977)

Duckett, G.F. (ed.), *Description of the County of Westmorland by Sir Daniel Fleming of Rydal AD 1671* (CWAAS Tract Series, vol. I, Quaritch: London, 1882)

Duff, M. and P., *Kendal in Old Photographs* (Alan Sutton: Stroud, 1992)

(Duncan, H.W.) D.K.K, *Reminiscences of people and places in Kendal, sixty years ago* (Titus Wilson: Kendal, 1890)

Dunderdale, J.W. (ed. A. Bonney), *Kendal Brown; the History of Kendal's Tobacco and Snuff Industry* (Helm Press: Natland, 2003)

Eden, F.M., *The State of the Poor*, 3 vols, 1797 (repr. Cass: London, 1966)

Eddershaw, M., *Grand Fashionable Nights: Kendal Theatre 1575–1985*, (CNWRS, University of Lancaster, Occasional Paper No.17, 1989)

Edwards, P., '"Blood Ran Down"; Early Drama in Kendal', in *A History of Kendal*, vol. 4, (Lectures by CWAAS and Kendal Civic Society, Kendal, 2000)

Ekwall, E., *Concise Oxford Dictionary of English Place-Names* (OUP: Oxford, 1960)

Evans, E., 'A nineteenth century Tithe Dispute and its significance; the Case of Kendal', *CW2*, LXXIV (1974), 159–85

Ewbank, J.M., *Antiquary on Horseback: the first publication of the collections of the Rev. Thos. Machell chaplain to King Charles II towards a history of the Barony of Kendal* (CWAAS Extra Series, vol. XIX, Titus Wilson: Kendal, 1963)

Farrer, W. (J.F. Curwen (ed.), *Records Relating to the Barony of Kendale* (CWAAS Record Series, Vol. IV, Titus Wilson: Kendal, 1923)

Faull, M.L. and M. Stinson (eds), *Domesday Book, Yorkshire* 2 vols (Phillimore: Chichester, 1986)

Fendall, C.P. and E.A.Crutchley, *The Diary of Benjamin Newton, Rector of Wath, 1816–1818* (CUP: Cambridge, 1933)

Ferguson, R.S. (ed.), *The Boke off Recorde of the Burgh of Kirkby Kendal* (CWAAS Extra Series, vol. VII, Titus Wilson: Kendal, 1892)

Ferguson, R.S., *A History of Westmorland* (Elliot Stock: London, 1894)

Ffinch, M., *Portrait of Kendal and the Kent Valley* (Robert Hale: London, 1983)

Fitzgibbon, T., *A Taste of the Lake District in Food and Pictures* (Ward Lock: London, 1980)

Frater, A., *Stopping-Train Britain; a Railway Odyssey* (Hodder & Stoughton: London, 1985)

Gerhold, D., *Carriers and Coachmasters: trade and travel before the Turnpikes* (Phillimore: Chichester, 2005)

Gibson, J.S.W., *Local Newspapers, 1750–1920, England and Wales, Channel Islands, Isle of Man. A Select Location List* (Federation of Family History Societies: Birmingham, 1987)

Graystone, P., *Walking Roman Roads in Lonsdale and the Eden Valley*, (CNWRS, University of Lancaster, Occasional Paper, 2002)

Greenwood, O., *The Quaker Tapestry; a celebration of insights* (Impact Books: London, 1990)

Gregory, C., *Favourite Lakeland Recipes* (Salmon: Sevenoaks, n.d.)

Handley, D.J., *Notes on Furness Branch Bells* (The Reminder Press: Ulverston, 1983)

Harbottle, B., 'Excavations at Kendal Castle, Westmorland, 1967', *Quarto*, 5/4 (Abbot Hall Art Gallery: Kendal, 1968)

Harbottle, B., 'Excavations at Kendal Castle, Westmorland, 1968, *Quarto*, 6 (Abbot Hall Art Gallery: Kendal, 1969)

Harbottle, B., 'Excavations at Kendal Castle, Westmorland, 1969', *Quarto*, 7/4 (Abbot Hall Art Gallery: Kendal, 1970)

Harbottle, B., 'Excavations at Kendal Castle, Westmorland, 1971', *Quarto*, 10/1 (Abbot Hall Art Gallery: Kendal, 1972)

Hartley, M. and J. Ingilby, *Life and Tradition in the Yorkshire Dales* (Dalesman Books: Clapham, 1981)

Hartley, M. and J. Ingilby, *Yorkshire Album; Photographs of Everyday Life, 1900–1950* (J.M. Dent: London, 1988)

Head, Sir G., *A Home Tour through the Manufacturing Districts of England in the Summer of 1835*, (repr. A.M. Kelley: New York, 1968)

Hey, D., *Packmen, Carriers & Packhorse Roads: trade and communications in North Derbyshire and South Yorkshire*, 2nd edn (Landmark: Ashbourne, 2001)

Hillman, A. (transcr.), *The Rake's Diary: The Journal of George Hilton* (Curwen Archives Trust: Kendal, 1994)

Hindle, P., *Maps for Historians* (Phillimore: Chichester, 1998)

Hindle, P., *Thomas Jefferys Historic Map of Westmorland 1770, reproduced in four sections from the original engravings* (CWAAS, Record Series, Kendal, vol. XIV, 2001)

Hindle, P., 'The first large scale county maps of Cumberland and Westmorland in the 1770s', *CW3*, I (2001), 139–53

Historical Manuscripts Commission, *Report on MSS in Various Collections*, VIII (HMSO: London, 1913)

Hitchmough, W., *C.F.A. Voysey* (Phaidon: London, 1995)

Hobbs, J.L., 'The Turnpike Roads of North Lonsdale', *CW2*, LV (1955), 250–92

Hodgkinson, J., *The Greater Parish of Kendal 1553–2002, during the patronage of Trinity College, Cambridge* (Little Trinity Publishing: Levens, 2002)

Hodgson, H.W., *A Bibliography of the History and Topography of Cumberland and Westmorland* (Joint Archive Committee for Cumberland, Westmorland and Carlisle: Carlisle, 1968)

Holden's Triennial Directory for 1805, 1806, 1807 (Holden: London, 1805)

Holloway, J., *The Oxford Book of Local Verses* (OUP: Oxford, 1987)

Homan, R., 'The Kendal Union Building Societies', *CW2*, LXXXII (1982), 183–90

Howard-Davis, C., *Kendal Castle; a guide* (South Lakeland District Council: Kendal, 2000)

Hughes, R., 'Social Housing: Local Authority and Housing Society providers in 1930s Kendal', MA Dissertation (Open University, 2000)

Hunt, I., *Old Lakeland Transport* (Rusland Press: Penrith, 1978)

James, S.E., 'Queen Kateryn Parr (1512–1548)', *CW2*, LXXXVIII (1988), 107–19

James, S.E., 'Parr memorials in Kendal Parish Church', *CW2*, XCII (1992), 99–103

James, S.E., 'Sir William Parr of Kendal: Part I, 1434–1471', *CW2*, XCIII (1993), 99–114

James, S.E., 'Sir William Parr of Kendal: Part II, 1471–1483, *CW2*, XCIV (1994), 105–20

James, S.E., 'Sir John Parr of Kendal, 1437–1475', *CW2*, XCVI (1996), 71–86

Jarvis, R.C., *The Jacobite Risings of 1715 and 1745* (Cumberland County Council: Carlisle, 1954)

Jervoise, E., *The Ancient Bridges of the North of England* (The Architectural Press: London, 1931)

Johnson L., *et al.*, *Holinshed's Chronicles of England, Scotland and Ireland in Six Volumes*, 1808 (repr. AMS Press Inc., 1965)

Jones, B.C., 'Westmorland Pack-horse Men in Southampton', *CW2*, LIX (1959), 65–84

Kelly's Directory of Cumberland & Westmorland (Kelly's: London, 1914)

Kidson, A., *George Romney, 1734–1802* (NPG: London, 2002)

Kightly, C., *The Customs and Ceremonies of Britain* (Thames & Hudson: London, 1986)

Kingwell, D. and B. Jameson, *Kendal Pubs: A Potted History* (Westmorland Gazette: Kendal, 1998)

Kingwell, D. and the Centenary Seven, *A Northern Stronghold—The History of Kendal Rugby Union Football Club, 1905–2005* (Kendal RUFC: Kendal, 2005)

Loomes, B., *Westmorland Clocks and Clockmakers* (David & Charles: Newton Abbot, 1974)

McLynn, F., *The Jacobite Army in England 1745; the Final Campaign* (John Donald: Edinburgh, 1998)

Mannex, P.J., *Directory of Westmorland and Lonsdale North of the Sands in Lancashire* (Simpkin, Marshall & Co.: London, 1849)

Margary, I.D., *Roman Roads in Britain*, 2 vols (Phoenix House: London, 1957)

Marshall, J.D., *Old Lakeland; some Cumbrian Social History* (David & Charles: Newton Abbot, 1971)

Marshall, J.D., 'Kendal in the late seventeenth and eighteenth centuries', *CW2*, LXXV (1975), 188–257

Marshall, J.D. and J.K. Walton, *The Lake Counties from 1830 to the mid-twentieth century. A Study in Regional Change* (MUP: Manchester, 1981)

Martin, G.H., 'The Town as Palimpsest', pp. 155–169 in H.J. Dyos (ed.), *The Study of Urban History* (Edward Arnold: London, 1971)

Martin, J., 'Mislet, the Braithwaites, and the Black Drop', *CW3*, II (2002), 201–7

Morgan, K. (ed.), *An American Quaker in the British Isles: the Travel Journals of Jabez Maud Fisher, 1775–1779* (OUP: Oxford for the British Academy, 1992)

Morris, C. (ed.), *The Illustrated Journeys of Celia Fiennes c1682-c1712* (Macdonald & Co.: London, 1982)

Morris, M.S., *An Honourable History: the story of Kendal High School* (p.p.: Kendal, 1991)

Munby, J., 'Medieval Kendal: the First Borough Charter and its Connexions', *CW2*, LXXXV (1985), 95–114

Murfin, L., *Popular Leisure in the Lake Counties* (MUP: Manchester, 1990)

Newman, R., 'Archaeology in Kendal, 1987/88', *Contrebis* (Journal of the Lancaster Archaeological & Historical Society), XIV (1988), 45–50

Nicholson, F. and E. Axon, *The Older Nonconformity in Kendal: A History of the Unitarian Chapel in the Market Place* (Titus Wilson: Kendal, 1915)

Nicholson, J. and R. Burn, *The History and Antiquities of the Counties of Westmorland and Cumberland*, 2 vols, 1777 (repr. EP Publishing: East Ardsley, 1976)

Nicholson, C., *Annals of Kendal, being a historical and descriptive account of Kendal and the neighbourhood with biographical sketches of many eminent personages connected with the town*, 2nd edn (Whitaker & Co.: London, 1861)

Nicholson, N., *The Lake District; an anthology* (Penguin Books: Harmondsworth, 1978)

North, O.H., 'The Roman Station at Watercrook', *CW2*, XXXII (1932), 116–23

North, O.H., 'Finds from the Roman Station at Watercrook', *CW2*, XXXIV (1934), 35–40

North, O.H. and E.J.W. Hildyard, 'Excavations at the Roman fort at Watercrook 1944', *CW2*, XLV (1945), 148–62

Oates, J.D., *The Jacobite Invasion of 1745 in North West England* (CNWRS, Lancaster University, Occasional Paper, 2006)

O'Connor, J., *Memories of Old Kendal; recollections and pictures of people of bygone Kendal, and the town and times they lived in*, 3rd edn (Westmorland Gazette: Kendal, 1962)

Palmer, J.H. (rev. and ed. W.T. McIntire), *Historic Farmhouses in and around Westmorland* (Westmorland Gazette: Kendal, 1952)

Parson W. and W. White, *History, Directory and Gazetteer of the counties of Cumberland & Westmorland, 1829* (repr. M. Moon: Beckermet, 1976)

Penney, N. (ed.), *The Household Account Book of Sarah Fell, 1673–78* (CUP: Cambridge, 1920)

Perriam, D.R. and J. Robinson, *The Medieval Fortified Buildings of Cumbria; an Illustrated Gazetteer and Research Guide* (CWAAS Extra Series, vol. XXIX, 1998)

Phillips, C.B., 'The population of the borough of Kendal in 1576,' *CW2*, LXXXI (1981), 57–62

Phillips, C.B., 'Town and county; economic change in Kendal *c.*1550–1700', pp. 99–132 in P. Clark (ed.), *The Transformation of English Provincial Towns, 1600–1800* (Hutchinson: London, 1984)

Phillips, C.B., 'The Plague in Kendal in 1598: some new evidence', *CW2*, XCIV (1994), 135–42

Pigot & Co's National Directory of the counties of Chester, Cumberland, Durham, Lancaster, Northumberland, Westmoreland & York (J. Pigot: London, 1834)

Piper, D., *The English Face* (NPG: London, 1992)

Poole, Bro. Rev. H., *Some Notes on the Trade Companies of Kendal in the 16th and 17th centuries* (no publication data, n.d.)

Post Office Directory of Westmorland & Cumberland (Kelly & Co.: London, 1858)

Potter, T.W., *Romans in North-West England; excavations at the Roman forts of Ravenglass, Watercrook and Bowness on Solway* (CWAAS Research Series, vol. I, Titus Wilson: Kendal, 1979)

Raistrick, A., *Quakers in Science and Industry*, 1950 (repr. Wm Sessions: York, 1993)

Rivet, A.L.F. and C. Smith, *The Place-Names of Roman Britain* (Book Club Associates: London, 1981)

Roberts, W. (ed.), *Thomas Gray's Journal of his Visit to the Lake District in October 1769* (LUP: Liverpool, 2001)

Robinson, J.M., *A Guide to the Country Houses of the North West* (Constable: London, 1991)

Rogers (ed.), P., *Daniel Defoe, A Tour through the Whole Island of Britain* (Penguin Books: Harmondsworth, 1973)

Rollinson, W. (ed.), *A Tour in the Lakes in 1797 by William Gell* (Smith Settle: Otley, 2000)

Rollinson, W., *Life and Tradition in the Lake District* (Dalesman Books: Clapham, 1981)

Rollinson, W., *A History of Cumberland and Westmorland*, 2nd edn (Phillimore: Chichester, 1996)

Rolt, L.T.C., *The Inland Waterways of England* (George Allen & Unwin: London, 1950)

Rosenfeld, S., *The Georgian Theatre of Richmond Yorkshire and its circuit: Beverley, Harrogate, Kendal, Northallerton, Ulverston and Whitby* (Society for Theatre Research/Wm Sessions: York, 1984)

Rowlands, M.B. (ed.), *Catholics of Parish and Town, 1558–1778* (Catholic Record Society: London, Monograph 5, 1999)

Royal Commission on Historic Monuments (England), *An Inventory of the Historical Monuments in Westmorland* (HMSO: London, 1936)

Rushforth, G., 'Churchwardens Accounts, Kendal', *CW1*, IX (1887–88), 269–83

Satchell, J., *Kendal on Tenterhooks* (Kendal Civic Society/Frank Peters: Kendal, 1984)

Satchell, J., *The Kendal Weaver* (Kendal Civic Society/Frank Peters: Kendal, 1986)

Satchell, J. and O. Wilson, *Christopher Wilson of Kendal; an eighteenth-century hosier and banker* (Kendal Civic Society/Frank Peters: Kendal, 1988)

Satchell, J., *Kendal's Canal: History, Industry and People* (Kendal Civic Society: Kendal, 2000)

Satchell, J., *Old Kendal: A Selection of Paintings, Drawings and Prints from the Collection of Kendal Town Council* (Kendal Civic Society: Kendal, 2003)

Shotter, D.C.A., 'The Roman Conquest of the North-West', *CW2*, C (2000), 33–53

Shotter, D.C.A., 'The Roman Fort at Watercrook (Kendal)', *Contrebis* (Journal of the Lancaster Archaeological & Historical Society), XXV (2000), 6–10

Smith, S., *The Kendal & Windermere Railway* (Cumbrian Railways Association: Barrow in Furness, 2002)

Smith, S.D., *'An Exact and Industrious Tradesman': The Letter Book of Joseph Symson of Kendal, 1711–1720* (Records of Social and Economic History, new series, vol. 34, 2002)

Somervell, J., *Some Westmorland Wills, 1686–1738* (Titus Wilson: Kendal, 1928)

Somervell, J., *Water-Power Mills of South Westmorland on the Kent, Bela and Gilpin and their Tributaries* (Titus Wilson: Kendal, 1930)

Stell, C., *Royal Commission on Historical Monuments (England): An Inventory of Nonconformist Chapels and Meeting-Houses in the North of England* (HMSO: London, 1994)

Storey, R.L., 'The Chantries of Cumberland and Westmorland, pt. II', *CW2*, LXII (1962), 155–70

Stuart, S.E., *Biographical List of Clockmakers, North Lancashire and South Westmorland, 1680–1900* (CNWRS, Lancaster University, 1996)

Stukeley, W., *Itinerarium Curiosum, Or, An Account of the Antiquitys and Remarkable Curiositys in Nature or Art, Observ'd in Travels thro' Great Brittan. Centuria II* (London, 1776)

Swainson Cowper, H., 'On some obsolete and semi-obsolete appliances', *CW1*, XIII (1895), 86–102

Taylor, A.C., 'Thomas Harrison and Stramongate Bridge, Kendal', *CW2*, LXIX (1969), 275–9

Taylor, J., *The Carriers' Cosmography* (A.G.: London, 1637)

Taylor, A. (ed. J. Martin), *The Websters of Kendal. A North-Western Architectural Dynasty* (CWAAS Record Series, vol. XVII, Titus Wilson: Kendal, 2004)

Thompson, B.L., 'Westmorland Church Bells', *CW2*, LXX (1970), 51–68

Toulmin Smith, L. (ed.), *The Itinerary of John Leland in or about the years, 1535–1543*, 5 vols (repr. Centaur Press: Fontwell, 1964)

Tusser, T., *Five Hundred Points of Good Husbandry, 1580* (OUP: Oxford, 1984)

Tyson, B., 'James Towers, a Kendal surgeon (1785–1846) and some of his medical colleagues', *CW2*, XCIII (1993), 197–213

Universal British Directory of Trade & Commerce (4 Vols) Vol. 3, (1794)

Vale, E., *The Mail-Coach Men of the late Eighteenth Century* (Cassell: London, 1960)

Vickers, R., 'Country Carriers in Victorian Lakeland', *CW2*, XCVIII (1998), 277–86

West, J., *Town Records* (Phillimore: Chichester, 1983)

Whaley, D., *A Dictionary of Lake District Place-Names* (English Place-Name Society: Nottingham, 2006)

White, A.J., 'Early Museums in Lakeland', *CW2*, LXXXIX (1989), 269–75

White, A.J., 'Actors, Heiresses, Architects and Charlatans', in *The History of Kendal, four lectures given at the Brewery Arts Centre, Kendal, 1994* (CWAAS, Kendal Group/ Kendal Civic Society; Kendal, 1995)

White, A.J., *Lancaster a History* (Phillimore: Chichester, 2003)

White, A.J., *Life in Georgian Lancaster* (Carnegie: Lancaster, 2004)

White, A.J., 'Fast Packet Boats to Kendal', *CW3*, VI (2006), 145–62

White, R., '"Sizergh to be burnt within two days": Sizergh Castle and the Gordon Riots', *CW3*, VI (2006), 103–12

Whitwell, J., *The Old Houses of Kendal, or the Local Perambulator* (Kendal Literary & Scientific Association/ Thos Atkinson: Kendal, 1866)

Whitwell, R.J., 'Chantries in Kendal and Lonsdale Wards, 1546', *CW2*, VIII (1908), 124–35

Wild, F., 'The Development of the Roman Road System in the North-West: the Evidence of the Samian Ware', *Britannia*, XXXIII (2002), 268–74

Willan, T.S., *An Eighteenth-century Shopkeeper, Abraham Dent of Kirkby Stephen* (MUP: Manchester, 1970)

Williamson, G.C., *Boyne's Trade Tokens issued in the Seventeenth Century in England, Wales and Ireland*, 1889–91 (repr. Seaby: London, 1967)

Wilson, C.A. (ed.), *Traditional Food East and West of the Pennines* (Alan Sutton: Stroud, 1991)

Wilson, E.M., 'Some Extinct Kendal Customs', *CW2*, XXXVIII (1938), 164–79

Wilson, P.N., 'Canal Head, Kendal', *CW2*, LXIX (1969), 132–50

Winchester, A.J.L., *Landscape and Society in Medieval Cumbria* (John Donald: Edinburgh, 1987)

Winstanley, M. and R. David, *A Guide to Cumbrian Historical Sources* (CNWRS, Lancaster University, 2006)

Wiseman, W.G., 'The Medieval Hospitals of Cumbria', *CW2*, LXXXVII (1987), 83–100

Wood, P. (ed.), *Science & Dissent in England, 1688–1945* (Ashgate Publishing: Aldershot, 2004)

Woods, J., *The North Road. A Brief History of the Kendal to Shap Road* (p.p., 2001)

Worrall, E.S., *Returns of Papists 1767 Diocese of Chester* (Catholic Record Society: London, Occasional Paper No. I, 1980)

Wright, J. (ed.), *English Dialect Dictionary*, 6 vols (Frowde & Amen Corner: London, 1898)

Yeadon, H.L., *The Motorway Achievement. Building the Network: The North West of England* (Motorway Archive Trust/Phillimore: Chichester, 2005)

Young, A., *A Six Months Tour through the North of England*, 4 vols, vol. III (London, 1771)

Websites

It is difficult to predict how the usage of the internet may develop in years to come. It may be much more massive than at the time of writing or may have been entirely superseded by some new technology in a few years time. However, supposing that it is still in use and that these websites have not been discontinued, migrated or changed out of recognition, here are a few I have found very useful.

Workhouses: users.ox.ac.uk/~peter/workhouse

Cumbria Record Office (and others): www.a2a.org.uk/search

Listed Buildings: http://www.imagesofengland.org.uk This is not only useful for the pictures of listed buildings, but also for the listing information which is usually hard to access except purely locally.

Churches: http://www.churchplansonline.com This gives access to the plans originally sent to the Incorporated Church Building Fund seeking grant. They include repairs as well as more radical rebuilds, and unsuccessful appeals as well as successful ones.

Censuses: accessed via the Library edition of ancestry.com, (http://www.ancestrylibrary.com) this gives free access to all the Census Enumerators' Returns, 1841–1901 for the whole country, including the facility to print or download images of the original pages. For IGI data and the 1881 Census the Mormon database is very useful (the latter can be searched more effectively than the Census data held on ancestrylibrary.com). This is to be found at http://www.familysearch.org

A very useful current source of websites is M. Winstanley and R. David, *A Guide to Cumbrian Historical Sources* (CNWRS, Lancaster University, 2006). This also contains a resume of what is available in the collections of various institutions inside and outside Cumbria.

Index

Numbers in *italics* refer to illustrations